Modern Britain:
Structure and Change

TREVOR NOBLE

Modern Britain: Structure and Change

B. T. Batsford Ltd.,
London & Sydney

'First published 1975

Copyright © Trevor Noble, 1975

Printed by Anchor Press, Tiptree, Essex
and bound by
William Brendon & Son Ltd, Tiptree, Essex
for the publishers
B. T. Batsford Ltd, 4 Fitzhardinge Street, London W1
and 23 Cross Street, Brookvale, NSW 2100, Australia

ISBN 0 7134 2987 9 (hardback)
      0 7134 2988 7 (paperback)

Contents

FOR FAITH

Preface

The present state of British society is the outcome of a long and complicated history. The sources of the contemporary social order can be traced from the latest products of modern technology to events following on the Roman occupation. This, however, is not primarily an historical account and I have tried only to delineate the forces presently at work in shaping this society. I have set out to describe Britain in the period after 1945 and especially in the 1960s, but with some reference to trends which had their origins before that period. As far as possible, given the evidence available at the time of writing, I have tried to bring the picture up to date for 1971. Sometimes, however, it has been necessary to rely on material which may no longer reliably reflect how things are, while by the time these remarks reach the reader events may have moved on to produce in one area or another noticeable differences from the account presented here.

Of course society is changing. That is one of the things this study is about. Yet we will recognise our future when it comes because it will be shaped by our own past. More important, however uncertain the times may be, not far behind the dazzling screen of daily alarms and excursions we can uncover social processes which economic crises may influence but cannot bring to a standstill, which bombings, political excitation and technological innovation may deflect but will not stop. Whatever the outcome of our present predicaments, while it makes sense to believe we are dealing with the same society we are likely to find ourselves constrained by the same sort of structural factors which can be discerned in the present. It is this pattern, demonstrated I think in the evidence up to the early 1970s presented here, which, even when local changes render details of the discussion obsolete, is likely to be of more lasting relevance.

The study which follows is concerned with British society as a whole rather than the problems and prospects of any part, and then primarily with Great Britain rather than the U.K. That is to say I can offer little fresh sociological insight into the distinctive current sufferings of Northern Ireland and have not here made the attempt. I shall therefore refer generally and loosely throughout to Britain, but where figures are presented in support of the argument, especially official statistics, it is necessary to note in each case the territorial basis of their reference. Apart from studies in particular localities many figures refer to the United Kingdom of Great Britain and Northern Ireland; others are published which describe only Great Britain, which includes England, Wales and Scotland, while still others refer only to England and Wales. Some figures from sample surveys and unofficial research refer only to England. The reasons for these inconsistencies are wreathed in the coils of administrative convenience, or lie in the outcome of battles long ago or the necessities of eking out frugal research funds. But the provenance of each set of figures will be made clear as we proceed.

My debts to other authors are too numerous to specify separately but will be all too evident throughout the book. I am particularly grateful however to those of my colleagues and former colleagues who have read and commented on parts of the typescript and to Mrs Thelma Kassel, Mrs Sylvia Lockey and Mrs Rene Shaw who deciphered so much of it from my original manuscript. Without the encouragement of my wife, Faith, and the patient understanding of Patrick Connell, the book could scarcely have been written at all.

Lastly, I should say that I am sure it is much more interesting to write a book like this than to read it, especially if the reading is connected with some examination or equally 'educational' aim. Teachers, I hope, may find here ground they will want to quarry or upon which they may, perhaps, even wish to build their own discussions, but the book is, of course, primarily intended for the student, whether formally enrolled as such or in the broader sense of one who pursues learning. For his or her sake footnotes have been provided so that topics which I have perhaps treated too briefly may be pursued in more proper depth and also so that issues on which the reader may disagree with me may be taken to the arbitration of the available evidence. In suggesting besides, some further reading in connection with each chapter, my aim has been to help extend a reader's acquaintance with the superabundant sociological material on modern Britain now available, giving some taste of the variety of viewpoint and interpretation which exists within it. At the same time it seems realistic to keep such a list fairly brief if it is to be useful. If in this connection, however, brevity should be a shortcoming, there again the footnotes to the text will, I hope, serve. In writing for the student, I have tried to avoid the condescending over-simplification of complex problems evident in some recent discussions of contemporary British society. You may feel, however, that at times this avoidance has been all too successful, and for those unnecessary obscurities that may remain I can only offer the small consolation of my apologies. The best I hope for is that the book should turn out to be what an old literary friend used to describe as a figgy pudding; in other words, that the reader may be able to discover some good things well worth chewing over in amongst the dough.

January 1975

Acknowledgements

The quotations from Mark Abrams' introduction to Daniel, *Racial Discrimination in England* on p.57, J. & E. Newson, 'Some Social Differences in the Process of Child-Rearing' in Gould (ed.), *Penguin Social Sciences Survey*, 1968, Clive Jenkins, 'Tiger in a White Collar?' in *Penguin Survey of Business and Industry*, 1965, are reproduced by permission of Penguin Books. That on p.59 from Banton, *White and Coloured*, 1959, is by permission of Jonathan Cape; the extract from Margaret Stacey, *Tradition and Change*, 1960, is by permission of Oxford University Press. p.118: Firth, Hubert and Forge, *Families and their Relatives*, pp. 213-14: F.M. Martin, from 'Some Subjective Aspects of Social Stratification' in Glass, (ed.), *Social Mobility in Britain*, 1954, p.260: S.John Eggleston, *The Social Context of the School*, pp. 266-7: Basil Bernstein, *Class Codes and Control*, 1971, are all by permission of Routledge & Kegan Paul. p.120, Dennis et al., *Coal Is Our Life* by permission of Tavistock Publications; p.183: Guy Routh, *Occupation and Pay in Britain 1906 to 1960* by permission of Cambridge University Press; pp.256 and 264-5: Davie, Butler and Goldstein, *From Birth to Seven*, p.276: *The Public Schools: A Factual Survey*, 1966, both by permission of Longmans; p.255: Alan Little and John Westergaard, 'The Trend of Class Differentials in Educational Opportunity in England and Wales', *British Journal of Sociology;* pp.270-71: Douglas, Ross and Simpson, *All Our Future,* by permission of Peter Davies Ltd; p.163: Dorothy Wedderburn, 'Inequality at Work' in Townsend and Bosanquet (eds), *Labour and Inequality*, 1972, by permission of the Fabian Society.

'. . . nations stumble upon establishments which are indeed the result of human action, but not the execution of any human design'.

Adam Ferguson,
An Essay on the History of Civil Society
1767

1 The Analysis of Social Structure

Introduction

The sociology of modern Britain is often regarded in these days as a ragbag of vaguely sociological snippets only suitable for those without a proper grounding in the discipline, an empiricist leftover from the days before a really profound modern theoretical sophistication had been achieved. I do not share these views. The attempt to understand the complexity of our own social experience and its structural setting in our own society is essentially in the tradition of social thought of which Weber and Durkheim are only two of the greater exemplars. Our problems of course are not identical but they overlap with theirs. Our historical circumstances, our intellectual inheritance, our cultural predispositions at once present us with distinct issues and a somewhat different approach from their analyses. Without making grandiloquent claims for this particular contribution, the themes which I have taken up here are related to the central concern which has been the root of that tradition of social thought, the understanding of the interrelated processes which frame the society in which we live. The book is of course incomplete as an account of Britain today. It attempts only to examine some of those aspects of the social setting in which we find ourselves which seem to have a structural importance inasmuch as they appear to me to bear on the current balance between the forces of change and the forces of stability and thus perhaps on the longer-run outcome of contemporary situations.

The time is not auspicious for a book like this, perhaps it never is. So many things are changing that, at best, one can only describe what was the case relatively recently. We live in times of political, economic and social change. New data; new theories; new interpretations burgeon on every side like bulbs in a sudden springtime. New findings and, in particular, the results of the 1971 census, should soon outdate many of my quantitative statements even if they confirm the direction of the changes I have described. There have besides been many other texts on British society published recently and one cannot avoid the question of the need for a further addition to this plethora. These other books fall into three main categories. There are, firstly, the social histories which in suitable sociological terms present a narrative account of some of the changes which have occurred in British society during the twentieth and in some cases the latter part of the nineteenth centuries. Then there are the selected readings, which provide a sample of research reports and sometimes more polemical pieces on various aspects of modern British society. Thirdly, there have been several attempts to present 'just the facts', mainly in the form of statistical compendia which select from official and unofficial sources usually quantitative information presented mostly without commentary for the reader to use as mortar in building his own arguments. Some of the works in each category are admirable pieces of scholarship and where I have myself drawn on them they are referred to in the following chapters. Most of them however, suffer from the limitations of their respective genres. None of them, I believe, helps us to understand the structure of the society they attempt to document. There is, on the one hand, a need to make much more explicit the framework of sociological concepts and the model of society used as a basis for the selection made in the readers or the statistical compendia. On the other hand there is the desirability of relating the historical descriptions to the sociological ideas about social processes which have usually emerged from synchronic analyses of social behaviour.

In this book I have sought to synthesise something of all three approaches together with some new findings and ideas of my own. My historical dimension is necessarily very short, indeed almost limited to the extended continuous present, while my account of the work of other interpreters of various aspects of modern British social structure is necessarily selective. As far as the original presentation or reinterpretation of the factual evidence is concerned I have tried to concentrate on those pieces of information which seemed to have a structural relevance. The selection of data in each section of the book has therefore been made with a view to its contribution to the whole rather than a concern with a thorough treatment of each separate topic.

Apart perhaps from some of the recent social histories, most books about contemporary Britain have dealt only with unrelated aspects of the social structure, so that any impression of the whole wood, as it were, has been lost in a detailed inspection of the separate trees. It is necessary to be selective but it is not necessary to seem disjointed. In writing this account of the structure of British society, I have been more concerned with the general pattern than with the particular component parts. Yet it seems to me that the structure of the whole cannot be discovered except through an examination of the interrelationships between the various pieces of evidence which a wide range of writers, researchers and official departments have painstakingly and separately gathered. Thus, in undertaking to describe the structure of present-day society, the first major problem I encountered, naturally enough, was the question of what to include and where to begin.

The Problem of Description

Published research in the last several years has poured out from the presses in an ever-expanding flood, and this has not altogether been a loss. Though I am afraid there seem to be more books and papers which I have not yet managed to read now than there were when I began the task, I have even so been forced to be more actively selective. The simple-minded idea of presenting all the available evidence and leaving the reader to make up his own mind can no longer be entertained and of course it never was a very good idea. Such a procedure would in any case have represented an arbitrary and fallible selection on the basis of whatever I might have been able to find at a given point in time rather than a systematic selection of information on the basis of some criterion of relevance to a carefully worked out interpretation of the facts. Let me be clear upon this matter, I am not proposing either that anyone should engage in an idiosyncratic selection of facts to fit some theoretical predilection or that the only way of going about things is to undertake a gross over-simplification of complicated issues in order to convince the ill-informed. The range of what might be relevant to our task is only restricted by our own resources of time and understanding. The crucial issue, however, is whether we are able to assemble the data we employ coherently in a way which will bear the critical examination of those who have access to the evidence for themselves. The reader must judge for himself whether the arrangement of evidence which I will present in the succeeding chapters in fact adds up to a coherent and convincing argument.

My first aim then was to describe, in so far as it is possible to do so, the social structure of Britain today, or at least very recently, on the basis of the available evidence. This may seem unfashionably empiricist in the eyes of some fellow-sociologists but somewhat regretfully I can still see no preferable alternative. Unless a description is closely founded on soundly established evidence, there can be no good reason for expecting anyone else to accept it as true. On the other hand, description is by no means the simple matter it may at first appear. Describing something, especially anything half so complicated and various as a society, is an active process of selecting those features which seem to be significant in some way. But what is significant is not self-evidently so but a matter of choice and so we come back again to the first problem of choosing what to include and where to begin.

In practice it is necessary to select the items of information which will be used in an account of British social structure from the huge amount of factual data which has been accumulated for various purposes. Even this mass of material is only a fraction of what one might know eventually.

But the choice of what is significant need not be entirely arbitrary and if one is going to make any sense at all to anyone else it must be neither entirely arbitrary nor entirely idiosyncratic. One clearly has to have some idea to start with about what it is important to observe; in other words, some conceptual schema which helps one choose some facts as more salient than others to one's description. It is necessary to employ some criterion of relevance related to the way things work or are thought to work if one's description is not to be altogether misleading.

The choice of those facts that seem to be important and the manner of their juxtaposition with one another is determined by the idea one has to begin with of what the social structure is like. At the same time, of course, one's idea of what the social structure is like will be determined or, at least we might hope strongly influenced, by what the available facts seem to show. But this is to go beyond pure description and it is in the resolution of this dilemma that the attempt to describe hopefully becomes sociology. The description of a social structure is pursued through the interaction of facts and ideas, ideas about the way society works, tested and where necessary rejected or modified in the examination of evidence about the society in question. Thus in a description — or at least one which does not seek to mislead — there is also an element of explanation. A useful description notes those features of the object or process under consideration which characterise its usual mode of operation or use, or which indicate the manner of its having attained its present state. This is implied in the very idea of the 'structure' of society. Thus when we use the term 'social structure' we employ a metaphor which, in describing the social relationships certain people have with certain others, implicitly includes the possibility of explaining at least some aspects of these relationships. Our description becomes in this way, if not what can properly be called an experiment, at least something of an exploratory diagnosis.

One cannot, then, simply describe a society, and particularly a society one has grown up in. Even before we encounter the problems of personal subjectivity, there are problems of sheer scale. This society, to begin with, is too big and too diverse. There are, that is, too many people and their relationships with one another are too complex. Their patterns of association, their customs and institutions are too varied and are, furthermore, too liable to continual change and mutation for even anything so apparently straightforward as a description to be undertaken without considerable care.

The problem of making meaningful statements, let alone true ones, about a society composed of such a wide diversity of unique individuals is serious but soluble. The answer partly lies in the numbers of people involved. We can talk about the general characteristics of groups, classes, generations rather than the particular and personal characteristics of each untypical member. Secondly, we can look at the pattern of relationships between these groups or categories of individuals rather than directly at the groups and categories or the individuals themselves. If we compare society to a network then, as a net is described as a lot of holes joined together by string, we can, concentrating on the strings, observe the overall pattern of relationships. Observing the overall pattern is not easy however, when one is unable to step back for an overall view, when, that is, one is entangled in the net. Even if one can talk sensibly about the structure of society the problem of convincing other people, who may look at things from a different point of view, is not resolved.

Subjectivity

In thinking about the society in which we ourselves live, we are dealing with the framework which shapes our own experience. In trying to grasp something of its shifting complexity, we use the beliefs and preconceptions, values and ideas which, in large part, it has first moulded for us. Our attitude to what we are trying to understand is, then, a curiously ambiguous one, a degree more problematic than the chicken and egg problem. To some extent our own experience will be a crucial touchstone for the validity of our conclusions about the society we are concerned with. After all, a description of a social situation which none of the participants can recognise is unlikely to be true. At the same time our own experience can be very misleading when we try to generalise from it. We may not always understand all the determinants of our own behaviour, far less that of the other people we encounter. Besides, in one way or another, the experience of each of us is unique. In the very act of opening this book, the reader has reduced by one more act the number of things he formerly had in common with the great mass of the general public, though I hope he will not be utterly alone in this respect.

There are both advantages and disadvantages in taking to the study of a society in which we ordinarily live. These both derive from familiarity. It is an advantage to be able to evaluate and interpret relationships, attitudes and goals in the way in which they are understood within the society in which they are current. We can readily do this because we, as citizens, have to choose for ourselves amongst them. If we can be honest with ourselves, we are less likely to impart inappropriate interpretations of the behaviour we observe than would be the case in studying another less familiar society. We should always be prepared on the other hand to discover things are not, in fact, as people say or think they are and familiarity will often reliably guide us past misleading appearances.

Familiarity at the same time presents serious difficulties. Firstly, in our own society live most of our closest and deepest friends as well as our bitterest and most despised antagonists. It is always difficult to be objective about those who know us best. Secondly, society is never still and the more closely we are involved the more obvious is its uncertainty and inconstancy. A social relationship must be continuously renewed if it is not to wither and fade away. Yet in the very process of sustaining a relationship over any length of time it is necessarily changed in quality.

Change is of the essence. On the one hand we are so close to events that it is difficult to see beyond their contingency. Every new day is always different. On the other hand, as we go about a daily routine, it may seem that one day is much like another, this year like the one before last; things don't change much around here. If we are to remain sane in the constant flux of social coming and going, however, we ourselves must adapt so easily and imperceptibly to our environment that we may not see how radically it is changing all around us. So one has the feeling that even if nothing new ever happens, things are not what they were.

The only way out of this morass of subjectivity is through the careful cultivation of a vigorous scepticism. It is necessary to develop a propensity to doubt what we are told until we have been able to examine critically the available evidence. We must treat the generalisations people make, whoever they may be, with especial caution until they have been verified, and if they cannot be verified at all we must be most suspicious about their truth. This, of course, applies equally to the utterances of parents, professors, politicians and prophets and to what I have written here.

As individuals we all necessarily have our different points of view but these do not add up to sociology. Subjective opinions are not enough. A sociological account aims at objectivity; that is to say its interpretations follow the available evidence and are accessible to criticism. One cannot of course ever claim to have shown the truth of any particular matter but only to have attempted to approximate to it. The meaning or significance of that approximation will depend upon the interpretation that can be given to it. On the other hand, if we cannot ever be certain of the truth we can show that some opinions are wrong and others very probably wrong while some may perhaps be true. But while we can never be sure of the ultimate truth, at least not through sociological enquiry, we should not conclude that objectivity is a chimera which will forever evade any pursuit. Objectivity is constructed in sociological investigation, it is a way of dealing with evidence by trying to set aside or take into account the preferences and prejudices we all individually possess.

Empirical enquiry and logical criticism are the techniques of object-ivity. Information and interpretations which can survive such examination can, provisionally, be relied on. Theoretical speculation in general can not, but when it is consistent with what is reliably known then there is at least the possibility that it too is true.

Change and Stability

Society is a set of relationships between people. These relationships are shaped by an inheritance of unevenly distributed material resources, a protean diversity of custom and belief, the privileges and prejudices of their history and the opportunities which the present provides. Society has as many aspects as its members' imaginations can conceive. Some have held it coterminous with everything that is human. To be concerned with the structure of one particular society is to address a more finite problem. We shall be dealing with relationships still but between categories of individuals, groups or social strata. Where the focus is on the characteristics of the whole pattern rather than its particular elements we shall find ourselves dealing with fairly general concepts, such as class, mobility and population, income, wealth and occupation rather than particular institutional complexes.

It is here that we have the joint focus of the book. Social structure is a tissue of changing relationships, of people doing things, changing things, planning and predicting the future as well as conserving a revered past. But social change is not fortuitous; with rare exceptions, it takes place within an ordered framework of expectations, traditions, respected and enforced rights and obligations, some of which are curtailed while others are expanded and elaborated. If it did not, the process of change would be purely accidental, random and unpredictable and there would be no point in trying to understand its outcome. What is more, we would all have been reduced to a state of anomic raving ages ago.

To render the development of an outline of British social structure more manageable a task, the inseparable have had to be treated separately. Those factors making for change and those resisting change, or from an opposite point of view those undermining and those conserving or stabilizing the social order, necessarily operate at the same time but they do not each cancel out the effects of the other. The orderly, familiar pattern persists from year to year while at the same time changes do occur. I have tried to keep these two sets of facts and two sets of factors in mind in developing the analysis which is presented in the succeeding chapters. The earlier chapters in particular deal with the areas in which some of the principal sources of contemporary structural change can be identified. In the later part of the book those features of social structure which tend towards the maintenance of its stability or resistance to change are more emphasised. To begin with I have tried briefly to describe the recent composition and growth of the population and the consequent changes it seems to be producing in social relations together with its interaction with the intrinsic dynamics of the industrial economy. Among the factors resistant to change the pattern of social stratification seems to be of primary importance.

Social Stratification

In one area after another one becomes aware of the fact that while people are not all alike, they are not just individually or idiosyncratically different. In addition to the other ascriptive characteristics and roles which unite and divide people, they are also socially differentiated in terms of a pattern of social stratification or what the man in the street calls class. In his profoundly sensitive study of British political culture, Professor Beer noted this deep and abiding social tendency: 'call it hierarchy, or precedence, or even the class system; we would hardly recognise English society or English politics without it, although more than one school of reformers has set up as its enemy'.[1] Social stratification may be described in general terms as the pattern of relationships which systematises the inequalities of opportunity and reward between groups and tends to perpetuate these inequalities from one generation to the next. This is obviously a central concern in the analysis of social structure. Just what the pattern appears to be like today and whether it seems to be changing will be a major theme in the remainder of the discussion.

The relations between social strata are multiplex and their elucidation is central to an understanding of the social structure. As I have already suggested, because our understanding of these matters is so closely linked with our political and moral interests, with our private ambitions and personal frustrations, objectivity is difficult to achieve. The first major step in the direction of objectivity is to give serious attention to the available evidence and to see what it may show. But before we can do that we must clarify some of the main concepts we shall have to employ.

In Britain 'class' or social stratification is a topic which is beset by a great amount of prejudice and many over-generalisations. Contradictory views on the regrettable behaviour or privileges of other classes and the non-existence or unimportance of class differences are often held by the same people at the same time. They bear witness even in denying its existence to the potency of the class system in shaping the way we see our social environment and judge our fellow citizens.

The term 'class' itself has of course been used by many writers to mean many, rather different, things. Related terms overlap in meaning and the whole field is one of the most terminologically confused of any in sociology. It is obviously essential to clear up what we mean when we use a term in common and frequent employment, frequently meaning different things. The term 'class' is an emotionally charged term, a politically loaded term. In England its very pronunciation proclaims to the hearer an ineradicable bias on the part of the speaker, from 'class' to rhyme with 'ass', to 'class' to rhyme with 'farce'. Pronounce it the first way to a respectable middle-class gent and you risk being dismissed as a red revolutionary; pronounce it the second way to a group of trade unionists and you are likely to be labelled a snob. To cut through this web of implied meanings, of political, social and even moral overtones, we have to define our terms more precisely. This may involve a somewhat outlandish vocabulary or the use of familiar words in rather restricted or unusual ways. It is a good example of the occasionally justified use of

---

[1]　Samuel H. Beer, *Modern British Politics*, Faber, 1969, p.35.

what may seem strange jargon about ordinary everyday experience in order to avoid ambiguity and misunderstanding.

Social stratification involves the differentiation of members of society into groups which are more or less privileged, which enjoy relatively more or less prestige, who are able to exercise authority or are seeking the right to do so. How can we recognise these groups? Clearly if we intend to make comparisons between them or to comment on the relations they have with one another, we must be able to identify them. This is not simply a question of defining boundaries or of deciding how to classify the impoverished peer or a trade union baron and similar anomalies.

We are concerned (I suppose in some ultimate way) with the distribution of power in society. Classes are stratified according to their economic power, their relation to the production and acquisition of goods. Clearly, as well as the ownership of property or wealth, income is a significant indicator of economic power. But the distribution of income is continuous. There are no sharp breaks or intervals which clearly divide the rich from the comfortably off or the latter from the poor. Wealth is easier from our point of view since it may be argued one either owns wealth or does not. But wealth ranges from a few pounds in a hole in the mattress to a controlling interest in a multi-million-pound industrial or commercial enterprise. From a sociological point of view it is not only the amount of wealth someone has which is likely to be significant but where it is invested or how it is made to work. Similarly with income, the amount is not the only or perhaps even the most important socially significant fact. In terms of the reliability of income and therefore its worth when trying to establish credit the source of the income may be of at least equal importance. The distribution of wealth and income is discussed in Chapter 6.

Occupation and employment status directly reflect the individual's involvement in the productive aspects of the economic process and in the context of his particular occupational responsibilities confer different degrees of authority or influence on the individual. Since his occupation usually determines the amount of income he receives and is usually readily discovered while income and wealth are often difficult to ascertain anyway, occupation is conventionally taken to be the best indication of the individual's position in relation to the distribution and acquisition of goods. The categorization of occupations presents some problems which will be dealt with at greater length in Chapter 5. Clearly the self-employed can be distinguished from those who sell their labour. Those whose employment involves the management of others may be classified separately from those who are only subject to such management. Distinctions can be made in terms of the nature of the industry which employs the worker; for instance, we can separate those workers engaged in productive processes and service industries from those in administration. Other distinctions can be made in terms of skill and qualifications or the degree of security of employment enjoyed. The problem is complex and will be avoided to a certain extent to begin with by adopting conventional definitions which at least make comparisons possible even though the precise evaluation of any differences then observed can be uncertain.

In discussing social stratification I shall be referring to differences within and between the upper, middle and working classes. Very little is known about the upper class and many people doubt the existence of such a class altogether except as a figment which politicians find useful when they need someone to denounce without actually hurting anybody's feelings. We shall explore this mystery further, particularly in the concluding chapter. For the most part then, I shall be discussing relations between the working class and the middle class and will use these terms in general to distinguish the members of families whose chief income earner is a manual worker and those in which he is in a non-manual job respectively. This general distinction between non-manual workers and manual workers is not just a convenient but arbitrary division. The precise boundary between these two social strata is in practice difficult to delineate but the difficulty should not prevent us considering the distribution of rewards and opportunities or the differences in social patterns and attitudes which divide them. The use of conventional groupings should mask 'real' divisions rather than exaggerate them. Thus, if we find that manual workers and non-manual workers differ in respect of some attribute or other, this is likely to be an underestimate of real social difference rather than the artificial contrivance of one. The manual/non-manual division does not only indicate economic or class differences, however. The terms 'middle class' and 'working class' are commonly used in a way which, following Weber's distinction, indicates differences between status groups rather than 'classes' in the strict sense.

Status groups are differentiated by their styles of life and these are still more difficult to be objective about than economic differences though a number of quasi-anthropological studies have described several different patterns or subcultures within British society. Occupation here too seems to be the major index of different styles of life. The level of income, the exigencies of clean and dirty work, variable or regular hours, the security of the job, the different kinds of educational background required, the future orientation or short-run hedonism encouraged by different market situations has encouraged the development of value systems associated with occupational groups which have absorbed or been absorbed into the other value patterns deriving from other traditions — regional, religious, historical and political — which have shaped the national culture.

Status groups, however, are innumerable and status signs shift with fashion or the inventiveness of those seeking to establish some new claim to social esteem. The main boundaries seem to coincide with class boundaries, however, inasmuch as economic resources seem to set the limits within which claims to prestige can be sustained. It is in this context perhaps that it is most appropriate to consider the idea of relative deprivation and reference-group behaviour. Invidious comparison would mostly appear to occur between groups whose status or prestige is close in comparison with other groups. Thus even in relation to income levels manual workers are more likely to compare themselves with other manual workers. The most affluent of manual workers' horizon does not extend beyond the lower ranges of white collar incomes while non-manual workers are unlikely to compare themselves with any but the most highly skilled, and highly paid, manual workers.[1]

In discussing the various aspects of modern British social structure dealt with in the following pages, I shall from time to time refer to different social status groups or subdivisions of social strata such as the traditional working class or the upper and lower middle class. For instance, as we shall see in Chapter 3, geographical mobility is related to socio-economic status and the quality of social experience in different social strata is coloured by the different incidence of geographical mobility. Life in the traditional close-knit working class communities will be contrasted with that of the estate-dwelling workers, perhaps owning their own homes, who have gone in search of better opportunities and left behind them the traditional loyalties of birthplace and community. Still more individualistic, and more detached from the ties of locality, large sections and perhaps the majority of the middle class, especially those in professional and managerial occupations, are still more likely to be orientated towards careers whose specialization demands mobility in pursuit of advancement. This discussion of traditional and geographically mobile working class, of upper and lower middle class, etc., is more schematic than descriptive, however. Many of the studies on which such an account can be based were carried out long since in communities which have, no doubt, been transformed out of all recognition by subsequent redevelopment, migration and affluence. The simplified and schematic representation of the life styles of social strata seeks mainly to fix marks in terms of which the processes of social change and transformation can be plotted. The divisions represent some attempt to secure the ends of dimensions along which change might possibly be measured.[2]

Max Weber distinguished three types of social stratification: classes are divided in terms of their economic resources, status groups in terms of the deference they enjoy and parties in terms of their *right* to have their way in matters affecting society as a whole. At the most general level parties may range from transitory movements associated with a particular

[1] See W.G. Runciman, *Relative Deprivation and Social Justice*, Routledge, 1966, ch. 10 and 11, and Dorothy Wedderburn and Christine Craig, 'Relative Deprivation in Work' in Dorothy Wedderburn (ed.), *Poverty, Inequality and Class Structure*, Cambridge University Press, 1974, pp. 141-64.

[2] cf. John Goldthorpe, David Lockwood, Frank Bechhofer and Jennifer Platt, *The Affluent Worker in the Class Structure*, Cambridge, 1969, p.86, n.1.

campaign, on entry to the Common Market or immigration for instance, to highly institutionalized quasi-permanent groups, like the Labour and Conservative parties. Party differences in the most general sense occur on a wide range of issues and, cutting across class and status boundaries as they do, are difficult to identify. The specifically parliamentary political parties themselves and the distribution of support for them represent this pattern only very crudely, obscuring much of the volatility of opinion and issue as these ebb and flow through the structure of society. This limitation arising out of their endurance and relative unresponsiveness to urgent matters lends a virtue to the study of the parliamentary parties as they seem to reflect the more enduring or longrun groupings within the competition for institutionalized power.

The system of social stratification in Britain is undergoing a continuous process of change. In the last century and a half some classes have grown and acquired a measure of power, while the economic bases of others were being undermined by the forces of economic change. Distinctions between some status groups have disappeared and new dimensions of different-iation have emerged and spread while others have become less important. Religion, nationalism both indigenous and transferred,[1] racialism and other ideological perspectives have divided opinion outside the usual party lines in the parliamentary sense from time to time. The historical process is complex and my account of it very selective in focusing on what seem to be the more enduring patterns and thereby attempting to grasp a sense of the whole.

Institutions

In exploring this particular society in order to understand how it works, it has not, of course, been possible to examine it in all its all too alluring detail. On the contrary; it has been necessary to cast away enormous areas of experience which for many will represent the most important and most interesting aspects of life in contemporary Britain. Only certain aspects of social life have been inspected, those which would seem, though not necessarily at first sight, most helpful in understanding how it is articulated. What remains may perhaps be compared to a bonesetter's view of a beauty queen or a geologist's account of the view over a rich and varied landscape. Much that might attract and engage our interest and affections has been ignored in order to emphasize what seem to be more enduring structural features below the surface.

The formal institutions of contemporary British society, Parliament, the churches, trade unions, the legal and education systems are among the many topics which will not be directly dealt with here. They have been described with admirable clarity and brevity in the Official Handbook

---

[1] See George Orwell, 'Notes on Nationalism', in *England, Your England*, Secker, 1953, pp.41-67.

produced annually by the Central Office of Information.[1] More critical and discursive accounts of these features of our society are legion and many will be referred to in the course of my discussion. But it is not only because these institutions have been so frequently discussed that I will pay them little direct attention but for a better and also more sociological reason. It involves the place of such forms in the societal model I hope to employ and it is this. The formal institutions of a society, the elaborate conventions, the imposing constitutions, the hallowed charters and the subtly drawn statutes may in general be considered as modes of establishing the legitimacy either of already existing structural relations between social groups, or of social procedures deliberately contrived for the pursuance of the interests of some group or the preservation of existing but vulnerable relationships. These formalised social procedures legitimately incorporated through the publication of written documents, and the observation of certain ceremonial formulae and public and private rituals, are merely expressions of some parts of the structure of society. This is not to argue that they are not part of the social reality with which we are concerned, but rather, to deny that they are the whole of that reality. The formal institutions of a society are not themselves the social structure but are conditional upon it and are likely to undergo change as the relations which they legitimate between social groupings change.

Again, this is not intended to deny the constraining effects of the institutions themselves or to argue that they are always dependent factors, never independent. Over and against the individual the formal institutions generally have an independent existence which, if not irresistible, is undeniable. At the level of the society as a whole the significance of the formal institutions is more conventional, more conditional and subject to modification. From the schoolboy's angle the educational system is a given fact of life. For the government in power, it is a matter of the most suitable means towards certain ends and subject to drastic modification should better or cheaper means be discovered or other ends be found more desirable. For interest groups between these extremes, the local authorities or the organised teaching professions, the 'sacred-ness' of the educational system is likely to have an intermediate status. Likewise the political constitution is not an absolute. Constitutional monarchy and the parliamentary system are the conventional arrangements adopted for various reasons in the government of Britain; elsewhere they manage things differently. The individual elector or party member must take these arrangements as given, however. To change them would involve a substantial shift in the balance of interests in the society out of which these particular arrangements have arisen and to the accommodation of which they have been continually modified. Such changes can occur, but they are not brought about by the action of an individual actor.

[1] *Britain: An Official Handbook,* H.M.S.O., annually.

In this study it is not these formal aspects of society but the informal relationships between groups which are of central concern. The way these are represented in the formal conventions of society, and the way these legitimating conventions may succeed or fail in adapting to the social patterns they represent, is in itself an area for investigation and one which may be most instructive to the student of social change. These questions we will, of necessity, encounter again in examining the outcome of the interactions between the forces of change and the factors of stability in British social structure.

In attempting to describe a whole society, as I said earlier, it is necessary to attempt to explain to some extent why at least parts of it are the way they seem to be. In terms of the people whose varied relationships with one another are the society that we seek to understand, this means ultimately that we must attempt to explain, at least in very general terms, why in certain respects they behave the way they do. Thus for those of my readers for whom Britain is a foreign country, I hope the remainder of the book will illuminate some of the strange things that go on here. For the others, for whom nothing that happens in Britain could be anything other than the most natural thing in the world, I offer no exotic surprises, no scandals in Scunthorpe or the Dolce Vita on the Dartford loop. Instead, less appetisingly, I propose to try to blow the dust off some rather dry data and offer what may be a number of new ways through some old facts and figures. This, then, is not a complete account of social life in contemporary Britain. I have written only about the structural aspects of society and only some of these. But in choosing these topics for consideration I have sought to give an impression of the complex whole.

2 The Population

Introduction

The study of social structure, at the most elementary level, is concerned with the pattern of interaction between people. Within a definable population of individuals the range of possible relationships and inter-relationships is certainly very large, and theoretically, possibly infinite but in practice it is limited since the existence of certain social configurations hinders the development of others. Some structural developments may emerge out of the necessities of cooperation for the sake of survival in a given environment with given resources. Others will be shaped by the composition of the population itself, by the proportions of various sorts of individuals it contains. An account of its leading demographic character-istics will therefore be an essential foundation for any systematic examination of a society. Although this is not an aspect of social structure which has always commanded universal interest, awareness of the fundamental significance of population growth and change has increased in recent years and even those readers still unconvinced of this may find much to recommend in dealing with the topic at the outset.

The size and composition of the population are the outcome of the interaction of the numbers of births, deaths and migrations over time. In Britain most of the relevant information on the operation of these factors is available from the regular statistical returns of the Registrars General and the census reports.[1]

Births

It seems appropriate to begin a discussion of the population with the evidence on births. Table 2.1 summarizes the trend in births and birth-rates in the present century. The table clearly shows the major change in the recent demographic history of Britain. This was the ending and reversal of the large and steady downward tendency of the crude birth-rate which had

---

[1] At the time of writing, however, most of the material from the 1971 census was not yet published.

continued from the mid-nineteenth century almost to the middle of the twentieth. The Second Great War and the large-scale mobilization of men and resources which it involved, like the First, naturally disturbed the continuity of civilian life in Britain. After the so-called 'bulge' in the

Table 2.1

Live Births in United Kingdom 1900-1971

	Total (000s)	Total per 1000 population	% Illegitimate
1900-2	1095	28.6	4.3
1910-2	1037	24.6	4.5
1920-2	1018	23.1	4.8
1930-2	750	16.3	4.8
1941	696	14.4	5.5
1951	797	15.8	4.8
1961	944	17.8	5.5
1966	980	17.9	7.6
1971	902	16.2	8.2

Source: *Annual Abstract of Statistics*

number of births in 1947, when many families whose foundation had been postponed due to the uncertainties of wartime were begun, the number of births at first fell. In the United Kingdom as a whole there were 1,025,000 live births in 1947 while in 1955 at the lowest point in the subsequent decline there were 789,000 live births. In Scotland the lowest point was reached in 1952 and in Northern Ireland as early as 1951. The number of births steadily increased thereafter in all parts of the United Kingdom until 1964, when for only the second time since 1920 there were more than a million live births. In England and Wales from the 1947 peak of 20.5 live births per 1,000 population, the crude birth-rate declined to approximately the low fluctuating rate typical of the 1930s. From 1955 to 1964, however, it rose steadily from 15.0 live births per 1,000 population to 18.5 per 1,000. In Scotland and Northern Ireland birth rates have remained higher than in England and Wales throughout the century but have followed a similar pattern of increase and decrease. Since 1964 there has been another reversal of the trend in the number of births, and by 1970 the crude birth-rate had again returned to the level of 40 years before. In the United Kingdom as a whole there were 1,015,000 live births in 1964, thereafter numbers declined to reach 902,000 in 1971.[1] While the trend of the crude birth-rate closely reflects the changing number of

---

[1] *Annual Abstract of Statistics*, No. 109, Table 26.

births, however, a more detailed examination shows that this is the gross outcome of a number of different social developments.

The long decline in fertility which has occurred in all western industrial societies reduced the United Kingdom crude birth-rate from about 35 births per 1,000 of the population in the middle years of the nineteenth century to about 15 births per 1,000 population in the middle 1930s. The Royal Commission on Population showed that 43 per cent of the brides married in Britain in the 1870s had seven or more children while less than two per cent of brides married between 1925 and 1929 had seven or more children.[1] Many explanations have been suggested. Some have sought to find the cause in the operation of environmental factors, others in changes in the genetic character of western man. Environmentalists have contrasted the nervous strain of modern life with the bucolic robustness and vitality of the rustic past, or have suggested that people can produce fewer children because of the synthetic foods now widely consumed as compared with the rich natural foods of former times. These arguments overlook the hardship and struggle for survival which were the lot of the majority of our forebears. They overlook the evidence which indicates that for the poor, even in the country, standards of nutrition were not high either in terms of quantity or quality. In the urban and industrial areas of Victorian England, in fact, food was freely and frequently adulterated sometimes with substances which were actually poisonous.[2]

These explanations are not then very satisfactory. As Dennis Wrong writes '. . . one can also find contemporary customs and conditions favourable to higher fecundity (the maximum biological capacity for reproduction) and fertility (the actual rate of reproduction), such as greater leisure, more adequate diets, and better obstetrical care'. Similarly, 'changes in genetic reproductive capacity great enough to account for the downward trend would probably require several generations, yet the decline was manifest within a much shorter period'.[3] The Royal Commission on Population concluded therefore that the decline in family size could not plausibly be accounted for by involuntary causes; '. . . the alternative view, that the decline in family size has been brought about wholly, or mainly by deliberate family limitation is far better supported'.[4]

The reduction in the birth rate which is the most important and

[1] *Royal Commission on the Population: Report*, H.M.S.O., 1949.

[2] See e.g. Peter Laslett, *The World we have Lost*, Methuen, 1965, ch.5; John Burnett, *Plenty and Want: A Social History of Diet in England from 1815 to the Present Day*, especially ch. 5, 8, 10, Pelican, 1968; E. Royston Pike, *Human Documents of the Industrial Revolution in Britain*, Allen & Unwin, 1966; John Yudkin, 'English Eating in the 1860's', *The Listener*, 30 January 1969, pp. 134-136.

[3] Dennis Wrong, *Population and Society*, Random House, 1961, pp. 54, 55.

[4] *Royal Commission on Population: Report*, paras 77-80, p.32.

influential feature of Britain's demographic history in the first part of the twentieth century was very largely the outcome of deliberate decisions by married couples to have smaller families than those they themselves had grown up in. In accounting for this change it is obvious that the spread of knowledge about and the use of contraceptive techniques has permitted an increasingly large proportion of couples to decide how many children they will have. The increasing proportion of illegitimate children in recent years (see Table 2.1) demonstrates, however, that such knowledge and practice may not yet have spread far enough.

Surveys carried out for the Population Investigation Committee show how approval of birth control has increased. The survey carried out in 1960 drew on a random sample of married men and women up to 59 who had married since the First World War. Fifty per cent of those marrying in the 1920s were without reservation in favour of birth control, but 70 per cent of those marrying in the 1950s unreservedly approved. Of the approvers 80.5 per cent had used one form of birth control or another and even 35.6 per cent of the non-approvers had done so. Middle class people, that is non-manual workers and the wives of non-manual workers, more commonly approved the use of contraceptive procedures but there was little difference between the classes in the extent of ultimate practice. Middle class couples apparently planned the number and spacing of their children from the outset of their marriage. Working class couples tended to begin birth control later in their marriages after they had had enough children.[1] In a subsample of 1,600 marriages within a larger survey carried out in 1967-68 it was found that 93 per cent of middle class couples who had married between 1961 and 1965 already practised contraception and 91 per cent of working class couples married a similar length of time did so. Comparison with marriages of longer duration indicated that the gap between middle class and working class families was rapidly closing and that allowing for those not yet using birth control amongst the most recently married couples the overall proportion deliberately controlling their family size would eventually be about 95 per cent.[2]

The evidence of studies such as these showing the now almost universal practice of contraception, of course only demonstrates how families have implemented their ideas about a desirable number of children. Other factors have been influential in determining what these ideas would be. The consequences of changing notions of what is a desirable number of children, however, have been both profound and far reaching.

The deliberate limitation of the number of children has produced a

---

[1]   See Griselda Rowntree and Rachel M. Pierce, 'Birth Control in Britain', *Population Studies*, 1961, XV, p.192.

[2]   See D.V. Glass, 'The Components of Natural Increase in England and Wales, *Population Studies: Supplement*, May 1970, Table 3, p. 17.

dramatic change in family life. Professor Titmuss[1] pointed out how the average working class woman who married in the 1890s could expect to go through ten pregnancies spread over a period of 15 years or so. A woman who married in the 1950s would on average spend only about four years pregnant or caring for an infant. In addition, and partly because of this change, women's expectation of life has increased giving them the opportunity to care more thoroughly for a growing family than their grandmothers could and nevertheless enjoy the choice of taking up other activities outside the home in the years of maturity and middle age. Increasingly in the 1950s and 1960s the childbearing years have been likely to occur earlier in a woman's lifetime, especially in the working class, so further extending the duration of a possible post-maternal career. It is this more than any purely statutory provision in respect of the franchise or other rights that has made for what Titmuss called 'the revolutionary enlargement of freedom for women'.[2] This emancipation of women from pregnancy has had important consequences for the status of women within the family and beyond it in the sphere of occupations and indeed in the whole of our culture.

It is evident, then, that the birth-rate, which has been the major component of population growth and change in twentieth-century Britain, is the aggregate and mostly unintended[3] outcome of the choices married couples deliberately make about the number of children they wish to have. These choices however are made within a framework of consideration shaped by the potential parents' social circumstances and personal and historical experience. When we consider birth-rate trends we must therefore make a more detailed examination of the kinds of choices being made.

The crude birth-rate can be somewhat misleading here. By relating the number of births to the total population it includes in the calculation children and old people and men as well as women. Especially when men, old people and children are increasing or decreasing as a proportion of the population this can give a distorted impression of demographic events. The crude birth-rate also obscures differences between newly established families and those which have endured for many years and between women of different ages. A better statistic for showing the pattern of decisions about having or not having children is therefore one which

---

[1] R.M. Titmuss, *Essays on the Welfare State*, Allen and Unwin, 1958, See especially ch. 5 'The Position of Women' and ch. 6 'Industrialization and the Family'.

[2] ibid. p.91.

[3] It is most unlikely that concern about population growth or decline enters into decisions about how many children a married couple want except among a tiny minority. Even within this narrow demographically self-conscious group such considerations have probably been widespread only for brief periods in respect of population decline in the late 1930s and the anxieties about population growth at the very beginning of the 1970s.

relates births to the number of women of childbearing age. The number of
live births per 1,000 women aged between 15 and 44 years reached its
lowest point in 1951 and then rose fairly steadily to reach a peak in 1964.

Table 2.2

Birth Rates Specific for Age of Mother in England and Wales

Live Births per 1,000 Women

Age of Mother	1939	1947	1951	1964	1971
15 - 44	61.3	90.6	71.6	92.6	83.6
15 - 19	16.0	19.28	21.03	42.31	50.4
20 - 24	92.7	145.99	126.19	179.50	154.1
25 - 29	113.4	169.65	134.23	185.06	153.0
30 - 34	81.4	117.58	89.04	107.09	77.5
35 - 39	46.6	65.64	45.74	50.00	32.8
40 - 44	15.3	19.44	13.36	13.08	8.1

Source: *Registrar General*

The greatest proportionate change in the number of live births between
1951 and 1964 was the increase from 29,000 to 77,000 to mothers aged
15 to 19 years. Just over half this increase may be attributed to the growth
in numbers of women in the age group together with the substantial
increase in the proportion of them who were married. While in 1951 there
were 1,628,000 women in the 15-19 age group and 42 in every thousand
were married, in the age group of 1964 this had increased to 2,085,000
and 70 in every thousand were married.

The largest *numerical* increase was in the number of births to mothers
aged 20 to 24 years, from 189,000 live births in 1951 to 276,000 in 1964.
Again the increase in the proportion of women in the age group who were
married, from 475 per thousand in 1951 to 578 per thousand in 1964,
together with an increase in the number of women in the age group would
account for approximately 52 per cent of the increase in legitimate births.
The remainder of the increase in legitimate births to women in these age
groups is the result of an increase in the fertility of young women in the
early years of marriage.[1] This could be partly the outcome of a tendency
to produce children earlier in the marriage rather than of an inclination to
produce more.[2] The decline in the fertility of women over 25 years of age
after 1964 might be taken to support this interpretation, though other

[1] See Registrar General's *Annual Statistical Review of England and Wales for 1966*,
    Part II, Table QQ(e).

[2] See D.V. Glass, op.cit., 1970, pp. 14 and 16, and cf. Conrad and Irene Tauber,
    The Changing Population of the United States, Wiley, 1956, pp. 267-8.

factors are involved too. From 1951 the numbers of women in the other relevant age groups declined but, though at all ages the proportion of women who were married increased, this would have been insufficient on its own to offset the decline in numbers except amongst the over 40-year-olds. In the latter age group fertility began to decline after reaching a low peak in 1962 and was already below the 1951 figure by 1964. Amongst women aged 35 to 39 years there was an increase in the proportion married and a rise in the fertility rate, but the overall decline in numbers brought the live births in 1964 to mothers in this age group below the 1951 figure.

Despite the decline of over 300,000 in the number of women aged between 25 and 34, mothers in this age range bore 64,000 more children than the 1951 age group had. Almost three fifths of this increase may be the consequence of the increase in the proportion of women at these ages who were married. Clearly however the increase in the number of third and subsequent children by some 65,000[1] must mainly have been the labour of women in their late twenties and early thirties. Almost one third of the total increase in births in 1964 compared with 1951 was, then, the result of an increase in family size.

The lowest point in birth rates for women in their most fertile years, between that is, 20 and 29, was reached in 1951. From then the rates rose steadily to 1964 and declined thereafter. For women aged 30 to 35, however, the rise did not begin until 1955 and for women over 35, not till 1960. Amongst women aged less than 20, the upward trend began earlier, apparently in the early war years. The onset of this rising trend clearly indicates the change in family building associated with the arrival of a generation of mothers born in the late 1920s and early 1930s and marrying for the most part in the later 1940s.[2]

After 1964 births to women over 20 years of age, and especially to those over 30, declined as Table 2.2 shows. This was certainly more than the consequence of other demographic changes alone. Although there were decreases in the number of women in the age groups at risk over the age of 30, the proportionate decrease in the number of births was greater still. The number of women in England and Wales aged 30-44 decreased by 8.4 per cent between 1964 and 1971 but the number of births to women in this range went down by 33.6 per cent, and while the number of women aged 25 to 29 increased by ten and a half per cent this age group produced eight and a half per cent fewer children. There was a less than four per

---

[1] See *Annual Abstract of Statistics:* Tables showing Legitimate Live Births.

[2] The onset of this trend clearly calls in question the assumption made by Boreham that fertility rates began to rise suddenly in 1955 and in consequence his speculative attribution of causal significance to post-1955 immigration, improving economic circumstances and extensions of social security benefits cannot be wholly accepted, ref. John Boreham, 'The Pressure of Population', New Society, 3 March 1966, p. 10.

cent increase in the number of births to women aged 20 to 24 in 1971 as compared with 1964 but the number of women in the age group increased by 21 per cent as the babies of the postwar bulge reached the age of their own highest fertility. The number of young women aged 15 to 19 on the other hand declined by nine and a half per cent, but by 1971 the number of births to mothers of this age had increased by almost eight per cent on 1964. Clearly a different pattern of decisions was being made about family building. Births of first-born children continued to increase, though only slightly. The numbers of second and subsequent children born, on the other hand, showed a progressive decline after the peak year of 1964.

Studies of changing intentions about family size naturally conform to this pattern. In a survey of over 6,300 married women all aged under 45 years carried out in 1967, Myra Woolf found that the ideal family size declined among those marrying after the early 1950s.[1] John Peel found that, among the more than 300 Hull newlywed couples he surveyed in 1965 and again in 1970, 70 per cent hoped to have one or two children at the later date compared with only 54 per cent when they first married five years earlier. The major change was among couples who had started out planning to have three or more children, though there was also a small reduction in the number planning to remain childless.[2] Still more recently women under 45 who had been under 25 when they married were asked in the 1971 General Household Survey about expected family size both at the time of the survey and when they had first married. Unsurprisingly the longer they had been married the closer their currently expected number of children corresponded to the number they already had. Expectations at marriage had been exceeded by women married before 1960 but for those married since then, so far with fewer children than originally expected, current expectations were less than they had been at marriage.[3] It is difficult to interpret these findings usefully since they may reflect the influence of the experience of married life in contrast with the hopes and dreams of the newlywed or alternatively they may represent a response to historically specific circumstances. Myra Woolf's findings and the sudden change of direction in birth-rates after 1964 suggest that external factors can change family plans dramatically. From the General Household Survey one can see how, at least among women married more than ten years, expectations are shaped by actual behaviour. The opposite is less clearly substantiated. As with other areas of life, expectations about how we will behave in the future no doubt have some

[1] Myra Woolf, *Family Intentions,* Office of Population Censuses and Surveys: Social Survey Division, H.M.S.O., 1971, p. 14.

[2] John Peel, 'Family Planning in the First Five Years of Marriage', *Journal of Biosocial Science,* 1972, 4. p.333.

[3] Office of Population Censuses and Surveys: Social Survey Division, *The General Household Survey,* H.M.S.O., 1973, pp.73-4.

influence on fertility too. But expectations can change quickly for many
reasons and it remains an open question how far studies of this kind can
take us beyond an understanding of fertility that has already occurred.[1]

Though potential parents' intentions offer at best a very uncertain
guide to the future, a good deal can nevertheless be learned from a closer
examination of the past. In the changing pattern of fertility since the
Second World War we can identify two sorts of factors which have had an
effect on birth rates. On the one hand there has been change in the age
cycle with the trend towards childbearing at younger ages, increasingly by
women under 20, and this has continued with increasing weight in
succeeding age cohorts. Then again, we can observe the impact of a
particular historical generation passing through their childbearing years,
whose high fertility at first augmented the age-cycle change to produce the
rising trend of the late 1950s and early '60s. The investigation of such
historically specific influences in the recent demographic history of Britain
has scarcely begun. For the time being the best that can be done is to
identify them and remind ourselves that we still lack any adequate
explanations. In addition there are on the other hand a number of
structural factors, particularly the distribution of age and marital
condition which influence the birth rate, though themselves historically
conditioned and scarcely better understood, they should be considered
independently.

Marriages

Among the major influences on the birth rate has been the changing
incidence of marriage. After the Second World War there was a sharp rise
in the number of marriages but about 1949 the rate returned to something
close to that of the late 1930s. In England and Wales the number of
marriages then increased steadily for ten years from 1958 to level off
around the level of the late 1940s. In Scotland and Northern Ireland where
economic uncertainties and the consequences of migration had greater
effects this trend was less clear. In the United Kingdom as a whole there
were almost 460,000 marriages registered in 1971. It is not the absolute
increase in the number of marriages that is so important however, but
rather the proportion of the population who are married. As Table 2.3
shows more than half the population is married these days compared with
about a third at the beginning of the century. Of more significance for
population growth is the fact that where only one in four women aged
20-24 was married in the early 1930s at the beginning of the 1970s almost
two out of every three in this age-range were married. At the same time,
due to the increased expectation of life more women remain married as

---

[1] See e.g. *Report of the Population Panel*, Cmnd. 5258, H.M.S.O., 1973, para. 163,
    p.44.

fewer marriages are broken by the early death of a husband.[1] On the other hand, having a longer life expectancy than their husbands, many more women survive into old age and elderly widowhood. This increase in the proportion of the population who are widowed contributes to the recent levelling-out of the proportion who are married.

Table 2.3

The Proportion of the Population Married in Great Britain

Census	Proportion of the Total Population Married	Proportion of Women Aged 20-24 who are Married
	%	%
1901	33.1	26.7
1931	40.9	25.4
1951	48.4	47.1
1961	49.5	57.1
1966	50.8	58.1
1971	50.8	62.1

Source: Calculated from *Annual Abstracts of Statistics*

One of the factors which has contributed to the increase in the proportion of women who marry is the changing balance of the sexes in the population. In 1971 there were only 943 males for every 1,000 females in Great Britain. This is mainly attributable to the fact that amongst the elderly there are many more old women than old men since women tend to live longer. In the younger age groups the situation is different. In the earlier years of this century there were about 104 males born for every 100 females. Since the Second World War there have been about 106 males born to every 100 females.[2] However, mortality in childhood, adolescence and early adulthood had always been much higher for males. Mortality statistics suggest that the male from at least the foetal stage on, is inherently more vulnerable than the female and is further subject to the hazards of a more aggressive culturally idealized personality,[3] generally

[1] See P.R. Cox, 'Changes in Ages at Marriage, Childbearing and Death: Preparation of Estimates', Appendix 4 in M. Young and P. Willmott, *The Symmetrical Family*, Routledge, 1973, pp.361-4.

[2] See *The Registrar General's Annual Statistical Review of England and Wales for the year 1971*, Part II, Table D1.

[3] In their survey of families in Dorset, Dundee, Glamorgan, Halifax and Haringey. Hunt and her colleagues found boys more likely to have health and 'other' problems than girls. The most common health problems reported were respiratory illnesses; 'other' problems were mainly behavioural. Audrey Hunt, Judith Fox and Margaret Morgan, *Families and their Needs*, H.M.S.O., 1973, Vol.I, p.38.

more dangerous or injurious working conditions and a greater likelihood of being a casualty of war.

Looking at the single population of an age likely to marry one can see from Table 2.4 the remarkable change that has occurred in the twentieth century.

Table 2.4

Bachelors per Thousand Spinsters aged 15 to 44 years in Great Britain

1901	981
1931	979
1951	1154
1961	1302
1971	1376

Source: Calculated from *Annual Abstract of Statistics*

The shortage of bachelors in 1931 represents an increase from the 1921 position when there were just over eight single men for every ten single women between 15 and 45. This was the result of the terrible destruction of young men in the war of 1914-18, witnessed in every parish war memorial throughout the country. In the early 1960s a generation of spinsters retired from many occupations and professions, in particular teaching, nursing, local government and commercial offices where they devoted their lives to a career instead of the families they might have expected to have had but for that war. In the war of 1939-45 the loss of life amongst British servicemen was rather less than it had been a generation before. In addition, the improvement in the physical welfare of children, through the provisions of the Welfare State made available to all social classes, has meant that fewer males have died in infancy and childhood. Improved working conditions and the National Health Service sustained the improvement in male mortality rates into adulthood. As a consequence there are now more males than females at every age up to 45 years in England and Wales. Scotland and Northern Ireland lag behind because the male expectation of life is not so high there but also as a result of the migration of young men to England and Wales. Thus in Scotland and Northern Ireland the number of females exceeds the number of males at all ages above 25.

The increasing surplus of bachelors is a new feature of this and other large scale urban and industrial societies. Its appearance suggests that in future we can look forward — however apprehensively — to some consequent changes in the still current social norms relating to marriage and family life. The events of the last two or three years would suggest possible developments may be in the direction of a greater acceptance of

male homosexuality or perhaps of a pattern of heterosexual relationships
of shorter duration — perhaps a pattern of serial polyandry of the much
publicized Hollywood variety. Have we here perhaps the demographic
basis of Women's Lib? Or perhaps a factor in the postwar increase in
violent crime? This is of course highly speculative. A study of some 785
adults in San Francisco, however, by Dr Genevieve Knupfer and her
colleagues[1], comparing married men and single men, married women and
single women, suggests that single men were the most unhappy. An
unmarried man was found to be seven times more likely than a spinster to
be a victim of a severe neurotic disorder, to suffer more from loneliness, to
be more aware of being unhappy and less contented with his job. More
discursive commentaries on the role of marriage have commented on its
crucial functions for the psychological well-being of the individual in an
increasingly impersonal society,[2] but I shall return to the evidence on that
aspect of family life in another chapter. In the context of the demographic
trends I have been discussing though, the outlook for young men in Britain
is not a very cheerful one.

Already the worsening of the competitive situation of men in the
marriage market has increased the chances of marriage for women. It has
become much easier than ever before for any woman who wishes to marry
to find a partner, but there are probably still more young men who would
like to marry than can find wives. This has almost certainly been an
important element in the reduction of the average age at marriage of both
men and women. The average age of both brides and grooms declined
steadily from 1945 until the late 1960s. Though there are signs that this
has now levelled out, the mean age for first marriages in 1971 was less than
24 for men and under 22 for women compared with over 26 and 23½
respectively only 20 years earlier. The proportion still in their teens had
fluctuated over a fairly narrow range through the first 40 years of the
twentieth century. About ten per cent of brides and two per cent of
bridegrooms throughout this period were younger than 20. After the
large number of young wartime marriages the proportions at first fell again
but from the mid-fifties continued to rise until the middle 1960s. Since
then over 30 per cent of women and about ten per cent of men marrying
for the first time have been under 20.

While the state of the marriage market is no doubt an important factor
it is, of course, not the only one affecting the decision to marry. F.M.
Musgrove has suggested that this increase in teenage marriage is one
indication of the rising status of the young.[3] In the period of relatively

[1]   Knupfer et al., 'The Mental Health of the Unmarried', *American Journal of
      Psychiatry*, 122, 8, 1966, pp.841-51.

[2]   See e.g. Peter L. Berger and Hansfried Kellner, 'Marriage and the Construction of
      Reality' in Hans Peter Dreitzel (ed.), *Recent Sociology No.2*, Collier-Macmillan,
      1970, pp.50-72.

[3]   F.M. Musgrove, *Youth and the Social Order*, Routledge, 1964.

low unemployment and rising wages especially for young people since 1948 they have become more economically powerful as a group and autonomous as individuals. Fostered no doubt by the commercial encouragement of a sense of independence through the media of the youth culture, their ability and willingness to undertake the complexities of adult life — marriage, children, a mortgage and hire purchase — has in consequence increased. All this is particularly true of young people in the working class.

Rachel Pierce, on the basis of a sample survey of over 700 marriages, described how her 'finding of earlier marriage among the manual worker couples is, of course, consistent with the class differences in contemporary society, where a shorter period of education, little if any further training, apart from apprenticeship, and a much quicker rise, particularly amongst the unskilled workers, to an adult rate of earning find the manual worker independent at a much earlier age than his non-manual contemporary'.[1]

Table 2.5

Socio-Economic Status and Age of Women at Marriage
England and Wales 1961

Socio-Economic Status*	All Wives	All Unbroken Marriages		Proportion of Women married 1959-61 who were less than 20 years old at marriage
		Brides at less than 20 years old	Brides at 20-24 years old	
	%	%	%	%
Upper Middle Class	16.8	8.6	51.7	11.6
Lower Middle Class	22.1	11.1	50.6	15.9
Skilled Working Class	35.5	18.6	54.8	30.3
Semi and Un-skilled Working Class	25.6	19.3	50.3	34.9
All	100.0	15.4	52.1	25.9

*Wives are grouped according to their husband's socio-economic group thus:
    Upper Middle Class: Groups 1, 2, 3, 4, 13.
    Lower Middle Class: Groups 5, 6, 12, 14.
    Skilled Working Class: Groups 8, 9.
    Semi and Unskilled Working Class   Groups 7, 10, 11, 15, 16.
These socio-economic groups are described more fully in Table 2.7.

Source: Calculated from *1961 Census of England and Wales, Fertility Tables,* Table 14.

[1] See Rachel Pierce, 'Marriage in the Fifties', *Sociological Review*, 1963, 11, p.218.

The 1961 Census confirmed Pierce's finding as Table 2.5 indicates. While in all social classes most women marry in their early twenties, far fewer middle class women are likely to have married very young. The final column of the table shows that in the years immediately before the census the proportion of women marrying while still in their teens had increased in all classes. The proportional increases in the working class however were much greater than in the middle class. Thus amongst those marrying in 1959-61 less than one in seven middle class brides was under 20 compared with one in three in the working class. Of course there has been an overall increase since then but we must await the results of the 1971 census to discover whether this difference between the classes has continued to widen throughout the 1960s as it was apparently doing at the beginning of the decade.

Doubtless the readiness with which increasing numbers accept the bonds of matrimony at such relatively tender years also reflects the vital importance of the marriage relationship in the lives of the vast majority of men and women in modern Britain. Perhaps its most weighty implication, however, derives from the apparent association between earlier marriage and larger families.

Table 2.6

Mean Family Size in 1971 by Age of Wife at Marriage and Duration of Marriage

England and Wales

Age at Marriage	Year and Duration of Marriage				
	1941 30 years	1951 20 years	1956 15 years	1961 10 years	1966 5 years
Under 20 years	2.86	3.05	2.82	2.41	1.58
20-24 "	2.18	2.28	2.29	2.10	1.33
25-29 "	1.71	1.87	2.07	1.96	1.34
30-34 "	1.22	1.37	1.53	1.56	1.16
35-39 "	.66	.67	.78	.83	.69
40-44 "	.24	.22	.25	.28	.25
All Ages under 45 yrs	2.04	2.21	2.29	2.11	1.39

Source: Registrar General's *Annual Statistical Review of England and Wales for 1971*, Part II, Table PP.

Table 2.6 shows that the brides of 1951, 1956 and even 1961 had on average by 1971 more children than those marrying in 1941. For each duration of marriage the younger brides had produced more children and the proportion of women remaining childless increases with their age at marriage. As a consequence of the increased proportion of women marrying under 20 years of age the proportion of childless marriages has declined.

Table 2.7

Family Size and Socio-Economic Status
England and Wales 1961

Husbands' Socio-Economic* Group	Mean Number of Children**	
	All Families†	1956 Marriages***
1 Employers and Managers (large establishments)	1.67	1.32
2 Employers and Managers (small establishments)	1.71	1.37
3 Professional workers – self-employed	1.91	1.69
4 Professional workers – employees	1.52	1.35
5 Intermediate non-manual workers	1.54	1.29
6 Junior non-manual workers	1.56	1.20
7 Personal service workers	1.81	1.61
8 Foremen and supervisors – manual	1.93	1.27
9 Skilled manual workers	1.86	1.36
10 Semi-skilled manual workers	2.04	1.47
11 Unskilled manual workers	2.36	1.74
12 Own account workers (other than professional)	1.82	1.50
13 Farmers – employers and managers	2.18	1.76
14 Farmers – own account	2.02	1.64
15 Agricultural workers	2.17	1.57
16 Members of armed forces	1.74	1.90

*For a fuller description of the Registrar General's Socio-Economic Groups see e.g. Census 1961: Great Britain Summary Tables, pp.xxii-xxiv.
**These figures refer to the mean number of children of women married only once and enumerated with their husbands.
†Marriages referred to in this column are those of any duration of wives first married when aged less than 45 years.
***These families are those of women married for five complete years who were aged at marriage between 20 and 24 years inclusive.

Source: 1961 Census of England and Wales: Fertility Tables, Table 14.

Since family size is associated with age at marriage and age at marriage is associated with social class it will surprise no-one to learn that family size also varies with the family's socio-economic status. The relationship, however, is not a simple one and this complexity itself is significant both directly in showing that family size cannot be the effect of any single cause, and indirectly in what it reveals of the complexity of social stratification in modern Britain.

The first column in Table 2.7 shows that in general the largest families tended to be either rural, that is those of farmers and agricultural workers (socio-economic groups 13, 14, 15) or to be fathered by the less skilled manual workers (groups 10, 11). The fathers of the smallest families were professional employees (group 4) and members of the lower middle class (groups 5, 6). Comparing these average family sizes is not an altogether straightforward matter, however, on account of the different age structures of the socio-economic groups. These are partly shaped by the typical career and recruitment patterns of the occupations which comprise any particular group, and partly by historical changes in the relative growth of different occupations. Socio-economic groups 1 and 3 (employers and managers in establishments employing 25 or more people in central and local government, industry, commerce, etc. and self-employed professional workers) and 8 (foremen and supervisors – manual) for instance have large proportions of older men because they recruit the more experienced and retain the more senior. Types of occupation which have more recently expanded such as those represented in socio-economic group 4 (professional employees) are more likely to include a larger proportion of younger members. Even allowing for differences in the average age at marriage in different social strata, older men are likely to have been married longer and on that account have fathered more children than younger men.

The figures in the second column of Table 2.7, which refer to wives married for the same length of time and at similar ages, to some extent evade these problems. Comparing on this basis fertility in different social strata during the late 1950s and early 1960s, a rather complex pattern emerges. The largest of these families still seemed to be in the rural groups (13, 14, 15), and manual workers (groups 9, 10, 11) apparently fathered more children than the average middle class male. The fairly simple status gradient noticeable in the case of marriage age is not apparent, however, for family size. Within the working class family size was inversely related to social status. That is to say, just as the wives of unskilled manual workers tended to be married younger than the wives of skilled manual workers, even holding age at marriage constant they also, on average, had larger families. Amongst the rural groups and in the middle class, the opposite situation generally prevailed. Farmers' wives married later than the wives of agricultural workers but, controlling for age, they had larger families by the time they had been married five years. Among the middle class groups it was the independent professionals (group 3) whose families were largest — larger than most manual workers' families, while the smallest families of all were those of junior non-manual workers (group 6). In other words, amongst these younger families in the middle class, in contrast with the working class, it was the higher status families which were largest.

The pattern of family size in the middle class is also to be contrasted with the pattern of marriage in the middle class — the wives of self-employed professionals were by a long way those least likely to marry when under 20 years old and uniquely at the beginning of the 1960s showed a declining tendency to do so.

Although we cannot place complete reliance on them, studies of anticipated family size suggest that this pattern persisted at least until the later 1960s. Myra Woolf found that the intended family size of professional and managerial workers' wives continued to increase among those who married in the 1960s while lower-middle class and working class women marrying after the middle 1950s showed continuously declining expectations.[1] Among the couples from Hull whom John Peel studied, it was the middle class and unskilled-working class families who changed their minds most dramatically however. At first, it seems, they wanted larger than average families but after five years intended to have fewer children than the rest of the sample.[2] Because the middle class were undifferentiated in this study there is a problem of comparability here and, as I have suggested, expectations or intentions may in any case change more rapidly and more radically than actual behaviour.

Referring back to the pattern of achieved family size in 1961, continuing prejudice against, or ignorance of, efficient means of family planning might help explain the pattern of family size within the working class at that time. In the rural groups and in the middle class, however, it was the more affluent who tended to have the most children. Thus fertility is neither a simple function of prosperity and poverty nor a direct product of market situation. Undeniably these factors constrain people's lives but the general attitudes and values that each particular couple have also enter into their family planning decisions. Religious beliefs and inherited cultural tradition have to be taken into account here. Kelvin and Butler and Stokes for instance found that in both the middle class and in the working class larger families were more common among Labour voters than Conservative voters.[3] What is evident is that class differences are complex and are changing but we must seek further evidence before we can be sure just how.

[1] Woolf, loc.cit., pp.30-31.

[2] Peel, loc.cit., 1972.

[3] See R.P. Kelvin, 'The Non-Conforming Voter', *New Society*, 25 November 1965 pp.8-12; David Butler and Donald Stokes, *Political Change in Britain*, Macmillan, 1969, p.271.

Illegitimacy and Pre-Marital Conception

Fertility is not only influenced by the changing pattern of marriage. A still small, though till recently increasing, proportion of children are born to unmarried mothers so that, in 1971, one child in every 12 born was illegitimate. The proportion was about one in 16 in Scotland and one in 32 in Northern Ireland.

Part of the increase in illegitimacy can clearly be attributed to the declining proportion of conceptions which lead to legitimate maternities. Getting a girl 'in the family way' was more likely to lead a young man into marriage in 1938 than in the fifties, sixties or seventies. Though there has been an overall increase in pre-marital conceptions, illegitimate maternities are more frequent in the larger urban areas and conurbations — particularly West Yorkshire, South East Lancashire and Greater London — and least common in rural areas though this may be due to the migration of unmarried mothers to the cities where facilities are better and it is easier to achieve some degree of anonymity.[1]

Table 2.8

Illegitimacy and Pre-marital Conception in England and Wales: All live Births*

Year	Percentage Illegitimate	Percentage Legitimate ·Births Pre-maritally Conceived	Pre-maritally conceived Legitimate Births as % of All Pre-marital Conceptions
1938	4.2	10.2	70.2
1951	4.8	7.5	60.1
1961	6.0	7.3	54.9
1971	8.4	8.6	50.6

*Pre-marital conception rates are calculated by the interval between the date of marriage and the birth of the first child. All women producing children within eight months of their wedding (8½ months up to 1951) are assumed to have conceived before marriage.

Sources: *Annual Abstracts of Statistics* and Registrar General's *Annual Statistical Review of England and Wales 1971*, Part I Tables D1 and UU.

Two thirds of all illegitimate maternities were to mothers over 20, less than a third to mothers in their teens. But more than one in four maternities to mothers under 20 years of age was illegitimate in 1971,

[1] See *Registrar General's Annual Statistical Review of England and Wales 1971*, Part II, Table GG.

three and a half times the proportion in any other age group.[1] I do not think one can deduce anything for the future from these high rates amongst the youngest fertile age group. That is to say illegitimate births should be seen as part of the generally high level of fertility amongst younger women. There is no sign of any lesser propensity to marry in later life. Neither can illegitimacy rates reasonably be treated as a sign of the imminent decline of the family as an institution in contemporary society as they have sometimes been by the cassandras of the small screen and the jeremiahs of the popular press. For a start perhaps half of all recorded illegitimacy in fact occurs within the context of family life. Professor Glass has referred to a special study made by the Registrar General of England and Wales which revealed that in one third of the births registered as illegitimate which were matched against the 1961 census, both mother and father were listed as present so that there was a *de facto* family unit while the subsequent re-registration of almost a fifth of all illegitimate births indicates that this proportion should perhaps rather be regarded as akin to pre-marital conceptions.[2] Others have taken a more political line on the subject. Hartley, for instance, has argued that the rise in illegitimacy in Britain was associated with the extension of Welfare State facilities! 'While I would not pretend to suggest', she wrote, 'that such aid is the *cause* of illegitimacy, I would suggest that its availability may reduce the motivation to prevent conception.'[3] This hypothesis is not well supported and further doubt is cast upon its plausibility earlier in Hartley's discussion of increasing illegitimacy by her observation that in the United States 'the same phenomenon seems to be occurring with the U.S. moving farther and faster'.[4] A sober comparison would not have suggested at that time that the United States was moving farther and faster than Britain in the provision of Welfare State aid.

Very little information is available on the class distribution of illegitimacy but the survey by Pierce referred to earlier provides data on pre-nuptial conception rates in the 1950s. As we have seen the proportion of pre-maritally conceived but legitimate maternities has increased since then but in the absence of better information we can probably assume that the relative proportions still hold good.

[1] ibid, Tables AA(a) and FF.

[2] D.V. Glass, 'The Components of Natural Increase in England and Wales', Memorandum to Select Committee on Science and Technology (Sub Committee C) — see *First Report: The Population of the United Kingdom,* H.M.S.O., 1971, p.190; Registrar General's *Annual Statistical Review of England and Wales 1971,* Part II, Table T3; and *Report of the Population Panel,* H.M.S.O., 1973, p.41.

[3] Shirley M. Hartley, 'The Amazing Rise of Illegitimacy in Great Britain', *Social Forces,* 1966, 44, p.542.

[4] ibid, p.538.

Table 2.9

The Incidence of Precipitated Marriages
amongst Couples Marrying 1950-1959

		Husband's occupation at marriage		
	All	Non-manual	Skilled-Manual	Other-Manual
Percentage of brides of all ages	16.3	7.6	18.9	21.1
Teenage brides	32.0	28.0	28.4	36.4
Brides aged 20-24	12.7	4.5	15.4	17.4
Brides aged 25+	11.6	5.7	17.8	13.5

Source: Rachel M. Pierce "Marriage in the Fifties", *Sociological Review,*
1963, 11, p.221.

It is evident that middle class brides, especially the older ones, were rather more prudent in one way or another than working class brides but that about one third of all teenage brides were pregnant at marriage. Comparing this rate with the frequency of pre-nuptial pregnancy for teenage brides marrying in the 1930s, however, Pierce found the proportion had scarcely risen. She points out that with the increase in teenage brides, this, of course, means that there are many more pregnant teenage brides now but not proportionately more.[1]

It remains uncertain whether the more 'permissive' pattern of sexual behaviour among young people which this reflects has itself helped to bring about the lowering of the average age at marriage or whether both are the result of more general cultural changes. It hardly needs pointing out that changes in pre-marital sexual activity are likely to have an effect on fertility rates. What it is important to note is that the effect still works on legitimate birth rates too.

Fertility and Social Change

Fertility has become substantially a matter of deliberate decision making on the part of parents though from time to time they may revise their ideas about how many children they would like to have. Family building, perhaps like most other deliberate human behaviour properly understood, is affected by two main sets of factors, namely those which comprise the circumstances within which decisions are made and, secondly, those which

[1] Rachel M. Pierce, op.cit., p.217; cf. Griselda Rowntree 'Teenage Marriage', *New Society,* 1, 1, 1963.

in the past shaped the way in which the individual is likely to perceive and respond to his present situation. As it is perceived by, or as it impinges on, potential parents the contemporary social environment includes such influences as the family's economic prospects, prevailing social customs, religious beliefs and secular attitudes relating to family life, and current fashions in the care and rearing of children. In addition to the contemporary scene, however, present behaviour may be shaped by the couple's past experience in circumstances which have ceased to exist, in their relationships with their own parents for instance, or their reactions or responses to the beliefs and behaviour of preceding generations. Such influences as these may endure throughout their lifetime, outweighing the exigencies of a changing social environment. As Butler and Stokes have noted, 'our evidence suggests that beliefs as to family size tend in an interesting way to be tied to a wider pattern of values and beliefs, of which political allegiance and aspirations of social mobility are also part'.[1]

The shortening inter-generational interval and the tendency toward earlier marriage can, to some considerable extent, be understood in terms of a secular change in the social status of adolescents and young adults associated in particular with the continuing improvement in their relative economic prosperity since the 1930s. Equallythe discontinuities in these trends in the years after 1968 may reflect the uncertainties produced by the increasing economic inflation with its particular impact on young married couples.[2] The fertile generation of women born around the year 1930, whose impact on the birth rates of the 1950s and early 1960s was so great, seems to require an historically more specific explanation. The women of that generation were and remained different from their immediate elders and from their juniors. Their family building was evidently less affected by contemporaneous circumstances and more by some set of factors which marked them early and continued to influence them in a particular way. Their parents' generation had deliberately limited its families, perhaps in reaction to the straitened circumstances and even frequent poverty of large families at the turn of the century. They themselves perhaps, in their turn, were reacting against the Stopesian views of their parents. On the other hand, the crucial experiences may have been associated with the economic circumstances of their childhood in the late 1930s, or perhaps their adolescent impressions of the war.

The reduction in fertility, except amongst adolescents after 1964 however, occurred both amongst the fertile generation, then in their later

---

[1] D. Butler and D. Stokes, op.cit., 1969, p.62.

[2] See Myra Woolf, op.cit. p.121, *Report of the Population Panel*, Table 14, pp. 44 and 45; and *Annual Statistical Review of England and Wales for 1971*, Part II, Table D. It is on the other hand, however, hard to see how inflation might have been a factor in the similarly fluctuating illegitimacy rate. In this case the effect of the Abortion Act 1968 has probably been of greater significance; see *Social Trends* No.3, 1972, Table 68.

thirties, and also amongst their younger successors. This seems to have taken most demographers by surprise and satisfactory explanations are still lacking.

Deaths

While fertility has been the major factor influencing the growth of the population, its composition has been significantly affected by the incidence of mortality. Of course death still comes to all of us sooner or later, the important demographic question is when? In the 30 years between 1880 and 1910, death rates in all age groups fell by about a third. This decline continued, though more slowly, until about 1930 since when the crude death-rate, that is for all age groups taken together, has fluctuated around 11 and 12 deaths per thousand in the population. If we look at death-rates for each age group separately it is nevertheless apparent that great improvements have been made. The improvement in mortality rates is most marked in the case of infant mortality. In the United Kingdom as a whole by 1971 the chance that a child under one year old would die was about one eighth what it had been at the beginning of the century and less than a third of what it was until 1941.

Table 2.10

Infant and Maternal Mortality in the United Kingdom
Rates per thousand live births

Year	Deaths of Infants under 1 year of age	Maternal Deaths (in pregnancy and childbirth)
1900-2*	142	4.71
1930-2*	67	4.54
1941	63.3	3.20
1951	31.1	0.82
1961	22.1	0.35
1971	17.9	0.17

*Annual Averages.

Source: *Annual Abstract of Statistics*, 109, 1972, Table 35.

As Table 2.10 shows too, deaths of women in pregnancy and childbirth in the U.K. were about 26 times more frequent in the 1930s and almost five times more frequent even in the 1950s than in 1971. Thus while childbearing has become much safer, it also has become productively more efficient than ever, since a higher proportion of children survive into physical maturity.

In England and Wales, the proportion of still-births has declined since 1930-32 when for every thousand live and still-births, 41 were still-births. In 1951, there were 23, in 1961 there were 19, and in 1971 in every thousand births only 12 were still-births. A study of over 14,000 still-births and more than 17,000 infant deaths registered in England and Wales between April 1964 and March 1965 showed that, though there was an improvement in the rates in all regions and all social classes, still-births were significantly more common in the working class than in the middle class. Social class differences were greatest in the North and in Wales.[1]

Death-rates amongst the older age groups in the population have not been amenable to such striking improvements. Nevertheless, for age groups above 55 years, taking males and females together, 1971 death-rates for the U.K. were only about four fifths of what they had been 40 years before. For age groups under 35 years old, death rates were between just less than a fifth and just over a quarter of what they had been in 1931. The number of people in the older age groups was of course enormously increased because of this improvement in the survival rates of the young.

The advantage of the female sex at all ages can be seen in Table 2.11, and despite the tremendous reduction in all mortality rates, this advantage has been increasing at all ages. This is clearly reflected in the average expectation of life, for mortality rates are but the sadder obverse of survival rates. The figures in Table 2.12 show the age which according to the Registrar General's calculation exactly half the children of each sex born in a given year or years could expect to reach.

Table 2.11

Death Rates by Age in 1931 and 1971 in the United Kingdom
Deaths per thousand at each age

Ages	1931		1971	
	Males	Females	Males	Females
0-4	22.3	17.7	4.7	3.6
5-9	2.3	2.1	0.4	0.3
10-14	1.5	1.5	0.4	0.2
15-19	2.6	2.4	0.9	0.4
20-24	3.3	2.9	1.0	0.4
25-34	3.5	3.3	1.0	0.6
35-44	5.7	4.6	2.4	1.6
45-54	11.3	8.3	7.3	4.4
55-64	23.7	17.6	20.6	10.4
65-74	57.9	43.7	52.3	26.9
75-84	134.2	110.1	118.2	76.6
85 and over	277.0	246.3	251.0	209.1
All Ages	12.9	11.5	12.2	11.1

Source: *Annual Abstract of Statistics, 109*, 1971, Table 41.

[1] General Register Office of England and Wales, *'Regional and Social Factors in Infant Mortality'*, H.M.S.O., July 1966.

Table 2.12

Expectation of Life at Birth in England and Wales

Year	Males	Females
1838-54	39.9	41.9
1901-10	48.5	52.4
1930-32	58.7	62.9
1951	65.8	70.9
1961	68.0	73.8
1971	69.0	75.3

Source: Registrar General's *Statistical Review of England and Wales for 1971*, Part II, Table B2.

The transformation since the middle of the nineteenth century is remarkable. Then half of the males born died before their fortieth birthday. By the beginning of the twentieth century, the improvement was considerable but even then less than half survived to their fiftieth year. It was another 50 years before the pattern of death rates permitted the prediction that half the males born would see out a full working life. It seems, however, that more than two thirds of the males born in 1971 will survive into the years of retirement. Throughout this period, as we have seen, females have survived longer than males so that by 1971 half the females born could be expected to reach the age of 75. At the same time, the difference in the average life expectation of two years in favour of women in the mid-nineteenth century had increased to probably over six years in 1971. Again while the rate of improvement in life expectancy has been slowing down, it has done so to a greater extent for men.

Mortality rates and social class are inversely related. Standardized mortality rates for 1959-63 of unskilled workers were double those of professional and managerial workers.[1] Indeed in 1971 unskilled men of working age were about three times more likely than professional men to say they suffered from a chronic illness and lost about five times as many days away from work due to sickness or injury. Children under five in unskilled workers' families were only about half as likely to be seen by their doctors in a two-week period as compared with those in all other strata, middle class or working class, though among older children and men of working age unskilled workers and their children were the most likely to consult their G.P., but not perhaps to the extent that the chronic sickness and absence from work figures might suggest.[2] The lesser extent to which they make use of the medical services despite the evidently

[1] Registrar General's Decennial Supplement, *Occupational Mortality Tables*, H.M.S.O., 1973.

[2] See *General Household Survey 1971*, pp. 279, 303 and 319.

greater frequency of sickness and injury among unskilled workers and their families represents a major problem in improving mortality rates to the level achieved by those more fortunately placed. It is also an indication of the self-sustaining processes of inequality in society which I shall return to in later chapters.

The Age Structure

The changing pattern of mortality rates has had some effect on the size but more particularly on the composition of the population. Obviously, the improvement in the survival of children has helped to sustain the growth of the population even through the period when the average size of families was declining. At the same time, this improvement doubtless made some contribution to the changing climate of opinion about the desirable number of children in a family. The more important direct effect of improvements in survival rates, both of children and adults, has been the alteration produced in the age structure of the population which in turn has produced secondary effects in many areas of life.

The decline in fertility in the late nineteenth and the earlier part of the twentieth centuries led to a decline in the proportion of children in the population. This was augmented by the increasing numbers of adults as more children than before survived into adulthood. The improvement in the average expectation of life has also meant that an increasing proportion of the population survives into old age and that an increasing proportion of the aged is very old.[1]

In Table 2.13 the under-15 year olds broadly represent the wholly dependent young, while men of 65 and over and women of 60 and over can generally be assumed to be retired. There has been a steep increase in retirement amongst men and whereas in 1959 only 47 per cent of men retired at 65 by 1969 more than 70 per cent did so at this age or earlier.[2] The dependency ratio expresses the ratio between these groups and the age groups which include almost all the economically active members of the population. This range from 15 to 64 for men and to 60 for women also includes, however, an increasing number of people enduring full-time courses of education (more than one and a half million of them in 1971), some threequarters of a million of the chronically sick and disabled who cannot work and about six and a half million full-time housewives, women, that is, with no paid work outside their own homes.

[1] See N.H. Carrier, 'Demographic Aspects of the Ageing of the Population', ch. 24. A.T. Welford et al. (eds), *Society*, Routledge, 1963.

[2] Brian Abel-Smith, 'Public Expenditure on the Social Services', *Social Trends*, No.1, 1970, p.18.

Table 2.13

Age Structure of the United Kingdom Population 1901-1971

Year	Total Population (millions)	Percentage in each Age Range			Dependency Ratio** (per thousand)
		0-14	15-64/59*	65/60* and over	
1901	38.2	32.5	61.3	6.2	632
1931	46.0	24.3	66.1	9.6	512
1951	50.2	22.5	63.9	13.5	564
1961	52.7	23.3	62.1	14.6	611
1971	55.4	24.2	59.8	16.0	673

*Retirement ages: 65 for men, 60 for women.
**The Dependency Ratio is the number of persons aged 14 and under and 65/60 and over per thousand persons aged 15-64/59.

Source: *Annual Abstracts of Statistics* 90, 1953 and 109, 1972 and *Social Trends, 3,* 1972, 'Social Commentary', Table 1, p.6.

In the earlier part of the century Britain had a young population. Almost a third was under 15 years of age at the beginning of the century but declining fertility reduced this to less than a quarter by 1931. Rising birth-rates again increased the absolute numbers of the young, who in 1964 for the first time reached a higher figure than in 1901, but as a proportion of the larger population their position advanced only slowly and that mainly as a consequence of the smaller numbers in the middle age ranges where the low fertility rates of the thirties were making their delayed impact. Perhaps the most striking feature of Table 2.13 is the dramatic increase during the first half of the century in the proportion of the population over retirement age. It is this which has maintained the trend in the dependency ratio since the 1930s. As Table 2.14 shows women outnumber men among the older age groups, and increasingly so beyond retirement age, though males outnumber females more in each succeeding age group under 40.

In 1971 the numbers in each succeeding age group were larger until we reach the 30-39 year olds. They were born in the years of low fertility rates in the 1930s and are fewer in number than any other age group under 60. It was this relatively small cohort, however, which includes many of those women whose fertility produced the rising birth-rates of the early 1960s. The larger numbers in the following cohorts means that even a reduction in age-specific fertility rates could nevertheless produce a similar or even growing number of births. As the Report of the Population Panel pointed out 'The age structure of the population is itself an almost

inevitable cause of further growth'.[1] The children born in the postwar
'bulge' and aged about 24 in 1971 are the cause of the sharp rise in
numbers in the 20-29 year old age group, while the high levels of fertility
during the 1960s account for the increase in the youngest age groups.
Among the older age groups people survive in ever larger proportions than
their seniors, though mortality rates, especially for men, begin to rise
increasingly steeply after the age of 45. In 1971 the number of men in
their fifties and sixties was less than it would have been but for the 1939-45
war and the effects of the 1914-18 war are apparent in the small
proportion of men amongst the elderly. Mostly, however, this is the result
of the generally better expectation of life women enjoy even in civil life.

Table 2.14

Age and Sex in the United Kingdom in 1971: Total Population *

Ages	Numbers (millions)	Percentage in Each Age Group	Female Surplus (in thousands)
70 and over	4.5	8.1	1391
60-69	5.9	10.5	525
50-59	6.6	11.9	214
40-49	6.8	12.3	45
30-39	6.4	11.5	−88
20-29	8.0	14.4	−110
10-19	8.2	14.7	−217
Under 10	9.2	16.6	−237
TOTAL	55.7	100.0	1523

*Including members of the armed forces temporarily abroad.

Source: Calculated from *Annual Abstract of Statistics 109*, 972,
            Table 13.

Change in the age structure of the population has consequences which
go beyond its implications for future population growth alone. The
pattern of change in contemporary Britain will by itself obviously demand
a continuing and increasing deliberate redistribution of resources from the
working population to the dependent groups because it is the economically inactive sections of the population which are increasing fastest.
Without any rise in standards there will thus be, through a widening of
demand, an increase in the amount of money which must be spent on
education; welfare services, in particular health; and pensions. In turn this
is likely to influence the distribution of employment amongst the working
population, reinforcing the trend toward the services sector. Then again,

[1] loc.cit., 1973, para.3, p.1.

the generation born in the 1930s and 1940s which will be at the peak of its occupational career in the 1970s and '80s will be succeeded by a generation whose larger numbers will mean worsening career prospects unless occupational opportunities expand at the higher levels too.

Less obvious, but socially no less significant, effects are likely to follow. For instance, just as the changing balance of the sexes, especially amongst the young and single, was likely, I suggested, to bring about some cultural change in relations between the sexes, so the changing age structure is likely to have consequences for the relations between the generations.[1]

The Balance of Migration

In addition to the changing patterns of fertility and mortality, the size and composition of the population is also affected to a certain extent by movements outward and inward, to and from other countries. Some of the social consequences of migration will be referred to in the next chapter but, for the present, I want to concentrate upon its demographic aspects.

Table 2.15

Net Gain and Loss from Migration
(in thousands)

Inter-censal period	Great Britain	England and Wales	Scotland
1901-1911	−755	−501	−254
1911-1921	−859	−620	−239
1921-1931	−562	−170	−392
1931-1951	+508	+757	−249
1951-1961	+150	+406	−256
1961-1971	−404	−106	−298

Source: *Annual Abstract of Statistics 109*, 1972, Table 18.

Comparing the natural increase of the population, that is the excess of births over deaths in a given period, with the actual increase or decrease, as observed say in the censuses, makes it possible to estimate the net gain or loss by migration. As in the nineteenth century, the growth of the population in the twentieth century has been slowed down by the net loss of population overseas. Between the beginning of the century and 1931 there was a net loss of well over 2,000,000 emigrants from Great Britain. After that, however, there was a substantial overall net gain as in the years

---

[1] See, e.g., Holger R. Stub 'Education, the professions, and long life', *British Journal of Sociology*, XX, 1969, pp.177-89. This question is discussed briefly in the context of family life in Chapter 4.

of depression many former emigrants returned after finding life in Canada, Australia or the United States even harder for the unsuccessful than they had known it here. At the same time with the rise to political power in Europe of parties employing political police, the persecution of minorities and other forms of oppression, there was a large-scale immigration from the continent including a quarter of a million refugees. After 1945 there was again a large amount of emigration to Canada, Australia, Rhodesia and South Africa and also to the U.S.A., but this is masked in the table by the large prewar inflows and the postwar immigrants particularly from Eastern Europe. Most of the settlement from overseas was concentrated in England and Wales. Scotland has been a country of net emigration throughout the twentieth century and since 1901 has lost overseas the equivalent of one third of her present population. Emigration from Scotland has been increasing though it did not in the 1960s reach the level of the 1920s, when it completely offset natural increase and the population for a time declined.

A second phase of immigration from 1954 to about 1962 or 1963 was boosted by a large influx from the Commonwealth countries, in particular the West Indies, India and Pakistan, but this was substantially checked by the Commonwealth Immigration Act which came into effect in 1962 and a number of more recent 'tightening-up' measures. At the same time emigration was increasing and by 1963 exceeded immigration even in England and Wales.

The International Passenger Survey introduced in 1964 and now carried out on behalf of the Department of Trade and Industry provides us with a fairly reliable basis for estimating the characteristics of immigrants and emigrants from year to year. International passengers are classified as migrants if they indicate their intention to reside in or be away from the United Kingdom for twelve months or more. The balance of recent migration, at least since 1964 has been consistently outward and is, of course, the product of large inward and outward flows. Table 2.16 shows that between 1964 and 1971 there were more than a 1,500,000 immigrants to and over 2,000,000 emigrants from the United Kingdom. Many immigrants – about a third – were of course British citizens returning after residence abroad. In addition to those in the table, however, there was also a net movement of citizens of the Irish Republic into the U.K. throughout the period who were not covered by the survey and have been estimated to average about 10,000 a year, so that in the period represented the total net loss was probably a bit under 400,000.

In 1971 there was a substantial movement of migrants in both directions between Britain and the U.S.A. and the countries of Western Europe. Immigrants from the United States and from Europe were for the most part aliens while emigrants to those destinations were fairly evenly divided between British citizens and aliens. There were large numbers, mainly of British citizens, moving in both directions between the U.K. and the

Commonwealth African countries. More than half of all the emigrants
from Britain in 1971, however, went to Commonwealth countries – in the
main British citizens going to Australia, Canada or New Zealand. Overall
there were more men than women amongst emigrants but this picture was
the result of the large numbers in the 25-44 years age range. In the 15-24
years age group, women, especially the single, were in a large majority and
again slightly exceeded men in number amongst emigrants over 45 years of
age. The largest proportion of emigrants naturally came from the South East
of England and by contrast with emigrants from the northern and midland
regions, Wales and Scotland, women overwhelmingly outnumbered men
among those from the South East.[1]

Table 2.16

Migration to and from the United Kingdom 1964 - 71* (in thousands)

Citizenship of Migrants	Inward	Outward	Net gain (+) or loss (−)
Australia, Canada and New Zealand	112	128	−16
Other Commonwealth**	488	134	+354
Aliens	438	272	+166
British U.K.	545	1513	−968
All migrants beyond British Isles	1584	2047	−463

*Excluding migrants to and from the Republic of Ireland.
**Including U.K. passport holders from E. Africa from mid-1967.

Source: *Social Trends No. 3,* 1972, Table 11.

Rather less than half of the net emigration of British citizens was
offset by the net inward balance of Commonwealth and alien immigrants
and census figures suggest that probably fewer than half of these stay as
much as five years in Britain.[2] Of the net inflow of aliens three quarters
came from the U.S.A. or Western Europe outside the six countries which
then formed the E.E.C., and just under half of the 1971 net inflow of
Commonwealth citizens came from India, Pakistan and Ceylon. There was
a small net outflow to the West Indies.[3]
    Emigrants are on average slightly older and more likely to be married

[1]   See Registrar General's *Annual Statistical Review of England and Wales for 1971,*
      Part II, Table S2(f.)).

[2]   See *1966 Census: Migration Summary Tables,* Part I, Tables 2A and 2B and *1961
      Census: Great Britain Summary Tables,* Table 30.

[3]   See Registrar General's *Annual Statistical Review of England and Wales for 1971,*
      Part II, Table S2(a).

than immigrants. In Table 2.17 it is clear that children under fifteen represented about a quarter and workers rather more than half of the net outward movement of British citizens. Children and housewives form similar proportions of the smaller net inflow of Commonwealth citizens, mainly the dependants of immigrants already here. Children and housewives make up a smaller proportion of the inflow of aliens the majority of whom, but for the students, would be workers. The majority of economically active Commonwealth citizens coming into the United Kingdom in 1971 were in the professional and managerial category as a result of the Department of Employment's voucher scheme. It would appear that more aliens than Commonwealth citizens in manual and clerical occupations were able to enter Britain even before her accession to the Common Market. Students were the largest group in the net gains of both aliens and Commonwealth citizens.

Table 2.17

Balance of Migration into (+) and out (−) from the United Kingdom in 1971 by Occupation and Citizenship

(in thousands)

Occupation	Citizenship			
	Total	British	Commonwealth	Alien
Professional and Managerial	−7.6	−12.4	+3.4	+1.3
Manual and Clerical	−31.8	−38.8	+2.6	+4.4
Armed Forces	−0.8	−1.0	+0.1	+0.1
Students	+21.4	+4.4	+8.9	+8.1
Housewives	−6.4	−8.9	+2.9	−0.5
No occupation (and not known)	+2.3	−0.1	+3.1	−0.7
Children under 15 years	−17.4	−21.9	+3.0	+1.5
Total numbers Inward	199.7	92.0	53.3	54.4
Total numbers Outward	240.0	170.6	29.3	40.1
Overall Balance	−40.3	−78.6	+24.0	+14.3

Source: Registrar General's *Annual Statistical Review of England and Wales for 1971*, Part II, Table S2(d).

To summarize, the balance of migration has generally been outward from the countries of the United Kingdom and this has tended to moderate population growth, though only to a small extent. Between 1961 and 1971 the population grew on average at about half a per cent per annum. The net loss from migration in 1971 was equivalent to a little less than 0.1 per cent of the population or about a sixth of population growth for that year.[1] Only in the 1920s was emigration overseas from Scotland on such a scale as, for a short time, to bring about a decline in the population there. Though net emigration from England has never reached such proportions as to offset the natural increase in the population about four fifths of all U.K. emigrants are from England and England has had a net loss from migration since 1963. Most of this loss overseas, however, is made up for by internal migration. In 1966 for instance there was an outward balance of 53,000 from England to countries outside the British Isles while during the twelve months preceding the 1966 census it was estimated that from the rest of the U.K. and Eire there was a net gain of a little under 52,000 people.[2] The immigration of people from elsewhere in the British Isles and from foreign and Commonwealth countries overseas, helps to compensate for the outflow of economically active British citizens, especially in the professional and managerial occupations,[3] and this accession of manpower is an important factor in maintaining economic growth. The numbers of children gained from the Commonwealth and foreign countries, though they may present special problems in education, amount to less than a quarter of the net outward movement of British children going to live overseas. If all migration ceased, therefore, British schools would be very much more overcrowded than at present.

Population Growth and the Future

The rate of population growth in the United Kingdom as a whole slowed down steadily until the 1930s and after that increased again to level off in the late 1960s. These changes in the rate of growth have in both cases taken demographers by surprise and predictions about the future size of the population have had to be drastically revised, upwards in the 1950s and mostly recently downwards again. The population has continued to grow

[1] These estimates are calculated from the same sources as Tables 2.13 and 2.17; see also the similar figures in *Report of the Population Panel*, H.M.S.O., 1973, Table 6, p.30.

[2] See Registrar General's *Annual Statistical Review of England and Wales for 1966*, Part II, Table S(i) and *1966 Sample Census of England and Wales: Migration Summary Tables, Part I*, Tables 1A and 2A.

[3] cf. the figures for science graduates and engineers in the period 1961-66 given in D.I. MacKay, *Geographical Mobility and the Brain Drain*, Allen and Unwin, 1969, p.205.

however; these changes are simply changes in the *rates* of growth and thus though it is not at present thought that there will be as many people in Britain at the end of the century as was predicted at the time of rising birth rates in the earlier 1960s it is as certain as anything can be that accommodation will have to be found for an additional seven or eight million people over the next 30 years. It is, however, too early to assess fully the consequences of the most recent demographic changes which may only have begun in the mid-1960s or even to judge whether they may perhaps represent only temporary fluctuations within more long-term trends. This general growth of population, as we have seen, has been brought about by the interaction of several factors. But the changes they have produced have not only been demographic. If one examines the secondary consequences of some of the demographic trends I have already referred to, it is apparent that they reach out into the structure of social relations and the culture which it enshrines.

Possibly in response to earlier criticisms of complacency[1] a small panel of experts was set up by the Government in 1971 to advise on population policy. They pointed out that, 'sooner or later, Britain must face the fact that its population cannot go on growing indefinitely' and concluded that the sooner stability was reached the better, although the present structure of the population of itself meant that this could not be achieved for several decades.[2]

Some of the consequences of further population growth are easy to foresee though their quantification, necessary if planning for the future is to be realistic, is more difficult and fortunately lies beyond my present aim. The most obvious outcome of continuing population growth is that in an already densely populated country the pressure on the available space will be intensified. This is a twofold problem of provision and preservation. Most immediately, there is the problem of provision of housing for a larger population with a larger proportion than ever before in independent family units. Along with the housing there is the provision of ancillary services — roads, drains, gas, electricity, water, refuse disposal, telephones, recreation space etc. — and all these things represent demands upon public funds and limited economic and natural resources. Most of the current pressure has been the result of rising standards rather than population growth, but increasing numbers exacerbate the problems. An example of the sort of issue we are already coming to realize cannot any longer be evaded is the problem of traffic and its consequent congestion, pollution and noise. The growth and spread of economic prosperity since the 1950s brought about a situation in which there were 15,000,000 vehicles registered in Britain in 1971, about four times as many as 20 years before

[1] See House of Commons Select Committee on Science and Technology, First Report, Session 1970-71, *The Population of the United Kingdom*, H.M.S.O. p.x.

[2] *Report of the Population Panel.* 1973, pp. 3 and 106.

and increasing steadily year by year.[1] The problem was generated by affluence but is likely to become more intractable with the growth of population.

Together with, and as a consequence of, the solution of these problems there is the further problem, more severe in the more prosperous and therefore more densely settled parts of the country, of the erosion of amenities which derive from the availability of land. The preservation of the countryside becomes progressively more difficult and at the same time more important, not least on account of the contribution of the agricultural industry to the national balance of payments. It is also obvious that with a population that is growing the output of the national economy must continue to expand if only to maintain even the present standard of living. The burden of this necessity is aggravated by the decline in output per head due to the fact that it is the numbers in the non-productive sectors of the population, those not yet working and those who have retired from work, that are growing fastest. Here we have yet another case of having to run ever faster merely to stay in the same place.

Control over population growth will not solve all the problems facing Britain now or in the future, as the Population panel pointed out.[2] These have more to do with rising expectations and the distribution of scarce resources among an already densely settled population. Yet it is clear that in the long run, and perhaps not so very long as to be beyond our own lifetimes, a continuing increase in numbers is likely to make their solution a great deal more difficult if not impossible.

---

[1] See *Social Trends, No.3,* 1972, Table 126.

[2] loc. cit., p.4 and ch. 5.

3 Geographical Aspects of the Social Structure

Introduction

Only an incorrigible optimist can still believe that movement and change are necessarily related. In this chapter, however, I want to examine some of the ways the shifting geographical distribution of the population may affect, and possibly help to change, the structure of British society. In the preceding chapter I dealt with some of the changes in the size and composition of the population which appear to be contributing to the progressive and continuous modification of our social milieu. The people of Britain are not a static population however, and their geographical mobility has substantial, if not immediately apparent, social consequences. These are brought about both directly and indirectly. The direct influence of geographical mobility may be felt through its disturbance and attenuation of existing social relations together with the impact of the new encounters it brings and the gradual creation of new bonds which it may lead to. People move, pull up roots and settle elsewhere, lose touch with old acquaintances and learn to cope with new neighbours. More indirectly, the changing pattern of relationships this represents can have effects far beyond the immediate problems of adjustment experienced by the migrants and their families themselves. The movement of people from one community to another changes the social environment they leave behind as well as the one they settle in. Changes in the rate and character of migration into or out of a community can be expected to alter the sense of continuity in the cultural setting within which the social experience of all those who live there becomes meaningful.

There are two sorts of geographical mobility which have some relevance for contemporary British social structure, sociologically distinguishable mainly in terms of the kind of boundaries crossed. The major concern in this chapter will be with internal migration within Britain, though for the most part concentrating on relatively long-distance movements. External migration is important too and this must be further subdivided between emigration and immigration. In looking at the pattern of internal migration I shall try to describe briefly who moves, where they move to and from, why they move and what the long-term effects on their social experience are likely to be. In examining emigration, the same sort of analysis would be less appropriate. Emigration does have important consequences for the communities the emigrants leave, though not perhaps so great as for the communities they make for. The leading characteristics of the recent flow of emigrants from Britain have been outlined in the preceding chapter. A short account was also given there of the smaller overall flow of immigrants. In this chapter I shall begin with a brief examination of what we can learn about Britain from their settlement here.

Immigrants

In 1971 less than six per cent of the population of Great Britain, about 3.1 million people, had been born in other countries. These immigrants can be divided between those born in Ireland, those born within the Commonwealth and those born in foreign countries. These three groups represented approximately 1.3 per cent, 2.4 per cent and 2.0 per cent of the total British population respectively. Though their proportions are so small however, their settlement here raises a number of important issues. Firstly, their settlement patterns indicate not only something about the needs and aims of the respective groups of immigrants themselves but also something about the needs of the society which attracted them and its capacity to absorb them. Secondly the kind of problems they have to contend with in establishing themselves here draws our attention to features of the British social structure which operate as constraints upon all its members. Thirdly, the early encounters immigrants have with a new society throw into relief many features of its way of life. The lack of acceptance experienced by recent groups of immigrants to Britain in particular illuminates several major aspects of British culture whose importance in structuring the overall pattern of social relations is crucial.[1]

---

[1] A great deal of work has deservedly now been done in this area in Britain. Studies have been published of Chinese, Italian, Indian, Irish, Jamaican, Pakistani and Polish immigrants. My aim here is not to introduce the reader to the subject of race relations or the sociology of migration but to select only the material from these areas which can be directly used in the account of British social structure. Among the many available sources I have found the following studies particularly helpful in this area: Michael Banton, *White and Coloured: the Behaviour of British People towards Coloured Immigrants*, Cape, 1959; Michael Banton, *Racial Minorities*, Collins, 1972; Raymond Firth, *Two Studies of Kinship in London*, Athlone Press, 1956; R. Hooper (ed.), *Colour in Britain*, B.B.C., 1965; Ernest Krausz, *Ethnic Minorities in Britain*, MacGibbon and Kee, 1971; J. Zybrycki, *Polish Immigrants in Britain*, Nijhoff, 1956; and among the many impressive books published for the Institute of Race Relations, particularly John Rex and Robert Moore, *Race, Community and Conflict*, Oxford, 1967, which deals with the Irish,

Settlement Patterns

The same factors which influence internal migration affect immigrants from overseas, except that the inhibitions of local ties or cultural roots in one or other of the regions of the remoter provinces do not operate. In consequence the attractions and economic and occupational opportunities of the great cities, and especially the west Midland conurbation and the economic pull of South East England, particularly the Greater London conurbation, attract most migrants from overseas.

Table 3.1 shows that the biggest single group of British residents born outside the United Kingdom continues to be those born in the Irish Republic. Of those born in the Commonwealth a minority came from the old Dominions, namely Australia, New Zealand and Canada and of the remainder from the 'new' Commonwealth countries two thirds have come

Table 3.1

Immigrants in Great Britain 1961-1971 and Proportions Resident in the Conurbations

	Total in Great Britain (thousands)			Percentage Increase 1966-71	Percentage Resident in the Seven Conurbations*	
	1961	1966	1971	%	1966	1971
Total population	51284	52304	53826	2.9	34.7	32.6
Residents born in:						
Irish Republic	n.a.	713	721	1.1	57.4	57.1
Australia, Canada and New Zealand	110	125	145	16.0	39.8	40.7
Remainder of Commonwealth, including:	336	853	1157	35.7	63.1	62.6
India	166	240	323	34.6	57.2	58.3
Pakistan**	32	75	139	85.4	66.9	65.5
West Indies	173	270	303	12.2	77.5	75.6
Foreign countries	804	887	1077	21.4	44.6	44.0

*viz. Central Clydeside, Greater London, Merseyside, Southeast Lancashire, Tyneside, West Midlands and West Yorkshire.
**The 1971 Census was made before U.K. recognition of the independence of Bangla Desh led to Pakistan withdrawing from the Commonwealth in 1972.

Sources: *1961 Census: Great Britain Summary Tables*, Table 9.
1966 Census: Great Britain Summary Tables, Table 6.
1971 Census: Great Britain Advance Analysis, Table 2.

West Indians, Pakistanis and English in Sparkbrook, Birmingham; and E.J.B. Rose et al., *Colour and Citizenship*, Oxford, 1969, which deals with the demographic, historical, legal educational, political and psychological context of race relations in contemporary Britain.

from India, Pakistan[1] and the West Indies. There have been increases among all these groups of overseas born residents in recent years though the proportion of the total population born in the area of the Irish Republic has declined slightly. The rate of growth appears to have declined however in all groups except amongst the foreign-born, who in the later 1960s were settling in Britain at about twice the rate of the earlier part of the decade. The final section of the table refers to the concentration of the population in the seven conurbations of Central Clydeside, Greater London, Merseyside, South East Lancashire, Tyneside, the West Midlands and West Yorkshire centred on the cities of Glasgow, London, Liverpool, Manchester, Newcastle-upon-Tyne, Birmingham and Wolverhampton, and Leeds and Bradford, respectively. All the immigrant groups were much more concentrated in these areas than was typical of the general population. The Australians, New Zealanders and Canadians were the most dispersed, followed by those born in foreign countries, mainly from Europe and the United States. Many of these people have been settled here for many years as large numbers of Europeans came here in the troubled years before and after the Second World War. The Irish, amongst whom there have always been a large number of relatively short stay immigrants, and even more the immigrants from the new Commonwealth countries were particularly concentrated in the conurbations. The proportions rose in 1966 to over two thirds of Pakistanis and more than three quarters of the West Indians.

The figures for the total population show that in the later 1960s the movement out from the centres of the great urban areas continued so that the proportion of the population remaining within the unchanged boundaries of the seven officially designated conurbations declined. Though they remained more concentrated than the native population most immigrant groups except for the Indians and those from the 'old' Commonwealth seem to have been subject to the same sort of dispersion process, albeit, as might be expected with some continuing immigration, to a slightly lesser extent.

A similarly uneven pattern emerges from an examination of the regional distribution of immigrant settlement. Table 3.2 compares the distribution of immigrants across the ten standard regions of Great Britain with the distribution of the whole population. Just under a third of the British population lived in South East England, the proportion remaining roughly constant from 1966 to 1971. Amongst the immigrants only the Pakistanis were not much more concentrated in the South East than this. The relatively low propensity of Pakistanis to live in the metropolitan region is accounted for by the very high proportions who lived in the West Midlands and Yorkshire and Humberside and the increasing proportion in the North

---

[1] References to immigrants from Pakistan refer to the situation in 1971 and include those from what are now Pakistan and Bangla Desh.

Table 3.2

Regional Distribution of Immigrants in Great Britain 1966-1971 by Birthplace*
(percentages)

Born in:		North	Yorks & Humber	N.West	E.Mid	W.Mid.	East Anglia	S.East	S.West	Wales	Scotland	
Irish Republic**	1966	1.4	4.8	13.6	4.4	12.7	1.2	50.2	4.2	2.1	5.4	100.0
	1971	1.5	4.9	13.5	4.5	13.0	1.4	50.3	4.1	2.0	4.9	100.1
Australia, New Zealand, Canada	1966	2.9	4.3	7.1	3.6	5.3	2.7	54.8	7.3	2.2	9.9	100.1
	1971	2.8	3.9	7.0	3.3	4.7	3.0	56.0	7.5	2.2	9.7	100.1
Remainder of Common-wealth	1966	1.6	6.2	6.4	4.4	13.2	1.5	58.3	4.5	1.2	2.7	100.0
	1971	1.5	6.6	7.1	5.3	13.8	1.5	56.2	4.1	1.2	2.7	100.0
India†	1966	2.1	6.2	6.9	6.0	16.1	1.4	52.4	4.8	1.0	3.3	100.2
	1971	1.5	6.3	7.4	7.1	19.0	1.2	49.8	3.7	1.1	2.9	100.1
Pakistan†	1966	2.1	19.9	11.3	3.4	23.0	1.0	33.6	2.0	1.0	2.7	100.0
	1971	2.0	18.9	14.3	3.5	19.9	1.3	34.7	1.6	1.2	2.7	100.1
West Indies†	1966	0.3	4.6	5.4	4.7	15.6	1.1	64.5	2.6	0.7	0.5	100.0
	1971	0.3	5.0	4.7	4.8	15.4	1.0	64.5	3.1	0.7	0.5	100.0
Foreign Countries	1966	2.4	6.0	7.8	5.3	6.1	4.8	53.5	5.8	2.8	5.4	99.9
	1971	2.3	5.5	7.2	4.8	5.6	4.9	56.0	6.0	2.6	5.2	100.1
Total Population of Gt Britain	1966	6.3	9.0	12.7	6.3	9.3	2.9	31.9	6.8	5.0	9.9	100.1
	1971	6.1	8.9	12.5	6.3	9.5	3.1	31.9	7.0	5.1	9.7	100.1

*Percentages are based on those resident members of the population for whom information on birthplace was available.
**Including Ireland – part not stated.
† Also included in proportion for 'Remainder of Commonwealth'.

Source: *1966 Census: Great Britain Summary Tables*, Table 6.
1971 Census: Great Britain Advance Analysis, Table 2.

West in relation to the distribution of the population as a whole. Among the groups identified in Table 3.2, the highest concentration was nearly two thirds of all West Indians in Britain who lived in the South East, though among some numerically smaller groups the concentration is even greater. Of all the Cypriots in Britain, for instance, 81 per cent were living in the South East region at the time of the 1971 Census. Apart from the Pakistanis who were more evenly distributed between the Greater London, West Midland, South East Lancashire and West Yorkshire conurbations, half or over of all the other Commonwealth and foreign born residents lived in the South East, mainly in the London area. There are a number of particular concentrations to note, the Bradford Pakistanis, the Indians of the East Midlands, the Manchester Irish, the Australians and Canadians in the South West and the foreign born, particularly around American air bases in East Anglia. With these exceptions only the South East consistently and the West Midlands to a lesser extent have attracted larger proportions of the immigrant populations than the proportion of the total population living there. This clearly reflects and magnifies the pattern of relative regional economic prosperity which will be referred to later in the chapter.[1]

Relations with the majority

In his historical account of Irish immigration into Britain, John Jackson described how even in the postwar period, 'the majority of the Irish entered those types of employment which were unacceptable to many British workers and the new arrival from Ireland was more mobile in his search for employment than the native worker'.[2] That has been a fairly typical pattern. Among the more recently arrived groups, with relatively low levels of skill and education among most of the immigrants brought up in India, Pakistan and the West Indies and a frequently hostile attitude on the part of the general public towards their employment, there has been a tendency for them to find semi-skilled or unskilled jobs in manufacturing industries. The more varied opportunities in London provided a slightly greater range of occupational achievement there than, for instance, in the West Midlands but as Rose concludes, '. . . between 1961 and 1966 the socio-economic status of the different immigrant groups did not rise and they continue to occupy a low position in our social hierarchy'.[3] Thus despite the control of immigration from these countries after the Commonwealth Immigration Act there are as yet few signs of their

[1] A more detailed account of the distribution of the coloured population in 1966, chiefly those born in India, Pakistan and the West Indies is presented in E.J.B. Rose et al., op.cit., ch.10.

[2] J.A. Jackson, *The Irish in Britain*, Routledge, 1964, p.97.

[3] Rose, op.cit., ch. 13 and particularly page 177; see also Peter Collison, 'Immigrants' Varieties of Experience', *New Society*, 26 June 1969, pp.990-92.

percolation up through the occupational structure.[1] This effective restriction in the range of occupational opportunities is matched by the limitations which operate in relation to housing.

In many areas, especially conurbations like London or the West Midlands, economic growth and an expanding number of jobs attract migrants from other parts of Britain and overseas while Welfare State standards have required the extensive clearing of older substandard housing. Public and private building together cannot provide enough accommodation for all the people requiring it. There is generally a waiting list for council houses and the cost of buying a private house will be beyond the means of most new immigrants. Mortgages are difficult to obtain for people with low wages or insecure employment and most recent immigrants are likely to be subject to both of these handicaps. For new arrivals the housing gap is filled by the development of lodging houses or multi-occupied large houses in what urban sociologists have called the 'zone of transition', that is in areas of older large houses near the city centre let off in separate rooms after their former middle class residents had moved out to more distant suburbs. In their 1970 survey in the London Borough of Haringey Hunt, Fox and Morgan found that coloured families were much worse housed than similar white families. They were less likely to have a whole house or self-contained flat to themselves, were much more overcrowded in the rooms they rented and yet usually had to pay higher housing costs than did white families. Hunt and her colleagues summed up the situation as follows:

'We have shown that the income levels of coloured families are no higher than those of white families and that the adequacy and amenities of the accommodation they occupy are in many ways inferior, so it appears that many coloured families are spending higher proportions of their incomes for housing whose standards are inferior to those of their white counterparts'.[2]

Rex and Moore point out however that the residents of the area like the one they studied in Sparkbrook, Birmingham, are ethnically mixed. Together with the immigrant families of various ethnic communities the zone of transition 'includes . . . transitional people awaiting rehousing and isolates and deviants of all sorts'.[3] It is the interaction of these groups,

---

[1] The optimism expressed in the Department of Employment's survey, *Take 7*, H.M.S.O., 1972, pp.102-103 may be sustained to some extent by some of the findings of the 1971 General Household Survey – see Social Survey Division: Office of Population Censuses and Surveys, *General Household Survey: Introductory Report*, H.M.S.O., 1973, Table 4.25.

[2] Audrey Hunt, Judith Fox and Margaret Morgan, *Families and their Needs*, H.M.S.O., 1973, vol.I pp.47-53.

[3] Rex and Moore, op.cit., 1967, p.279.

primarily on a basis of competition over housing resources, new and already existing, which creates the hostilities of such areas. This was borne out by Mark Abrams' 1969 Five Boroughs survey for the Institute of Race Relations. In the London boroughs of Ealing and Lambeth where the housing shortage was most acute more people opposed council tenancies for coloured people and more sympathized with discrimination against coloured people on the part of private landlords.[1]

At least since the Romans came to Britain people from other countries settling here have found the already resident population somewhat standoffish and distant, if not always actually hostile, neighbours. It is true that agrarian populations have usually migrated with swords in their hands looking for what others had already considered their best lands and have, as should be expected, been met with no welcome. Peaceable migrants in contrast have usually settled in the towns where trade and industry have presented the readier chance of income. In Britain immigrants have been the refugees from political or religious persecution and increasingly with industrialization and the growth of population associated with it, refugees from village and rural poverty.

During the twentieth century, after the gradual absorption of refugees mainly from Russian and Polish pogroms of the late nineteenth century many of whom settled in East London, the flow of immigration from Europe was first severely restricted by the Aliens Act of 1920 although this did provide for special consideration to be given to political and religious refugees. Throughout the 1920s and especially the 1930s many did seek refuge here from both Fascist and Communist purge and persecution. After the war many more settled here, those from Eastern Europe especially, for political reasons, but others increasingly for economic reasons, basically that there were jobs here paying wages better than those to be had at home. The Poles and Hungarians, Germans and Italians, Spaniards and Ukrainians who entered Britain before and after World War Two, and in particular the largest group of immigrants, the Irish, whose entry has never been limited, have largely been either absorbed into the population or have at least ceased to be noticed by the native majority. The problems of assimilation in these cases have generally been temporary only, disappearing completely with the maturing of a second generation here who have become almost wholly anglicized.

There is less likelihood of this occurring so readily in the case of the more recent Commonwealth immigrants in consequence of the degree of racial prejudice which has been aroused and the discrimination which has been practised against them. A P.E.P. report *Racial Discrimination in Britain*[2] describes a survey by Research Services which showed widespread

---

[1] See E.J.B. Rose (ed.), op.cit., 1969, pp.579-82.

[2] Published by P.E.P. in 1967; see also W.W. Daniel, *Racial Discrimination in England,* Penguin, 1968, an extended account of the same research.

discrimination against coloured applicants for housing, employment and a number of commercial services including car hire, motor insurance and house mortgages. In a series of tests

'. . . first a coloured immigrant, then a white immigrant of Hungarian origin, and finally a white Englishman applied for what seemed to be available to all people irrespective of colour or ethnic origin. In each test the three applicants had equivalent occupational qualifications or housing requirements. The results from the housing test speak for the whole survey. When applications were made for private letting or purchase, the West Indian was discriminated against on two thirds of the occasions when the Englishman received a positive response; the white alien was also discriminated against, but on many fewer occasions.'[1]

This experience of rejection obviously aggravates the difficulties of settling into a strange society. Many immigrants come to terms with it, in a sense, by avoiding as far as possible situations in which they are likely to encounter humiliation through discrimination. The attitudes of the native English towards immigrants were investigated in the same piece of research. 'The white respondents', Abrams summarized, 'tended to base their acceptance of discrimination on the grounds that, despite their own preference for equality of treatment, they were the prisoners of other people's prejudices.'[2]

Racial prejudice, either expressed or latent, may underlie much of the discriminatory behaviour which the British display towards coloured people but does not necessarily do so. Prejudices can only be explained at a psychological level and are perhaps equally likely to arise from discrimination as a rationalisation or self-justification as to cause it. Racial discrimination is a matter of social behaviour and may vary independently of people's personal prejudices. Racial discrimination involves relationships between people not only in terms of their individual personal characteristics or worth, but in terms of their positions or roles within a social structure. Like any other kind of role behaviour involving patterns of evaluations and expectations, customs and conventions, we shall at best turn up only half the story by delving in the psychological case histories of those who practise discrimination.[3] We therefore have to distinguish four issues: the extensive practice of racial discrimination; secondly, the growth of attitudes which may take the form of racial prejudice; thirdly, the conditions under which the expression of these attitudes is rewarded or disrewarded; and lastly the relation between these three. Discrimination is

[1]   Mark Abrams, 'Introduction' in W.W. Daniels, op.cit., p.13.

[2]   ibid.; cf. Michael Banton, *White and Coloured: the Behaviour of British People towards Coloured Immigrants*, Cape, 1959.

[3]   cf. Banton, *Racial Minorities*, Collins, 1972, pp.83-4.

likely to be less widespread than prejudice in the circumstances of the majority believing most people to be unprejudiced. Conversely discrimination is likely to be more widespread than prejudice in the situation described by Abrams' white respondents where the majority appear to believe that most people are prejudiced, even though most claim (truthfully or not) to be themselves unprejudiced. If their account of themselves can be accepted then people feel that prejudice is more common than is in fact the case. They believe that others are antipathetic to coloured people while they themselves are not, while the others are themselves under a similar misapprehension. This systematic or pluralistic ignorance can make a numerically minority view into an effectually dominant one. It is to the dominant view that people tend to conform in their behaviour.

If racial discrimination arises from the nature of the social system in which people live, it is in terms of at least some of the principles of the organization of this social system that such behaviour can be understood. Conversely, given the same premise, an understanding of racial discrimination should shed some light on the way the social system works.

Michael Banton has argued that it is possible to understand relations between immigrants and the host society in terms of the way relations between Britons are managed, '. . . norms relating to coloured people differ from the others only in degree . . . they are consistent with other aspects of British culture'.[1] Perceived social status is clearly one element in the attitudes and behaviour of the British towards coloured immigrants. Most of the immigrants are identified as lower class. The majority are in unskilled manual work and they live in what were already undesirable areas to most people in Britain long before the recent immigrants ever got there.[2]

The immigrant to Britain, however, does not merely have to fit himself into some available slot in the social structure as an extra competitor for the same jobs, houses or education and welfare facilities. If he is fully to become a member of this society, he has to be accepted by its members and in order to achieve this it is necessary for him to learn the customary ways of doing things here, including competing. John Rex and Robert Moore argued that we should stop thinking in terms of relations between immigrants and the host society. The host society cannot be understood as a unitary group but must be seen, they wrote, 'as compounded of groups in a state of conflict with one another about property and power, as well as of groups with differing styles of life arranged in a status hierarchy'.[2]

---

[1] Banton, 1959 op.cit., p.91.

[2] cf. Michael Banton, 'Social Acceptance and Rejection', ch.9 in R. Hooper (ed.), *Colour in Britain*, B.B.C., 1965.

[3] J. Rex and R. Moore, op.cit., p.14; they themselves in fact used this rejected framework, however, e.g. in discussing the assimilation of the Irish. ibid.. p.85.

Though this is a substantially fair account of the host society, it nevertheless tends to obscure the extent to which these groups share a common mode of conflict. The customs, norms, value patterns and assumptions which are shared by the conflict groups, and which in fact serve to maintain the conflict, themselves may present problems for the immigrant. In some fights, especially those which have become traditional, strangers are not welcome.

A member of society has to come to know the expectations that people will have of him in certain situations, the assumptions they make about what can and cannot, what should and should not be done at certain times and occasions. In other words, he has to learn the culture. Michael Banton described how

'It is hard, very hard, for a stranger to become British . . . the new norms of conduct round which the stranger would have to rebuild his personality were he to mix with complete freedom are the less easily apprehended because they are not made explicit, and for this very reason Britons are not sufficiently conscious of them to be able to teach them. Learning to be British is made even more difficult in that the newcomer has to learn, not a uniform national culture, but a class and perhaps a regional culture appropriate to his position, which, while sharing many common features with the other subcultures, differs from them in important respects.'[1]

Acceptance is decided in terms of conformity to a whole complex of norms which are not made explicit even when they are broken. The sanctions which enforce them are silence, avoidance or non-recognition. This is difficult enough for the British to cope with, small wonder that the new immigrant or overseas visitor, with little or no experience of the system to guide him, finds it difficult to establish himself in British social life. In her Banbury study Margaret Stacey found that not only were the norms of the social status system not made explicit, but most people denied that the system existed at all although they were perfectly aware of it in regulating their own behaviour. 'There are certain social rules which say that the existence of status and class differences should be assumed but not spoken about. One effect of this is to make people pretend, to themselves as well as others, that the differences do not exist or are less pervasive than is in fact the case.'[2] It is these culturally conventional disjunctions between avowed belief and actual behaviour which are the cause of the not infrequent accusations of inherent hypocrisy on the part of the British. Given a status system which depends upon being opaque even to those who maintain it, it is unsurprising that Englishmen find it difficult to accommodate their behaviour to the stranger whose very ignorance of

[1] M. Banton, *White and Coloured*, Cape, 1959, p.178.

[2] Margaret Stacey, *Tradition and Change*, Oxford, 1960, p.145.

the system questions one of its fundamental assumptions. Banton writes '. . . In any society the network of social relations is maintained by common agreement about the behaviour appropriate to particular relationships. Strangers are people who are unaware of these norms of conduct. The coloured man is considered the most distant of all strangers'.[1] This, he argues, is because on sight they are thought of as being unfamiliar with the norms of behaviour which British people assume each other to be familiar with, as well as the subtle and indirect means of communicating their expectations and interpretations of behaviour. Racial discrimination in Britain, at least in part then, is one example of a central feature of the culture, the avoidance of strangers. This occurs most generally with regard to private or intimate relationships, where the conventions of social behaviour are least formalized but in which their disregard can be the most disturbing. 'Avoidance is most marked in relationships based on implicit norms and in which sanctions on deviant behaviour are weak.'[2] Since informal behaviour is governed by implicit norms which are sanctioned by avoidance rather than overt criticism it is very difficult for any newcomer to learn what he has done wrong if he offends his new neighbours. Partly, then, because they are seen as lower class, partly because they are strangers who, it is thought, will probably not know the proper course of conduct if a friendship or neighbourly relationship is entered into there is a tendency to avoid contact with immigrants. This interpretation may excuse little but is consistent with the general impression that the ruling passion of the English is the avoidance of embarrassment at all costs.

All immigrant groups tend to settle at first in ethnically homogeneous areas where housing is available to them and there are other immigrants who can help them in the early stages of coping with a strange new society. Gradually as they gain in confidence and security they come into contact with members of the host society. Through the acquaintanceships they make at work and with neighbours, through the friendly approaches and rebuffs they meet, they learn the culture within which they must operate. At the same time the native population becomes accustomed to the immigrants. Among respondents to the Five Boroughs Survey, Abrams found those who had worked with coloured people were much less inclined to favour automatically making them redundant before white workers.[3] Re-analysing this material Bagley noted a slightly lower level of prejudice among those with coloured neighbours living close by.[4] In a

---

[1] Banton, *White and Coloured,* p.178.

[2] ibid., p.180.

[3] See Rose (ed.), *Colour and Citizenship,* Oxford, 1969, p.577.

[4] Christopher Bagley, *Social Structure and Prejudice in Five English Boroughs,* Institute of Race Relations, 1970, and cf. Robin Ward, *Coloured Families in Council Houses: Progress and Prospects in Manchester,* Manchester Council for Community Relations, 1971, p.15.

small study in three London boroughs, C. S. Hill found it was in the borough with the fewest coloured immigrants that the rate of racial prejudice was highest. Familiarity breeds acceptance '. . . when the initial period of settlement and adjustment has been made', he wrote, 'and the immigrants begin to adjust themselves to their new environment and to conform to local customs and the host community begins to get used to the sight of the newcomers and to accept their presence, the level of overt prejudice . . . begins to fall'.[1] These processes of mutual adjustment and accommodation are retarded in a society where avoidance of strangers is the norm by the fact of visibility. Sheila Patterson wrote, 'Long after Polish, Italian and Jewish ghettos have blurred and merged in the rest of the city, a coloured ghetto can remain. It can remain not as an area where temporary migrants as people of a different subculture prefer to live, but as a depressed area regarded by the majority society as suitable for people who, however much they have come to share the same living patterns and cultural values, are still visibly different and socially unacceptable to that society.'[2] The danger for British society and for its recent immigrants lies in this direction.

Regional Differences

The three countries of Great Britain are governed more or less directly by the same government under the Queen and vote in the same elections; have a single language commonly understood, the same or similar newspapers, radio and television programmes, are overwhelmingly urban residentially and more so occupationally and are educated in very similar educational systems.

Despite these familiar facts, it is impressive to observe how much regional diversity persists. Scotland preserves its own administrative departments and its own educational and legal systems which differ in some respects, mainly terminological, from those prevailing in the remainder of Great Britain. In both Scotland and Wales there are proportionately larger rural populations than in England while in both religious affiliations play a rather more prominent part within the subdivision of society than in England.[3] In Wales, of the 2,750,000 population, one per cent speak only Welsh, while almost a fifth can speak the language, and in some areas it remains an important means of communication[4] and, rather more widely, a focus of national sentiments.

[1] C.S.Hill, *How Colour Prejudiced is Britain?*, Gollancz, 1965, p.43.

[2] Sheila Patterson, *Dark Strangers*, Penguin, 1965, p.214.

[3] For a more thorough account of these divergences see *Britain 1973: An Official Handbook*, H.M.S.O., 1973, ch.1.

[4] *Census 1971; Report on the Welsh Language in Wales*, H.M.S.O., 1974, Table 6.

Yet even in England homogeneity does not everywhere prevail. Fertility and mortality rates, the incidence of different types of illness and the frequency of industrial injuries vary from one part of the country to another. The availability of doctors and dentists and public expenditure on medical and educational services varies too – the poorest provision, not entirely by definition, usually being in the areas of greatest need. In general it is the industrial regions of northern England, Scotland and Wales where the situation is most depressed and depressing. Incomes are lowest, while infant mortality and the fatal illnesses of middle age are more common in the north as are industrial accidents.[1]

The distribution of the population between the regions is changing. Nineteenth-century industrialization based on the resources of coal and water shifted the balance towards the northern regions of England, Central Scotland and South Wales. In the twentieth century this has changed and the new technological basis of society has tended to restore the distribution of our larger population to the earlier pre-industrial pattern.[2] Table 3.3 shows how the direction of regional population growth has changed during the present century. The region where the industrial revolution made the greatest changes earliest in the preceding century, the North West, declined proportionately after the First World War. The North and Wales continued to grow until the 1920s and Yorkshire and Humberside until the 1930s but the economic crises of the interwar years marked an ending of the first phase of British industrialization and the regrowth which followed was predominantly located elsewhere. Reading

[1] A most impressive examination of the statistical evidence on regional differences will be found in Edwin Hammond, *An Analysis of Regional Economic and Social Statistics,* Rowntree Research Unit: University of Durham, 1968. A good deal of useful material on the differences and inequalities between northern and southern England, particularly as they influence educational experience and achievement, has been brought together in George Taylor and N. Ayres' study in what they describe as 'educational ecology', *Born and Bred Unequal,* Longmans, 1969. B.E. Coates and E.M. Rawstron's important study *Regional Variations in Britain – Studies in Economic Social Geography,* Batsford, 1971, covers similar ground in even greater detail. In addition a large amount of statistical information on economic, demographic and social matters is published each year by the Central Statistical Office in *The Abstract of Regional Statistics,* in which the ten standard regions are defined in some detail, and regional analyses of other data are provided in *Annual Abstract of Statistics; Social Trends; Report of the Commissioners of H.M. Inland Revenue; Family Expenditure Survey,* all published annually and of course the less frequently appearing *Census* reports. The observations in the paragraph above are based on: Hammond, ch.5; Taylor and Ayres, ch.1; Coates and Rawstron *passim* and the *Abstract of Regional Statistics,* No.6, 1970, Tables 11, 15 and 16. I have for the most part confined myself to comparisons between the standard regions with all the loss of detail which working on such a large scale implies. For simplicity in presentation I have sometimes grouped these into still larger units as shown in Table 3.5.

[2] See Department of the Environment, *Long Term Population Distribution in Great Britain – A Study,* H.M.S.O., 1971, ch.1.

Table 3.3

Population in the Regions of the United Kingdom 1901-1971

Standard regions of England:*	Census						
	1901	1911	1921	1931	1951	1961	1971
	%	%	%	%	%	%	%
North	6.5	6.7	6.9	6.6	6.2	6.2	5.9
Yorkshire and Humberside	9.2	9.3	9.3	9.4	9.0	9.0	8.7
North West	13.8	13.8	13.6	13.4	12.8	12.5	12.2
East Midlands	5.3	5.3	5.3	5.5	5.8	5.9	6.1
West Midlands	7.8	7.8	8.0	8.1	8.8	9.0	9.2
East Anglia	3.0	2.8	2.8	2.7	2.8	2.8	3.0
South East	27.5	27.8	27.9	29.4	30.2	30.8	31.0
South West	6.7	6.4	6.2	6.1	6.4	6.5	6.7
Wales	5.3	5.8	6.0	5.6	5.2	5.0	4.9
Scotland	11.7	11.3	11.1	10.5	10.1	9.8	9.5
Northern Ireland	3.2	3.0	2.9	2.7	2.7	2.7	2.8
Total *de facto* %	100.0	100.0	99.9	100.0	100.0	100.0	100.0
Population of the U.K. (millions)	38.2	42.1	44.0	46.0	50.2	52.7	55.4

*Boundaries as at 1971.

Source: 1901-1931 *Social Trends*, 3, 1972, Table 14.
1951-1971 from *Annual Abstract of Statistics* 109,
1972, Table 11.

along the rows of the table we can see that it was this period which saw a shift in the main focus of population growth to the East and West Midlands and a spurt in the continuing growth of the South East which later was to spill over into the neighbouring South West and East Anglia. Like the other regions with large rural populations, Scotland and Northern Ireland, these began the century with a declining proportion of the total population but in the thirties and especially during the forties they began to grow while the decline in Scotland continued and only levelled off in Northern Ireland. Thus at the beginning of the 1970s Scotland, Wales and the three northern regions of England were inhabited by still growing numbers but a declining proportion of the total population, while the proportion living in the Midlands and the Southern part of England and, rather surprisingly, in Northern Ireland, was increasing.

Occupational Distributions

What seems to underlie this pattern are the economic differences between the regions. The coalmining, iron and steelmaking, shipbuilding and wool and cotton textiles, which were the basis of British industrialization in the nineteenth century, were chiefly concentrated in Northern England, Central Scotland and South Wales. The decline of these industries over the middle years of the twentieth century has broadly coincided with the growth of industries such as oil and petro-chemicals, electronics, motor vehicles and others in the services sector which have, in large part, been concentrated in the Midlands and South of England. The pattern of growth and decline obviously influences the relative prosperity of the different regions. Of particular importance in this inter-regional distrib-utive process has been the growth of public and private administration with its consequent bureaucracies located pre-eminently in the Greater London area. Besides most of the major government departments, almost all the large corporations, public and private, have their headquarters and principal offices in London, however far away the main centres of their industrial operations may be. Even the National Coal Board has its headquarters at the end of Buckingham Palace's back garden. Of the thousand largest British firms in 1971, ranked by turnover, 85 of the largest 100 had their head offices in the Greater London area ranging down to 30 of those ranked 901 to 1000.[1] Hammond shows that over 80 per cent of the rateable value of all office accommodation was accounted for in the South East region, and this, of course, is to exclude crown and local government offices.[2] More than half the net increase in commercial office space in England and Wales between 1964 and 1967 and almost two thirds of the net increase in government office space went to the South East region.[3] The concentration of commerce and administration in the South East, which as these figures suggest, is increasing, is reflected in the distribution of occupations in the different parts of Britain in 1966 shown in Table 3.4.

The table indicates considerable differences between the regions. Seventy per cent of men working in the northern region of England were manual workers. At the other extreme, in South East England only 56 per cent were manual workers. From a different point of view, this not only represents a much higher proportion of non-manual workers in the South East region than in other regions, but when the different sizes of the regions are taken into account it also means that a very large proportion of all non-manual workers was to be found there. Thus in 1966, in Wales

[1] See *The Times 1000*, Times Newspapers 1971, Table 1.

[2] Hammond, *An Analysis of Regional Economic and Social Statistics*, Rowntree Research Unit: University of Durham, 1968, Table 2.6.1.

[3] *Abstract of Regional Statistics*, 6, 1970, Table 38.

there were fewer than 100,000 men in the managerial and professional groups, compared with almost a million in the South East of England. The two southern regions of England, the South East followed by the South West, again had large proportions working in the clerical and technical occupations and teaching. It was in the Midlands followed by the Northern regions of England and Scotland that the proportions who were skilled manual workers were highest. East Anglia had a high proportion in the semi-skilled and unskilled manual category but in this case they were mainly agricultural workers. The more industrial regions, Wales followed by the Northern region of England and Scotland, had the largest proportions of their men in unskilled and semi-skilled manual jobs.

Table 3.4

Socio-Economic Status in the Regions: Economically
Active Males in Great Britain 1966

	Total Econom. Active Males	Manag. and Prof.*	Clerical, Technical and other Non-man.**	Skilled Manual†	Semi-and Unskilled Manual***	Total
	(000's	%	%	%	%	%
England & Wales	14,491	15.4	21.7	35.0	28.0	100.1
Northern	975	12.0	18.1	38.2	31.9	100.2
Yorkshire and Humberside	1,433	13.2	18.3	38.6	30.1	100.2
North West	1,988	14.0	21.2	36.5	28.2	99.9
East Midlands	1,032	13.1	18.5	39.8	28.7	100.1
West Midlands	1,584	13.8	18.0	40.2	28.0	100.0
East Anglia	476	14.4	19.3	31.2	35.0	99.9
South Eastern	5,158	18.6	25.5	31.1	24.8	100.0
South West	1,053	15.5	23.1	31.7	29.8	100.1
Wales	792	12.2	20.6	34.7	32.4	99.9
Scotland	1,503	13.3	18.8	36.5	31.6	100.2
Great Britain	15,994	15.1	21.4	35.1	28.3	99.9

*The Managerial and Professional Group consists of socio-economic groups 1, 2, 3, 4 and 13.
**Clerical, Technical and other Non-manual workers are those in socio-economic groups 5, 6, 12, 14.
†Skilled Manual workers are those in socio-economic groups 8 and 9.
***Semi and Unskilled Manual workers include all those in socio-economic groups 7, 10, 11, 15, 16, 17.
For a fuller description of the socio-economic groups used in the Census see Table 5.4 – below or 1966 *Census, Economic Activity Tables*, Part II, pp. xvii-xviii.

Source: *1966 Census Economic Activity Tables Part III*, Table 31.

Table 3.5

Regional Distribution of Male Non-manual Workers* in Great Britain 1961 and 1966

		1961		Economically Active Males 1966 Direction of change in actual numbers given in brackets		
Regions**	Total	Non-manual	Manual	Total	Non-manual	Manual
	%	%	%	%	%	%
Northern England	27.9	24.7	29.8	27.5(−)	24.6(+)	29.1(−)
English Midlands	16.0	13.7	17.3	16.3(+)	14.3(+)	17.6(−)
South East England	34.7	40.2	31.7	35.2(+)	41.5(+)	31.5(−)
South West England	6.5	6.8	6.3	6.6(+)	6.9(+)	6.4(−)
Wales	5.1	4.7	5.3	5.0(−)	4.5(−)	5.2(−)
Scotland	9.8	9.9	9.6	9.4(−)	8.2(−)	10.1(+)
	100.0	100.0	99.9	100.0(−)	100.0(+)	99.9(−)
N @ 100 per cent in thousands	16,232	5,713	10,519	15,994	5,854	10,140

*These categories are the four used in Table 3.4 combined.
**These regional groupings are based on the standard regions. Though these were redefined in 1965, this has been taken into account in drawing up the table.
In 1961: *Northern England* refers to the following old standard regions – Northern, North Western and East and West Ridings plus Lindsey except Lincoln County Borough.
   English Midlands refers to West Midlands and North Midlands less Lindsey (except for Lincoln County Borough) and less the Soke of Peterborough.
   South East England refers to London and South Eastern, the Southern and Eastern Regions plus the Soke of Peterborough.
   South Western England refers to the South Western standard region.
In 1966: *Northern England* refers to the following standard regions, North, North West, Yorkshire and Humberside.
   English Midlands to West Midlands and the East Midlands standard regions.
   South East England to East Anglia and South East standard regions.
   South West England to the South West standard region. Details of the composition of the standard regions will be found, for example, in Appendix I of a current *Abstract of Regional Statistics*. Wales and Scotland retained their boundaries unchanged between 1961 and 1966.

Sources: 1961 *Census of England and Wales: Occupation Tables*, Table 28; *Occupation Industry and Socio Economic Groups – Lincolnshire*, Table 5; *Occupation Industry and Socio Economic Groups – The Soke of Peterborough*, Table 5.

   1961 *Census of Scotland: Occupation Industry and Workplace Tables*, Table 28.

   1966 *Census: Economic Activity Tables*, Park III, Table 31.

The concentration of the non-manual workers in South East England is brought out in Table 3.5. There was a general shift towards non-manual occupations amongst economically active men. The total number of manual workers has declined in all the regions except Scotland, and the absolute increase of some 10,000 manual workers there is difficult to reconcile with the evidence of a continued net outflow of men from that country (see Chapter 2). Within the general decline there was a shift in the regional distribution so that the proportions of all manual workers living in the South West and the Midlands increased slightly. The growth of non-manual employment has occurred only in England. In Scotland and Wales there were fewer men in non-manual jobs in 1966 than in 1961. The proportions of all men in non-manual jobs who were working in the Midlands, the South East and South West England increased at the expense of the other regions while their concentration in South East England in particular became more marked. The shrinkage in the number of manual workers produced an overall decline in the number of economically active men between 1961 and 1966. In South East England and to a lesser extent in the Midlands and the South West, the growth of non-manual jobs completely offset this trend and brought about a growth in the numbers of occupied males. Thus the general contraction of the male labour force was concentrated in Northern England, Scotland and Wales while the rest of England, and particularly the South East, accounted for an increasing proportion of the growing number of non-manual workers. This is also reflected in the regional distribution of unemployment with the lowest level in the South East and at the end of 1971 rates more than twice as high in the West Midlands, Yorkshire and Humberside, the North West and Wales, and three times higher in the North and in Scotland.[1]

Incomes

The changing pattern of employment is to some extent a reflection and partly a cause of the inter-regional distribution of personal incomes. Table 3.6, based on the Earnings Survey carried out by the Department of Employment, shows the distribution of median gross weekly earnings for a two per cent sample of all non-manual and manual workers in all industries and services in April 1971. Manual workers' earnings, on average, were highest in the West Midlands and the South East. In North West England and Wales their earnings were on or close to the national average. Manual workers in the East Midlands, the North region, Yorkshire and Humberside and Scotland had below average earnings while with their substantial proportion of agricultural workers, median earnings were particularly low in South West England and East Anglia. The median gross weekly earnings for non-manual workers corresponds to the figure for the West Midlands. Only in the South East was there a higher figure – five and a half per cent

1 See *Abstract of Regional Statistics No.8*, H.M.S.O., 1972, Table 27.

above this. In all the other areas median non-manual earnings were lower. It is worth noting that despite the high level of manual workers' earnings the gap between non-manual and manual incomes is widest in the South East.

Table 3.6

Median Weekly Gross Earnings by Region 1971

| | Full-time men over 21 years old | | |
Region:	Non-manual workers	Manual workers	Differential
	£	£	£
North	32.5	27.8	4.7
North West	33.7	28.4	5.3
Yorkshire & Humberside	32.4	27.0	5.4
East Midlands	32.2	27.3	4.9
West Midlands	34.4	30.1	4.3
East Anglia	32.3	25.3	7.0
South East	36.3	29.0	7.3
South West	32.8	26.3	6.5
Wales	33.5	28.4	5.1
Scotland	33.4	27.2	6.2
Great Britain	34.4	28.1	6.3

Source: *Abstract of Regional Statistics*, 8, 1972, Table 67.

The relative prosperity of the South East in comparison with other regions lies not just in average wages and salaries being generally higher than elsewhere, but, as the earlier tables showed, in the higher income occupations being increasingly disproportionately represented there. Hammond points out that the ratio of salaries to wages is approximately 1:2 in the South East, while in other regions it is 1:3 or 1:4.[1]

Board of Inland Revenue statistics, based on income tax returns, show that the distribution of personal wealth too is in favour of the South East. In 1970, of all personal income from investments and savings, 45 per cent went to South East England, 20 per cent to the regions of Northern England, 12 per cent to the Midlands, 10 per cent to the South West, 9 per cent to Scotland and 4 per cent to Wales. From an examination of wills published in *The Times* in 1965, Hammond estimated that almost 54 per cent of personal wealth was left in the South East. Not surprisingly, over 50 per cent of all personal incomes over £5,000 per annum before tax was

[1] See Hammond *An Analysis of Regional Economic and Social Statistics,* 1968, p.24 and Table 7.4.2.

taken in the same quarter.[1] As a rough and ready measure of the regional distribution of poverty, Hammond shows that authorizations of National Assistance allowances per 10,000 of the population were highest in Wales, followed by Northern England, Scotland, South West England and the South East. On this measure the Midlands were least susceptible to poverty.[2]

Coates and Rawstron argue that the trend towards proportionately more and more people with higher and higher incomes in metropolitan England has some far-reaching economic consequences of a mostly inflationary nature.[3] Economic growth in one particular region creates a relative scarcity of labour. Locally, the competition between employers for workers has the consequence of raising wages offered and this reverberates throughout the country as wages agreements in one area set the pace for wage demands elsewhere. Secondly, and partly because of this, goods and services produced in the London area whose costs have high labour and land components have their prices forced up not only in the London area but generally. Economic growth which is not related to the geographical distribution of labour resources can thus be inflationary. The processes which raise the cost of living lead to increases in wages and salaries which attract more workers and the affluent market encourages commercial development which increases the demand for labour. It is a process which feeds upon itself.

The areas of relative industrial decline are losers in this situation. Redevelopment may be hindered by the fact that many costs rise in response to the inflationary situation in regions with a more buoyant economy. The problems of attracting investment to the depressed areas are thus increased. The employment prospects of the workers who remain in the region are thus worsened while skilled manpower is attracted away to the better opportunities elsewhere. But it is not just the economies of the poorer provinces which suffer. In the prosperous South East and especially in inner London the poorest members of the community also have severe problems.

Housing

Some of the consequences of the increasing concentration of the more affluent in South East England, particularly in the area focused on London, have operated through the effects they have had on the land and housing markets. This may be seen in Table 3.7. The cost of land for

[1] These figures refer to the regional groupings described in Table 3.5. See *Abstract of Regional Statistics,* 8, 1972, Tables 61, 62 and Hammond, op.cit. 1968, Table 7.1.4.

[2] Hammond, op.cit., Table 7.2.1.

[3] Coates and Rawstron, *Regional Variations in Britain,* Batsford, 1971.

private housing is above average in the South, and in London is nearly five times the national average. This has led to a higher density of private housing development in the London area though otherwise new developments are at a lower density in the South. Though land prices are so much higher in the London area than elsewhere, during the sharp rise in prices after 1970 it was there that prices were increasing fastest. Figures published by the Nationwide Building Society showed that in 1972 the average price of new houses ranged from over £13,000 in London and the South East to less than £7,000 in North East England. The cost of the site varied from 39 per cent in London and the South East region down to 11 per cent in Scotland. The price of existing houses increased most steeply in the five years from 1967 to 1972 in the Southern area.[1]

Table 3.7

Housing Land Prices in the Private Sector 1969

	Price per acre	Price per plot	Average No. of plots per acre	Average Increase in price per plot 1966-1969
	£	£		%
North*	4,170	460	9.1	76
Midlands and Wales	5,530	630	8.9	25
South (except London)	7,940	990	8.0	52
London	31,520	2,470	12.8	23
England and Wales	6,510	760	8.6	47

*The *North* comprises the Northern, Yorkshire and Humberside and the North Western Standard Regions; *Midlands and Wales* comprise East Midlands, West Midlands and Wales; *the South* comprises East Anglia, South Eastern and South Western Standard Regions.

Source: Department of the Environment: *An Index of Housing Land Prices*, H.M.S.O. 1970.

The loss of half a million people from the Greater London conurbation in the 20 years since 1951 has not eased the problem. The expansion of office building has intensified the competition for limited land resources. At the same time slum clearance has reduced overcrowding and population densities have fallen, but the growth of professional, managerial and white collar employment has maintained a steady demand for lower density accommodation. As land prices in the older suburbs have increased under these pressures, people in the middle income ranges have moved out from

[1] Nationwide Building Society, *Occasional Bulletin 115*, January 1973.

the conurbation to the newer dormitory communities in search of a desirable residence they can afford. This has had the effect that the daily flow of commuters from further out has increased. Travelling times to and from work of four hours a day are not uncommon, while housing costs in outer suburbia have risen under the increasing demand. Over the period 1964-66 average household expenditure on housing in the Greater London area was nearly half as much again as the U.K. average but was only 18 per cent above the U.K. average in the remainder of the South East region. Average expenditure on housing rose by just under two thirds in the relatively short time between then and 1971. The increase was slower in Greater London at 50 per cent but in the remainder of the South East — commuter land — average expenditure on housing increased by 68 per cent in the same period.[1]

Some of the more affluent members of the middle class have responded to the economics of this situation, partially no doubt under the influence of all those magazine articles of the 'squalid terrace-house into colour-supplement dream-home' type, and have moved back into the older nineteenth-century suburbs which the middle classes had long since abandoned. In parts of Islington and Camden Town and many similar areas, property prices have risen especially steeply and rents once freed from control have soared as large old Victorian terrace houses and artisans' cottages have been eagerly sought by younger middle class families.

As a consequence by the early 1960s many poorer people could no longer afford to live even in the more decayed areas. In 1963 the Ministry of Housing set up a special committee under Mr Justice Milner Holland to investigate the matter.[2] The committee found that despite the enormous amount of local authority house building, there were still 180,000 applicants on the housing lists in Greater London in June 1962, a number equal to more than a third of the then current total of local authority tenants whose accommodation had taken 60 years to build. The wait for a council house in London is generally much longer than in other parts of the country. The social survey which the committee commissioned found that almost a fifth of all the households in Greater London were too poor to be able to afford to live even in local authority housing if one assumed that rent and rates should not account for more than a third of household income. From this survey the committee also estimated that, because of overcrowding, unsuitable conditions and the present likelihood of eviction there were in 1964 about 190,000 households in London urgently in need of new or improved housing and, in addition, something between 40,000 and 80,000 living with relatives or friends. Besides the 190,000 in urgent need, the committee estimated that there were between a third and half a

---

[1] See *Family Expenditure Survey*, Reports for 1966, Table 11, p.78 and for 1971, Table 53, p.100.

[2] *Report of the Committee on Housing in Greater London* (The Milner Holland Report), Cmnd 2605, H.M.S.O., 1965.

million households in need of new or improved housing because they had
no access to a bath. The report makes clear that for many people in
London eviction may mean not simply a move to another house but being
made literally homeless. 'The extreme consequence of housing stress in
London is homelessness. In 1964, seven thousand people were living in
local authorities' welfare accommodation (1500 families) and 1,000
children had to go to Local Authority care as a direct result of housing
difficulties.' These families, the committee points out, 'were not, at least
initially, "problem families". The most common case is the unskilled
worker with a wife and several children, often with a below average
income which has been reduced by unemployment or sickness. But the
distress and disruptive effect on family life of being evicted and having to
go to welfare accommodation can be easily imagined.'[1] A more recent
study of homelessness in London showed that while Inner London
contained six per cent of the population of England and Wales in 1966 it
had 37.5 per cent of the registered homeless.[2]

These circumstances tend to drive out those among the lower paid who
can escape and do not encourage workers from other parts of Britain to
take their place. The availability of jobs for less skilled workers, with
wages that may not be especially attractive by British standards but are
preferable to unemployment and real poverty elsewhere, has attracted
many of the recent immigrants from overseas. Without them many service
industries and particularly some of the public services, transport, health
etc., might well have been unable to continue effectively. Immigrants are,
however, peculiarly vulnerable to the economics of the situation I have
been describing. A lot of them have found themselves trapped in a
situation where relatively low incomes have to support a family here and
often dependent relatives 'back home' and also pay for scarce high cost
but sub-standard accommodation they have not the means to leave. As a
result they may find both themselves and their children not merely
segregated residentially but handicapped by their social conditions in any
attempt they make to integrate themselves with the rest of society. There
are some signs of a slow improvement but most of the coloured
immigrants who arrived in Britain in the early 1960s still find themselves
distinctly worse housed than is typical for the rest of the population.[3]

We are faced with the paradoxical situation that the very real housing
problems which remain in many of the older industrial cities and towns of
Scotland and Northern England are rooted in their relative economic and

[1] ibid.

[2] John Greve, Dilys Page and Stella Greve, *Homelessness in London,* Scottish
Academic Press, 1971.

[3] See Social Survey Division O.P.C.S., *General Household Survey: Introductory
Report,* 1973, pp.143-6 and A.H.Vanags 'The Household Expenditure of
Immigrants', ch.14 in E.J.B. Rose, *Colour and Citizenship*, Oxford, 1969, also ibid.
ch. 12.

social decline[1] while in Inner London the problem is a consequence of rapid economic growth. The Milner Holland committee found that the move of the 'better off' middle classes to the inner districts of London was a major cause of the eviction of sitting tenants as owners wanted to sell with vacant possession and get a higher price for middle class residential property. The pressure of the better-paid occupations on the housing resources of the metropolitan area has thus raised the prices of houses and of land which they themselves have to pay and which poorer people cannot pay at all.

Cultural

It is not only the economic aspects of regional difference and their direct consequences we are concerned with. The economic and demographic variations I have already referred to seem to be part of a more all-embracing pattern of cultural or at least sub-cultural variation. Even within England there are different names for similar things in different parts of the country and differences of dialect and accent survive at least amongst the working class. Different customs and tastes in food, dress and entertainment have been extensively if not systematically examined, mostly by market researchers.[2] Despite the survival of some traditional attitudes and practices from former times perhaps the most noticeable differences are not differences in actual behaviour, however, but the differences in regional stereotypes. The northerner's view of people in 'the South' as soft, smooth-tongued and snobbish is matched by the southern view of the northerner as unmanageable, unimaginative and uncouth. While similar views go back at least to the eighteenth century, they retain a fairly widespread currency today.[3] A divorce court judge remarked during a case at Sheffield in June 1966[4], 'A bit of wife-thumping on a Saturday night may not amount to cruelty in some parts of England. I am sure it is not so in Sheffield, but a bit of thumping in Cheltenham may be cruelty. The social background counts.' The sociological significance of these remarks lies not so much in their value as evidence of regional variation in family norms but in the ethical relativity they express based, as it is, on social perception.

The increasing concentration of the middle class in the South and especially the South East of England provides a congenial social, cultural and physical environment which attracts more middle class people from

[1] See Taylor and Ayres, *Born and Bred Unequal,* Longmans, 1969, ch.2.

[1] A wide ranging account of many examples of regional differences will be found in D. Eliston Allen, *British Tastes,* Hutchinson, 1968.

[3] cf. Graham Turner, *The North Country,* Eyre and Spottiswoode, 1967, p.12 and ch.28; see also George Orwell, *The Road to Wigan Pier,* Gollancz, 1937, ch.7.

[4] See *Morning Telegraph,* Sheffield, 22 June 1966.

elsewhere. This is why, for example, the arts flourish in London, where the audiences are, while in the provinces only the subsidized repertory theatre survives; only four cities can maintain an orchestra and for the most part non-mass entertainment is confined to an annual 'festival'. The metropolitan aesthete's image of the provinces as a cultural wasteland where, apart from the annual performance of 'The Messiah', people are likely to prefer a brass band to Boulez and 'Coronation Street' to *Coriolanus* is not completely unjustified. It is in the main the result of the difference in the distribution of the social classes. The predominance of what remains of working class culture in the provinces is due to the predominance there of the working class.

Geographical Mobility

About ten per cent of the population move house every year. Over a period of five years 30 per cent and over ten years 53 per cent will have moved their place of residence at least once, and some more often. Two-thirds of these moves are within the same town and half of the remainder involve moving no more than ten miles. Moves within the same locality are particularly common in the north of England and Scotland, rather less so in the South and South East of England, where more moves are to a different town. Only about five per cent of moves are over distances of 100 miles or more.[1] In 1971 the General Household Survey of a random sample covering almost 26,000 people in Great Britain over the age of 15 showed that 8.8 per cent had lived at their current address for less than a year. The survey of labour mobility carried out in 1963, in which a national random sample of just under 20,000 people aged 15 and over was interviewed, found that only 7.6 had lived at their current address for less than a year. In 1963 32 per cent had moved in the five years before the survey but in 1971 37 per cent had moved in the preceding five years. Thus geographical mobility is increasing.[2] Apart from the satisfaction all this must give to the removals trade, in aggregate it amounts to very large amount of geographical mobility and it is worth considering the extent of some of its less obvious social consequences.

Some Reasons for Moving

From the labour mobility study and the General Household Survey we can learn some of the social characteristics of those who move and the sorts of reasons they have for moving. In 1963 it was found that less than half

[1] See *1966 Census of Great Britain: Migration Summary Tables,* Part I; Amelia Harris and Rosemary Clausen, *Labour Mobility in Great Britain 1953-1963,* Government Social Survey, 1966, p.12.

[2] Harris and Clausen, op.cit., and *General Household Survey*, 1973, p.149.

those aged 15 to 19 years had moved in the ten-year period before the survey while two thirds of the 20-24 year age group and 86 per cent of the 25-30 year olds had moved, half of them more than once. Among the older age groups, mobility declines. Of the 31-44 year old respondents, 70 per cent had moved at some time during the ten years between 1953 and 1963. In the 45-54 year old group more than half had not moved and only one in eight had moved twice or more often. The relative stability of residence amongst this group repeats the pattern found amongst the youngest age group in the survey whose parents might be expected to be found among those over 45 years old. Even fewer in the 55-64 year old age range had moved, though amongst the oldest age group, 65 years and over, there was rather more mobility. 'It is not unreasonable to assume', write Harris and Clausen, 'that this is caused by moves on retirement and those necessitated by old age and infirmity'.[1]

People move for a great variety of reasons. First of all, people will generally change their residence on their marriage. Secondly, in a society in which most people earn a living while they can in contributing to a competitive economy, technological changes, the growth or failure of industries or even particular firms, security, the chance of richer opportunities somewhere else or a dislike of their managers will all be influences on where people choose to live. Other reasons — to be nearer grandparents, to find a pleasanter neighbourhood — are important too, but for most people the main motivation is connected directly with the question of housing. A council house may have become available or somewhere with an extra bedroom, or a bath, with a smaller, more manageable garden, nearer the shops, more convenient, less draughty, or an almost infinite range of similar grounds may lead people to move. Harris and Clausen found there was little difference between the sexes in the reasons they gave. Of those who had moved, 63 per cent had moved for housing reasons or to find better surroundings; 17 per cent for reasons connected with work; 11 per cent at marriage; six per cent to be near relatives and the remaining three per cent for a wide range of other, sometimes vague, reasons.[2] The General Household Survey classification of reasons is not exactly comparable. Many of those counted in 1971 as moving at marriage, for instance, would have been classified as moving for housing reasons in 1963. Nevertheless 40 per cent of those who had moved in the year 1970-71 gave grounds connected with housing and 42 per cent marriage, retirement, to be near friends or other 'personal' reasons. Again, 17 per cent had moved in connection with their work and a variety of other reasons made up the balance.[3] The 1963 survey showed 'housing' was the most usual impetus for short moves and was as likely to be a

---

[1] Harris and Clausen, op.cit., p.11.

[2] ibid., Table 16.

[3] *General Household Survey* 1973, Table 5.58, p.165.

reason for moving amongst single or widowed as amongst married people. Work was the most likely spur for single people moving, while amongst the widowed and divorced, especially those over 60 years of age, the desire to be near relatives or friends was of particular importance.[1] Though most moves connected with work were within the same region, work and the desire to be near relatives or friends were much more likely to bring people to contemplate long-distance moves. Almost a quarter of those who had moved for either of these reasons had in consequence moved over 100 miles. Of all last moves of more than 100 miles, 57 per cent were for reasons connected with work and 19 per cent to be near friends or relatives.[2] London and the South East attracted the highest proportion of movers for those moving in connection with work. Women expressed much less readiness to move on account of their work than men. Half the men and three quarters of the women said nothing would persuade them to move for a job[3] (twenty-five per cent of women were prepared to move on account of their work compared with 52 per cent of men who were so willing.)[4] Though their marital status made little difference to men's readiness to move on these grounds, only 19 per cent of married women· compared with 34 per cent of single women said they would be prepared to move for work reasons.

Movement Between the Regions

Of all the people who change their residence in any year, just over an eighth move from one region to another. Some of these moves may be over fairly short distances, from one side of a regional boundary to the other. Moving from end to end of a large region on the other hand will probably mean leaving friends and relatives a very long way away and such moves probably balance the short-range boundary crossing. Nevertheless, inter-regional migrants for the most part will usually be effectively geographic-ally mobile in a way that the majority who move within a region are not. Geographical mobility can be considered to be socially effective when the migrants detach themselves from one social environment and settle in another different one. The process of detachment implies the attenuation or severance of social contacts with a range of former workmates, acquaintances, neighbours and possibly even relatives, while settling in a new community involves encounters with a new set of neighbours and potential friends as well as fellow workers. In considering the sources of structural change in society then, inter-regional migration is worth examining for its effects both on the redistribution of the society's resources and on the individual members' sense of social location.

---

[1] ibid., Table 18.
[2] ibid., Tables 24, 19, 20, 21.
[3] ibid., Table 25.
[4] ibid., Table 28.

Table 3.8

Total Inter-regional Gains and Losses of Population within Great Britain by Birthplace at 1966

England

Net gain of 300,000 from Wales

Net gain of 455,000 from Scotland

North Region

Net loss of 420,000 to all other areas in England and Wales, nearly half to the South Eastern Region. Net loss equivalent to 12.8% of the resident population at the 1966 census.

Yorkshire and Humberside

Net losses to all other areas except the Northern Region of England, Wales and Scotland. Overall net loss equivalent to 4.7% of the resident population at the 1966 census.

North Western

Gains only from Scotland, Northern Region and Yorkshire and Humberside. Overall net loss equivalent to 3.7% of the resident population at the 1966 census.

East Midlands

An overall net gain equivalent to 3.1% of the resident population at the 1966 census. Net losses, however, to East Anglia and the South Eastern and South Western Regions.

West Midlands

Gains especially from the Northern Region and Wales, but larger losses to East Midlands and the South Western and South Eastern Regions virtually balance overall.

East Anglia

The only net losses were to the South Eastern and South Western Regions. Overall net gain equivalent to 1.8% of the resident population at the 1966 census.

South Eastern

An overall net gain from other parts of Great Britain of 793,000 amounting to about two-thirds of all interregional migration. A net loss of population only to the South Western Region. 4.8% of 1966 resident population gained from elsewhere.

South Western

Net gains from all regions totalling about 280,000 and representing 7.9 per cent of the 1966 resident population.

Wales

Net gains from Scotland and the Northern and North Western regions of England. Overall net loss equivalent to 11.3% of the resident population.

Scotland

Net losses to all regions of England and Wales. Overall net loss to rest of Great Britain equivalent to 8.9% of resident population at the 1966 census.

[1] Net gains or losses between Scotland and the various regions of England are estimated.

Source: Calculated from *1966 Census Great Britain Summary Tables*, Table 6.

Table 3.9

Proportion of residents native-born in each Region of England or Scotland and Wales: Great Britain 1966

Region or Country of Residence	Percentage of present population native-born within the Region or Country
Scotland	91.9
Northern	86.0
North-Western	84.0
Wales	83.1
Yorkshire and Humberside	81.2
West Midlands	77.9
South Eastern	75.2
East Midlands	73.6
East Anglia	68.8
South Western	67.8

Source: Calculated from *1966 Census Great Britain Summary Tables*

Over a long period, namely the lifetime of the present population, the outcome of all this movement has been the geographical redistribution of the population. Table 3.8 summarizes this long-run redistribution in comparing the birthplaces of the 1966 population with their place of residence at the time of the census. The broad pattern of gain and loss between the regions is consistent with the distribution of economic advantage which I briefly discussed earlier in this chapter. These long-term trends in inter-regional migration show up in the present homogeneity of regional population. Table 3.9 shows the proportions of native-born residents within each region in 1966. Scotland had the most homogeneously native-born population, followed by the northern regions of England and Wales. This of course reflects the relative attraction the southern and midland regions of England have had to migrants for a considerable period of time. On the other hand more than one eighth of the populations of both East Anglia and the South Western region were born in the neighbouring South Eastern region, though this probably represents the expansion of the metropolitan area across the regional boundaries rather than what might more properly be thought of as an interregional redistribution of population. In the East Midlands, another area of relatively recent industrial development, five per cent of the population had come at one time or another from the South Eastern region and another five per cent from Yorkshire and Humberside.

We can examine this pattern from the opposite point of view, an outflow analysis instead of an inflow analysis. Thus for those still resident in Great Britain we can examine the distribution of all those born in each region.

Table 3.10

*Proportion of natives of each region enumerated
in the region of their birth: Great Britain 1966*

| Region or Country
of Birth | Percentage of all
born in each Region
still resident there |
| --- | --- |
| South Eastern | 89.6 |
| Scotland | 87.0 |
| North Western | 85.3 |
| West Midlands | 84.0 |
| Yorkshire and Humberside | 81.5 |
| East Midlands | 81.0 |
| Northern | 78.8 |
| South Western | 78.7 |
| Wales | 76.6 |
| East Anglia | 74.8 |

Note: Percentages refer to the proportion of those born in each region of England or Wales or Scotland and resident in Great Britain in 1966.

Source: Calculated from *1966 Census Great Britain Summary Tables*, Table 6.

Table 3.10 shows that nine out of ten of those born in South East England had remained within the region. The place of Scotland in the table may seem surprising but is accounted for partly by the high proportion of emigrants from Scotland who go overseas rather than to other parts of Great Britain. Of all Scots resident in Britain, 13 per cent lived in England. The Welsh were much more likely to move within Great Britain and 23 per cent of all those born in Wales in fact were living in England, ten per cent in the South East. East Anglia and the South

Western region, both with extensive rural populations bordering on the prosperous South East, also had lost relatively large proportions of their natives living away from the region of their birth. Of people born in East Anglia, 15.5 per cent were living in the South Eastern region, as were 13 of the natives of the South West.[1]

Men and Women

In four of the five areas surveyed by Hunt, Fox and Morgan in 1970 fatherless families had been much more geographically mobile than other families. Proportionately half as many again had moved at least once during the preceding five years.[2] Poverty, insecurity of tenure, the many problems of lone mothers are certainly contributory factors here but it is necessary to recognise that women seem generally much more inclined to move than men. This may readily be confirmed by examining the 1966 Sample Census.

Everywhere there was a larger proportion of men than women resident still in their native region.[3] The inference which may plausibly be drawn is, of course, that women had been distinctly more geographically mobile over their lifetimes than men. Equally this is confirmed if we consider only the long-range mobility which shows up in changes of residence between regions over one and five years. That is to say there are more women than men whose address at the time of the Census was in a different region from where it had been a year or five years before.[4]

Over the first half of the 1960s migration increased by about 12½ per cent and in 1966 more than 705,000 people moved from one region of Great Britain to another. Migration by the middle-aged and elderly increased but only by a small amount. Most inter-regional migrants, about a quarter, were young adults but it was family migration that was increasing at the fastest rate. That is to say, people between 15 and 24 were the most likely to make these long-distance moves and part of the increase in migration can be attributed to the larger proportion of the population represented by this age group in 1966 than in 1961. However their migration rate increased too and the proportions of those in the 25-44 age group and their children (in the 1-14 age group) who moved from one region to another increased still more.[5]

In both years more women than men made these relatively long-distance moves between regions. While the general balance of migration for

[1]   *1966 Sample Census Great Britain: Summary Tables,* Table 6.

[2]   Hunt et al., op.cit., 1973, p.46.

[3]   *1966 Sample Census Great Britain Summary Tables,* Table 6.

[4]   *1966 Sample Census Migration Tables.*

[5]   See Department of the Environment, *Long Term Population Distribution in Great Britain — A Study,* H.M.S.O., 1971, pp.101-2 and 129.

both sexes remained towards the South East there was a significantly different emphasis in their orientation. In 1965-66 males exceeded females amongst inward migrants from the rest of Great Britain to the Northern, Yorkshire and Humberside, North Western, and the East and West Midlands regions of England and to Scotland. Females outnumbered males amongst migrants to East Anglia, the South Eastern and South Western regions of England and to Wales and the largest proportion was in the 15-24 age group. In 1960-61, migrants were classified according to the old Standard Regions. The divergence between the sexes in the direction of net migration was similar to that in 1965-66 however, save that there was a small majority of women amongst migrants to the North Western region from other areas of England and Wales and a small majority of men amongst English immigrants to Wales.[1]

This sad situation, with men and women apparently going their separate ways, is less apparent but its assortive effects are perhaps still more significant when we consider migration over a more extended interval. Part of the picture has already been sketched in when I compared residence and birthplace a little earlier. The 1966 Census provides more detail in its evidence on geographical mobility over five years which for the first time is presented alongside data for the last year preceding census day. Over this longer period, females outnumbered males amongst those moving from other parts of Great Britain to all the regions and sub-regions of England, Wales and Scotland, except for the West Midlands conurbation. In the same period, more females than males had left every region except Scotland and East Anglia.[2] Thus women outnumbered men in more of the migration flows in the long run than in the short run. In all, about 1.8 million people were living in a region different from the one they had lived in five years before. This is only about three and a half times the number who moved from one region to another in the year preceding the 1966 Census. A shortfall is, of course, to be expected as against a simple multiplication of the 1965-66 figure as the effect of deaths is more important over the longer period and return moves after less than five years away which show up in a single year would not appear in figures over the longer interval. In this case, however, there is an important discrepancy between the sexes which cannot be accounted for in this way. In 1966 there were nearly 44 per cent fewer men and 38 per cent fewer women five-year migrants than a multiplication of the 1965-66 moves would have

[1]   See *1961 Census of England and Wales: Migration National Summary Tables,* Part II, Table 5; *1966 Sample Census: England and Wales Migration Summary Table,* Part I, Table 24, and Department of the Environment, op.cit. 1971, Appendix 2, p.129.

[2]   See *1966 Sample Census: England and Wales Migration Summary Tables,* Part I, Table 2B. The population structure of the West Midlands conurbation is unusual in a number of ways: see Trevor Noble 'Family Breakdown and Social Networks', *British Journal of Sociology, XXI,* 1970, n.22.

led one to expect. A number of explanations are possible but the simplest is that women are not only in the majority amongst long-distance migrants but are more likely to move long distances, to be less likely to stay for only a short time and are even more likely than men to be drawn towards South East England.

Class and Education

Although in general people who own their own homes appear to be less likely to want to move than those who live in rented accommodation, both Harris and Clausen and the 1971 General Household Survey found that owner-occupiers were more ready to move for job reasons than local authority tenants.[1] The explanation lies in the different career patterns and expectations of the different social classes. Eighty-seven per cent of local authority tenants are manual workers and their families or retired or unoccupied people. The majority of middle class families are owner-occupiers.[2]

The same factor lies behind the positive relationship between moves for work reasons and educational attainment. Seventy-one per cent of respondents with university education had moved at least once in the ten years preceding the Ministry of Labour survey compared with 53 per cent for the whole sample and 37 per cent of all the graduates had moved at least three times compared with 17 per cent of the respondents with only non-selective education.[3] D. I. Mackay made a study of 1955 Scots graduates from the University of Aberdeen and found that, without taking into account those women who had married and were no longer in employment over the period 1955 to 1960, these graduates had been between two and a half and three times more likely to move to England than the Scots population in the same age group.[4] Similarly, in a survey of education and geographical mobility in north east England, Professor House and his colleagues found that technical college and grammar school leavers were more prone to leave home – the latter for further education – than secondary modern school leavers. In consequence, they concluded, the home area was drained of its ablest and most highly educated

[1] Harris and Clausen, *Labour Mobility in Great Britain 1953 – 1963*, 1966, Table 27; General Household Survey, 1973, Table 5.59 and cf. D.V. Donnison, *The Government of Housing*, Penguin 1967, Table 15.

[2] See Donnison, op.cit. Table 14 and cf. Mark Abrams, 'Some Measurements of Social Stratification in Britain', Table 2 in J.A. Jackson (ed.), *Social Stratification*, Cambridge, 1968, p.139.

[3] Harris and Clausen, op.cit., Tables 8 and 11.

[4] D.I. Mackay, *Geographical Mobility and the Brain Drain*, Allen and Unwin, 1969, ch.9.

manpower.[1] As Musgrove has remarked, 'Whatever sense of belonging the most highly educated in the nation possess, it is ever less likely to be with a community rooted in a territorial division of the land'.[2]

Selective or higher education is, of course, a major factor in recruitment to professional and managerial occupations. Higher education is related to geographical mobility through the demands made on the individual in the pursuit of a career. Musgrove found that only six out of 26 senior local government officers and one of the seven grammar school heads in a large 'Midland City' were locally born.[3] In R. E. Pahl's study of a commuter village in Hertfordshire, we are told that only two per cent of the professional status residents and their wives had been born in the county.[4] H. E. Bracey found in his study of a Bristol middle class housing estate that almost half of his respondents expected to move fairly soon, mostly for career reasons, and a third had moved more than 80 miles in coming to their current address.[5] On the basis of data from the 1958 and 1962 studies of housing carried out for the Joseph Rowntree Memorial Trust, D. V. Donnison showed that middle class families are more likely to move, while in the 1958 study 42 per cent of the administrative, professional, managerial and proprietorial households gave job changes as a reason for having moved in the past, compared with only 11 per cent where the household head was employed in other occupations.[6] The General Household Survey confirms this comparison but its findings suggest the possibility of some convergence since 1958 with other social strata becoming more subject to occupational influences in their movement from place to place. Professional workers were still the most mobile. Between 1966 and 1971 half of those families where the head of the household was in this kind of job had moved, one in five of them at least twice. Thirty-five per cent of heads of households who were professional and managerial workers who had moved in the preceding year had done so for

[1] J. W. House, A. D. Thomas and K. G. Willis, *Where did the School-Leavers go?* A Report to the Ministry of Labour. Papers on Migration and Mobility in Northern England, University of Newcastle-upon-Tyne Geography Department, 1968.

[2] F. Musgrove, *The Migratory Elite,* Heinemann, 1963, p.103.

[3] ibid. pp. 65-87.

[4] R. E. Pahl, 'Class and Community in English Commuter Villages', *Sociologia Ruralis,* 1965, 5-23. The percentage refers to residents in the Registrar General's Social Class I.

[5] H. E. Bracey, *Neighbours,* Routledge, 1964.

[6] See D. V. Donnison, *The Government of Housing,* Penguin, 1967 p.202 and 'The Movement of Households in England', *Journal of the Royal Statistical Society* (Series A), 1961, 124, pp.68-9. See also Raymond Illsley, Angela Finlayson and Barbara Thompson, 'The motivation and characteristics of Internal Migrants', *Millbank Memorial Fund Quarterly,* 1963, 41, 2 and 3 in which women moving into or out of a Scottish city are compared with stable residents. The association of class and education with geographical mobility was found to be most pronounced among married women with children.

reasons connected with their work. Of those who had moved only 20 per cent of intermediate and junior non-manual workers, including people like non-graduate teachers and clerical workers, 16 per cent of foremen and skilled manual workers and 12 per cent of less skilled manual and personal service workers had done so because of their employment.[1]

Within Britain then, those between 15 and 24 years old, women, the better educated and those in middle class jobs are more likely to be effectively geographically mobile than older people, men, the less well educated and the working class. The net balance of internal migration favours the South East of England, and these characteristics are even more marked in the flow of migrants to the South East region than generally. Over half a million people from elsewhere in Great Britain moved to that region during the years 1961-66. About half a million immigrants from overseas (including Ireland) joined them and about half a million people left the region for other parts of Britain. A large proportion of those leaving were economically inactive, particularly retired people and, increasingly, dependent wives and children in younger households. In these five years, 188,000 economically active men moved into the region, many of them bringing wives and families with them, while 178,000 left. In the same period, 113,000 economically active women arrived in the region, while only 82,000 left. There are, of course, fewer women in the working population than men so that the migration of working women is also less. Nevertheless the South East region's labour force showed a three times greater gain of women than of men.[2]

The comparison at the foot of Table 3.11 of net gains and losses in the South East region in the year preceding the 1966 Census with the five years 1961-66 suggests that among the economically active the gain of population to the South East was slowing down and, for men, even reversing. In the year 1965-66 there was in fact a net loss of economically active men from the region though the net gain of economically active women was twice as great. An examination of the socio-economic distribution of net gains and losses is revealing however. Over the whole five-year period, the main gains were among managers in large establishments, professional employees and white collar and personal service workers. The major losses were of skilled and semi-skilled manual workers and the self-employed, together with a continuing loss of owners and managers in small establishments, including farms. The pattern amongst women workers exaggerates that of men except that there were small net inflows of women manual workers. At the end of the period the net inward flow of men in professional employment and unskilled manual and indefinite occupations was reversed, while the gain of male managers and military personnel slowed down or ceased. Amongst men only managers,

[1] *General Household Survey* 1973, pp.158, 168.

[2] See 1966 Sample Census: *England and Wales Migration Summary Tables,* Part I, Table 6.

white collar workers and personal service workers continued to show gains. The continuing inflow of women workers, however, offset the loss of men in professional employment and helped sustain the regional growth of management. There were also gains of women in semi-skilled and unskilled manual work and indefinite occupations and, surprisingly, of both men and women in agricultural jobs. Ninety per cent of the net gain of women workers however was accounted for by those in non-manual and personal service jobs.

Table 3.11

Net Gain (+) or Loss (−) of Economically Active Men and Women to the South Eastern Region by Socio-Economic Group: Migrants to and from elsewhere in Great Britain 1966

	OVER 5 YEARS		OVER 1 YEAR	
	Men	Women	Men	Women
1. Employers and managers (large establishments)	+1,410	+500	+40	+130
2. Employers and managers (small establishments)	−1,040	−390	−490	−240
3. Professional workers – self-employed	−240	−40	−100	−30
4. Professional workers – employees	+3,570	+770	−220	+220
5. Intermediate non-manual workers	+5,240	+10,610	+1,190	+2,830
6. Junior non-manual workers	+6,040	+14,890	+1,350	+3,120
7. Personal service workers	+1,310	+4,260	+170	+1,440
8. Foremen and supervisors – manual	−1,150	−140	−520	−60
9. Skilled manual workers	−2,990	+620	−2,590	–
10. Semi-skilled manual workers	−1,020	+720	−990	+280
11. Unskilled manual workers	+990	+290	−290	+290
12. Own account workers (other than professional)	−2,540	−1,040	−850	−190
13. Farmers – employers and managers	−460	−20	−60	−30
14. Farmers – own account	−800	−180	−170	−70
15. Agricultural workers	−60	+70	+70	+90
16. Members of armed forces	+1,770	+20	–	–
17. Indefinite	+270	+170	−20	+50
Gains	20,600	32,970	2,820	8,450
Losses	−10,290	−1,810	−6,300	−620
Total Net Gain (+) or Loss (−)	+10,310	+31,160	−3,480	+7,830

Source: 1966 Census England and Wales: Migration Summary Tables, Part I, Table 6.

In brief, then, the occupational structure of the South East region is changing and this is reflected in the pattern of migration. The balance is shifting towards the employment of women and the region is attracting them from elsewhere in the country while in relation to the rest of Britain more men are leaving than arrive. This is the outcome of the growth of white collar and service employment which is sufficiently great to continue to draw British men in that sector too. The net gains and losses of men in different socio-economic groups are closely connected with the problem of incomes and living costs in the region. Women workers lacking dependents continue to be attracted into the region. Men, particularly those in lower income occupations who have dependents, have an incentive to leave. There cannot be much doubt that this is an important factor in the recent check to net migration into the region from the rest of Britain. This pattern of migration, then, reflects a continuing increase in the dominance of the middle classes within the South East and an increasing concentration of the middle class there.

Geographical Mobility and Cultural Change

The effects of changes in the distribution of the population, though frequently indirect, are subtle and penetrate to the most intimate social and personal levels of experience. Within the overall pattern of population redistribution relationships between colleagues, neighbours, relatives and friends are subject to far-reaching change. The redistribution of the population is, in large part, a matter of differential growth, with the population of southern England growing more quickly than that elsewhere, but this is materially reinforced as we have seen by the pattern of migration. But, through the individual experience of geographical mobility, migration has a still more important indirect effect on social norms and social structures. Migration affects the character of the social environment, not only in terms of its economic consequences in the labour market or in concentrating certain sorts of consumers in particular areas; the movement of new people into any area is likely to bring about a change in the quality of social life there, and not merely in terms of increasing the numbers trying to squeeze into the Underground, while their loss from their original community is likely to have concomitant effects there too.

From a sociological point of view, the changes in the social environment which are likely to have the most far-reaching consequences are those which bring about a change in the structure of social relationships. Elizabeth Bott pointed out that 'the effective social environment of a family is its network of friends, neighbours, relatives and particular social institutions'.[1] These external relationships form a network focused on the family in question. All the members at the periphery of such a network

[1] E. Bott, *Family and Social Network*, Tavistock, 1957, (2nd Edition 1971), p.159.

may know one another and be in independent contact with one another. Such a network would be described as close-knit. At the other extreme, a family's social network may be so loose-knit that none of the people they count as members know one another save through their common acquaintance with the members of the particular family in question.

The inter-connectedness of the network of external relationships will be affected by a wide range of factors. The economic, demographic and social characteristics of the area the family lives in would clearly be important. The geographical and social mobility of the members of the family as well as of the people they know together with their opportunities for making new social contacts are also directly relevant.[1] Geographical mobility in particular is likely to affect the individual's or his family's social contacts and in this way to shape his experience of the wider social system.

An overwhelmingly working class community which has perpetuated itself over several generations, depending upon employment in a single industry, is clearly more conducive to a high density of extra-familial relationships and the total network is likely to be more close-knit than in a more socially heterogeneous area with an unbalanced age structure and a rapid turnover of population dependent on a wide variety of occupations. Many working class families, for instance, live not only near the husband's workplace but near his workmates' families too, and have most of their relatives and even most of the people they have ever known living fairly close around them. Though individual families are not all equally affected or necessarily affected in the same way, it is more than likely under these circumstances that a family would have a very close-knit social network of external relationships. Not all working class families' social relationships are so densely inter-connected, especially not those who have moved from one part of the country to another in search of work. But among urban families most of the families with a very close-knit social network are likely to be working class.[2]

Middle class families are more likely to have moved in the course of husbands' careers, especially in the professions. In consequence, perhaps even more than geographically mobile working class families they are likely to have and retain contact with friends, relatives and former colleagues in different parts of the country who remain unknown to their current neighbours and associates.[3]

[1] ibid. p.113 and Christopher Turner, 'Conjugal Roles and Social Networks: A re-examination of an hypothesis', *Human Relations*, 1967, 20, pp.121-30.

[2] See Bott, op.cit., 1971 p.42 and ibid. second edition, 1971, p.250; also Gordon Rose, *The Working Class*, Longmans, 1968, pp.10-11.

[3] Bott, op.cit., 1971 and Colin Bell, *Middle Class Families*, Routledge, 1969, pp.52-3; also Jane Hubert, 'Kinship and Geographical Mobility in a Sample from a London Middle Class Area', *International Journal of Comparative Sociology*, 1965, 6, pp. 61-80.

Families in close-knit social networks have multiple relationships, direct or indirect, with each other. They can observe, discuss and evaluate many aspects of one another's behaviour. It may seem almost as if everyone not only knows everybody else, but everybody else's business too. The high 'visibility' of behaviour thus facilitates social control[1] and appropriate role behaviour can be specified and sanctioned in many spheres of life. The individual with a loose-knit social network has a much more fragmented role set. Each relationship is compartmentalised from the others. As it is much harder for any third party to observe how the individual behaves in any social situation, communal norms are more difficult to enforce. Ideas about a woman's place in the home or what is inappropriate for a man to do about the house are harder to maintain. At the same time, the segmentary character of other contacts emphasizes the socio-emotional singificance of the conjugal relationship. The husband and wife are dependent on one another for psychological gratifications such as sympathy, understanding and security and this encourages a greater amount of cooperation and sharing. This change may be a liberation or an intolerable burden for those not prepared for it,[2] but it is only readily maintained, it seems, where geographical mobility continues to separate one adult generation of kin from another.[3] For families from a traditional close-knit community leaving the long-settled areas where family life follows a traditional pattern, where a husband's obligations are clear and a wife's duties unquestioned, is a more complex process than the substitution of one lot of environmental influences, a new pattern of social norms and a new set of relationships, for the old. The old relationships are not altogether relinquished, the old norms not altogether forgotten. A close-knit network cannot be immediately replaced by another. For a time at least, the migrant must adapt to a less densely interconnected network of social relations. This is likely to prove especially discouraging for those who have been accustomed to the personalized and particular relationships of a familiar neighbourhood, and they may feel ill-equipped to deal with a more impersonal environment. As Elizabeth Bott has noted, '. . . one move, even a comparatively short move . . . will be a social and psychological upheaval for a family if it involves the breakup of close-knit networks, where families who have moved before or who have been brought up to expect geographical mobility will be much less upset'.[4]

[1] See R.K. Merton, 'The Role Set: Problems in Sociological Theory', *British Journal of Sociology*, 8, 1957, p.114 and *Social Theory and Social Structure*, The Free Press, Glencoe, 1957, pp.336-56; cf. the discussions of gossip as a vehicle of social control in Leo Kuper, *Living in Towns*, Cresset, London, 1953, pp.79 ff; Max Gluckman 'Gossip and Scandal', *Current Anthropology* 4, 1963, pp. 307-316, and Colin Bell op.cit. pp.139-44.

[2] See M. Young and P. Willmott, *Family and Kinship in East London*, Routledge, 1962, and John Mogey, *Family and Neighbourhood*, Oxford, 1957.

[3] See Peter Willmott, *The Evolution of a Community*, Routledge, 1963, ch.4.

[4] Elizabeth Bott, *Family and Social Network*, 1971, p.279 and cf. p.305.

What evidence there is which is relevant here mostly comes from studies of fairly short distance moves, especially where people have moved from an old part of town into a new housing estate on the edge. This has been a very common experience in postwar Britain and it was estimated in 1961 that more than a third of the population were then living in houses built since 1945.[1]

Young and Wilmott for instance, described how on the new council estate they studied, called Greenleigh in their book, people were less likely to spend their leisure time visiting relatives because they no longer lived close at hand. Friends and neighbours however did not replace the company of now distant relatives and the Greenleigh families in consequence simply spent more time at home with their own immediate family than they had in the old neighbourhood in London's East End where they had lived before.[2] Especially for the women the separation and loss of daily contact with their relatives was felt to be the most serious problem of the families who had come to live at Greenleigh. Similarly on the Barton estate, the then new council estate in north Oxford studied by Mogey, a third of the women found that the loss of ready contact with close relatives – and especially with their mothers – was a source of strain.[3] In traditional working class communities this easy accessibility and frequent interaction among relatives has been of the very greatest importance. Thus in their study in the Sparkbrook area of Birmingham, Rex and Moore discovered that relationships with neighbours mattered more amongst the lower middle class and even among the immigrant population than in the working class neighbourhoods. For the Sparkbrook working class their own families and relatives retained their primary importance even as day-to-day social contacts, though they might be dispersed over the whole of Birmingham rather than all living in the same neighbourhood.[4]

Not only do relationships with neighbours not substitute for the reduced level of contact with relatives, on the estates there appears to have been a reduction in interaction with neighbours as compared with the old inner city areas where most of the tenants had come from. Mogey noted that on the new estate children played at home more because parents were more concerned about selecting their children's friends and discouraging them from playing with the rough kids at the other end of the road. Young and Willmott observed that men spent less leisure time in the public houses at Greenleigh, partly because they knew fewer people, partly

---

[1] See J.H. Nicholson, *New Communities in Britain*, National Council of Social Service, 1961.

[2] M. Young and P. Willmott, *Family and Kinship in East London*, Routledge, 1962.

[3] John Mogey, *Family and Neighbourhood*, Oxford, 1957.

[4] John Rex and Robert Moore, *Race, Community and Conflict*, Oxford, 1967, pp.76-77 and cf. Gordon Rose, *The Working Class*, Longmans, 1968, p.59.

because being fewer the pubs were on average further away than they had been in Bethnal Green. At the same time married men found their pocket money reduced because the cost of living on the new estate proved to be higher than it had been in the old area. Travel to work back in Inner London obviously cost more and rents were higher too. But the move to a new house with a garden had meant that for most families a good deal of new expenditure was incurred. In the house new floor coverings, curtains etc. were necessary and the improvement in housing usually made the old furniture seem shabby and inadequate. A similar discontent was observed by Mogey among the Barton residents. What surprised him was that despite the considerable improvement in their housing, they were more discontented than similar families still in the old houses in St Ebbes in central Oxford. The St Ebbes families seemed to accept the inadequacies of their old houses and put up with the lack of facilities they had grown used to. Many of the Barton families were much less contented with what seemed to Mogey very much better conditions and this he attributed to the raising of their aspirations due to the discovery that improvements were possible. He described their condition as one of status dissent, an unwillingness to accept their situation in contrast with the status assent of the St Ebbes families who were prepared to make do and did not complain.

In contrast with the familiar neighbourhood of the long-settled Bethnal Green or St Ebbes where, even apart from the likelihood of a large number of relatives living close by, neighbours were likely to have known one another all their lives, to have grown up and gone to school together, on the new estates neighbours were people from different districts and seemed strangers to each other. The intimacy of the old relationships was gone. The old community had given a sense of identity, of belonging and also, to quote Mogey, 'a traditional set of behaviour patterns and a mechanism to find out what is expected'.[1] As Nicholson has pointed out, 'in the new setting there are no longer commonly accepted standards'.[2] Young and Willmott found that on the estate families withdrew into their own households all the more as a result and the concern with new standards of interior decoration and furnishing seemed to become competitive, as was observed earlier by Kuper in his study of council estates in Coventry. 'Keeping up with the Joneses' became apparent and there was a general shift away from the Bethnal Green way of life which Young and Willmott describe as a move from 'people centred' existence to a 'house centred' one, a change from the judgment of neighbours on a personal basis, as people one has known all one's life and whose family and foibles one has known, to a tendency to assess the behaviour of others

---

[1] Mogey, *Family and Neighbourhood*, Oxford, 1957. See also Josephine Klein, *Samples from English Cultures*, Routledge, 1964.

[2] J.H. Nicholson, *New Communities in Britain*, National Council of Social Service, 1961, p.31.

largely in terms of the only information readily available about them, their visible possessions — the furniture which can be seen being moved in, the car, the perambulator, the children's clothes and toys.[1] The proximity of a nearby private estate apparently intensified the drive among the Greenleigh residents towards more lavish expenditure as a sign of improving social status.[2] In this kind of situation the locality in which a family lives is less a source of social support than yet another arena for social competition. The absence of a sense of community denies the individual the opportunity to find a sense of identification there. He may turn still more towards those areas of life where he can still find some rewarding and personally affirming involvement. Writing of the experience of the migrant professional Musgrove argued, 'His career and his domestic life are called upon to provide an ever greater measure of personal significance and failure in either becomes increasingly catastrophic'.[3] The stresses to which the migrant is particularly exposed may themselves induce further peregrination, ' . . . the next town, the next job (perhaps even the next wife) may be different, more satisfying, easier to live with'.[4] This romantic belief is certainly a major theme in contemporary folklore but how far it actually influences behaviour it is so far impossible to judge.

Margaret Stacey's study of Banbury[5] describes the relationship of the traditional Banbury residents, those who worked in the traditional trades of the ancient market town and had been born there and had grown up there, and the non-traditionalists, the newcomers who had come to settle in the town and work in the new industries. She remarks that 'Apart from rifts between groups of neighbours of widely different social status, the greatest social distance was found between northerners and other residents'.[6] However the division is not a universal one. She emphasizes that ' . . . it may be said with a fair degree of certainty that working class families from the north of England or from Scotland are very unlikely to settle on intimate terms as neighbours [to natives of Banbury]. No such prediction can be made for the middle class . . . the middle class concept of neighbouring is, apparently, sufficiently nearly common to north, south and midlands.'[7] It is among the working class that regional differences exist, differences in speech, manners, customs, and these divide even the newcomers to the town. Thus the assimilation of the working class migrant is likely to be difficult and the sense of belonging to a community is particularly likely to be destroyed for the northerners, to the extent that they are not accepted by their new neighbours.

[1] cf. Kuper, *Living in Towns*, Cresset, 1953, p.46.

[2] Young and Willmott, *Family and Kinship in East London,* Routledge, 1962, p.152.

[3] F. Musgrove, *The Migratory Elite*, Heinemann 1963, p.155.

[4] ibid.

[5] Stacey, *Tradition and Change*, Oxford, 1960.

[6] ibid. p.109.

[7] ibid. p.110, cf. Musgrove, op.cit., pp.105-106.

Migration for the middle class family is likely to be easier. In the middle class it is the migrant who is likely to make the changes rather than suffer from them. To start with, as Jane Hubert noted, ' . . . a migrant middle class population differs from a working class one. Professional men and women apply for appointments and usually only move when they have accepted the job. An unskilled or even skilled labourer will usually come to London to look for work.'[1] This economic advantage of the middle class, or at least of the upper middle class, migrant is reinforced by other features of middle class culture. Their relative psychological independence of kin contact and greater facility in verbal communication helps to account for the fact that middle class people are more likely to occupy their leisure time and social life with friends and colleagues rather than relatives and neighbours. As Goldthorpe and his colleagues emphasize, middle class people are more likely to *make* friends 'through personal choice and initiative from among persons with whom no structured relationship already exists'.[2] This is not a common feature of working class life. In comparison with the working class, middle class families are much more likely to entertain in their homes friends who are not relatives; their members are more likely to belong to clubs, societies and formal associations of one sort or another and to have more committee memberships than even the more participatory of the working class.[3] This readiness to join groups, to associate with others who are neither related to him, near neighbours or workmates makes it easier for the middle class individual to move from one community and from one set of relationships to another. But for the migrant middle class, the quality of the relationships he leaves or takes up is not the same as those enjoyed or endured by his settled peers. Margaret Stacey contrasted the traditionalist middle class, who judge a man in terms of his antecedents, and the non-traditionalist middle class – mainly the newcomers to the town bringing new standards to judge their own and others' behaviour in the existing community.

[1] Jane Hubert, 'Kinship and Geographical Mobility in a Sample from a London Middle Class Area', *International Journal of Comparative Sociology*, 1965, 6, p.68.

[2] See John Goldthorpe, David Lockwood, Frank Bechhofer and Jennifer Platt, *The Affluent Worker in a Class Society*, Cambridge University Press, 1969, and cf. Mogey, *Family and Neighbourhood*, Oxford, 1957, ch.5; Stacey, op.cit., 1960, pp.114-5, 155, and Peter Willmott and Michael Young, *Family and Class in a London Suburb*, Routledge, 1960, pp.127-9.

[3] See the next chapter on further middle class and working class family comparisons; Goldthorpe et al., op.cit., 1969, Table 9, p.93; C. Rosser and C.C. Harris, *The Family and Social Change*, Routledge, 1965, pp.106-7; P. Willmott, op.cit., 1963, Appendix 2, Table 19, p.135 and Table 28, p.139; Willmott and Young, op.cit., 1960, and Michael Young and Peter Willmott, *The Symmetrical Family* Routledge, 1973, pp.229 and 222. Musgrove found high status migrants substantially over-represented among the leaders of five voluntary associations in a large midlands city – *The Migratory Elite*, Heinemann, 1963, ch.5.

'Many non-traditionalists do not apply 'Who is he?' as a test of a man's social acceptability. Their test is rather 'What does he do?' judging him on his merits as an individual both at work and at home, rather than on his family connections and original social background. And on this basis they wish to be judged. Occupation is, therefore, more important for them that it is for the traditionalist. Furthermore, they do not belong to, or they do not accept the status structure of Banbury. That is not to say they do not recognize status. They do, and in one way or another are deeply concerned about it.'[1]

Social status for the migrant middle class is not ascribed to anyone on the reputation of their relatives, the rectitude of a father, the dignity of uncles or the prowess of a cousin. For them social status has to be achieved in terms of what a man can show for his efforts, each man for himself or at least for himself and his immediate dependents. This then, for the working class and the middle class migrant alike is, in general, a more impersonal, more competitive world not only economically but socially.

Movement out of the close-knit communities, where traditional ways are established and familiar, to new communities without tradition or without a collective awareness of a common way of life is not a new phenomenon. It is a theme which may be traced in the literature of the past two centuries. It is associated with the shifts in population consequent on the rapid urban expansion and transformation which has continued since industrialization got under way. Nor are the traditional ways, with which the experience of mobility is contrasted, of very long standing. The traditional working class communities in the East End of London or round the great industrial conurbations or the mining towns mostly date only from the latter part of the nineteenth century, perhaps four generations ago. Hobsbawm has described the origins of what we now describe as the traditional working class life style which emerged only between 1870 and 1900 and lasted with very little change until the affluence of the late 1950s and 1960s.

'Its most complete expression was to be found in the characteristic centres of late nineteenth century working class life, the industrial north or proletarian areas of large non-industrial cities like Liverpool and South or East London, which did not change very much, except for the worse, in the first half of the twentieth century. It was neither a very good nor a very rich life, but it was probably the first kind of life since the Industrial Revolution which provided a firm lodging for the British working class within industrial society.'[2]

---

[1] Stacey, *Tradition and Change*, Oxford, 1960, p.16.

[2] E.J. Hobsbawm, *Industry and Empire*,, Weidenfeld, 1968, p.137. For a rather more favourable evaluation of this 'traditional' working class life-style see, e.g., George Orwell, *The Road to Wigan Pier*, Gollancz, 1937, pp.147-50.

Wilmott's study of council-house tenants in Dagenham showed that, if it is possible at all, a 'traditional' community of close-knit social networks and extended families is likely to establish itself in only two generations. The intervention of 'rational-legal' procedures for the bureaucratized allocation of scarce publicly owned housing, however, tends to move each generation on to a new community and inhibits the growth of 'traditional' norms by loosening social networks and limiting the extension of extended families over three or four generations in daily contact. But in an expanding population this has been the experience of a substantial proportion of each generation of families since the mid-nineteenth century. The twentieth century differs to the extent that, as the pace of change quickens and geographical mobility increases, such processes may enmesh an ever larger proportion of families.

Geographical mobility is encouraged by the growth in scale of organizations in industry, commerce and public administration, which means that when employees join a company, they are much less likely to find themselves settled for life with an interest in participating in the local community that their firm serves. Increasingly and, as we have seen, especially in the upper ranks of the middle class, the pursuit of a career in a world dominated by great industrial corporations and administrative bureaucracies focuses attention away from the residential community. In this kind of setting the executive employee and perhaps even his family, is more likely to become career orientated than community orientated and the career will generally entail the series of moves and transfers which inspired Watson's description of such people as *spiralists*.[1] In addition, the redevelopment of the older inner urban areas and long-term technological change bringing about the decline of older staple industries in some areas and economic growth elsewhere, augment the upheaval of traditional patterns by affecting not only each new generation, new families setting up for the first time, but the older and apparently more established generation too.

It may be, as C. C. Harris has suggested, that 'the more mobility destroys local groups, the more important kinship relations may become'.[2] But this is not to argue that the loosening of relationships within a local community strengthens kin ties, only that kin ties have a residual importance which may survive separation. Family life certainly retains its importance in society at large and Rex and Moore, Colin Bell and Young and Willmott found that car-owning families unsurprisingly were able to keep in touch with their relatives despite geographical dispersion,[3] but

[1] See W. Watson, 'Social Mobility and Social Class in Industrial Communities' in Max Gluckman and Ely Devons (eds), *Closed Systems and Open Minds,* Oliver and Boyd, 1964 and Colin Bell, op.cit., 1969, ch. 2 and 3; p.82 ff. above.

[2] C.C. Harris, *The Family,* Allen and Unwin, 1969, p.141, n.29.

[3] Rex and Moore, *Race, Community and Conflict,* 1967; Colin Bell, op.cit., 1969, and Young and Willmott, op.cit, 1973, pp.229-30.

family life and some of the changes it is subject to will be considered at greater length in the next chapter.

In so far as the experience of geographical mobility has effects upon the structure of social relations, then the pattern of migration discussed earlier in the present chapter can be seen to have several socio-cultural consequences. Migration can be identified as one of the sources of change in local cultures not only in bringing new people into contact but, through the loosening of social networks both for the migrant and the stationary, in the normative pattern which is expressed in the qualitative aspects of their social interactions. Secondly, the experience of geographical mobility may be most disturbing for someone brought up within one of the more traditional working class communities, and this helps explain the reluctance of many workers to move. Third, the much greater amount of mobility, especially of those in professional and managerial occupations, is an important factor differentiating the culture of the middle classes, which emphasizes individualism, ambition, independence and achievement, from that of the working class with its greater emphasis on the individual's obligations to his group and the here and now. With the increasing mobility of sections of the working class one might expect some move towards the middle class in terms of the values expressed in the way of life of the most mobile and this is a topic to which we shall return in Chapter 7. The progress of professionalization and bureaucratization, which go with the growth in scale and the centralization of administration in commerce and industry as well as the public services, is likely to intensify the geographical mobility among the middle classes to a still greater degree, however, and for the majority this is likely to widen the differences still further rather than reduce them.[1]

Geographical mobility within Britain, as we have seen, is increasing. Though generally under-estimated as a factor in social change, it is, nevertheless, likely to prove of increasing importance in shaping British society in the later years of the twentieth century not only in terms of the quality of individual social experience but in terms of the larger issues of community cohesion and class relations too.

[1] cf. Musgrove, *The Migratory Elite*, Heinemann, 1963, p.105.

4 The Structure of Family Life

Introduction

With an increasing proportion of a growing population married, there are more distinguishable family units now than ever before. Most people live in family groups. According to the 1971 census, 52.3 million people, out of a total of 53.8 million in Great Britain, lived in 18.5 million private households, the remaining 1.5 million resided in various kinds of institution: barracks, convents, hospitals, hotels, prisons et cetera.[1] More than 3,000,000 of these private households, however, were in fact people living alone, and there were also a further 300,000 households whose members declared themselves on the census schedule to be unrelated. The definition of a family used in the census refers only to parents and children. Usually, however, a family group might be defined more broadly to include people living with their spouses and their children or their parents, grand-parents, aunts, uncles, cousins or other relatives. In these wider terms over 14,000,000 of the households identified in the 1966 census, containing more than 48,000,000 people, may be designated as family groups,[2] and in 1971 with more but slightly smaller families there should turn out to have been about 48.6 million people living in about 15,000,000 family groups. Many of those living alone or with unrelated persons are not, of course, isolated but may be in frequent, even daily contact with members of their families. In addition, many of those without any relatives or living away from their own kinsfolk, nevertheless live within the framework of a family environment. Besides those households where two or in some cases more families lived together, in 1971 over 300,000 family groups had non-relatives living with them and sharing meals with them.[3] These included households where there were

[1] from *1971 Census Advance Analysis*, Table 3.

[2] *1971 Census Great Britain Summary Tables (one per cent sample)* Table 26 and cf. *Sample Census 1966 England and Wales, Household Composition Tables*, Appendix A Table 1. At the time of writing complete data from the 1971 Census were not available. For a cautionary note on the use of census data, though now somewhat out of date as far as British material is concerned, see J. Hajnal 'Family Size' in Julius Gould and William L. Kolb (eds), *A Dictionary of the Social Sciences*, Tavistock, 1964.

[3] *1971 Census Advance Analysis*, Table 26 and p.XVIII for the definition of a private household used in the census.

lodgers, foster children, *ménages à trois* and other arrangements not separately distinguished in the census tables.

Though the overwhelming majority of the population may live at home with their families, the nature of their domesticity is various. This is not the place to discuss the psychological factors in family relationships, though the temperamental and personal idiosyncracies of the individual members are likely to shape the quality of relationships within the family, perhaps more so than in any other group. But the structure of the family, in the sense of the pattern of desirable and expected behaviour within which these psychological variables operate, is dependent on cultural and social factors. The relationships between husbands and wives, parents and children, brothers and sisters, and between people who, by extension of these bonds, are reckoned as relatives, are in large part functions of the ideas they have about how they ought to behave in those relationships. These ideas are acquired through their involvement in other relationships both in their family life and also outside it in the wider social system.

The Family and Change

Despite the many cultural assumptions common through most of British society, the structure of family life varies according to the diverse patterns of social relationships which occur within a highly differentiated social structure. At the same time, however, the family group remains effectively the immediate social environment within which most people live. But it is not an unchanging environment. The changes to which the family is subject are both secular and cyclical. The family is subject to secular change within the society at large as a result of demographic, economic, political, cultural and other developments. In the absence of reliable and detailed historical evidence, it is difficult to be certain about the exact nature of these changes in the long term, but the more recent changes in family life in response to some of the current changes in British society will be discussed later. Cyclical family changes are for all of us more readily recognizable within our own personal experience. Though our most profound and earliest social experience is that of family change, and although the crises of our family life are the source of our most intimately satisfying, most joyful and most painful hours, the essential transience of family life is something we too easily, perhaps in some kind of self protection, forget.

From the individual point of view and overstating somewhat, it might be said that for most of us the first 15 or 20 years of life are spent in an intensifying struggle to free ourselves from one family which is usually achieved only by setting up another one we will spend the remaining years more or less desperately trying to maintain. At the level of the family group, Stacey writes, 'of its nature the immediate family is a short-lived unit, which lasts only for a part of the life of its members'.[1]

The family group moves through a cycle of foundation, growth, change and dissolution. Children are born, grow up and leave home, spouses may part, parents die. Only 8,000,000, or 56 per cent, of the families recorded in the 1971 census included married couples and their children. The other family groups were at either earlier or later phases in their development. Stacey found in her Banbury study that less than half of the families in her sample were what she called 'whole families', that is, consisted of married couples with all their children still living at home. She presented the first available account of the proportion of families at various stages of the family cycle in a community in Britain. These proportions are based on a sample of 898 families living in Banbury in 1950.[2]

Table 4:1

Families and the Family Cycle in Banbury

	No Children	All Children at home	Some Children left home	All Children left home
Couples with wife under 45 years old	7%	36%	1%	—
Couples with wife over 45 years old	5%	11%	9%	9%
Widowed Parents (including divorced and separated)	3%	7%	7%	5%

Source: Stacey, *Tradition and Change* Ch. 7, chart XVII, p.134.

As the table shows, in only 47 per cent of the Banbury families were all the children still at home with both parents still living. If we add those couples who still had some of their children living with them we find the proportion almost exactly corresponds to the 1971 national figure. It is also clear from Table 4:1 that the ageing of the married couple and the process of producing and rearing children can be represented as a matrix of possibilities through which the careers of different families may take rather different paths. The demographic changes already discussed, in particular the trends toward earlier marriage and an increased expectation of life, are likely to have affected the distribution of families within this grid so that if the survey were conducted now a number of differences in the proportional distribution would probably appear.

Rosser and Harris in a later study carried out in Swansea also discuss

[1] Margaret Stacey, *Tradition and Change,* Oxford, 1960, p.133.

[2] ibid., Appendix 7, p.209. These and the figures from the census refer not merely to dependent children but to those of all ages.

the family cycle. They distinguish four phases of development. These are: firstly, the Home-Making phase which they define as the period from marriage to the birth of the first child; secondly, the phase of Procreation, from the birth of the first child to the marriage of the first child; thirdly, Dispersion, the phase covering the marriage of the first child to the marriage of the last child; and the Final phase, from the marriage of the last child to the death of the original partners. They found the 1725 families in their sample were distributed as follows; 17 per cent in the Home-Making phase, 47 per cent in the phase of Procreation, 16 per cent in the phase of Dispersion and 20 per cent in the Final phase.[1] It is worth noting the figure of 47 per cent in the second phase coincides with the proportion of Banbury families at a similar stage of development some ten years earlier and described as 'whole families'. The single dimension of Rosser and Harris's analysis, however, does not allow for the diversity of experience between different families[2] and produces some small anomalies in their findings which make an exact comparison with, or confirmation of, the Banbury results impossible.[3]

The shortening of the intergenerational cycle, which I mentioned in a preceding chapter, is changing the duration of each phase of the family cycle however these may be defined. If parenthood begins earlier in life then so does grandparenthood. Other things being equal, increasingly in the future children are likely to grow up in an environment which includes all their grandparents and even some great-grandparents. Townsend considered that the number of grandparents had more than doubled since the beginning of the present century[4] and estimated that 22 per cent of those over the age of 65 in Britain in 1962 had great-grandchildren[5]. Firth and Stacey both noted that in the communities they studied kinship ties generally extended over three generations, linking grandparents, parents and grandchildren in regular contact. The lateral range of kin known

---

[1] C. Rosser and C.C. Harris, *The Family and Social Change,* Routledge, 1965, Table 4:5, p.164; see also C.C. Harris, *The Family,* Allen and Unwin, 1969, ch.7.

[2] cf. Christopher Turner, *Family and Kinship in Modern Britain,* Routledge, 1969, p.82.

[3] For instance they show that two per cent of the Swansea households in the Procreation phase consisted of married couples living alone, that five per cent of families in the phase of Dispersion were like this and that two per cent of families in the Final phase were made up of parents and unmarried children; op.cit., Table 4:6, p.166. These proportions are of small account it is true but suggest that the reported findings must be interpreted with some care.

[4] Peter Townsend, *Sociological Review Monograph No.8,* (ed. Paul Halmos) 1964, p.92.

[5] In Denmark the proportion was similar at 23 per cent, but in the U.S.A. 40 per cent of the national sample of over 65 years olds were great-grandparents. ref. E. Shanas, P. Townsend, D. Wedderburn, H. Friis, P. Milhoj and J. Stehouwer, *Old People in Three Industrial Societies,* Atherton, 1968.

usually did not go beyond first cousins[1]. By enlarging the depth of generations in the kinship network it is obvious that the lateral extension of kinship is increased too, though whether this will be manifest in actual effective social groupings is dependent on the operation of other factors. It may be that, as Townsend suggests, a degree of vertical splitting may occur, but evidence is as yet lacking and rather than the weakening of sibling relationships which this would imply some limitation of inter-generational interaction is equally likely. As Harris has pointed out however, the character of intergenerational relations depends to a considerable extent on the stage each has reached in their respective life cycles.[2] The achievement of parenthood changes the relationship between the young adult and her or his own parents; arrival at retirement may transform relationships with children and especially grandchildren. As we all have felt, involvements outside the family impinge on our response to our relatives, and our needs for one another — as well as our capacity or willingness to respond — change as we move through our life-cycle. A shortening of the intergenerational interval and the increasing survival of the elderly can throw this gearing out of mesh, so that new assumptions about one another and new patterns of behaviour have to be evolved if the family is to adapt to the consequences of such demographic change. It is on these grounds that Townsend argued that 'the data about the emergence of the four generation family suggest that the structure of the kinship network has been changing more rapidly than has been supposed. It is therefore likely that changes in family organisation and relationships may have been affected less by changes in industrial and economic organisation and relationships may have been affected more by changes in population structure.'[3] The changes in the structure of the population which have brought about the emergence of the four-generation family thereby have produced a change in the environment within which children are socialized into the customary social expectations — the culture of the society of which these families are part. In particular, this represents an alteration in the context within which the relations between the generations evolve[4]. If married couples are freed of parental responsibilities while still in the prime of life, they are likely to want to pursue new interests, possibly outside the home, if the opportunities are available. This, as has been suggested, is especially likely to influence the status of women as the period of their full commitment to motherhood is done with earlier in their lives. The effects on the occupational structure, on the structure of

---

[1] Raymond Firth, *Two Studies of Kinship in London,* Athlone Press, 1956, p.62; Stacey, op.cit., p.117.

[2] C.C. Harris, op.cit., p.188.

[3] Peter Townsend, 'The Four Generation Family', *New Society,* 7 July 1966, p.13.

[4] ref. Kingsley Davis, 'The Sociology of Parent-Youth Conflict', *American Sociological Review,* 1940, 5, pp.523-35 and W.E. Moore, *Social Change,* Prentice-Hall, 1963, pp.51-2.

husband-wife relations and the stability of marriages have yet to be calculated. At the other end of the cycle, the earlier embarkation upon matrimonial and parental careers by an increasing proportion of young people may affect their relations with the members of older generations as well as the pattern of youth culture too. But all this remains an area for future research as far as Britain is concerned.

In so far as the time interval between the generations is shortening more in the working class than in the middle class, the differential effect on the family cycle and on inter-generational relations is likely to widen class differences in family patterns. Against this, some have suggested that other factors, including changes in family size and the break-up of traditional communities under the impact of geographical mobility, are tending to reduce class differences.

Definitions and Distinctions

Before proceeding to discuss secular changes in family structure and variations between different sectors of society there are some preliminary distinctions which have to be made. Family structure can be examined at two levels. These are, firstly, the elementary family and secondly the wider kinship system. The group made up by a husband and wife and any dependent children they may have is termed the elementary family (this group has also been described by various writers as the nuclear, immediate, primary or conjugal family). I should say that the definition of the elementary family as 'the two adults surrounded by one child or more' which I came across recently must have been founded on hard-won personal experience, but in this discussion the term will be used to include childless couples too. In 1971, there were about 13,000,000 elementary families in Great Britain.[1] Most people expect to belong, at some stage, to at least two elementary families. These are the family into which they are born, which may be described as their 'family of orientation' or 'family of origin'; and the family which they themselves establish when they marry, described as their 'family of procreation' or 'family of marriage'.[2]

Any elementary family, however, is embedded in the wider networks of relationships which involve its members with other people outside the family boundary. On the foundation of a family of their own people do not, on that account, usually sever connections with their family of origin. On the contrary, though relationships may be changed by their new status they generally continue to find throughout their lives an important part of their social activity within the ambit of those they regard as their relatives. Larger groupings of relatives by blood (kin) or marriage (affines) may be analysed in different ways. The whole range of genealogical connections

[1] *1971 Census Great Britain Summary Tables (one per cent sample)*, Table 34
[2] G. P. Murdock, *Social Structure*, Macmillan, New York, 1949, ch.1.

which an individual can be shown to have is rarely of any sociological significance, however, especially when he may remain in ignorance of many of them. There is rarely any sociological value in going beyond the range of all the relatives whom a person knows to exist. This group has been called by Young and Willmott the 'kinship network', though it includes both kin and affines.[1]

Within the kinship network, the frequency of contact and the salience for him of the relationships an individual may have with his various relatives can vary enormously. While some may be very dear to him, visited often, sharers in the day-to-day commerce of his domestic and private life, others, perhaps far away, are likely to be little more to him than a half-familiar face at someone else's wedding or receive no more acknowledgement than the annual tribute of a Christmas card, if that.

The Extended Family

The relatives with whom closer relationships are maintained in many cases can be distinguished as a more or less cohesive grouping within the wider kinship network. This grouping is generally of three or four generations, grandparents, parents and grandchildren, and has been termed by Firth a 'close kin unit' or 'set', but is commonly described by British sociologists as an 'extended family'.[2] This may seem to be to labour the obvious but the clarification of terms is of some importance. After all the effect of sociology, unless it is in error, can never be to astonish us about the familiar, the aim is only to see things more clearly.

[1] M. Young and P. Willmott, *Family and Kinship in East London*, rev.edn., Penguin, 1962, p.13.

[2] See Raymond Firth, 'Family and Kinship in Industrial Society' in Paul Halmos (ed.), *The Development of Industrial Societies: Sociological Review Monograph No.8.*, Oct. 1964, p.83 and note 28 p.87; Raymond Firth, Jane Hubert and Anthony Forge, *Families and Their Relatives: Kinship in a Middle-Class Sector of London*, Routledge, 1970, pp.281-8; Peter Townsend, *The Family Life of Old People*, rev.edn., Penguin 1963, p.126 and in Halmos (ed.), op.cit., note 29 p.96 Townsend uses the term to apply to a group of relatives who may reside in separate households but are in frequent contact, seeing one another every day or nearly every day. Firth, op.cit., 1964, restricts the term further 'to refer to groups of kin of three generations or more having a fairly well defined corporate lineal character, such as co-operation in ordinary productive activities, common ownership of assets, recognised common responsibilities'. Other writers, on the other hand, have used the term more loosely 'to refer to any grouping related by descent, marriage and adoption that is broader than the nuclear family' – N.W. Bell & E.F. Vogel, *A Modern Introduction to the Family*, Free Press of Glencoe, 1960, p.1.; cf. the virtually identical formula used by Rosser and Harris, *The Family and Social Change*, Routledge, 1965, p.32, and Colin Bell, *Middle Class Families*, Routledge, 1969, ch. 4 and 5, where the term in practice is used to apply to all recognised kin or the whole kinship network, e.g. pp.100-101.

The extended family then, looked at one way, mainly involves the maintenance of contact with members of the families of origin of a pair of spouses. It is, from the opposite point of view, in general the result of the persistence of elementary family ties beyond the marriage of the second generation and often especially of the continuing strength of the mother-daughter tie.[1] Sometimes other, genealogically more distant, kin may also be included on account of some particular mutual affection, but this is not very common. Jane Hubert, for example, found that amongst the upper middle class in Highgate, while contact was maintained with only 32 per cent of known kin outside the family of origin, in over 90 per cent of the cases contact was maintained with parents and siblings.[2]

Interaction between relatives is socially more significant than residential proximity alone. Geographical distance is not of itself a social fact. Even so, frequency of contact is no certain guide to the importance of the services kinsmen render to one another or to the strength of the feelings which bind them together.[3]

It is important to keep the matter in perspective however, and the role of the extended family should not be over-emphasized however much it may have been overlooked in the past.[4] Ties with relatives beyond the circle of the elementary family are not in Britain of any obvious structural importance at the macro-social level. At the level of individual social relations they are of considerable significance, but they do not have the moral inflexibility or the all-embracing character they have in less urban and particularly less industrialized societies. The essential basis of these sustained relationships is the affection born within the elementary family. There is considerable variability from one individual to another and, for each, participation in extended family relationships may not have the same significance at every phase of his or her life.[5]

Relatives continue to interact with one another, however, partly in the exchange of services, reinforced by the sense of reciprocal obligation so created between one family and another. Thus, where a married woman co-operates with her mother in the performance of household tasks, the

---

[1] See Raymond Firth, *Two Studies of Kinship in London,* Athlone Press, 1956, p.63; Margaret Stacey *Tradition and Change,* Oxford, 1960, p.116; Townsend, op.cit., 1963, p.92.

[2] Jane Hubert, 'Kinship and Geographical Mobility in a Sample from a London Middle Class Area', *International Journal of Comparative Sociology,* 6, 1965, pp.72-3, and see Firth, op.cit., 1956, pp.62-3.

[3] See Hubert, op.cit., p.78, and Bell, op.cit., 1969, p.161.

[4] See Raymond Firth, 'Introduction to Family and Kin Ties in Britain and their Sociological Importance', *British Journal of Sociology,* Vol.XII, 1961, p.305; Rosser and Harris, op.cit., 1965, p.287; W.M. Williams, *A West Country Village: Ashworthy,* Routledge, 1963, p.158; Margaret Stacey, op.cit. p.111.

[5] See C.C. Harris, *The Family,* 1969, p.188, and Raymond Firth, et.al., op.cit. 1970, pp.153 and 451-3.

members of the two families may feel some sense of duty to keep up a level of sociability even when initially the warmth of positive sentiments between them is not great. The range of kin with whom any contact is maintained varies as these duties involved in inter-family relations among kin are non-obligatory and their observation, except possibly in relation to parents, is permissive.[1] In his account of kinship in one of the older working class districts of London, Firth observed that 'personal selectivity is shown to a high degree in the recognition and maintenance of kin relations. This tends to operate for elementary families as units.' And in their later study of upper middle class families in north London Firth and his colleagues noted that ' . . . the *effective* social ties of kinship tend to be shared. Kinship as a basis for social action tends to involve married couples and families, not individuals alone.'[2] When related families live in the same neighbourhood, they will find it especially difficult, however, to combine a close association with some relatives with having little to do with others without some members of the kinship network feeling offence or embarrassment. This will likely lead to social control and when families are dependent on one another for the exchange of mutual aid in household management and family care such sanctions can carry considerable force. Where geographical mobility has separated families selectivity on personal grounds amongst them is much more readily achieved. Firth has pointed out the role played in defining a family's effective kinship network by such instruments of social recognition as wedding invitations and Christmas cards 'which by being sent or withheld in initiation or exchange serve to acknowledge or disavow interest in the relationship'.[3]

In spite of this element of selectivity, of migration and the decline in the average size of the elementary family compared with the beginning of the century, the extended family is nevertheless a vital element in the social experience of the majority of people in Britain. This has been particularly well illustrated in studies of the social circumstances of the elderly. Most old people in modern Britain, as in other industrial societies, are in close and frequent contact with their relatives, especially, of course, with their own, probably married, children. This appears to be the case irrespective of class or region and in urban as much as in rural areas.[4] In 1962 a study of a national sample of 2,500 old people indicated that more than two thirds of those with children saw at least one every day and about another 17 per cent usually saw one or more of their children weekly.[5]

[1] See Firth, op.cit., 1956, p.62 and Stacey, op.cit., p.117 and p.132.

[2] Firth, op.cit., 1956, pp.62-3 and see Firth et al. op.cit., 1970, p.197.

[3] Firth, op.cit., 1956, p.63.

[4] See Townsend, *The Family Life of Old People*, 1963, p.238, Table 28.

[5] ibid pp.241-2.

Mother and Daughters

Relationships between kin are, in effect, generally between family and family rather than between individuals, but the responsibility of sustaining these bonds is mainly carried by wives and mothers rather than by husbands or children. In all social classes women tend to have a wider knowledge of their relatives and have more frequent contacts with them than men do.[1]

The structure of extended family relationships differs from one social class to another and to some extent within classes too. In long established urban working class communities studied in the 1950s, the most immediately impressive feature was the dominance of the bond between mothers and their married daughters. This kind of family pattern has been described at some length in the studies of Bethnal Green in east London by Townsend in his survey of 203 old age pensioners[2] and by Young and Willmott, who carried out a larger survey of a random sample of almost a thousand of the adult population of the borough, together with a more intensive study of 45 couples with young children. Mothers were focal points in the kinship networks. With a mother's death contact with uncles and aunts would be quickly lost and when aunts died, contact was lost with cousins. Even the relationships of married sisters were loosened as they became the mothers of married children and grandmothers in their turn. In Banbury too, Stacey noted the same pivotal importance in the extended family of the tie between parents and their married children. 'When parents die, the family focus goes with them and contact with married siblings weakens'.[3] Stacey refers to families focused on the parents in Banbury but she is generalizing about families from all social classes. In the old urban working class communities, the focus of the family was specifically the mother or grandmother. It was this which led Firth to describe the kinship system of the working class in South Borough, London, as matri-centred or 'matral'.[4]

It was in the Bethnal Green studies that it was made clear how misleading it was to confine consideration of the extended family to groups resident in the same dwelling. Seventy-eight per cent of the old age pensioners in Townsend's survey saw at least one of their children daily. Only four per cent of those with children did not see at least one of them every week. Again, it was chiefly daughters visiting their mothers who maintained this frequent contact.[5] Half of the married women in Young

---

[1] See Stacey, op.cit., 1960, Tables 24, 25; Rosser and Harris, op.cit., 1965, Table 6:4 and pp.220-21; Firth et al., op.cit. 1970, pp.202 and 425-37.

[2] Townsend, op.cit., 1963.

[3] Stacey, op.cit., 1960, p.121.

[4] Firth, op.cit., 1956, p.62.

[5] Townsend, op.cit., 1963, Tables 5 and 6.

and Willmott's Bethnal Green survey had seen their mother in the 24 hours preceding their interview and 80 per cent had seen their mother in the previous week. The intensive interviews with the smaller 'marriage sample' showed that a married woman would see her mother, usually at her mother's house, on average four times each week. Mothers and daughters had an important bond in their common role as housewives and with the advent of the daughter's children this was strengthened in their common role as mothers. An exchange of services between the female generations was established. Women received a great deal of advice and often considerable assistance in caring for a young family, running a household, and in some cases working outside their homes, from their own mothers. The willingness of a mother to look after her daughter's children or prepare meals for her son-in-law may often be the crucial factor in permitting a woman to seek a paid job and so help 'make both ends meet'.[1] But the exchange is not one-sided. Mothers and daughters living in close proximity are able to help one another with the heavier chores, make use of one another's household equipment, be on hand to help with shopping expeditions, see that the rent collector, the tallyman or the milkman gets paid, share information and exchange a host of other services. In their old age and in sickness or infirmity, with this kind of relationship, mothers are able to depend on the personal care of their daughter. Harris has suggested that their exchange of domestic services with close relatives in this way is an important factor in the reluctance of many working class families to move away from their familiar surroundings.[2]

The kinship structure observed in Bethnal Green has been noted in other of the older working class communities. Firth's account of South Borough also in London has already been mentioned but the pattern recurs in widely separated parts of the country. Summarising Rosser and Harris's extensive survey in Swansea in his introduction to the book R. Huws Jones says

' . . . it is tempting to say that family and kinship in Swansea are just like Bethnal Green only more so. The frequency of face to face contacts, for all the difference in the areas, is almost identical. The 'mam', typically the wife's mother, holds the family together, 'the dominant centre of the web of kinship'. There is a powerful tendency for a married daughter to live with her mother or get a house close to her. As in East London, the pattern of reciprocal support reveals itself in myriad ways, mostly similar to those in Bethnal Green.'[3]

[1] See C.C. Harris, op.cit., 1969, p.128 and Audrey Hunt, Judith Fox and Margaret Morgan, *Families and Their Needs*, H.M.S.O., 1973, vol.I, p.27.

[2] ibid., p.104 and see Townsend, op.cit., 1963 and Young and Willmott, op.cit., 1962.

[3] Rosser and Harris, op.cit., 1965, p.vi.

Madeleine Kerr in her study of some 60 households in 'Ship Street' in Liverpool's dockland area described the brief adolescent rebellion of daughters in these families. With more household duties than their brothers, their rejection of parental authority was the more defiant but it was also short-lived. After marriage and especially after the birth of a first child the relationship with their husbands quickly lost its romance. They turned back to their mothers, even going back to live in the same house if there was space and as one woman said to Kerr, 'I could do without me husband but not without me Mam'.[1]

In Ship Street as in Bethnal Green and in the mining town of Ashton described by Dennis and his colleagues[2], the menfolk had a strong tie to their own mothers, second in importance in family life only to the mother-daughter bond. Husbands nevertheless tended to be drawn more into their wives' families. Young and Willmott, for instance, found that two-thirds of the men in their Bethnal Green general sample had seen their own mother in the preceding week. The 45 husbands in the marriage sample saw their mothers on average twice a week but their mothers-in-law they saw on average three times each week.[3] Young and Willmott noted the tension frequently inherent in the relationship between a man and his mother-in-law. In the extended family pattern typical of Bethnal Green this tension was grounded in competition between their respective claims on the time and affection of the wife and daughter and it is, of course, at the root of a good deal of once-popular humour.

Fathers and Sons

Where the menfolk of a family work together ties of kinship between them are reinforced and counterbalance the position of the women in the extended family. This is perhaps most likely to occur when the family is engaged in some common enterprise, running a family business, shop or farm.[4] Among wage workers, the situation is most likely to arise where the range of available occupations is small. In Ashton, despite a common reluctance, lack of other opportunities and the whole local system of cultural values conspired to make sons follow their fathers into the pits.[5] Young and Willmott suggested that in Bethnal Green among an older generation, there had been a closer relationship between fathers and sons

[1] M. Kerr, *The People of Ship Street,* Routledge, 1958. See also the discussion of adolescence and marriage in the same area in J.B. Mays, *Education and the Urban Child,* Liverpool University Press, 1962, pp.89-104.

[2] See N. Dennis, F. Henriques and C. Slaughter, *Coal is Our Life,* Tavistock, 1956, ch.5.

[3] Young and Willmott, *Family and Kinship in East London,* Penguin, 1962, p.73.

[4] See Stacey, op.cit., 1960, pp.123, 137; Bell, op.cit. 1969, pp.58-60; W.M. Williams, *A West Country Village: Ashworthy,* Routledge, 1963, p.182.

[5] Dennis et al., op.cit., 1956, ch.5.

than they were able to observe directly. Before the Second World War many men had worked in the London docks, as Billingsgate market porters or in the printing trades. In all these occupations it was hard in those days for a young man to get a job at all unless he had someone already there who could 'speak for him' to a foreman or employer. Usually this would be done by his father or another relative.[1] Comparatively low levels of unemployment in the postwar period, the increasing differentiation of jobs and the increasing ability of workers to travel further to work, together with residential mobility, have contributed to the separation of working class men from their relatives in the work situation. As a result of these changes, relations between working class fathers and sons are less and less reinforced by the common experience, interest and concern of a shared job and the significance of the mother-daughter tie in the extended family structure is heightened. The husband, away from his family during working hours and possibly at his leisure too in the working-men's club, has become a less central figure in the extended family. Meanwhile, the ties of sentiment linking one family with another in the kinship network, reinforced by interaction and common activities among the women, in the older working class areas, have come to be more and more the preserve of the women. Only where, perhaps as a result of their distance from close relatives and friends, wives have come to depend more on the company of their husbands is the balance between husbands' and wives' kin connections restored.

Where family property is involved though, family ties are generally close. The link between fathers and sons in farm families, if not always cordial, is particularly strong. In Gosforth (Cumberland), Williams noted that farmers' sons were much less likely to belong to juvenile peer groups than village boys and they tended to spend their leisure at home. The strength of these male family bonds derives not only from the fact that from before they leave school, sons work with their fathers. As Williams observed in his study of a farming community in the west country, the link between fathers and sons is re-inforced by the patterns of inheritance of land, goods and skills. Nalson found in his survey of a west Pennine farming area that two thirds of farmers' sons went into farming themselves and, though not necessarily inheriting a family farm, more successful fathers would often help set a son up on a farm of his own.[2]

[1] cf. University of Liverpool Social Science Department, *The Dock Worker,* Liverpool University Press, 1954.

[2] W.M. Williams, *The Sociology of an English Village: Gosforth,* Routledge, 1956, pp.142 ff.; W.M. Williams, op.cit., 1963, p.182 and see p.142; W.M. Williams, *The Country Craftsman,* Routledge, 1958, pp.136-41; J.S. Nalson, *The Mobility of Farm Families,* Manchester University Press, 1968, ch. 5. Comparable succession figures for 1880 relating to tenants on the Northumberland estates are given by F.M.L. Thompson, *English Landed Society in the Nineteenth Century,* Routledge, 1963, pp.202-3.

In the urban environment, however, occupational skills are learned on the job. Even when working class fathers and sons work for the same employer, sons rarely inherit useful skills let alone productive property. With the exception of a declining number of sons going into their own families' businesses, middle class men rarely have close kin among their colleagues as a result of their wider opportunities to enter a highly differentiated range of occupations. The greater relative wealth of the middle classes means, on the other hand, that property is a more significant element in the relationships between the generations than in the working class and in this respect, as we shall see, the father-son relationship seems to be particularly important.

Kinship and Geographical Mobility

People who settle at a distance from the neighbourhood where their parents and possibly other kin live cannot maintain the same kind of interaction as those who remain in lifelong proximity to their close relatives. Jane Hubert has noted that 'geographical distance may enable ties to be dropped without, generally, upsetting the relationships between other kin'.[1] It is not that migrant couples must necessarily sever the bonds of kinship, though it may be easier for them to do so if they wish; nor is it that their relatives become less emotionally significant to them simply because they have moved. But geographical distance (as well as social distance) changes the quality of the relationships. Kin who are not at hand cannot quite be taken for granted in the same way. It is harder to simply 'drop by'. Conscious and deliberate attempts must be made to sustain relations. Visits must be arranged, letters written, telephone calls made, cards sent. These acts all take care, effort and time. The ownership of telephones and cars, or a ready facility in letter writing, are still mainly features of middle class life.[2] Even given the easy availability of these private media of communication, geographical mobility reduces the frequency of contact between kin.

In their study of the Sparkbrook area of Birmingham, Rex and Moore found that even in the traditional working class streets extended families were no longer concentrated within the one locality. As the city corporation took over the old houses from the private landlords, they were allocated to families who had to be rehoused from slum clearance schemes

[1] op.cit., 1965, p.80 see also Bell, 'Mobility and the Middle Class Extended Family', *Sociology,* 1968, p.182; John Goldthorpe, David Lockwood, Frank Bechhofer and Jennifer Platt, *The Affluent Worker in the Class Structure,* Cambridge, 1969, p.104; Young and Willmott op.cit., ch.11, and Willmott and Young op.cit., 1960, ch.7.

[2] See Willmott and Young, op.cit., 1960, p.73; Rosser and Harris, op.cit., 1966, pp.106-7, and Michael Young and Peter Willmott, *The Symmetrical Family,* Routledge, 1973, pp.226-30.

in other parts of the city. Young Sparkbrook families with a different position on the city's housing list had therefore to move elsewhere if they were to find a house. In consequence, while less than a third of the English had any relatives living in the same neighbourhood, almost nine out of ten had relatives in Birmingham as a whole. As in other working class communities, men were quite likely to spend much of their leisure time out of the home, usually in clubs or pubs with an informal group of friends. Women saw their relatives significantly more often than the men did but fairly regular visits were made to relatives living out of the neighbourhood by husbands and wives together.[1]

Young and Willmott studied 47 couples who had moved out of Bethnal Green to 'Greenleigh', a postwar council estate on the metropolitan fringe. Settling into Greenleigh was a slow process and most missed the sense of their extended family around them. The time and expense of travel back into the East End, together with the higher cost of living on the estate, reduced the frequency of contact between women and their mothers very considerably. Husbands, still working in or near Bethnal Green, maintained contact with relatives there but visiting became a two-way process with fortnightly visits to and from Mum.[2] This sort of development was observed in Oxford by Mogey, who also noted the greater formality of kin visiting on the new estate, with set teas and best clothes and behaviour compared with casually 'just popping in' in the older area when relatives lived in the same neighbourhood.[3] Nevertheless, kin ties remained important and were not displaced by sociability with neighbours and friends but merely changed in quality in the way described.

Some working class families, perhaps the majority of those who move away from the centre of their kinship networks, move not out of the need for housing but in search of better jobs or at least of jobs with better rewards.[4] While the bonds of kinship and community are thus not enough to prevent families moving, they are neither abandoned nor displaced by new relationships with workmates or friends in the middle class sense. Among the sample of Luton manual workers and their wives, the majority of whom had moved to the town from elsewhere, Goldthorpe and his colleagues noted the continued importance of relatives. 'Those of their kin who were *reasonably* available represented a major source of friends and companions, despite the fact that these kin rarely lived in such proximity that contact could be maintained with them in a largely casual and unplanned way'.[5] At the same time, in most cases these families retain 'the

[1] John Rex and Robert Moore, *Race, Community and Conflict*, Institute of Race Relations, Oxford, 1967, pp.75-9.

[2] loc.cit., ch.9.

[3] Mogey, *Family and Neighbourhood*, 1956.

[4] See Amelia Harris and Rosemary Clausen, *Labour Mobility in Great Britain*, the Government Social Survey, H.M.S.O., 1966, Table 21, p.18.

[5] Goldthorpe, Lockwood, Bechhofer and Platt, op.cit., 1969, p.89, and also see p.38.

traditional working class belief that the home is a place reserved for kin and for very special friends alone'.[1] While this was so, geographical mobility is likely to segregate relationships with kin all the more effectively from relationships with the families' new neighbours and acquaintances. A family's effective social environment would, of course, therefore coincide less with its immediate residential neighbourhood and the total structure of social relationships in which the family was involved would become less closely interconnected.[2] Some of the consequences of this for the mobile family will be considered later in the chapter.

But the experience of geographical movement need not be perpetual. The old working class areas we have looked at had been new developments sometimes only three or four generations before the time when they were studied. Indeed 'traditional' working class communities may take only two generations to establish.

Willmott studied a housing estate which had been started 40 years earlier to house families from East London. In that time, he wrote, 'Local extended families, which hold such a central place in the older districts, have grown up in almost identical form on the estate . . . In part, Dagenham is the East End reborn.'[3] But Dagenham differs from the older working class communities in part because for many families it has not been possible to extend themselves locally due to the lack of houses available in the area for the children of the earlier residents. Many of the second generation have had to move away, with the consequent reduction in contact and the attenuation of kinship relationships. Thus, though the older traditional areas may be swept away by housing redevelopments only to be replaced by new 'traditional' communities, even after the lapse of three or four generations, an exact replication is unlikely. The population trends I have outlined in an earlier chapter, together with the processes of technological change and its consequences, suggest that the experience of mobility and upheaval is likely to come to an increasing proportion of families.

Middle Class Kinship

Middle class people typically have a pattern of relationships with their relatives different from the traditional working class pattern. The expectations relatives have of one another are different in the middle class in part because of the different role expectations such people have for themselves. They have been socialized into a different set of norms from

[1] Goldthorpe, et al., 'The Affluent Worker and the Thesis of Embourgeoisement', *Sociology*, vol.1, 1967, pp.21-2; and op.cit., 1969, p.92.

[2] ref. C.C. Harris, op.cit., 1969, p.133, and cf. Eugene Litwak, 'Geographical Mobility and Extended Family Cohesion', *American Sociological Review*, 1960, vol.XXV.

[3] Peter Willmott, *Dagenham: The Evolution of a Community*, Routledge, 1963, p.109.

those which characterize the traditional working class sub-cultures. These are in turn partly the outcome, partly a contributory factor, in the greater residential mobility of middle class families. Apart from their role expectations and their residential mobility, the significance of property in the structural continuity of middle class — particularly upper middle class — families distinguishes them still more crucially from the working class patterns.

Relatives are much less predominant in the ordinary everyday sociability of most middle class families than is the case in the working class. Young and Willmott's London regional survey however suggests that there may be an exception to this in the case of the wives of clerical workers. This could be the consequence of the more limited geographical mobility of the lower middle class and is almost certainly connected with their economic circumstances. Men and women in the professional and managerial stratum not only travelled further to work but frequently travelled considerable distances, mostly by car, to meet their scattered friends. Contacts with relatives were much less frequent. In contrast, people in the less affluent section of the middle class on average had fewer contacts with either friends or relatives than did the working class respondents, but within their small social circles relatives played a proportionately more important part. The wives of clerical workers were the only group out of two middle class and two working class strata who had on average seen more relatives than friends in the week preceding the interview.[1] Goldthorpe et al., however, found that even white collar workers and their wives were much less reliant on kin for leisure time companionship than the very geographically mobile workers they studied in Luton.[2] A comparison between higher status members of the middle class and less mobile members of the working class could be expected to have produced a still greater contrast.

Middle class extended families are more often scattered than working class families; the degree of scatter is most marked in the upper middle class. In Swansea, as elsewhere, working class families showed a strong tendency toward matrilocality but, in contrast, middle class married women tended to have moved further from their parents' homes than their husbands had.[3] Nevertheless, even in the middle class, daughters still see

[1] Young and Willmott, op.cit., 1973, pp.229-30.

[2] Goldthorpe et al., op.cit., 1969, Table 7, p.88 and p.90. Luton lies within the region covered by Young and Willmott's survey.

[3] See Bell, op.cit., 1968, p.175, and *Middle Class Families*, Routledge, 1969, p.80; Rosser and Harris, *The Family and Social Change*, Routledge, 1965, pp.212-13 and compare P. Willmott and M. Young, *Family and Class in a London Suburb*, Routledge, 1960, ch.6, Table IX. Willmott and Young do not distinguish residential proximity to parents for either sex by class and as more than a third of their sample were working class, differences between the classes in this respect could very well be obscured.

their parents rather more frequently than sons do. Comparing the young professional and managerial families he studied in west Swansea with Rosser and Harris's earlier findings in the same town for non-manual workers' families taken all together, Bell found there seemed to be large differences within the middle class. In terms of residential proximity and frequency of contact with parents and siblings the lower middle class, in Swansea at least, appear to be more like the working class taken as a whole than like the upper middle class.[1] This may be associated in some way with their readiness to marry young.[2]

In general, though the mother-daughter tie is, as in other social strata, the major structural feature of the close-kin unit, in the middle class it is to a greater extent counterbalanced by other important relationships. The contrast with the old working class communities I have previously considered can quite properly be emphasized. Sharing a less traditionally structured and usually more intimately responsive relationship with their husbands, middle class women need to rely less on their children for emotional gratification especially in the middle years of life. Middle class men, through an active participation in the socialization of their children[3], establish the basis for closer relationships with them later. Even where the upper middle class training in psychological independence from the family involves some delegation of the children's socialization and sending them away to school at nine or 13, this may weaken relationships with the mother at least as much as with the father. This balance of more intimate ties in the lower middle class, and sometimes more distant ones in the upper middle class, persists into the adulthood of both sons and daughters, who retain closer relationships with their fathers than is typical in the traditional working class extended family.

Willmott and Young described how in Woodford the reciprocity of inter-generational aid noted in Bethnal Green seemed to have been destroyed by the typical 'kinship career pattern' of the middle class. As middle class daughters mostly lived at a distance from their mothers they were not able to depend on them for more or less continuous help or moral support as was the case in Bethnal Green. Of course, mothers were likely to come to assist if a daughter was ill or during a confinement but such occasions would in the normal course of things be rare. On the other hand, while most young and middle aged women in Woodford lived some distance away from their parents, paradoxically most of the old people had a relative, and most commonly a daughter, living quite close at hand. Thus, while children moved away from their parents when they themselves married or even before, when they reached old age the parents generally moved so as to live with, or at least near to, one of their children. This is

[1] See Bell, op.cit. 1968 pp.175-7 and op.cit. 1969, ch.4.

[2] See ch. 2 above, in particular Table 2.5.

[3] See the brief discussion of conjugal roles and the socialization of children below.

indeed the most common reason for the widowed and the elderly, especially women, moving; a high proportion of them moving a hundred miles or more in the process.[1] In this way in the middle class the older generation was quite as likely to receive in their old age personal care and attention from their relatives as in a working class community. On the other hand in very many cases this must result in an uneven distribution of assistance among the network of relatives. Not all will be evenly burdened. But the extended family operates as a system not merely as a series of bilateral exchanges. Firth and his colleagues describe how, among the middle class, relatives assist one another without necessarily expecting any complementary return from the same individual. Support ' . . . is often conceived as one-way. If the ideal of friendship is equality, the ideal of a kinship relation allows of asymmetry. Differences in age, capacity and economic position may all be regarded as valid reasons why one party should give and the other receive, without necessary reciprocation.'[2]

Upper middle class women, like those in Highgate, often have had some kind of professional training and have usually been residentially independent of their parents long before marriage. The independence of outlook associated with this kind of background means that however strong their emotional ties with their mother, under normal circumstances they do not want or expect the moral support of daily contact any more than they need her assistance in the day-to-day management of their households. Their mothers would travel great distances, even from abroad, to be with their daughters at the birth of a child — especially the first. But in this social stratum it seems the ties of sentiment which exist between the generations are not lessened by distance nor by their relative infrequency of contact. As compared with the situation in Bethnal Green, the upper middle class housewife's relationship with her mother is expressed, as Hubert puts it, 'perhaps in maturer ways, with dependence only in times of crisis e.g. in confinements and illness, not in the daily running of their lives'.[2] If not a matter of dependency, except sometimes perhaps for the very old, the exchange of aid between adult generations in the middle class is not all one way. Middle class parents do provide assistance to their married children of a kind which is not restricted by geographical separation, and indeed some kinds of assistance may be facilitated by it.

People who have achieved a social status higher or lower than that of

[1] See Harris and Clausen, op.cit., 1966, Appendix VIII and ch.2, Tables 17, 18, 20.

[2] Firth, Hubert and Forge, *Families and Their Relatives*, Routledge, 1970, p.387.

[3] See Hubert, 'Kinship and Geographical Mobility in a Sample from a London Middle Class Area', *International Journal of Comparative Sociology*, 6, 1965, p.64; Firth et.al., op.cit., 1970, pp.458-9 and cf. the similar conclusion reached about public schoolboys' relations with their parents in B.M. Spinley, *The Deprived and the Privileged*, Routledge, 1953. Some of this material is discussed more fully in Josephine Klein, *Samples From English Cultures*, Routledge, 1965, vol.II, pp.611-29.

their family of origin may find that relationships with their relatives undergo a change. The socially mobile individual, moving from one class or status group to another is faced with the problems of having to behave in different ways according to the norms prevailing in the different milieux he moves in. Maintaining relationships with his kin and former acquaintances as well as with his new peers faces him with a continual problem of choosing the correct response appropriate for the momentary situation. Because someone who is socially mobile in Britain has to cope with sets of people who normally maintain a degree of social distance from one another there is a persistent risk for him of inconsistency and consequent rejection by either set. Furthermore, the sort of behaviour which seems appropriate to relationships between people of different social status can get mixed up with the norms governing relationships with kin unless the situations where one set of norms or the other operate can be compartmentalized. Among the Highgate sample, it would appear, those families who had been upwardly mobile maintained contact with fewer of their relatives.[1] For men, occupational roles are the principal focus of their social position and experience. In consequence vertical mobility or significant discrepancies between a man's occupational status and that of his father is likely to make this kind of problem more acute than is usually the case for women. A married woman's roles as housewife and mother play a more central part in her life and social mobility is likely to make less difference between her and her mother's day-to-day activities than between a man and his father. As Willmott and Young found for their predominantly lower middle class Woodford sample, 'movement from one class to another creates a barrier inside the family only for men, not for women'.[2] Social mobility, especially downward social mobility, led to sons in Woodford seeing less of their fathers. It had made little difference to daughters' frequency of contact with their parents or to sons' contact with their mothers, though apparently there was some tendency for the downwardly mobile of both sexes to see their mothers rather more often than others did.[3]

A career or a marriage which takes someone into a different social class from the one they grew up in, usually of course takes them to live in a different neighbourhood, often in a quite different town. Occupational mobility mostly entails geographical mobility. Bell found that all the upwardly mobile families in his west Swansea sample had been geographically mobile too.[4] Thus while geographical mobility reduces the frequency of contact between kin and may lead to a slightly more distant

---

[1] This inference is based on the evidence presented in Firth et al., op.cit., 1970, pp.186 and 196.

[2] Willmott and Young op.cit., 1960, p.78.

[3] ibid. pp.74-8, and Appendix 3, especially pp.148-51.

[4] Bell, *Middle Class Families*, 1969, p.44.

kind of sociability between them in all social classes, for the socially mobile this may, in fact, make it easier for them to combine the continuation of those relationships which remain important to them with a claim to acceptance as equals in their new status situation.

· The early years of married life tend to be the most difficult financially for most middle class couples. The purchase of a desirable residence in a desirable neighbourhood, its equipment with tasteful furnishings and up-to-date labour-saving devices, the acquisition of a car and the establishment and insurance of a suitably civilized style of life are all incurred at a time when the husband's income is at its lowest, and are likely to become increasingly worrying with the loss of the wife's income and the additional expense associated with the arrival of children. Colin Bell has described how many middle class parents in their more prosperous middle age are able to assist their newly married children through this period with contributions towards the deposit for their house or with large pieces of expenditure such as the installation of central heating. Alternatively, financial assistance may take the form of status-conferring gifts. The general effect of these transactions is to raise the living standards of the young family above what they could afford on the husband's own earnings. The parents of couples who have been upwardly mobile into the middle class cannot provide this kind of help and in consequence, first generation middle class couples are usually older by the time they can achieve appropriately middle class patterns of consumption.

This situation is to some extent at odds with the middle class values of individualism and self-reliance. Bell points out, however, that the geographical separation of the giver and receiver makes such transactions easier to reconcile with these principles. The fact that a couple's life-style may be subsidized by their parents is less obvious when the parents live far away (sometimes even to the couple themselves) and often the giving may ostensibly be to grandchildren – a layette, expensive toys, riding lessons, school fees, etc. Since much of the aid is essentially financial, it is typically from father to son or his children (or occasionally from father-in-law) and thus helps balance the mother-daughter bond to a considerable extent. The inability of the parental families of the upwardly mobile to give this kind of help of course meant that this particular bond between fathers and sons was lacking. As Bell observed, 'Because the families from a working class background could not be in receipt of the same kind of aid as those from middle class backgrounds, there was not a corresponding increase in emphasis on the male part of the extended family structure that I have been able to demonstrate for the entirely middle class extended family'.[1]

In all social strata, inter-generational aid is a factor in the maintenance of life-styles. In the working class we have seen this typically is through the direct exchange of domestic or semi-domestic services between mothers and daughters. In the middle class aid to the elderly may take a

[1] See Bell, 1968, pp.182-3, and 1969, ch.4 and pp. 160-61, 182-3.

similar form. Aid to the younger generation serves particularly to raise the level of consumption and the acquisition of goods through financial assistance and, of course, at a later stage through the inheritance of property. In this way, despite the more frequent migration of middle class families, the generations are linked in a way beyond the means of the working class. Once dispersed beyond the possibility of social interaction geographically mobile working class families and the upwardly socially mobile remain linked with their kin only by the continuing bonds of affection.

We have seen how the existence of contacts between relatives continues to be important in all social strata. I have emphasized the role of the extended family not just in the crises of life or on ritual occasions, weddings, baptisms, funerals; but as a continuing agency of sociability and help in the ordinary mundane affairs of people. Colin Bell writes that the middle class extended family 'works continually, if not day to day then month to month, to maintain and/or advance the status of its members'.[1] Somewhat earlier and primarily in respect of the working class, but still generally true, Professor Firth argued 'the significance of kin ties outside the elementary family in contemporary British society lies primarily in the positive social contacts in visiting, in recreation, in exchange of news and advice, in attendance on ceremonial occasions and at crises of life, and in the moral obligations that frequently attach to such contacts.

'Kinship recognition and relations are important as a part of social living in general . . .'[2] Even when the exchange of services or indeed actual face-to-face contact is infrequent, the extended family and kin ties in general, for the middle class and the migrant as well as for the traditional working class, remain important.

This brings us to an important function of kinship in contemporary society which so far has not been explicitly referred to. Their kinship network, and the extended family in particular, provides people with a structured framework for coping with the problems of social identity. In contemporary society perhaps it alone provides for most people an experience of continuity and unconditional belonging. For many of the upper middle class respondents in Highgate there was somewhere a particular district or community in which a number of their relatives still lived while others like themselves had moved away. It was with these relatives resident in this local area that contact tended to be maintained rather than with other migrant kinsmen even though the individual might have more in common with the latter.[3] Visits back to these places were described as 'going home'. The significance of the particular location for many of the mobile and highly individuated professional and managerial

---

[1] Bell, op.cit., 1969, p.88.

[2] Firth, *Two Studies of Kinship in London*, 1956, p.19.

[3] Hubert, op.cit., 1965, pp.75-6 and Firth et al., op.cit. 1970, pp.142-3, 151, 187-190 and 203-210.

workers and their wives can be understood as a place of origin establishing and sustaining for them a sense of identity. It is this enduring continuity, symbolized in the place of origin, which distinguishes kinship relations from all others and appears to account for their importance. Firth, Hubert and Forge make a comparison with the role that friends can play in the lives of their respondents,

'. . . the tie of friendship seems to be conceived as definitely positive, affective. Some of the kin roles may well involve receiving unpalatable views; and tension may be generated between the parties. The friendship bond is looked upon frequently as too frail to bear much weight of tension and negative affect. With kin, however, a certain imperative appears. They 'ought' to be available to supply this separate role; even if a certain amount of tension, criticism and unpopularity is risked in this exchange of views, this tends to be regarded as a proper risk. This attitude, which forms an important part of the quality of kin relations, would seem to be associated with the recognition of the kinship bond as one marked by continuity.'[1]

It is this need, more than the help or assistance given that seems to explain the survival of such ties outside the elementary family, maintained at some effort despite, or indeed perhaps because of, the greater mobility of the middle class and even of many of the younger working class families.

Husbands and Wives

Though the elementary family pattern is commonly accepted as normal and proper throughout British society, nevertheless the relationships between spouses and between parents and children vary a good deal in quality from one social milieu to another. The norms parents seek to establish in bringing up their children depend, at least to some extent, on both the internal structure of the family and its inter-relationships with the external social environment.

It is the marriage relationship which is the key to the internal structure of the elementary family. The relationships between spouses can be described in several different ways. One of the simplest, which has also proved one of the most illuminating, has been to examine the degree of overlap or differentiation in the role behaviour of husbands and wives. This idea was explored by Elizabeth Bott in her study of 20 married couples living in London in the early 1950s.[2]

[1] ibid., pp. 386-7.

[2] Elizabeth Bott, *Family and Social Network*, Tavistock, 1957, 2nd Edition 1971. Platt and others have, however, argued that this approach must be used only with considerable caution. See Jennifer Platt 'Some Problems in Measuring the Jointness of Conjugal Role Relationships', *Sociology*, 3, 1969, pp.287 ff. and C.C. Harris, *The Family*, 1969, ch.6.

At the one extreme Bott observed, many household chores and attending to the children were interchangeable tasks between husband and wife, family decisions were taken jointly and leisure activities were commonly shared. Other couples had a much more clearly defined division of labour between the husband's tasks and the wife's tasks, joint decision-making was much less stressed and they were more likely to spend their leisure time separately and independently. Most of the couples Bott studied fell between these extremes. For some of them, activities might be sharply segregated in one sphere and much more fully shared in another. Thus household duties, cooking and cleaning etc., might be considered the wife's exclusive responsibility while caring for the children or leisure activities might involve both spouses cooperating together. Others had inconsistent or uncertain patterns of behaviour.

The pattern of clear demarcation and almost complete division between the roles of husband and wife has been chiefly observed elsewhere in rural areas, especially among farm families[1] where a fairly strict division of labour seems to be carried over into purely domestic affairs from the division of tasks between husband and wife in the work of the farm, and also in studies of long-established working class communities. This older pattern of working class family life has become familiar beyond the social strata where it formed the common basis of experience, through the contributions to literary culture of a number of socially mobile writers.[2]

More general and more detached accounts are quite numerous too. Many of those features of family life described by Florence Bell at the beginning of the century in her study of Middlesborough steelworkers and their families persisted in several communities studied more than 50 years later.[3]

[1] See C. Turner, 'Conjugal Roles and Social Networks: a Re-examination of an Hypothesis', *Human Relations*, 20, 1967, 121-30; W.M. Williams, *The Sociology of an English Village: Gosforth*, 1956; and W. M. Williams, *A West Country Village: Ashworthy*, 1963.

[2] Some of the best known examples include D.H. Lawrence's description of a Nottinghamshire miner's family at the turn of the century in *Sons and Lovers*, Raymond Williams's description of a Welsh railwayman's family between the wars in *Border Country* and see also Richard Hoggart's descriptions of working class life in Leeds in the thirties in *The Uses of Literacy*. Alan Sillitoe on the life of a factory worker in Nottingham in the 1950s in *Saturday Night and Sunday Morning* and the continuing adventures of Ron Smythe's 'Andy Capp' in the *Daily Mirror* describe equally sympathetic but less admirable characters within similar working class sub-cultures in more recent times.

[3] See Florence, Lady Bell, *At the Works*, Arnold, 1903, republished by David and Charles, 1969; D. Chapman, *Home and Social Status*, Routledge, 1955; N. Dennis, F. Henriques and C. Slaughter, op.cit., 1956; Josephine Klein, op.cit., 1965, vol.1; J.M. Mogey *Family and Neighbourhood*, Oxford Univ.Press 1956; John and Elizabeth Newson, *Infant Care in an Urban Community*, Allen & Unwin, 1963, published as *Patterns of Infant Care*, Penguin, 1965; and *Four Years Old in an Urban Community*, Allen & Unwin, 1968; Rosser and Harris, op.cit., 1965; Townsend, op.cit., 1963; Young & Willmott, op.cit., 1957; C.C. Harris has described the pattern of family life we are concerned with here as typical only 'of a small, rather old-fashioned segment of the working class', see Harris, op.cit., 1969, p.166, n.31.

The segregation of conjugal roles was perhaps most marked amongst the Yorkshire miners' families in 'Ashton' where, it was said, 'husband and wife live separate, and in a sense secret lives'[1], but it was also evident in 'Ship Street' and 'Crown Street' in central Liverpool, in St Ebbes, central Oxford, in east Swansea and particularly the older families in Bethnal Green.

Employment and the Elementary Family

The impact on the family of industrial employment is enormous. Home and work are separated. The more demanding and dangerous occupations in particular place severe strains on the worker and through him on his dependents.[2] In the colliery village, Dennis and his colleagues emphasized the importance of the fact that the world of work was a man's world. Amongst miners working together, the heavy and hazardous work created a bond that others could not share which carried over into life out of the pit. This had the effect of excluding the women from more than marginal participation in the leisure time life of their menfolk except during courtship and early marriage and in so doing weakened the elementary family as a cohesive unit.

> 'The strict sexual division of labour in Ashton emphasized by the nature of mining, has extension in the range of social contacts and the ideas available to the two sexes. Just as most women see further than the home and the tasks of its maintenance on only one or two occasions each week, the husband is very often a comparative stranger to his home. One wife of thirty said of her husband, 'the only time I see anything of him is in bed'. Her neighbour described her husband as always being 'at work, at the club, or in bed'. Other men spend all their non-working hours in the garden, or, a very small number silently pottering about at home.'[3]

Their long experience until comparatively recent times of relatively low incomes and insecure employment has marked the value systems in all these communities. The rights and obligations of a husband's role emphasized his status as breadwinner and the chief virtues of a good husband were above all that he should have a steady job and be a reliable provider, though his actual earnings were generally his own affair. Apart from some of the heavier jobs, he was not expected to be bothered very much with the running of the household. In St. Ebbes '. . . the emphasis was on having a husband, a quiet docile man who kept his regular place

[1] Dennis et al., op.cit., p.228.

[2] See ibid., and also Peter G. Hollowell, *The Lorry Driver*, Routledge, 1969, ch.6: J. Tunstall, *The Fisherman*, McGibbon & Kee, 1962, and Michael Banton, *The Policeman in the Community*, Tavistock, 1964.

[3] See Dennis et al., op.cit., 1956, pp.204 and 224-5.

and was there when needed, either to discipline the children or to take over the wife's work in an emergency'.[1] Away from the textile manufacturing areas, wives did not traditionally work outside the home. With larger families and before rising living standards spread labour saving machinery to working class households during the 1950s, a married woman had less opportunity to seek paid employment. In the home, however, a wife was not merely wholly responsible for the housework and the family budgeting, the general care and control of the children, but also for the management of family affairs in relation to schools, welfare services, the rent collector, the juvenile court, the wider kinship network and prospective in-laws.[2] In Ship Street the romantic togetherness of early marriage was soon overwhelmed in the wife's day-to-day business of attending to a growing family and the husband's withdrawal into the world of work and his 'mates'. The partnership became increasingly segregated and wives came to refer to their husbands impersonally as 'him'.[3]

Conjugal relations in the middle class generally speaking seem very much to be contrasted with those of the traditional working class families we have so far considered. In most of the middle class families in Bott's sample and those in Willmott and Young's Woodford study, there was much less differentiation of activities as exclusively appropriate to the husband's or the wife's role. Cooperation and the sharing of experience was emphasized.[4] Young and Willmott investigated how far husbands' and wives' roles were segregated in their London regional survey in 1970. The proportion for whom meeting friends and relatives was a joint activity declined across the social hierarchy from the upper middle class through clerical workers and their wives to skilled manual workers' families and least of all among the less skilled working class.[5] In their studies of child rearing in Nottingham, the Newsons found that middle class fathers were somewhat more likely than working class fathers to be highly participant in caring for their young children, and a good deal less likely to take little or no interest at all. The marked differences within classes observed during the children's first twelve months evened out as they grew older. Unskilled working class fathers who were much less likely than others to take any great interest in putting to bed, feeding, changing or bathing the baby, were as likely to be highly involved by the time their children were four as

[1] Mogey op.cit. 1956, p.62.

[2] See Dennis, Henriques & Slaughter, op.cit., 1956, ch.5.; Kerr, op.cit., 1958, ch.4, 8, and p.122; Mogey, op.cit. 1965; pp.62-3; Newson & Newson, op.cit., 1968, ch.15; C. Rosser and C.C. Harris, op.cit., 1965; Peter Townsend. op.cit., 1956, ch.6; Young & Willmott, op.cit., ch.1.

[3] Kerr, op.cit., 1958.

[4] See E. Bott, op.cit., 1971, ch.3; P. Willmott & M. Young, op.cit., 1960, ch.2; C.C. Harris has pointed out that 'so far no British sociologist has dared to try to study the domestic habits of the upper class', op.cit., 1969, p.178.

[5] Young and Willmott, op.cit., 1973, Table 47, p.230.

other working class fathers. Over a similar period, upper middle class fathers' interest in their children increased, non-participation declined very considerably so that they surpassed fathers in the lower middle class in sharing in the care of their children. Leisure activities were more usually shared in the Nottingham middle class too, where husbands and wives were more likely to spend an evening out together than was the case amongst working class couples.[1] Middle class mothers were less likely to think their husbands were more strict with the children than they themselves were. This, the Newsons were at pains to emphasize, was not because middle class fathers were more easy going than their wives but because usually they agreed on matters of discipline. In the working class, and especially in unskilled working class families, husbands and wives were much more likely to disagree on these matters, mostly because wives thought their husbands tended to be too strict. The Newsons also note that, 'fathers rated as "highly participant" in the objective terms of the schedule tend to be thought by their wives to be closely in agreement with themselves on discipline, whereas less participant fathers are more likely than others to be regarded as "stricter".[2]

Though consistent with other evidence in illustrating the differences between the social classes in the role behaviour of husbands and wives, the Newsons' findings, on the other hand, also indicate that about half of all working class fathers were also highly participant in the care of their children while a majority shared their leisure with their wives at least to a minimal extent. The degree of conjugal role segregation is not related then to social status in any simple way and we must consider how the apparently complex relationship which exists can possibly be explained. Cotgrove argued that a husband's work situation, especially if he is employed in one of the more exhausting manual jobs, on the one side, and on the other the mutual help pattern imposed on working class mothers by the demands made on them by the larger families usual up to two generations ago, and not uncommon now, were primarily responsible for the traditional segregation of conjugal roles in these older working class communities.[3] In the middle class too it is apparent that a man's job has profound effects on his marriage and his family life. The salience of family life is perhaps greater for women than for men. Almost two out of every three of the 184 managing directors interviewed in Young and Willmott's London regional study found that work interfered with their home and family life. As most of them found their main satisfaction in life at work this perhaps is hardly surprising. Those running family-owned concerns were least likely to find work interfering with family life but amongst the

---

[1] See Newson and Newson, *Patterns of Infant Care* 1965, pp.225-9 and Table 29; also *Four Years Old in an Urban Community*, 1968, p.514, Table LIII.

[2] ibid., 1968, pp.516-17.

[3] S. Cotgrove, *The Science of Society*, Allen & Unwin, 1967, pp.44 ff. and Rosser and Harris, op.cit., 1965, p.207.

THE STRUCTURE OF FAMILY LIFE

rest men in the larger firms generally found themselves in this situation.[1]
J.M. and R.E. Pahl, in a survey of 86 middle managers and their wives,
noted that, while for the wives their family and the marriage relationship
was typically of paramount importance, the husbands' involvement in
their work was often of greater significance for them as a central life
interest. For some of the wives at least, this divergence engendered a
degree of ambivalence towards their husbands' careers, questioning
whether his success was worth what it cost in his preoccupation and time
spent away from herself and the family.[2] Different kinds of employment
evidently have different effects on out-of-work life, including family life,[3]
and a changing occupational structure with a reduction in the number of
the more physically arduous jobs or an overall drop in working hours may
have changed the pattern of family life of the workers affected.

Cotgrove's emphasis on the influence of economic and demographic
factors in the family's environment has been valuable in drawing attention
to the interaction between roles within the family and those performed by
the same individuals elsewhere. Harris has also underlined this point in
arguing that conjugal roles are aspects of the wider sex roles people play in
all their social relationships.[4] But in considering the roles people play we
are dealing not only with how people actually behave but with how they
feel they ought to behave. Roles are patterns of normative expectations
applied to people in particular relationships. Roles are defined not
descriptively but prescriptively so that, for instance, we describe a man as
a father in terms of the obligations he has, not because of the way he
actually behaves but because of the way it is felt he ought to behave.[5] In
order to analyse the influence of external factors on family roles it is
necessary, therefore, to consider how they might shape the normative
expectations members of the family have about themselves and one
another.

[1] Young and Willmott, op.cit., 1973, pp.251-5.

[2] J.M. & R.E. Pahl, *Managers and Their Wives*, Penguin, 1971, ch. 8 and 9.

3 See e.g. S. Cotgrove, 'The Relationship between Work and Non-Work among
Technicians', *Sociological Review*, 13, 1965, pp.121-9; S. Cotgrove and S.R. Parker,
'Work and Non-Work', *New Society*, 11 July 1963.

[4] Harris, *The Family*, 1969, p.174.

[5] Primarily that is, in terms of the expectations people in this particular culture have
in general about the way a man in his position ought to behave. A man actually
plays the role of a father not just in terms of these expectations but also in terms of
the more specific expectations of other members of his family, what the people he
knows outside the family are likely to expect, and the views he has himself about
how he ought to behave — cf. N. Gross, W.S. Mason and A.W. McEachern,
Explorations in Role Analysis, Wiley, 1958, p.60.

Change and the Conjugal Relationship

In Bethnal Green, Young and Willmott concluded that the old-style working class family though it still survives is rapidly disappearing.

'There are still plenty of men who will not do 'women's work' and women who state 'it's not a man's place to do it'. But for most people, it seems, the division is no longer rigid. Of the 45 husbands, 32 gave some regular help to their wives with the housework; 29 had, to take an index trivial enough in itself but perhaps significant, done the washing-up one or more times during the previous week.'[1]

The process would appear to have gone furthest in the lower middle class. In their 1970 survey Young and Willmott found 80 per cent of men in clerical jobs, 73 per cent of skilled manual workers, 70 per cent of the professional and managerial workers and 64 per cent of the semi-skilled and unskilled manual workers gave some help to their wives with household tasks, cleaning, cooking, child care etc., with or without washing up. The old sharp division of labour has been abandoned by the majority in all classes but more influential than the husband's job in differentiating those with a strict segregation of roles from the majority was whether the wife herself went out to work. As more wives go out to work (see Chapter 5 below), most husbands were prepared to take some share in helping about the house and in looking after the children.[2] But according to Young and Willmott the younger married couples were, in general, much less likely to have a sharply differentiated division of labour. This was notably the case in their parental roles. Both took pride in their children's turnout and shared in hopes and plans for their future.

'The younger husband of today does not consider the children belong exclusively to his wife's world or that he can abandon them to her (and her mother) while he takes his comfort in the male atmosphere of the pub. He now shares responsibility for the number of children as well as for their welfare after they are born.'[3]

Some American writers have interpreted similar differences between older and younger couples as evidence of cyclical change, in that role segregation increases with marriage duration, rather than of a secular change in family norms.[4] This is a question which cannot be satisfactorily resolved without

---

[1] loc.cit., p.27, and see ibid., p.30.

[2] Young and Willmott, op.cit., 1973, Table 8, p.95, and Table 15, p.115.

[3] loc.cit., 1962, pp.21, 28-9.

[4] In their more recent study Young and Willmott too have realized some of the difficulties of this kind of argument – see op.cit., 1973, pp.14-15, and cf. Robert O. Blood and Donald M. Wolfe, *Husbands and Wives,* Free Press, 1960, pp.41-4 and Reuben Hill, 'Decision making and the Family Cycle', ch.6 in Ethel Shanas and Gordon F. Streib (eds), *'Social Structure and the Family in Generational Relations',* Prentice Hall, 1965. Elizabeth Bott has also argued that role segregation

a controlled longitudinal study. But simply to note differences between older and younger married couples is unilluminating. Even if such a long-term trend were identified, it would still be necessary to try to account for it. The cultural and social environment in Bethnal Green was in any case undergoing considerable change in the fifties with large-scale rehousing and emigration from the borough and increasing contact with alternative and non-traditional norms for conjugal behaviour especially through women's magazines, television, etc.

The closer and more intimate relationship between younger married couples described in these studies may partly be attributable, as Dennis, Henriques and Slaughter suggested, to an improvement in living standards.[1] The improvement in wages and in the security of employment since the 1930s has removed or at least reduced one important source of conflict in family life. A husband and wife are no longer to the same extent likely to be in weekly competition over the contents of his wage packet.[2] Yet, though it may be a product of this improvement, there does seem to be in some areas a progressive change occurring in the norms relating to family life.

This was evident in Mogey's comparison of two working class areas in Oxford in the early 1950s previously referred to. One was an older area near the city centre, the other a newly built council estate on the city's northern outskirts. The traditional family pattern survived in the older area but companionate marriages were more frequent on the estate and he argued represented not so much a difference between generations as a response to the new environment.[3] On the estate '. . . a husband who is prepared to take his part in routine household tasks, who will share experiences, and who will take the wife out occasionally, is preferred. The co-operative family unit where necessary jobs are done by anybody rather than the rigid unit where the division of labour is insisted upon, has become a numerous type.'[4] Married couples who had moved from Bethnal Green to the 'Greenleigh Estate' in the outer metropolitan area, the families who had moved into the West Durham rural parish of 'Leadgill'[5] and the families of the geographically mobile 'affluent workers' of Luton were much closer to this type of cooperative family unit than to the traditional pattern. Goldthorpe, Lockwood, Bechhofer and Platt note that among the geographically mobile 'affluent workers' of Luton '. . . in comparison with what is known of the more traditional worker, the

increased through the family cycle (op.cit., 1971, pp.55-6), but C. Turner in his study of 'Leadgill' found no evidence that this was so, 'Conjugal Roles and Social Networks: a Re-examination of an Hypothesis', *Human Relations*, 20, 1967, p.128.

[1] op.cit., 1956, p.186ff.

[2] See also Young and Willmott, op.cit., 1973, pp.70-84.

[3] Mogey, *Family and Neighbourhood*, 1956, p.58.

[4] ibid., pp.62-3.

[5] C. Turner, op.cit., 1967.

amount of time spent by the men in our sample on leisure pursuits with "mates" outside the home is very small; and that within the home many appear to take part in — or indeed to have taken over — activities which in the traditional view would be usually regarded as "women's work" '.[1] Geographical mobility, then, would seem to be an important influence on family life but the question remains of how this influence works.

As we saw in the previous chapter, geographical mobility is likely to attenuate relationships between neighbours, friends and even relatives. People who have been geographically mobile are therefore generally likely to find themselves with a relatively loosely interconnected network of relationships outside their family as compared with those who have never moved away from the community they grew up in. For the geographically mobile, family life cannot simply comform to the time-honoured and unquestioned pattern of the local community because their involvement with it is only marginal. The question of conformity to any particular pattern becomes a matter of choice. In loose-knit networks each couple has to work out the proprieties of their own relationship for themselves, guided, if at all, only by the very general standards internalized earlier during their own primary socialization[2], and the generally vague ideas available through their uncertain interpretation of the content of the mass media or other secondary sources. As Bott says 'Couples in close-knit networks . . . knew, more or less, what the agreed standards were and could make them explicit. Couples with loose-knit networks were more aware of variation. Since many of the people they knew were not acquainted with one another, there were fewer norms of common consent.'[3] In consequence 'when networks become more loose-knit, the type of conjugal relationship becomes unpredictably variable.'[4]

These couples, rather than conforming to culturally prescribed and socially supported patterns of behaviour, come to work out the best relationship for themselves they can on the basis of their own particular psychological needs and resources. In these circumstances, the vulnerability of the marriage to the strains probable in any intimate relationship in a changeable environment is likely to be increased.[5]

In summary then, the degree of specificity of a married couple's conjugal roles seems to depend on the existence of norms of common consent amongst their acquaintances and thus of the connectedness of the network of social relationships they maintain outside the family. This

[1] J. Goldthorpe, D. Lockwood, F. Bechhofer and J. Platt, op.cit., 1969, p.105, and cf. Jennifer Platt, 'Some Problems in Measuring the Jointness of Conjugal Role Relationships', *Sociology*, 3, 1969, Table 1 p.289.

[2] See Barbara Harrell-Bond 'Conjugal Role Behaviour', *Human Relations*, 1969, 22, pp.77-91.

[3] loc.cit., 1971, p.202 and also see ibid., pp.208-210.

[4] ibid., p.290.

[5] See Trevor Noble 'Family Breakdown and Social Networks', *British Journal of Sociology*, XXI, June, 1970, pp.135-50.

pattern itself however is a function of the economic, demographic and
social structure of the community in which the family lives, the work
situation in which the husband earns their livelihood, the family's
geographical and social mobility and the way in which husband and wife
choose to respond to these influences. In other words, relationships within
the elementary family are to be understood sociologically in the context
of the members' set of relationships outside the family.

The idea that conjugal role relations vary with the connectedness of the
family's social network has, however, been criticized. Turner has shown
some of the problems involved in the concept of social network and in
particular in the measurement of connectedness[1], while Platt has indicated
some of the methodological and conceptual difficulties involved in
measuring as jointness what must necessarily be an abstraction from a wide
range of disparate behaviour[2].

Fallding took up Bott's point that where conjugal role segregation
occurs there is often little mixing between the sexes outside the family
either. 'The role segregation of the sexes within the family', he wrote,
'goes with sexual segregation outside it.' He argued that, 'there thus
appears to be a sharp cleavage by sex right across the network, so that it
can hardly be called connected'.[3]

Turner too found that, though husbands and wives tended to include
the same set of kin in their social networks, if kin are discounted in the
parish he had studied, there were a number of mainly farm families where
there was this sharp separation between a husband's friends and his wife's
friends. These husbands spent most of their leisure time away from home.
In these families, as in the miners' families, described by Dennis, Henriques
and Slaughter, there was a high degree of conjugal role segregation. Among
non-farming families, those with segregated conjugal roles generally had
close-knit networks but the relationship was complicated by a number of
other factors, geographical mobility in particular[4].

Though a great deal more clearly needs to be done to clarify the issues
which have emerged since Bott's original study it remains one of the most
illuminating contributions to recent British sociology. In her later
discussion Bott herself summed up the current balance of evidence:'. . .
The original hypothesis holds for cases of high network density, which is
typically found to be associated with a marked degree of conjugal role
segregation in both norms and behaviour. But the relationship between
networks and conjugal roles becomes unpredictably variable once one

---

[1] Turner, op.cit., 1967.

[2] Platt, op.cit., 1969.

[3] H. Fallding, 'The Family and the Idea of a Cardinal Role', *Human Relations* 14,
1961, pp.343, ref. Bott, op.cit., 1971, pp.65-70.

[4] Turner, op.cit., 1967; see also Goldthorpe et al., 1969, who note that even among
the affluent and geographically mobile workers of Luton, there was a tendency for
husbands and wives to have separate friends: op.cit., pp.91-2.

steps outside the realm of families living in close-knit networks.'[1] To put this another way, in loosely inter-connected networks the social constraints on conjugal relations are so reduced that the roles of husband and wife no longer correspond to a culturally prescribed pattern and the relationships between spouses cannot be reliably predicted. Instead spouses can only evolve a relationship which seems congenial to themselves and apparently capable of satisfying their personal needs and expectations. In so far as this may become increasingly common one may reasonably wonder if we should not anticipate the increasingly more widespread experience of familial anomie.

Socialization and the Family Setting

The family is the immediate social context of most of the behaviour which is merely summarized in the processes of demographic change we have already discussed. The changes, that is, in the composition and distribution of the population take place at the level of individual experience mainly in the setting of our family life. The family is founded by marriage, is enlarged by births and is affected, perhaps more than any other group, by the death of its members, or indeed by their prolonged survival. But readiness or reluctance to marry is influenced by the relationships with parents and siblings and the desire for children by pre-existing or anticipated family circumstances[2]. Even survival can be affected by the material and emotional conditions of a family environment.[3]

Above all, however, the family is important as a set of institutionalized relationships which constitute the structural setting within which most people learn the social norms and expectations which enable them to participate in the society to which they come to belong. It is in the context of family life that we grow up as members of society, where we acquire our social identity and our notions of how to behave in our relationship with others. It is in and for our family that most of our waking life is ordered. It is in the family that we come to care for those we care for most. Goode has pointed out the importance of the family as an agency of socialization and social control. Through the family, he argues, individuals are brought to serve collective needs or to conform to social norms while apparently responding chiefly to the needs and feelings of particular affectively significant others. A man sticks to a boring job for the sake of the wife and children he has to support, a lad stays out of further trouble so as not to break his old mother's heart. Reasons such as

[1] op.cit., 1971, p.313.

[2] See J.S. Nalson, op.cit., 1968; Geoffrey Hawthorn and Joan Busfield 'A Sociological Approach to British Fertility' in Julius Gould (ed.), *Penguin Social Sciences Survey 1968*, Penguin, 1968, p.200.

[3] See Peter Townsend, op.cit., 1963, pp.201ff.

these, more than the sanctions of communal disapproval or legal retribution, preserve the cohesion and stability of the social structure.[1]

As an agency of both socialization and social control, the family serves to transmit and maintain the pattern of culture. It is evident that in Britain the way mothers bring up their children and the norms and expectations they transmit varies across the social status hierarchy. The process of cultural differentiation between status groups begins even before children learn to talk,[2] and continues increasingly as they grow older. This is brought about not only through the different standards children may be deliberately taught. These may vary less than the values a child can infer indirectly from what his parents do or say and even from the mode of language used and the way it is employed as a medium of communication and expression[3]. An emphasis on explicit verbal communication with the child and an encouragement of a critical evaluation of his own and other people's behaviour is a more usual feature of a middle class upbringing as compared with the working class. The Newsons argue that this is not so much due to verbal inadequacy amongst working class mothers as a matter of the different attitudes they have about how their children ought to behave. Parents, they write,

'differ not so much in their basic aims as in the stress which they lay upon certain aspects of behaviour. The middle class style of parental control puts greater emphasis upon reasoning, adjudication of quarrels, fairness in the sense of 'do as you would be done by' and general good manners; values are transmitted by means of a pattern of reciprocal rights and obligations which the mother continually brings to her child's attention in words and by the example of her own actions. The working-class style of control emphasises authority, self-reliance in quarrels, fairness in the sense of 'be done by as you did' and respect for adults.'[4]

[1] See W.J. Goode, *The Family*, Prentice-Hall, 1964, p.2.

[2] See Newson and Newson, op.cit., 1965; Josephine Klein, op.cit., 1964, vol.II.

[3] Ref. in particular: John and Elizabeth Newson, 'Some Social Differences in the Process of Child-rearing' in Julius Gould (ed.), op.cit., 1968; also see J.W.B. Douglas, *The Home and the School*, McGibbon & Kee, 1964. Among the papers of Basil Bernstein his 'Socio-Linguistic Approach to Social Learning' in Julius Gould (ed.), *Penguin Survey of the Social Sciences 1965*, and reprinted as ch.7 in Bernstein, *Class, Codes and Control*, Routledge, 1971, is perhaps most useful in the present context; see also Denis Lawton, *Social Class, Language and Education*, Routledge, 1968. A great deal of the empirical material on the importance of parental values in a child's subsequent educational performance has been admirably summarized in Olive Banks, *The Sociology of Education*, Batsford, 1968, ch. 4 and 5.

[4] See Newson and Newson in Gould, op.cit., 1968, p.89 and cf. W.P. Robinson and S.J. Rackstraw, 'Variations in Mothers' Answers to Children's Questions, as a function of Social Class, Verbal Intelligence Test Scores and Sex', *Sociology*, 1, 1967, pp.259-76.

Social norms, what is expected of one in a given situation, thus differ from one class to another. But the contrast the Newsons describe is essentially one of orientation around a core of similar values. These elementary values of a common or national culture are adapted to, or reinterpreted from different positions within the hierarchically differentiated social structure. What is particularly impressive in their findings is how soon in life the individual's position in the social structure begins to shape his view of the world. As they put it, 'Men may be born equal; but within its first month in the world, the baby will be adapting to a climate of experience that varies according to its family's social class'[1]. But the culture learned at a mother's knee does not originate there. Parents communicate the values of their society through the example of the way they see their obligations to one another and to their children. In bringing up their children in the way they should go, parents are agents only. Their values are profoundly influential, impressed upon the uncritical child and reinforced by the irresistible sanction of parental love. But their values are only those of their kind, of their community, their generation, their status group.[2] The standards, expectations and moral norms which parents pass on to their children are only partly those they themselves learned in their own upbringing. These will have been modified and added to in their social relations with others beyond the circle of their immediate family. In view of the differences in family patterns, we have already considered however, it will be apparent that what is passed on is likely to differ not just in content but qualitatively too.

Class differences, differences in mobility, in contacts with close kin, in family phase, will all be important as well as the particular historical circumstances. But the division of labour between husband and wife within the family is of crucial importance in structuring the setting within which the primary socialization of their children occurs. This represents not just a different pattern of norms or role definitions to be learned, but a qualitative difference in the degree of definition which the roles are given and the assurance with which parents can make norms of behaviour explicit for a child. The parents in a more traditionalist family, with a greater certainty about their own roles and a greater sense of 'objective' or externally defined norms, are more likely to require conformity from children, emphasizing the supposed virtues of self-expression much less. In the older working class communities, families were adult-centred rather than child-centred. 'Discipline is administered not with an eye to the development of the child but to the immediate needs of the parents and

[1] J. & E. Newson, *Patterns of Infant Care*, Penguin, 1965, p.230.

[2] See Goode, op.cit., 1964, p.5; Frank Musgrove, *The Family, Education and Society*, Routledge, 1966; and the discussion of the profound political influence on the family in D.E. Butler and D. Stokes, *Political Change in Britain,* Macmillan, 1969, pp.44-52.

the household routine.'[1] The more joint conjugal relationships likely in the middle class and geographically mobile working class families lead to a greater focus on the child.

In so far as traditional and more authoritarian family patterns in both the middle class and the working class are changing, with increasing geographical and social mobility, family norms become less clearly defined. The Newsons have emphasized both the greater child-centredness and the uncertainties young mothers have, particularly in the middle class, about how to behave towards their children and how they should expect their children to behave.[2] The child is thus brought into less immediate contact with the apparently unambiguous realities of an adult world.

Children learn from the inferences they make from adults' behaviour, from what they do more than from what they say. Their parents' relative uncertainty is one of the characteristics of their normative environment they are most likely to be influenced by. The results for the young generation might equally be a disabling ambivalence in the face of problematical situations in later life or a tolerance of ambiguity which could be highly adaptive in a rapidly changing world. Whatever the consequences for the individuals, those for the society they will create will, without doubt, be profound.

[1] Dennis, Henriques and Slaughter, op.cit., 1956, p.237.

[2] See Newson and Newson, op.cit., 1965, pp.257-8 and op.cit., 1968, p.498 ff. and p.523; cf. Pahl and Pahl, *Managers and Their Wives*, Penguin, 1971, ch.9.. Young & Willmott have associated this with increasingly work-centred fathers and mothers and, at least in the case of older children, increasingly active parental leisure: op.cit., 1973, pp.279-80.

5 Industrial Change and the Occupational Structure

Introduction

At this point in the book I will take up some of the more directly economic aspects of British social structure. The aim here is not to set out all the leading features of the economic system but only to examine some of the ways that economic change influences other aspects of the social structure. In this chapter then, I will concentrate on the ways the British earn a living through employment and in the next go on to look at the distribution of incomes that ensues. To begin with I will deal with the composition of the working population and the relationship between work experience and other aspects of social life. Then I will briefly discuss the changing economic order within which changes in the pattern of employment can be seen as consequences firstly of the changing industrial basis of the economy and secondly of the growth in scale of economic operation and organization. Lastly in the present chapter, I want to consider the consequences of these changes in the distribution of occupations for the system of social stratification in Britain.

The economic system involves and influences everyone. We are all consumers. Fewer are producers. In Britain some 25,000,000, slightly less than half the population, are economically active, either producing the goods and services on which all depend or unemployed but seeking work. The means of livelihood for everyone lies in the productive employment of this economically active part of the population. It is worth noting, therefore, that in absolute terms the economically active part of the population has been increasing more slowly than the dependent or inactive part, and is indeed declining as a proportion of the population as a whole. As I noted in Chapter 2 this is mainly the result of the increasing expectancy of life for both men and women so that more and more survive longer into the years of retirement. The trend is, however, substantially reinforced by the effects of the extension of education for more and more young people beyond the statutory minimum age.

Looked at as a whole, perhaps the most important fact about the economy of Britain is that its viability depends on overseas trade. More than half the food eaten in Britain and most of the raw materials used in industry have to be imported from abroad. In consequence, the export of manufactured goods overseas and the provision of financial, commercial and communications services for foreign customers is vital if such a large population is to be maintained at anything like the present standard of living. More than any other major industrial country, except Switzerland, Britain is dependent in this way on external trade and therefore the industries and services which supply that trade have a central, though sometimes unappreciated, importance in supporting us all in the style of life to which we have become accustomed. In this situation, considered purely as a housekeeping operation, some of the trends in the deployment of manpower resources in contemporary Britain may seem rather disturbing. This is not the place however to attempt to evaluate the economic health of the U.K. nor to discuss the problems of the balance of trade and payments – even if I were sufficiently competent to try. What I want to do in this discussion of the occupational structure is to examine some of the processes which, generally without any deliberate intention on anyone's part, are directly bringing about changes in the pattern of social relations in the day-to-day life of large numbers of ordinary people and indirectly in the shape of the society as a whole.

Industrial Change

Expansion and contraction of sectors of the economy

The distribution of types of employment among the economically active population reflects the progress of the continuous change taking place in the industrial economy. New means of providing for consumer demand displace older, less efficient or less pleasing sources and methods. Inventions or organizational innovations bring within reach of the market newly desirable goods. New enterprises, expansion and new occupations take place alongside bankruptcies, closures and redundancies. It is in the consequently changing pattern of employment that these changes in the structure of an industrial economy have their most profound direct and indirect effects both on the structure of society and the day-to-day experience of individual men, women and children.

The figures in Table 5.1 summarize some of the recent trends. The number of employees in employment increased especially rapidly in the period around the Second World War with the growth of employment opportunities of wartime and the postwar reconstruction of the economy. Unemployment fell very steeply from the high prewar levels and an increasing proportion of women as we have seen, especially married women, took up jobs outside the home. After the slow growth of the working population in the 1950s, the relatively steep increase in the first half of the 1960s mainly reflects this increasing employment of married woman, particularly in the services sector, together with the increase in clerical jobs in other sectors. At the very end of the sixties and the beginning of the 1970s the rise in the level of unemployment contributed to the decline in the numbers at work, although a shrinkage in the numbers available for work, an effect of the succession of generations, helped to ameliorate its impact.

Since the 1930s, the primary industries, coalmining, agriculture and the fishing industry, have been in relative decline employing not only proportionately fewer but, since 1951, absolutely fewer workers. Though coal still provides for almost half the U.K. energy needs, the mining industry has declined as the demand for coal has beeen reduced in the face of competition from other fuels.[1] As output has fallen with the closure of

Table 5.1

Distribution of the Working Population* of Great Britain by Industry 1938-1971

Industry Orders**	Men and Women Percentages				
	1938**	1951**	1961	1966	1971†
Primary Industries (Orders I & II)	10.4	9.0	5.9	4.5	3.4
Manufacturing (Orders III – XVI)	36.6	39.2	39.5	38.1	38.3
Construction and Utilities (Orders XVII & XVIII)	8.7	8.3	8.3	9.0	7.3
Transport & Services (Orders XIX – XXIV)	44.4	43.4	46.4	48.4	51.0
Total Employees in Employment	100.1	99.9	100.1	100.0	100.0
N = 100% (in thousands)	17,378	22,313	22,329	23,301	22,027

*Refers to Employees in Employment
**Figures for 1938 and 1951 on which these percentages are based are not fully comparable with the later series due to changes in the industrial classification.
†Further changes in classification make exact comparison unreliable – see text.

Sources: Ministry of Labour and National Service, later Department of Employment estimates for the end of June each year; see *Annual Abstracts of Statistics*: 90, Tables 119 and 120; *105*, Table 129 and *109*, Table 146.

[1] See *Annual Abstract of Statistics, 109*, 1972, Table 174.

uneconomic collieries, employment decreased by more than half between 1951 and 1966[1] and a further 37 per cent between then and 1971[2]. Much of this decline has been accounted for by natural wastage, that is retirements and people leaving the industry for other jobs, but many miners from the older coalfields of the north of England, Scotland and South Wales have either had to move to newer, more productive, coalfields or have had to adjust to involuntary changes of both job and industry or cope with the equally difficult problems of early retirement. The consequences for some of the older mining communities have sometimes been severe.[3]

Employment in agriculture has been affected by two trends. Mechanization in the industry and the drift away from the countryside to the amenities and better wages in the towns have reinforced one another so that in 1971 agriculture, forestry and fishing together employed less than two per cent of the labour force. While output has increased, these industries accounted for less than a third of the jobs they had provided as recently as 1951. In construction and utilities — that is to say, the building industry together with gas, electricity and water — the numbers grew only slowly until after 1961 and consequently until then represented a declining proportion of the working population. The steeper increase between 1961 and 1966 reflects the building boom of the early 1960s. After 1966, a reclassification of undertakings followed by some amendment of the Standard Industrial Classification in 1968 has had the statistical effect of transferring over 100,000 workers, mostly formerly counted in construction and distribution, to the manufacturing sector. The effect of this on the figures in Table 5.1 can only be roughly estimated but it is evident on all measures that the numbers in the building industry in fact declined quite sharply in the later 1960s.

Despite the reclassification of some undertakings and the continued contraction of some industries such as the railways, the proportion of the working population employed in the transport and services sector has grown steadily. Industries such as catering and a number of miscellaneous services also showed declines in the numbers employed in the years after 1966 due, no doubt, to the effects of the Selective Employment Tax[4], one aim of which was to encourage the redeployment of workers into those areas of activity where their contribution to the overseas balance of payments might be most effective. Throughout the period there have been, on the other hand, particularly large increases in employment in insurance, banking and finance, and professional and scientific services — especially the education service. By 1971 the services sector employed more than

[1] See *Annual Abstract of Statistics*. 106, Tables 162-3.

[2] See *Annual Abstract of Statistics, 108,* Table 169.

[3] See e.g. Department of Employment and Productivity, *Ryhope: A Pit Closes*, H.M.S.O., 1970.

[4] Discontinued in 1973.

half of the British working population.

In the manufacturing sector some of the traditional industries of the older industrial areas, mainly in the north of England and in Scotland, on which the industrialization of the nineteenth century was mainly based, e.g. shipbuilding, woollen and cotton textiles and more recently iron and steelmaking, have been in decline under the impact of modern alternatives or more vigorous competition from overseas producers. Other manufacturing industries, and particularly those associated with the motor industry, have been increasing both in output and also in the proportion of employment they provide. After a fairly steady, if slow, overall growth however the proportion employed in the manufacturing sector as a whole began to decline in the 1960s though the numbers employed in fact continued to increase up to 1966. In the interval between then and 1971, industrial reclassification has added, at a rough estimate, about 0.7 per cent to the proportion of the working population counted in the manufacturing sector. The rest of the statistically apparent change is real and is the consequence of the sharper contraction in construction and the primary industries within a working population which is shrinking overall. Still the broad direction of these changes from manufacturing and the primary industries to the services sector continues and suggests that, figuratively speaking, in Britain we are still increasingly making a living by taking in one another's washing.[1]

The change in the structure of the industrial economy is paralleled by change within the organization of industry which shows up in almost every industry we care to examine. The shift towards the services sector in the economy is matched by the increasing proportion of managerial, technical and administrative workers in each separate industry. That is to say the trend is towards an increase in the proportion of non-manual workers. The implications of this for the class structure will be considered at the end of the chapter.

Table 5.2 shows in summary how the proportion of non-manual employees has been increasing in all industries, even those which are contracting in terms of output and employment (cf. Table 5.1). The only exception to this has been in professional and scientific services, where it is manual workers who are the auxiliaries, the porters and cleaners, furnacemen, gardeners, security men and car park attendants. In the first report of the Manpower Research Unit set up by the Ministry of Labour, the connection between this general trend and the increase in female employment is pointed out. Changes in industrial structure on the one hand and in the occupational structure within each industry together account for the changing pattern of occupations. The Manpower Research

[1] This parallels and reinforces the persistent tendency in much of British industry in the twentieth century to turn to the home rather than export markets. See e.g. E.J.Hobsbawm, *Industry and Empire*, Weidenfeld and Nicolson, 1968, ch.13, 'The Long Boom'.

Unit has shown how the services sector has accounted for an increasing proportion of all manual workers while correspondingly manufacturing industries have come to employ an increasing proportion of 'white collar' workers.[1]

Table 5.2

Percentages of Non-Manual Employees* by Industry Group

| Industry Group | Men and Women | | |
| | England and Wales | Great Britain | |
	1951** †	1961	1966
	%	%	%
I Agriculture, Forestry and Fishing	5.8	9.0	10.6
II Mining and Quarrying	5.2	8.1	9.4
III–XVI Manufacturing	17.6	22.9	26.1
XVII Construction	9.7	14.4	17.2
XVIII Gas, Electricity and Water	23.6	30.3	30.7
XIX Transport and Communications	25.1	26.3	29.0
XX Distributive Trades	34.2	35.3	35.3
XXI Insurance, Banking and Finance	87.7	88.5	89.2
XXII Professional and Scientific Services	72,4	69.0	67.1
XXIII Miscellaneous Services	15.5	22.0	27.4
XXIV Public Administration	46.9	47.0	49.1
All Industries and Services	27.1	30.9	32.9

*Managerial, Technical and Professional Staff and Clerical Workers as a percentage of all salary and wage earners.
**Salary/wage-earner distributions are not available for Scotland in 1951.
†Industry Order classifications were revised in 1958 and again in 1968 and additional caution is necessary in making particular comparisons across these points.

Sources: Calculated from: 1951 Census of England and Wales, *Industry Tables*, Table 9; 1961 Census of England and Wales, *Industry Tables*, Table 6; 1961 Census of Scotland, *Occupation, Industry and Workplace Tables, Part II*, Table 6; 1966 Sample Census, *Economic Activity Tables*, Table 36.

[1] See Manpower Research Unit, *Occupational Changes 1951-61*, Manpower Studies No.6, 1967 and *Growth of Office Employment*, Manpower Studies No. 7, 1968. The trend has been continuous at least since the beginning of the twentieth century and probably longer. Bonner presents statistical evidence for manufacturing industries in the period 1907-51, see John Bonner 'Administrative Overheads in British Manufacturing', *The Manchester School of Economic and Social Studies*, 1961, 29, pp.57-78, Table II.

The Working Population

The structure of the economy, particularly as it is represented in the distribution of occupations, is significant for the social structure of society at two levels. Firstly, at the level of the distribution of economic resources and therefore as a basic feature of the structure of power in society; secondly, at the level of individual experience in the work situation and the consequences this has in structuring the opportunities of the worker in the other areas of his life as an individual, in his family and in the wider community. In this chapter, it is the second of these aspects I will concentrate on, returning to the more general issues later.

If, first, we consider the demographic characteristics of the working population we can immediately see how economic and other social changes often interact. Fertility trends, marriage rates, the spread of secondary and higher education and the increasing expectation of life together with the requirements of a changing economy all interact upon one another and, in so doing, determine the composition of the working population.

Table 5.3

Age and Sex of the Working Population of Great Britain

	1951	1961	1966	1971
Total (millions)	23.2	24.8	25.6	24.8
	%	%	%	%
All aged 15 — 19	10.8	11.1	11.8	9.2
20 — 44	55.2	49.8	49.0	50.4
Women 45 — 59)	29.8	34.4	34.3	35.5
Men 45 — 64)				
Women 60 and over)	4.3	4.8	4.7	4.9
Men 65 and over)				
	100.1	100.1	99.8	100.0
Males	68.0	66.1	64.7	63.9
Married Women	13.7	18.0	20.3	22.7
Other Females	18.3	16.0	15.0	13.4
	100.0	100.1	100.0	100.0

Source: *Social Trends,* 3, 1972, Table 20.

The 'working population' as defined by the Department of Employment is numerically slightly larger than what the Office of Population Censuses and Surveys describes as the 'economically active' population. Both include everyone in a regular job whether employed or self-employed as well as those laid off through illness or an industrial stoppage and also the unemployed who would be at work if a job was available. The 'working population' however, is based on National Insurance card holders and therefore includes those who, like many students, are employed for only a few weeks in the year and are regarded in the population census as 'economically inactive'. This will not trouble us too much in the present discussion as I am mainly concerned with proportionate changes, though it does illustrate the difficulties that can arise in comparing statistical information from different sources even when both are 'official'.

The changing demographic composition of the working population is indicated in Table 5.3. The increasing proportion of teenagers in the working population up to the mid 1960s indicates the movement into employment of the 'bulge' babies of the immediate postwar period. The decreasing proportion through the later 1960s reflects not only the fertility syncline of the middle 1950s but also the tendency for increasing numbers to stay on at school after 15. The rise in the average age of the working population is evident in the changing proportions in the 20-44 and the over-45 age groups as the numerically small generation born in the 1930s and the early 1940s have continued their careers. This ageing of the working population has been reinforced by the improvements in health and life expectancy among the older age groups also reflected in the slightly greater proportion, mainly women,[1] at work over the statutory retirement age. The trend has depended, of course, less on the greater availability for work *of* older people but rather on the greater availability of jobs suitable *for* older people, a consequence of greater mechanization in manufacturing and, above all, of the growth of the service industries.

The changing industrial structure — the growth of the service sector and the expansion of both public and private administration — has provided the employment opportunities for an increasing proportion of women. The situation has changed since the 1950s however. With the reduction in the average age at marriage, the majority of the growing number of women in employment are now married. Not only are married women becoming an increasingly large proportion of the labour force but also an increasing proportion of all married women are working. This has unquestionably been facilitated for many by their achievement of control over their own fertility but equally certainly the increasing opportunities for employment have provided an important incentive to do so.

---

[1] In fact the proportion of men retiring at 65 or earlier increased during the 1960s — see Brian Abel-Smith, 'Public Expenditure on the Social Services', *Social Trends* No.1, 1970, p.18. This may in part be the result of structural change, with a decreasing proportion of men in manual occupations. Young and Willmott describe how in their 1970 survey '. . . of the 96 men who had retired, 46 per cent in the top class had done so before sixty-five compared with 18 per cent of former clerks, 17 per cent of the skilled and 11 per cent of the semi-skilled and unskilled' — Michael Young and Peter Willmott, *The Symmetrical Family*, Routledge, 1973, p.124.

Table 5.4

Economically Active Married Women in Great Britain by Husbands' Socio-Economic Group

Socio-Economic Group	% of Wives Economically Active			% of Wives Economically Active amongst couples with children	
	1961	1966	1971	1961	1966
1 Employers and Managers in central and local government, industry, commerce, etc. – large establishments	21.2	30.4	38.9	18.9	28.1
2 Employers and Managers – small establishments (less than 25 employees)	27.9	39.1	41.1	25.7	36.7
3 Professional Workers – self-employed	16.8	27.8	32.5	17.8	30.7
4 Professional Employees	23.6	31.0	37.8	14.8	23.2
5 Intermediate Non-manual Workers	31.3	39.7	48.4	25.8	34.6
6 Junior Non-manual Workers	32.3	40.0	45.5	26.1	35.4
7 Personal Service Workers	36.5	45.0	50.4	30.5	39.6
8 Foreman and Supervisors – manual	28.9	40.3	45.0	27.9	38.7
9 Skilled Manual Workers	32.3	41.4	44.3	26.1	35.0
10 Semi-skilled Manual Workers	30.8	39.8	45.4	27.8	37.2
11 Unskilled Manual Workers	27.9	35.4	39.1	25.6	33.4
12 Own account Workers (other than professional)	23.2	35.7	39.9	21.3	32.7
13 Farmers – employers and managers	8.7	20.2	27.6	8.7	22.7
14 Farmers – own account	8.3	16.9	27.0	8.2	18.6
15 Agricultural Workers	15.0	25.3	28.9	12.4	23.0
16 Members of Armed Forces	18.5	22.1	n.a.	8.7	17.4
17 Indefinite	16.4	11.9	n.a.	21.7	26.9
TOTAL	28.7	37.6	42.3	24.5	33.7

Sources: Calculated from: *1961 Census Great Britain Summary Tables*, Table 47; *1966 Census Household Tables*, Table 25. *1971 Census Great Britain Summary Tables (One Per Cent Sample)*, Tables 33, 36 and 13.

A comparison of the 1961, 1966 and 1971 censuses shows that the percentage of wives who were economically active increased from 29 per cent to 38 per cent in the first half of the decade and to 42 per cent in 1971.[1] Table 5.4 shows also that an increasing proportion of women with children were also going to work. Mothers still tend to stay at home during their children's early years, but once the children start school are much more likely to seek employment outside the home. In 1971 51% of women with dependent children aged 11-15 went out to work compared with only 19% of mothers whose children were aged less than five. Amongst these however, lone mothers are more likely to have to seek employment away from home as compared with women living with their husbands. According to the 1971 Census, 30% of divorced women, 31% of unmarried mothers and 33% of widows with children under five were in employment as compared with only 18% of similar still married mothers. In 1971, there were some 6,900,000 women with dependent children and of these 13.5 per cent worked full time and 24.4 per cent worked part time, i.e. less than 24 hours per week. Widows and unmarried and divorced mothers, it is clear, are much more likely to need to work full time. In 1971, while 18 per cent of married women with children worked full time and 16 per cent worked part time, 30 per cent of widows with children worked full time and 20 per cent worked part time; 34 per cent of other women with children worked full time and a further 12 per cent worked part time. Most of the children of widows were 11 years old or more but most of the children of unmarried or divorced mothers were younger than ten years old.[2] Thus children lacking a father are also much more likely to be brought up by a mother with a full-time job outside the home.

Amongst married women two in every five wives with one child in 1971 had a job as well, almost the same proportion as that of childless wives at 42 per cent and 43 per cent respectively. With two children, the proportion of wives going out to work fell to 37 per cent, with three children 33 per cent and 27 per cent with four children. Even with five or more children one wife in four went out to work, almost a third of them full time.[3] *Prima facie* this would seem to be rather hard on the mothers concerned but there is no evidence that it is particularly harmful to their children. For instance, as Viola Klein has pointed out,

---

[1] See Table 5.4 and *1971 Census: Great Britain Advance Analysis*, Table 1.

[2] See *1971 Census Great Britain: Summary Tables, (One Per Cent Sample)* Table 37 and Audrey Hunt, Judith Fox and Margaret Morgan, *Families and their Needs*, H.M.S.O., 1973, vol. 1, p.25, and Table 11, p.75; cf. Dennis Marsden, *Mothers Alone*, Allen Lane, 1969 and V.Wimperis, *The Unmarried Mother and Her Child*, Allen and Unwin, 1960.

[3] *1971 Census Great Britain: Summary Tables (One Per Cent Sample)*, Table 37.

'. . . in some working class areas, the employment of mothers has been traditional and widespread − e.g. in Lancashire − for a century or more. Life in these districts is geared to the fact of mothers going out to work. There is no evidence that the rate of juvenile delinquency or the incidence of other behaviour disorders among young people is higher than elsewhere.'

Indeed it seems that working mothers may be generally less possessive or neurotic about their children than mothers who stay at home as full-time housewives.[1]

What Hannah Gavron called the emancipation of women from their domestic captivity[2] through employment has proceeded at different rates in different social strata. This is shown in Table 5.4 where, as an independent measure of their social circumstances, the proportions of married women who work are related to their husbands' socio-economic group. It was in the ranks of the lower middle classes and the more skilled and generally better paid working class that wives were most likely to go out to work; more evidence, perhaps, of some convergence in the life-styles of the two strata. Farmers' and soldiers' wives were least likely to be working. In the period covered by the table, the proportion of women going out to work increased in all social groups except amongst those with 'indefinite' occupations but most rapidly amongst the upper middle class[3], the more skilled working class, own account workers' wives and farmers and agricultural workers' wives.

The right-hand half of Table 5.4 indicates the declining tendency for married women not to work when there are children in the family. Significantly, perhaps surprisingly, the practice of giving up work seems to be most marked amongst the wives of professional employees, a relatively well educated group whose highly vocal frustrations have been so widely publicized lately.[4] Curiously, among the wives of self-employed professionals.− that is the wives of doctors, lawyers and such − there has been an increasing tendency for women with children to be more likely to have

[1] Viola Klein, *Britain's Married Women Workers*, Routledge, 1965. p.147 and p.149; see also Hunt et al., op.cit., 1973, pp.24-5; P.Jephcott, N. Seear and J.H.Smith, *Married Women Working*, Allen and Unwin, 1962; and S. Yudkin and A.Holme, *Working Mothers and their Children*, Michael Joseph, 1963.

[2] Hannah Gavron, *The Captive Wife*, Routledge, 1966.

[3] At this level, in their sample of managers and their wives J.M. and R.E.Pahl found an association between the decision to go out to work and a wife's own level of education; see J.M. and R.E.Pahl, *Managers and their Wives*, Penguin, 1972, p.132. Hunt and her colleagues, on the other hand, found that while this was also true of non-married mothers, it was not generally so for mothers living with their husbands (op.cit., 1973, p.23).

[4] cf. R.K.Kelsall, Anne Poole and Annette Kuhn, *Graduates: The Sociology of an Elite*, Methuen, 1972, ch.4 and M.P.Fogarty, Rhona Rapoport and Robert N.Rapoport, *Sex Career and Family*, Allen and Unwin, 1971, ch.6 and p.474.

a job than amongst wives in this stratum as a whole. In this case this is probably connected with the age of the women concerned, younger wives being those who still have children at home and at the same time being more orientated towards employment than their older social peers. The same may be true of farmers' wives who are also more likely to have a job when they have children, though again this may be associated with generational differences as well as the changing nature of farm work and increasing opportunities for employment away from home, at least for the more mobile women, in rural areas. The 'Indefinite' socio-economic status group is a residual category about whom no generalizations can be made, but their curious social characteristics might repay a systematic examination some day.

The employment of married women has, at least until recently, sustained the growth of the working population by exploiting an increasingly available and previously neglected labour supply — the consequent addition to the earning power of families has been socially distributed unevenly and has contributed to recent shifts in the relations between the consumption patterns of different social strata and the general sense of relative affluence compared with the experience of earlier generations. The consequences for women themselves have also been substantial. The earning power of a working wife, as I suggested in the preceding chapter, has some bearing on the relationship she has with her husband. Her assumption of a new role in the family through her contribution to the household income is reflected in the enhancement of woman's status in society at large. The resolution and adjustment to the conflicting demands of her roles as worker, wife and mother create problems of identity for the contemporary married woman exceeded only by those faced by women frustrated by the lack of opportunity for paid employment.[1]

Work and Non-Work

It is not only for married women that employment, or the lack of it, presents problems in the context of leisure time or domestic roles. The loss of employment through unemployment or retirement presents a continuing trauma for many a man who has always thought of himself till then as a 'workingman'.[2] For men and women however, married or single, the

[1] See M.P.Fogarty et al., *Sex, Career and Family*, Allen and Unwin, 1971, and Hannah Gavron, op.cit., 1966. Still the clearest and most searching general account of these issues is to be found in: Alva Myrdal and Viola Klein, *Women's Two Roles*, Routledge, 2nd Revised Edition 1968. See also Viola Klein, 'Industrialization and the Changing Role of Women', in *Current Sociology*, 1963-64, vol.XII, pp.24-34.

[2] See Young and Willmott, op.cit., 1973, pp.148-50; Peter Townsend, *The Family Life of Old People*, Routledge, 1957, and W.G.Runciman, *Relative Deprivation and Social Justice*, Routledge, 1966, p.61 ff., and Tony Gould and Joe Kenyon (eds), *Stories from the Dole Queue*, Maurice Temple Smith, 1972, pp.10-56.

experience of employment even in ordinary, unexciting jobs is in itself an important element in their lives and a shaping influence in their opportunities to pursue one pattern of life or another away from the working situation.

For a long time now industrial sociologists and psychologists have been aware that the behaviour of men and women at work is influenced by the relationships existing amongst themselves in the work group and between the work group and others in the works or office. Increasingly, it has become evident, however, that the social structure within the factory cannot be studied in isolation from the world beyond the boundary wall nor the worker's behaviour on the job out of the context of his life before clocking-on and after clocking-off. Our response to the situation we find ourselves in at work derives in part from the attitudes and expectations, feelings and preconceptions we bring into the office or factory from outside. Gradually an obvious fact has become apparent, namely that work is part of our lives and our experience at home in the family, in the neighbourhood, in our leisure time, is likely to be at least as important to us as what occurs at work and may influence the way we behave there as much as anything in the work situation itself.[1]

On the other hand what happens to us at work, the demands the job makes on our energy, skills and temper, the relationships we develop with colleagues or our employers' behaviour towards us also have profound effects on us which carry over into the other areas of our life. It is not merely that we may expect compensation in our leisure and comfort in our family after the hardships of an arduous and dangerous job. The experience gained at work, whether we find it satisfying or frustrating, may shape our perception of the world and our place in it, and indeed the kind of person we believe ourselves to be.

An increasing number of British studies have sought to draw out the connections and interconnections between what happens at work and the other major areas of activity, especially relationships in the family and community, leisure interests and political orientation. I want to stress the *interconnections* here because while the conditions of work may have far-reaching 'out of work' consequences for a man and his dependents, at the same time the selection of a particular job and his qualitative experience there is likely to be shaped very much by the expectations and attitudes the worker brings with him from the world beyond the factory gates. We cannot ignore the importance of the structure of the community and the subculture within which the workers live and into which they have been socialized. When the workers' present residence and childhood home are within the same subculture and even within the same community as most of his workmates we may expect that their effects upon him will be

[1] See Sylvia Shimmin, 'Extramural Factors Influencing Behaviour at Work', *Occupational Psychology*, 1962, 36, pp.124-31 and David Guest and Roger Williams, 'How Home affects Work', *New Society*, 19 January 1973, pp.114-17.

reinforced. Professor Cotgrove has written, 'The worker's involvement in the work situation depends not only on internal factors such as the nature of the work task and of supervision, but also on the needs and expectations which he brings with him, derived from experience external to the work situation'.[1] Together with S.R. Parker, however, Cotgrove has been one of the chief exponents in Britain of the shaping influence of work experience on the other aspects of life.[2]

Studies of a coalmining community, of trawlermen, policemen, architects and railwaymen, shipyard workers and long-distance lorry drivers have emphasized the way these jobs create separate occupational communities and in many cases have drawn attention to the strains they generate between spouses either as a direct consequence of the separation or the risks the jobs entail or indirectly in creating distinct 'men's worlds' into which their wives cannot enter. Miners, fishermen, policemen, shipbuilders, long-distance lorry drivers, railwaymen and architects generally take some pride in their jobs. Typically their work roles are important to them in defining their social and personal identity.[3] This is, however, very much a matter of the level of intrinsic satisfaction which the worker gets from his work which in turn is related to the amount of autonomy he has and the level of skill involved in the job.[4] Salaman for instance describes how both 'the architects and railwaymen were strongly and positively emotionally involved in their work skills and tasks, and the main satisfaction that they derived from their work came from the actual performance of their work tasks, the usage of their valued work skills or from the nature of the work itself – e.g. its responsibility or autonomy'.[5] Outside the professions, probably most occupations are less psychologically salient in this way for those who follow them.

[1] S. Cotgrove, 'The Relationship between Work and Non-Work among Technicians', *Sociological Review*, 1965, 13, p.128.

[2] ibid; also S. Cotgrove, *The Science of Society*, Allen and Unwin, 1967, ch.2 and 4; S.R.Parker et al., *The Sociology of Industry*, Allen and Unwin, 1967, ch.3-6; S.Cotgrove and S.R.Parker, 'Work and Non-Work', *New Society*, 11 July 1963.

[3] N. Dennis, F.Henriques and C.Slaughter, *Coal is our Life*, Tavistock, 2nd Edition, 1970; G.W. Horobin, 'Community and Occupation in the Hull Fishing Industry', *British Journal of Sociology* 1957, VIII, pp. 343-56; J.Tunstall, *The Fishermen*, MacGibbon and Kee, 1962; M.Banton, *The Policeman in the Community*, Tavistock 1964; P.G. Hollowell, *The Lorry Driver*, Routledge, 1968; R.Brown and P.Brannen, 'Social Relations and Social Perspectives amongst Shipbuilding Workers: A Preliminary Report', *Sociology* 1970, 4, pp.71-84 and 197-211, and J.Cousins and R.Brown, 'Patterns of Paradox: Shipbuilding Workers' Images of Society', *Working Papers in Sociology No. 4*, University of Durham, Department of Sociology and Social Administration, 1972; G.Salaman, 'Two Occupational Communities: Examples of a remarkable Convergence of Work and Non-Work', *Sociological Review* 1971, 19, pp.389-407.

[4] See S.R. Parker et al., op.cit., 1967, pp.155-7.

[5] loc.cit., 1971, p.401.

The attitudes, opinions and behaviour patterns of people in several other occupations have been studied, though there is still a need for considerably more research of this kind. Among the occupations represented are bank clerks, youth employment and child care officers, managers, industrial technicians and a range of manual workers, mostly skilled or semi-skilled and in manufacturing industries.[1] These occupations may be less elemental in their day-to-day performance than those of miners, fishermen or even policemen and may also have a less dramatic influence on the lives of those who work in them. Nonetheless, they interact with other areas of life if only by allowing the development of relationships or interests which some occupations might inhibit. Parker found that youth employment officers and child care officers made a much less absolute distinction between work and other activities than bank clerks did. Asked to rank work, leisure activities and family life as a central life interest everyone except a few unmarried women child care officers ranked family life first. The bank clerks ranked leisure activities before work while the child-care officers and youth employment people rated work as a central life interest before leisure activities. The bank clerks found satisfaction in the security their jobs gave them and the people they came into contact with. The child care and youth employment officers were much more likely to find their work intrinsically satisfying and spent a great deal of their own time with colleagues.[2] This seems to be characteristic of more professionalized occupations in the middle class and in general those involving greater levels of skill and individual autonomy for workers. In their 1970 London regional survey Young and Willmott found that the professional and managerial stratum had most discretion in planning their working time while less skilled manual workers had least with clerical and skilled workers between.[3] This relative autonomy would appear to be an important component in the worker's sense of involvement in his job and parallels the increasing sense of separation of work from non-work activities across the same strata[4] which in turn is clearly associated with the extent to which work was felt to interfere with home and family life.[5] Those least involved in their work unsurprisingly were least likely to feel it made much impact on the rest of

---

[1] See S.R.Parker, 'Work and Non-Work in Three Occupations', *Sociological Review*, 1965, 13, pp.65-75; J.M. and R.E.Pahl, *Managers and Their Wives*, Penguin, 1972; S.Cotgrove, 'The Relationship between Work and Non-Work among Technicians', *Sociological Review*, 1965, 13, p.128; F.Zweig, *The Worker in an Affluent Society*, Heineman, 1961; J.H.Goldthorpe, D.Lockwood, F.Bechhofer and J.Platt, *The Affluent Worker: Industrial Attitudes and Behaviour*, Cambridge, 1968, and *The Affluent Worker in the Class Structure*, Cambridge, 1969.

[2] S.R. Parker, op.cit., 1965.

[3] Young and Willmott, op.cit., 1973, Table 27, p.160.

[4] ibid., p.173.

[5] ibid., Table 29, p.165, and Table 53, p.253.

their lives, even though the hours they spent at work were relatively long. Young and Willmott found that, leaving aside travel to work and work done at home, among those with set hours of work the length of time actually worked per week was greatest for the less skilled manual workers and successively less for skilled manual workers, clerical and the professional and managerial group. People without standard working hours, who could to a large extent make their own choices about the times when they worked, people like some social caseworkers, many of the self-employed either in the professions or in business and some senior managers, in fact worked the longest hours of all.[1]

But we should not be misled into generalizing from these occupations to the whole of the middle class. The sample of men from a training course for middle managers described by the Pahls were mostly highly ambitious and outside their own immediate families they too were interested in little but their work. In this respect they would not appear to be typical of all managers however.[2] Parker has pointed out that for British managers 'the picture of the "organisation man" sacrificing leisure and family life for the firm is largely a myth. T. Burns found that the average total commitment to work in his sample (94 managers in 10 British firms), including home work, business lunches, reading and travel for the firm was only 43½ hours per week. In a sample of 66 'middle managers', in ten varied companies, Horne and Lupton found the average working week to be 44 hours.'[3] This may be compared with an average working week for industrial manual workers throughout the 1960s of 46-7 hours.[4]

For probably the majority of industrial workers work is not in itself a primary source of interest. In their Luton inquiry Goldthorpe and his colleagues found a predominantly instrumental orientation to work among the highly paid factory workers they interviewed.[5] These men working in large-scale mass or process production plants did not, that is to say, value their work for its own sake but only as a means to other ends. Rather than any intrinsic interest it might have held for them they emphasized the

[1] ibid., pp.135, 140, but see ibid., pp.248-9.

[2] J.M. and R.E. Pahl, op.cit., 1972, pp.10 and 258.

[3] See S.R.Parker et al., op. cit., 1967, p.93. His references are to W.H.Whyte, *The Organisation Man*, Penguin, 1960; Tom Burns, 'What Managers Do', *New Society*, 17 December 1964; J.H. Horne and T.Lupton, 'The Work Activities of "Middle" Managers', *Journal of Management Studies*, 1965, 2, pp.28-30.

[4] See *Annual Abstract of Statistics*, 107, 1970, Table 153. Of course this does not include daily travelling time to and from work which may typically be greater for managers than for manual workers. See Young and Willmott, op.cit., 1973, pp.138-139. It is fair to point out however that in living further away managers thereby indicate a greater concern with non-work considerations rather than the converse.

[5] J.Goldthorpe, D.Lockwood, F.Bechhofer and J.Platt, *The Affluent Worker: Industrial Attitudes and Behaviour*, Cambridge, 1968, ch.7.

extrinsic satisfactions of their jobs, chiefly the money they earned. Two thirds gave the high level of pay as their main reason for staying in their present job and 73 per cent of the semi-skilled workers had in fact left previous jobs of higher skill or prestige but lower pay. While only a minority gave liking the nature of their work as a reason for staying in their present job, this was strongly associated with the skill it involved. Twice as many skilled workers (29 per cent) as semi-skilled workers (14 per cent) referred to the importance of their interest in the job.[1] Not expecting much from their jobs apart from the money, most were prepared to accept the pressurized boredom they endured in their employment as long as the money was good.[2] Though craftsmen were slightly more often interested in promotion than were semi-skilled men, neither thought their chances of promotion were very high and did not seek it. Skilled men were more inclined to join works clubs and societies (23 per cent were members as against eight per cent of semi-skilled workers) and were more often active in their union. They were also more likely to have friends among their workmates whom they met away from the works (40 per cent of the skilled workers met workmates away from work during their leisure time as against 20 per cent of semi-skilled men) but were less likely to be bothered much at the prospect of leaving them behind should they move on to another job elsewhere. In the context of this commitment to work mainly for the money, the low level of interest in union or other activities and the low level of contact with workmates away from the job itself, it is easy to see why Goldthorpe and his colleagues typified these affluent workers as 'privatized'.

The nature of the job and the industrial setting within which it is pursued are, thus, evidently associated with the kind of attitudes the worker is likely to have not only toward the job itself but towards his workmates, the union and in many of his activities outside work too. It is clear, however, from the fact that many of the semi-skilled workers in the Luton study had preferred the opportunities for high wages to the rewards of higher status or more skilled jobs elsewhere, that the work situation does not have an unambiguously causal role. There is often at least some degree of choice, whatever the limitations may be in any individual circumstances. Rather than a unidirectional influence in either direction it is probably more helpful to think of an interaction between the worker's experience in the course of his job and the expectations and predisposition he brings with him from outside. We have to recognize that the spatial boundaries of the workplace or accounting divisions between time paid for

---

[1] ibid., p.145.

[2] Parker defines satisfaction as 'a function of the discrepancy between what a worker expects, or thinks he should get, and what he actually experiences in the work situation', S.R.Parker et al., *The Sociology of Industry*, Allen and Unwin, 1967, p.148. In these terms most of these workers were quite satisfied.

and his own time are only external distinctions the worker has to cope with; they do not describe some schism in his awareness. He may behave differently at work and by his own hearth but he is the same man and the differences in his behaviour have to be made sense of in the context of the same life.

Changes in Scale

A major trend which affects the immediate social environment within which people work is the growth in scale of the undertakings they are employed by. This trend embraces not only the increasing size of factories, product divisions, etc. – what we may call plant size – but also the increasing scale of the organizations which may operate and manage a number of separate plants. As living standards rise so labour costs increase together with other 'overheads'. Smaller undertakings and establishments in all sectors of the economy, public and private, find it increasingly difficult to remain economically viable. Larger undertakings grow to take advantage of economies of scale and, in a market situation, of the weaknesses of their smaller competitors. Even public services, health and welfare, educational and legal, transport and communications, all become uneconomical to run on a small scale.

This process is, of course, one of the most distinctive features of that continuous social and economic transformation beginning in the late eighteenth century which we conventionally refer to as the Industrial Revolution. That transformation still continues. The growth in the scale of social organizations was, by present-day standards, at first slow, and in the twentieth century its acceleration seems to have brought about a qualitative change in social experience in some ways comparable with the original transition from a predominantly agricultural to a predominantly industrial society.[1]

---

[1] See Harold Perkin, *The Origins of Modern English Society 1780-1880*, Routledge, 1969, pp.107-124 and cf. E.J.Hobsbawm, *Industry and Empire*, Weidenfeld and Nicolson, 1968, pp.148-9, 180-183 who argues that in trade and manufacturing the growth in scale was comparatively slow until the 1890s and later. The consequences of this process in the countryside were already being deplored by Cobbett in his *Political Register* in 1806, quoted in Raymond Williams, *Culture and Society*, Penguin, 1958, pp. 14-15, but more recently it has been pointed out that farm mechanization and the drift away from agricultural employment has had the effect of reducing slightly the average size of the work group on British farms, despite the trend towards amalgamation and increased acreage per unit; see Howard Newby, 'Agricultural Workers in the Class Structure', *Sociological Review*, 1972, 20, pp.413-39 and Colin Bell and Howard Newby, 'The Sources of Variation in Agricultural Workers' Images of Society', *Sociological Review*, 1973, 21, pp.229-53.

Table 5.5

Size of Manufacturing Firms in Great Britain

Size of Plant by number of Employees	1953 %	1961 %	1968* %	Percentage Change 1953 − 1968 %
a) *Establishments*:				
11 − 99	75.1	72.6	72.2	−12.8
100 − 499	20.7	22.1	21.4	−6.4
500 − 999	2.6	3.1	3.2	+9.5
1000 or more	1.7	2.2	3.3	+72.3
Total	100.1	100.0	100.1	
N = 100.0% (thousands)	56.4	55.2	51.1	−9.4
b) *Employees*				
11 − 99	21.4	20.0	17.0	−18.7
100 − 499	33.6	31.2	31.9	−3.2
500 − 999	14.1	14.2	15.1	+9.2
1000 or more	31.0	34.5	36.0	+18.4
Total	100.1	99.9	100.0	
N = 100.0% (millions)	7.2	8.2	7.4	+1.9

*Estimate based on U.K. figures. The inclusion of a number of undertakings, particularly smaller ones, in the Manufacturing category after 1966 make exact comparisons with earlier figures hazardous. The general effect of reclassifications would however be to moderate the trend evident in these figures.

Source: Calculated from *Annual Abstracts of Statistics* 90, Table 138; *106* Table 143 and *109* Table 160.

In the manufacturing industries, as the figures in Table 5.5 indicate, though most plants with more than ten workers still had fewer than a hundred in 1968, these accounted for only 17 per cent of all employment or 19 per cent if plants with ten or fewer employees are included.[1] At the other extreme, just over three per cent of all plants, those with a thousand or more employees, by 1961 provided more than a third of all employment. The trend is clear and steepened during the 1960s. In the 1950s the total number of establishments declined by two per cent while

---

[1] The 1968 survey of manufacturing firms in the United Kingdom for the first time included plants with ten or fewer employees which accounted for 38 per cent of the total. These have been excluded from Table 5.5 for the sake of comparison with earlier estimates.

the number of employees increased by 13 per cent. Between 1961 and 1968 the number of manufacturing plants declined by 7.5 per cent while the number of workers decreased by nearly ten per cent, but the number of small plants continued to decline most steeply, and naturally, so did the number of employees working in small plants. Though most plants remained of moderate size with between 25 and 100 employees, more than half the workers were in plants employing over 500. The number of large plants increased most rapidly while the proportions and numbers of workers in the larger plants consequently increased most rapidly too.

This pattern is not only to be found in the manufacturing industries. Workers in all sectors of the economy are increasingly likely to be employed in larger plants, part of still larger organizations. This can be seen very vividly in retail distribution. In recent years an increasing proportion of the retail trade has been accounted for by firms with ten or more outlets, the multiple retailers. Between 1950 and 1966, the number of independent retailers declined by 100,000 to 404,000. The total number of shops decreased over this period by 80,000 while the number of people engaged increased by about a quarter of a million.[1] In the public services the trends in education may be taken as an example for the same tendency toward larger organization. Between 1961 and 1971 in England and Wales the number of pupils in schools went up from 7.7 million to 8.8 million and the number of teachers increased by 21 per cent, while the number of schools decreased from 35,000 to 33,000. Averages can be misleading, but clearly there was a tendency for an increase in the numbers in the larger schools and a reduction in the numbers of smaller schools.[2]

The growth in scale of industrial organizations goes beyond the increase in plant size. A single firm will often own several depots, factories or branches which are managed as parts of a single organization. Such firms themselves may be subsidiaries of larger industrial or commercial organizations with activities in a number of different fields. To consider only the size of separate plants is, in consequence, likely to lead to a substantial underestimate of the extent to which workers are employed in relatively large organizations but also of the size of the organizations themselves.

The public sector, employing in national and local government services and the nationalized industries just over a quarter of the working population,[3] can be considered mostly to comprise fairly large organizations. Among the thousand largest British industrial organizations listed by *The Times* in terms of the number of employees the Post Office ranks first followed by the National Coal Board, British Rail and the nationalized steel industry. In terms of capital employed, the Electricity Council and Electricity Boards in England and Wales are the largest

[1] See *Annual Abstract of Statistics, 109*, 1972, Table 277.

[2] ibid., Table 105.

[3] See Central Statistical Office, *Economic Trends*, 246, April 1974, pp.xxx-xxxi.

industrial undertaking in the country followed by the Post Office, then Shell and British Petroleum; I.C.I. is fifth.[1]

Through mergers, takeovers and the natural growth of the more successful companies, the private sector is also increasingly dominated by larger undertakings. This is perhaps most readily indicated in financial terms rather than in terms of employment, though the largest firms in terms of assets are generally among the largest employers. Thus the Monopolies Commission made a survey of mergers among large companies, defined as those with assets of £500,000 or more in 1961. As a result of mergers, and excluding takeovers by foreign firms, the 2,024 of these large companies which had existed in 1957 had been reduced to 1,253 at the end of 1968. In contrast with American experience, the growth of most of the larger United Kingdom companies was increasingly the result of mergers and takeovers. 'In 1958/60 companies with assets of more than £50 million acquired 10 per cent of the total companies and 27 per cent of the net assets involved but in 1968 the same group of companies acquired 38 per cent of the total companies acquired and 73 per cent of the net assets involved'.[2] The largest 80 companies held 53 per cent of the net assets of all the companies studied at the end of 1957 but at the end of 1967 the largest 80 companies held.62 per cent.[3] One third of the increase came from takeovers of other smaller companies in the sample.

Where this sort of development leads to the monopolization or domination of the market in some particular product or the provision of some service the consequences may be apparent not only in the prices charged to consumers but also in the opportunities for employment in certain kinds of occupation. The pattern of an increasing overall concentration suggested by the Monopolies Commission findings similarly has far-reaching economic effects.[4] From a more narrowly sociological perspective, its significance lies chiefly in the location of economic power and its consequent potential for influence over a wide range of questions thus increasingly concentrated within a narrowing social compass. But this will be discussed again in a later chapter.

The increasing scale of organizations and the reduction in their overall diversity is evident on the other side of industry, in the trade unions. In

[1] See *The Times 1000*, 1971, Tables 3 and 1.

[2] Monopolies Commission, *A Survey of Mergers 1958-1968*, H.M.S.O., 1970, paragraph 10, p.7.

[3] Utton has pointed out that the Monopolies Commission estimate overestimated the association between growth and company size by comparing the proportion of all assets held in the two years in question by what were the biggest 80 companies in 1968. The figures presented here are from his corrected estimate which compares the top 80 in 1968 with the (different) top 80 of 1957. See M.A.Utton, 'Mergers and the Growth of Large Firms', *Bulletin of the Oxford University Institute of Economics and Statistics*, 1972, 34, pp. 189-97.

[4] See, e.g., M.A.Utton, *Industrial Concentration*,Penguin, 1970, pp.88-9.

British industry, the employees' interests are chiefly represented through the trade union movement. Trade unions operate within the limits of the changing industrial system and occupational structure. The pattern of change there has important consequences for the pattern and process of workers' representation.

The trade union situation in Britain is complicated in that unions recruit on different principles. Some unions are occupational in that they recruit, for example, electricians or draughtsmen wherever they may be employed. Other unions are industrial unions in that they set out to organize all the workers in a particular industry – such as coal mining or the railways – irrespective of their particular jobs. Some unions combine these principles in representing a particular occupation or range of occupations in a particular industry, colliery overmen, railway clerks, etc. Some of the largest unions however are general unions and represent workers in a range of different occupations in many different industries.

'The Transport and General Workers' Union, for example, organizes the great majority of all grades of worker in one or two industries, such as the bus industry, process workers in most manufacturing industries and labourers in shipbuilding and building. In addition, it has a thriving section for clerical and supervisory staff. Its members are to be found in nearly all the country's major industries and services, and in most of them the members of the General and Municipal Workers' Union are to be seen alongside, for its structure is roughly similar. Both began as 'labourers' unions. Starting from a very different origin two one-time 'craft' societies, the Amalgamated Union of Engineering and Foundry Workers and the Electrical Trades Union, now appear more and more like the general unions in their make-up. Their members also work in nearly every industry and service in the country. In many of them they cover the maintenance craftsmen, and perhaps also their mates, but in engineering and elsewhere these two unions compete with the general unions in organizing production workers, both men and women. In addition, each of them is developing its own white-collar section. The coverage of many other large and middle-sized unions is only somewhat less irrational and complex than the coverage of these four.'[1]

In 1900 there were 1,325 trade unions with, altogether, less than two million members amongst them.[2] In 1970, there were only 481 unions but their membership was 11,000,000. While the labour force had grown from 16 million to almost 24 million the proportion who were trade unionists increased from 13 per cent in 1900 to 47 per cent in 1970. Membership fluctuated until shortly before the First World War, when the numbers

[1] *Report of the Royal Commission on Trade Unions and Employers' Associations 1965-1968* (The Donovan Report), H.M.S.O., 1968, para. 115.

[2] See D.Butler and J.Freeman, *British Political Facts 1900-1967* Macmillan, 1968, pp.211, 216, 219.

increased rapidly until there were over eight million trade unionists in 1921. Increasing unemployment and economic recession in the later 1920s and 1930s virtually halved this by 1934. The gradual improvement in trade saw increases in trade union support but it was only with the Second World War that membership again reached the 1921 level, with around 45 per cent of the labour force organized in unions.

Table 5.6

Trade Unions in the United Kingdom

	1951		1961		1970	
Number of Unions	735		646		481	
Membership (000s)						
Total	9,535		9,897		11,000	
Males	7,745		7,905		8,296	
Females	1,790		1,992		2,704	
Size of Unions by Numbers of Members	No. of Unions	Membership (000s)	No. of Unions	Membership (000s)	No. of Unions	Membership (000s)
less than 1,000	417	121	348	90	256	68
1,000 to 9,999	223	724	202	612	139	470
10,000 to 49,999	63	1,319	58	1,173	47	1,010
50,000 to 99,999	15	1,065	21	1,414	16	1,111
100,000 and over	17	6,305	17	6,609	23	8,343

Source: *Annual Abstracts of Statistics*, Nos. *100*, Table 150; *104*, Table 149; *109*, Table 168.

Table 5.6 sets out the recent part of this development. The most significant feature there is the pattern of growth in organizational size which we find echoed in the trade union movement as it is evident in almost every other institutional order in society.[1] Together with the continued, if slow, growth in the numbers of people involved, the number of units into which they are grouped is declining and it is among the smaller units that the decline is most pronounced.

The trend towards larger organizational size is associated with the growth of more formal and impersonal systems of coordination and control. In relation to their employees, this implies an increasing segregation between managers and workers and a lowering of most employees' intrinsic satisfaction with their work. Geoffrey Ingham has reviewed a large number of studies which like his own survey of workers in eight Bradford firms, show that there is proportionately more absenteeism amongst workers in larger plants. Je argues that this indicates a comparatively low level of interest in or loyalty to the relatively more

---

[1] The major exception is the case of the family where, in contrast, the tendency is towards a reduction in unit size at the same time as the number of separate units is increasing.

bureaucratized larger organizations on the part of their workers.[1] The more formal and impersonal systems of management seem to create much more of an 'us and them' situation in the industrial relations of the larger organization. Ingham writes, 'Evidence also suggests that relationships of the kind in question have the effect of restricting unionisation in small plants which may, in turn, limit further the level of bureaucratisation. For example, grievances are more likely to be dealt with on the basis of "particularistic" criteria in small plants, whereas formal procedures, based on "universalistic" criteria, are more probably found in large, unionised organisations.'[2] The experience of seemingly impersonal management and a loss of autonomy in the large organisation is not limited to manual workers. White collar or clerical, and increasingly many management personnel find themselves in the same kind of situation. In the 1950s, David Lockwood sought to account for the social and political conservatism of clerical workers, partly at least, in terms of their work situation which brought them into close contact on a personal basis with their employers or managers. The situation he described has been changing. Organizational growth, with larger offices, increases in the scale and complexity of corporate hierarchies and the centralization of administration within large corporations in a head office has led to decisions about personnel, their pay, promotions, privileges, as well as other policies and decisions generally being made far away from the scene of their implementation. It is only locally that personal knowledge and mutual consideration can demonstrably be factors which are taken into account in such matters. In the middle 1960s, Clive Jenkins described a work situation very different from that of the employee in the traditional small works or office.

> 'Questions of pay, promotion and fringe benefits, once within the personal prerogative of the works manager to negotiate, are now snatched from him to a central department in London. There *are* no channels (of communication) in the local works. With this comes a realisation that there is, for want of a better description, an affluent proletarianization of technicians, supervisors and clerks chugging along. It is *not* that they have been reduced to the poverty line. On the contrary, they are better paid than ever before; but they have less

---

[1] Geoffrey K. Ingham, 'Organisational Size, Orientation to Work and Industrial Behaviour', *Sociology*, 1967, 1, pp.239-58, and *Size of Industrial Organisation and Worker Behaviour*, Cambridge, 1970; see also John Child, *The Business Enterprise in Modern Industrial Society*, Collier-Macmillan, 1969, pp.70-71.

[2] Ingham, loc.cit., 1967, p.245; see also A.I. Marsh and E.E. Coker, 'Shop Steward Organisation in the Engineering Industry', *British Journal of Industrial Relations*, 1963, 1, who also noted the more informal relationships between management and workers typical of the smaller workshops, p.188.

freedom of action due to their very specialization, just as the manager has less flexibility in his approach due to centralization'.[1]

Jenkins may overstate the situation. The important point is that organizational growth and centralization affects not only manual workers but clerks, technicians *and* management. On the other hand, the proletarianization of these groups has not proceeded as far as their evident loss of autonomy due to the centralization of decision-making and the growth of organizational size and complexity, might have led us to expect.

It is true that increasing numbers of white collar workers are joining trade unions. G.S. Bain showed that between 1948 and 1964, while manual worker trade unionists increased in number 0.6 per cent, white collar unionism grew by 33.6 per cent. Seen in the context of the rapid extension of non-manual employment in this period, Bain wrote, 'White collar unionism in general has done little more than keep abreast of the increasing white-collar labour force'.[2] At the end of the 1960s, however, trade union membership began to overtake the growth in non-manual employment and between 1964 and 1970 the proportion of white collar workers who were union members increased from 29 per cent to 38 per cent.[3]

A.J.M. Sykes described two distinct sets of attitudes in an engineering works he studied in Glasgow. There were the clerks who identified with management but disliked management trainees and the manual workers who did not identify with management and indeed opposed management interests.

'It would appear', he wrote, 'that the clerks and the industrial workers see the work situation very differently and, accordingly, react to it very differently. In brief, each has a different industrial ethos. The question is, how has this difference arisen? They are members of the same company, they come from the same geographical area, and have similar, in some cases, identical, social backgrounds. The one major factor in which they differ is in the opportunities for promotion each has had.

---

[1] Clive Jenkins, 'Tiger in a White Collar?', *Penguin Survey of Business and Industry*, Penguin, 1965, p.62; cf. David Lockwood, *The Black-Coated Worker*, Allen and Unwin, 1957.

[2] G.S.Bain, 'The Growth of White Collar Unions in Great Britain', *British Journal of Industrial Relations*, 1966, 4, p.330; see also G.Routh, 'White Collar Unions in the United Kingdom' in A.Sturmthal (ed.), *White Collar Trade Unions*, University of Illinois Press, 1966; and R.M.Blackburn and K.Prandy, 'White Collar Unionisation: A Conceptual Framework', *British Journal of Sociology*, 1965, XVI, pp.111-22.

[3] This gain mainly occurred after 1968 and was most apparent among women workers. See G.S.Bain and R.Price 'Union Control and Employment Trends in the U.K. 1964-70', *British Journal of Industrial Relations* 1972, X, pp.366-81.

The clerks have had such opportunities for a long time, over fifty years; the manual workers have not had such opportunities'.[1]

Again we must note the interaction between work experience and the larger society which shapes the expectations workers bring with them through the factory gates. While the opportunities for upward movement remain open to the white collar workers, their view of the social structure of the factory is likely to differ from that of the manual workers, inheritors of a long experienced barrier to advancement into the ranks of managerial responsibility and opportunity. The ways in which such experiences are likely to carry over into life outside the factory, shaping and perhaps confirming experiences in other situations, will be taken up again in Chapter 7.

Thinking of Sykes's clerks, the crucial question seems to be whether the opportunities for promotion retain the same significance in a changing industrial environment. Whether their identification with management can survive the loss of direct communication indicated by Jenkins must represent a major difficulty for human relations in industry.

An analogous problem besets the trade unions. Professor Ben Roberts found that in the larger unions in the 1950s in most cases only between four and seven per cent of members attended meetings of their union branch.[2] More recently, Goldthorpe, Lockwood, Bechhofer and Platt found that in their sample of affluent workers in Luton, seven per cent of the trade unionists were regular attenders at their branch while 85 per cent never attended or had not attended in the previous year. Among the skilled craftsmen, participation was much greater, with 22 per cent regular attenders.[3] Sixty one per cent of the craftsmen thought the unions should be concerned to gain a say in management for the workers compared with only 33 per cent of other workers, and only among the craftsmen did a majority support the unions' association with the Labour Party.[4] All these workers were employed in relatively large firms, Vauxhall Motors, Skefko Ball Bearing Company and Laporte Chemicals, each part of a much larger

[1] A.J.M.Sykes, 'Some Differences in the Attitudes of Clerical and Manual Workers', *Sociological Review*, 1965, 13, p.307. This distribution of perceived opportunity is evident among the married men in full-time employment surveyed in the London region by Young and Willmott. Of those in professional and managerial jobs 76 per cent believed there was a career ladder open to them, as did 70 per cent of the clerical workers. In comparison only 48 per cent of the skilled and 45 per cent of the semi-skilled and unskilled manual workers took the same view of their own situations, loc.cit., 1973, Table 26, p.156.

[2] B.C.Roberts, *Trade Union Government and Administration in Great Britain*, Bell, 1956, p.95.

[3] John Goldthorpe et al., *The Affluent Worker: Industrial Attitudes and Behaviour*, Cambridge, 1968, pp.98-9.

[4] ibid., pp.145-6.

organization. Wedderburn and Crompton described much the same pattern
of participation on the part of craftsmen and more instrumental
membership for the sake of what the union could do for them among the
semi-skilled and unskilled workers on a complex of large chemical plants in
north-east England.[1]

A post-war study by Political and Economic Planning had shown that
voting for union officials was related to branch size. In the National Union
of Vehicle Builders, for instance, of those in branches with over a
thousand members, only eight per cent voted in union elections compared
with 46 per cent of those in branches less than a hundred strong.[2] Goldstein showed how as a result of this low level of active interest in the
routine affairs of the union, effective control of a branch could be won by
a small clique even when their views on matters of general policy might be
quite unrepresentative of the majority of branch members.[3] Once in office
however, such unrepresentative leadership has a position to defend and
may be unsusceptible to influence and difficult to remove. The iron law of
oligarchy affects trade unions as inevitably as political parties or other
participative organisations and is the more irresistible the larger the scale
of operations. The sort of schism Goldstein described at branch level, it is
easy to infer, may develop between the ordinary membership and the
national leadership of a union with more serious consequences.

Unofficial strikes or other forms of industrial conflict are not always a
bad thing, however, either for the union leadership or even for the
management or the economy in general.[4] Yet they do represent a loss of
earnings for the workers concerned and are more likely to occur when
communication and understanding between workers and their official
representatives and leadership is unsympathetic. The problem is not only
one of 'unofficial' action. A trade union leadership with interests of its
own distinct from those of the ordinary members, whether more
revolutionary or more managerial in orientation, is unlikely to serve them
well in the long run. The E.T.U. before 1957 is a well-known, even
infamous, example of a union oligarchy of the extreme Left. Not all such
self-perpetuating cliques are communist however and a number of firmly
anti-communist union leaders have been notably unresponsive to the

[1] See Dorothy Wedderburn and Rosemary Crompton, *Workers' Attitudes and Technology*, Cambridge, 1972, and Dorothy Wedderburn, 'What Determines Shop Floor Behaviour?', *New Society*, 20 July 1972, pp.128-30.

[2] P.E.P., *British Trade Unions*, London, 1955.

[3] J.Goldstein, *The Government of British Trade Unions*, 1952, pp.157-8.

[4] See H.A.Turner, G.Clark and G.Roberts, *Labour Relations in the Motor Industry*, Allen and Unwin, 1967, and H.A.Turner, *Is Britain Really Strike Prone?*, Cambridge, 1969, ch.5.

opinions of large sections of their members.[1] This is not to argue, of course, that all unions have lost touch with their ordinary members or that they have been taken over by unrepresentative political cliques. What it does indicate is that this is a serious problem for all trade unions and one which in some cases has not been solved. The problem of relations within trade unions between the elected leadership, full-time officials and shop floor members has been the focus of much recent concern and was one of the major areas discussed in the Donovan Report.[2]

Occupational Status Structure

The pattern of economic change, which has brought about the growth and decline of whole industries, in combination with the changing nature of industrial organization itself has produced the changing pattern of occupational status groups set out in Table 5.7 In the present century, the growth in scale of industrial and commercial enterprises as a result of mergers and competition together with the extension of the public sector has reduced the numbers of private businessmen making a living by employing labour and living on the profits of their trade. Self-employed artisans, traders and professionals, without employees but living on their own independent enterprise, have similarly declined since the 1930s as both trade and professional services became increasingly subject to the trends of increasing scale. The apparent reversal of this trend in the later 1960s probably derives, paradoxically, from rising wages amongst manual employees. Better wages in industry and rising labour costs must have left an increasing number of farmers replacing hired labour by machinery. Most probably, however, the new pattern mainly reflects the growth of 'the lump'. This is a practice mostly encountered in the building industry where rising earnings provided the incentive and the job situation the opportunity for workers to avoid taxes by moving from one contractor to another while remaining technically self-employed.

The growth of organizational size and the increasing administrative complexity and bureaucratization which it has entailed is reflected in the rapid increase in managers and clerical workers, particularly after the Second World War. The rapid increase in professional employees also is partly attributable to this cause, but is mainly due to the expansion in the public sector of the education, health and welfare services with their new

---

[1] See for example J.E.T.Eldridge and G.C.Cameron, 'Unofficial Strikes: Some Objections Considered', *British Journal of Sociology*, 1964, IV, 1, pp.24 ff. with reference to A.E.U. and B.I.S.A.K.T.A. More recent examples may be found again in the case of the A.E.U. executive committee's overriding of union conference decisions following the measures taken by the Labour Government in July 1966 and the leadership of the National Union of Seamen before the 1966 seamen's strike, ref. *Final Report of the Pearson Committee*, Cmnd. 3211, H.M.S.O., 1967.

[2] loc.cit., ch.3.

armies of teachers, doctors and nurses and social workers. Foremen and supervisors have tripled as a proportion of the working population since 1911 — also in part a consequence of the growth in plant size and the need for more formalised supervisory systems. 'Wage-earners', the remainder of the labour force, were more than three-quarters of the occupied population before the First World War. Their proportionate decline has continued even if we were to re-allocate to them all the recent growth of the self-employed, and since 1951 their actual numbers have been decreasing even while the economically active population continued to grow.

Table 5.7

Occupational Status Groups in Great Britain 1911–1971

	1911**	1921	1931	1951	1961	1966	1971**
			Men and Women				
			*Percentages**				
Employers	4.6	3.8	3.7	2.0	3.0	2.3	1.9
Self-employed without employees	5.2	6.2	6.0	5.0	4.2	4.1	5.3
Managers	3.3	3.5	3.5	3.8	5.4	6.0	6.7
Professional Employees n.e.c.	3.5	3.8	3.8	5.5	7.3	8.3	9.4
Clerical Workers n.e.c.	4.8	6.7	7.0	10.3	12.3	12.9	13.0
Foremen and Supervisors	1.3	1.4	1.5	2.5	3.6	3.8	3.9
Wage Earners†	77.3	74.4	74.5	71.1	64.2	62.6	59.8
TOTAL	100.0	99.8	100.0	100.2	100.0	99.9	100.0
Economically Active N = 100 per cent (in thousands)	18,347	21,029	21,029	22,579	24,014	24,857	25,003

*Rounding to the first place after the decimal point means that percentages do not always add to exactly 100.0
**Data for professional workers 1911 incomplete and estimated.
Data for employers 1971 estimated from household chief economic supporters.
†This is a broader category than 'manual workers' as defined for other tables. Wage earners here include a proportion of personal and domestic service occupations (especially amongst women) and other non-industrial employees. See Routh, *op.cit.*, p.157. Types or grades of wage earners have not been distinguished as it has proved impossible to reconcile the classification used in the earlier part of the series with any of the usual census distinctions between skilled, semi-skilled and unskilled manual workers.

Sources: 1911-1931 adapted from Guy Routh, *Occupation and Pay in Great Britain, 1906-1960*, 1965, Table 1 and Appendix A; *1951 Census One Per Cent Sample Tables*, Tables II.1 and II.2, *1961 Census, Great Britain Summary Tables*, Tables 31 and 32. *1966 Census, Economic Activity Tables*, Part I, Table 13. *1971 Census, Great Britain Summary Tables (One Per Cent Sample)*, Tables 13, 14 and 27.

It should be noted that this last group — those I have described as 'wage earners' — are mostly manual workers but the group also includes members of the armed services, postmen and telephone operators, policemen and firemen, domestic servants, shop assistants, waiters, cleaners and others mainly in service trades. In other tables in this book for the most part the categories used are based on the Registrar General's 17 socio-economic groups and are not exactly comparable. In particular, some of these occupations are elsewhere included as 'junior non-manual workers' along with some routine clerical jobs. Where to draw the line here is a problem made more difficult by the fact that it has been drawn at different points by different writers. This classification has been adopted in Tables 5.7 and 5.8 for the sake of continuity with Routh's impressive historical reconstruction,[1] though elsewhere for ease of comparison with census and other data, I have used the socio-economic groups and divided 'junior non-manual workers' from personal service workers and manual workers.

Table 5.8

Occupational Status of Economically Active Men and Women in Great Britain 1971

			Percentages
	Men	Women	Women as a Proportion of each Group
Employers*	2.3	0.9	17.3
Self-Employed* without employees	6.6	3.1	21.3
Managers	8.8	3.1	16.9
Professional Employees n.e.c.	9.0	10.1	39.3
Clerical Workers n.e.c.	5.6	25.9	72.8
Foremen and Supervisors	4.9	2.2	20.8
Wage Earners**	62.8	54.8	33.5
TOTAL	100.0	100.1	36.5
N = 100 per cent (in thousands)	15,867	9,136	

*Provisional figures
**see Note 3 to Table 5.7
Source: Calculated from *1971 Census Great Britain Summary Tables (One Per Cent Sample)*, Tables 13, 14 and 27.

[1] Routh, *see* Sources, Table 5.7.

There are important sex differences in the pattern of employment which are set out in Table 5.8. In 1971 more than a third of all those economically active were women. Women are concentrated in a more restricted range of jobs than men and some jobs are mainly 'women's work'. Men are about four times more likely to be in skilled manual jobs than women and much more likely to be in supervisory and managerial positions. More than half of male manual workers are in skilled jobs but only a quarter of women manual workers are skilled. Women, however, are almost five times more likely to be clerical workers than men and nearly three quarters of all clerical workers are women. They outnumber men by about ten to one in personal service jobs, such as shop assistants, domestic service etc. Women are also more likely to be in professional employment than men, but mainly in what are sometimes called the lower professions, with large numbers in primary teaching, social work and nursing. Men are predominant among employers and the self-employed.[1]

Between 1966 and 1971 though the proportion of the growing number of economically active women who were in management and the professions increased, the trend among men was still greater so that, as a proportion of these expanding occupations, women fell back. Conversely, though the proportion of women workers who were wage earners and supervisors declined, the decline amongst wage earning men was still greater and consequently the proportion of all wage earners who were women increased. Besides wage earners and employers the percentage of men in clerical jobs went down so that, with the continuing, if slow, growth in clerical employment, women became still more predominant there than before. Though the numbers of women in senior jobs, the professions or management, has increased, the recent expansion of women's employment has mainly been in more routine and less skilled occupations. There can be no doubt, therefore, that the increasing economic activity of women outside the home in recent years has, paradoxically, produced a distribution of apparently greater occupational inequality with men than before.[2]

There is another way of looking at this data on occupational status which is worth pointing out before we go on, as it will be relevant to a later chapter. I have been describing the distribution of occupations very much as a consequence of an interaction between demographic and economic change. It can also be seen as a structure of opportunities. While the opportunities may not be equally available to everyone, the expansion of professional, managerial and clerical occupations has required a change in occupational recruitment of some consequence in determining the pattern of social mobility. The nature of these consequences will be considered in Chapter 8.

[1] See also *1966 Census Economic Activity Tables, Part III*, Table 31 (for men), and ibid. Table 27 (for women).

[2] Table 5.8; cf. *1966 Census Economic Activity Tables, Part I*, Tables 2 and 3.

Occupation and Class

The distribution of occupations, for several reasons, should not be immediately identified with the class structure. In the first place whereas the distribution of occupations refers only to differentiation, when we talk about class we are dealing with relations of inequality. Throughout this book I have made comparisons between classes and it must be acknowledged that these have usually been very broadly sketched impressions of the working class *vis-à-vis* the middle class rather than a more discriminating exploration of the circumstances of all the strata one might wish to distinguish. I believe this cruder approach is justified, however, not simply because that is the way most of the available evidence is already classified but because that classification realistically corresponds to the underlying basis of social inequality in this society. There are many manifestations of difference between the classes as I have already shown and will enlarge upon in the succeeding chapters and these are reasonably clearly represented by a division between the strata which is based on occupational criteria. But there is more than a matter of statistical convenience in grouping the population in this way, there is the claim that the underlying inequality amongst them is a product of their involvement in the economic processes which sustain the society as a whole and allocate its benefits amongst its members. In the next chapter I will compare some of the material advantages gained from the ownership of property and the financial rewards of employment. For the present to proceed from the distribution of economic activity to the class structure it is necessary to refer to the unequal privileges accruing to those with different skills to offer in the labour market. These inequalities are evident in housing and the home environment, in education, in access to financial and welfare facilities and in the pay packet or salary cheque, but they begin in the workplace.

On the matter of working conditions Dorothy Wedderburn has commented that:

'. . . it does not require much documentation to establish that many more manual workers are exposed to worse noise levels, extremes of temperature, unpleasant smell as well as lower standard amenities, such as lavatories, canteens, etc. than their non-manual counterparts. Industrial accidents are a matter of great concern. They are showing a steady rate of increase and occur principally to manual workers. The total of reported accidents under the Factories Act increased in 1969 for the seventh year in succession . . . Not only does such a difference in the risk of accident have its economic aspects in terms of earning power, but it also results in differences in terms of physical and psychological suffering.'[1]

[1] Dorothy Wedderburn 'Inequality at Work', ch. 10 in P.Townsend and N.Bosanquet (eds), *Labour and Inequality*, Fabian Society, 1972.

Together with a colleague, Christine Craig, Dorothy Wedderburn has shown that it is not only the physical working conditions of manual workers which compare unfavourably with the provision made for non-manual grades. In a survey of over 400 manufacturing firms carried out in 1968 they found that in relation to holidays, hours of work and time-keeping, pension and sick-pay benefits both managerial and clerical staff typically enjoyed a more privileged position than manual workers. Manual workers are typically subject to stricter discipline and enjoy less autonomy over working hours and time off as well as generally enjoying fewer work-related benefits than other workers. In respect of typical male workers in their late thirties with over five years' continuous service in their firms, they compared the terms and conditions of employment of semi-skilled manual workers, foremen, clerks, technicians and senior and middle managers. Ninety-eight per cent of the firms required their semi-skilled operatives to clock-on or book-in and nine out of ten deducted pay for any lateness on their part. Over 40 per cent had no checking-in requirement for foremen, clerks and technicians and only six per cent required it of senior managers. Persistent lateness was generally regarded as grounds for dismissal where manual workers were concerned while no senior managers suffered deductions from their salaries and only 40 per cent risked their jobs for persistent lateness. Only eight per cent of firms followed the practice of deductions for clerical workers though persistent lateness was commonly treated very seriously. In less than 30 per cent of firms could operatives take time off for personal reasons, though over 80 per cent allowed this for all the other grades. The normal working week for the semi-skilled manual workers was 40 hours or more in 97 per cent of the firms and this was usual for foremen but clerks normally worked these hours only in nine per cent of the firms, technicians in 23 per cent, middle managers in 27 per cent and senior managers in only 22 per cent of the firms in the survey. In over 80 per cent of the firms' managers had a choice about when they would take their holidays and had 15 days or more per year. The same applied to clerks and technicians in well over 70 per cent of cases but to less than 40 per cent of the manual workers. More than half the firms operated a sick-pay scheme and two-thirds a pension scheme covering their semi-skilled manual workers while more than nine cases out of ten had such schemes for all the other grades studied.[1] Quite apart from the physical conditions of work then, or from earnings differentials, it is clear from these figures that the firms generally treated their manual workers less favourably in every

---

[1] See Dorothy Wedderburn, op.cit., 1972, p.177, and 'Workplace Inequality', *New Society*, 9 April 1970, p.593; and D.Wedderburn and C.Craig, 'Relative Deprivation in Work' in Dorothy Wedderburn (ed.), *Poverty, Inequality and Class Structure*, Cambridge University Press, 1974, pp.141-64. Outside the manufacturing industries employers' provision of sick-pay benefits for workers below professional and managerial levels is still less widespread — see *General Household Survey*, Table 6.18, H.M.S.O., 1973.

respect.

The Labour Mobility survey showed that manual workers and the less skilled in particular are also much less secure in their employment. Harris and Clausen found that unskilled men were the most likely to have changed jobs in the ten years preceding the survey, a fifth of them having had at least five jobs in that time. Men in managerial and executive jobs were least likely to have made a move and two-thirds of them had held the same job throughout the period.[1] It seems unlikely that this was a function of age as there was a higher proportion of older workers amongst the unskilled group. [2] Nor can it be attributed to relative shiftlessness or other supposedly psychological characteristics. The distribution of job instability on the contrary is a product of forces over which the workers themselves have little control. The poorer working conditions and terms of employment of manual workers in general are a reflection of their weaker position in the labour market and this is most clearly indicated by the relative possibility of being without a job altogether. This is much less common in professional and managerial or clerical occupations. Harris and Clausen noted that:

'. . . Professional and administrative people ensure in nine cases out of ten that they have a job to go to before leaving the one they hold, compared with three out of four of managerial and executive and clerical workers. In about two-thirds of cases, skilled workers have a job to go to before leaving, while 61-62 per cent of partly skilled workers ensure they have a job to go to before leaving. The group least likely to have a job lined up are the unskilled workers, only just over half of them having a job to go to when they leave'.[3]

These differences between occupational groups directly represent their relative security from the forces of economic circumstance based, at these levels, not on the ownership of wealth but on occupational skills in greater or lesser demand. Occupational groups are thus related to one another not only cooperatively through the social division of labour, but also competitively over the distribution of society's resources through the operation of supply and demand in relation to diverse skills in a changing industrial economy. Thus in a market economy a man's job may be treated as an index of his class position and the distribution of occupations as an outline of the class structure.

Having referred to the structural inequalities of class relations we should perhaps be wary of proceeding directly into the moral philosophy of the subject (whatever our obligation to do so as responsible citizens) if

---

[1] Amelia Harris and Rosemary Clausen, *Labour Mobility in Britain 1953-1963*, Government Social Survey 1966, p.59.

[2] ibid., Appendix I, Table 128.

[3] ibid., p.70.

that leads us to neglect the remaining sociological questions which arise in relation to the degree and distribution of inequality and whether or not these are changing. Some of these issues are considered further elsewhere in the book but for the remainder of the present chapter I want to examine some of the practical and empirical difficulties which beset discussions of present trends. Without a careful use of evidence discussion of the pattern of social stratification in modern Britain is little better than an exercise in propaganda or, at best, in imaginative literature. The evidence however, even when we use material as 'objective' as the census derived distribution of occupations, is not without its ambiguities and problems.

We must be cautious in identifying, from Table 5.7 for instance, the employers and the self-employed as the capitalist class and the service class or middle class in their managerial, professional, clerical and supervisory helpers, with the mass of the proletariat or working class in the wage-earning group. To start with this leaves out of account rather more than half the population who are not economically active. But there are further difficulties, which the table may obscure, in arguing from the occupational structure to the class structure.

I proposed earlier on that occupation may be taken as an index of class and social status but it is not altogether a simple matter to do so. We have already encountered the problem of how to categorize some occupations on the manual/non-manual boundary — jobs such as policeman, shop assistant, foreman. We ought not to make these allocations simply on the basis of what best produces statistical support for what we may be trying to prove at the time, the poverty of the lower middle class, the invidious discrimination against the workers, or whatever.[1] That there is a problem of classification is itself an important social fact. David Lockwood pointed out that, 'the work situation involves the separation and concentration of individuals, affords possibilities of identification with some and alienation from others, and conditions feelings of isolation, antagonism and solidarity'.[2] In general, this separation and concentration divides the classes and creates a sense of sharing a way of life with social equals. Some occupations however may be genuinely marginal in that the situation the worker finds himself in may be ambiguous in affording him possibilities of alienation from some and identification with other aspects of the same social groups, or involving a degree of separation from one group without locating him clearly in another either in his own eyes or anybody else's. Policemen, shop assistants and some foremen, for instance, may find themselves in this sort of situation. The foremen and supervisors are an heterogeneous lot in any case. Some of them may be engaged in manual jobs with some general responsibility for reporting when things go wrong

---

[1] See G.S.Bain and R.Price, 'Who is a White Collar Employee?', *British Journal of Industrial Relations*, 1972, X, pp.325-39.

[2] David Lockwood, op.cit., 1957, p.205.

while others carry junior administrative responsibilities and never 'get their hands dirty'. In other words, some foremen and supervisors could be considered to be manual workers and 'working class' while others are unambiguously in lower managerial positions and would generally be considered 'middle class'. It has become conventional to divide manual workers from non-manual workers and then sometimes to subdivide these groups further. Though this does not resolve the problem of whether, for example, foremen or policemen are manual workers or not, it does seem to correspond to real social differences. While it may or may not coincide exactly with the division between working class and middle class[1] such a classification would remain a useful instrument in the analysis of social structure, since it is less likely to fabricate apparent social differences than to mask real ones. Since most of us effectively have a social horizon which includes very little beyond our own immediate experience we are likely to treat detectable exaggeration in an account of the unfamiliar as grounds for disbelieving in it altogether. In describing social differentiation a procedure of minimal estimation should therefore prove a more convincing strategy.

In trying to describe either the class structure or the relative extent of social status groups the allocation or classification of children, housewives and the retired also has to be resolved. One cannot simply assume that these groups are distributed proportionately with the occupied population. Even amongst the employed there are ambiguities, apart from the sort of marginal cases I have just referred to. These are especially important when considering social status groups where the differentiating factor is sharing a common life-style. If they live at home, single men, particularly the younger ones, in any given occupation may belong to different social status groups. This is particularly the case at the lower margin of the middle class. The junior clerical worker who lives with his working class parents is, at least in his leisure time, likely to move in different social milieux from a young man in a similar job living with his parents if his father is, say, a successful estate agent. Such differences may or may not be less probable if the young men in question have left home to live on their own.

The problem of categorizing women workers is more difficult. The working wives and daughters of manual workers are quite likely to be in non-manual occupations but in terms of life-style and social prestige may remain 'working class'. In some studies, particularly those concerned with estimating rates of social mobility, the problem has been 'avoided' by looking only at distributions of occupied males. Another solution is to categorize individuals according to the occupation of the head of their household. This is more satisfactory in encompassing the whole population

---

[1] In 'Social Mobility and Class Relations in Britain', *British Journal of Sociology*, 1972, XXIII, pp.422-36, I have discussed this problem with reference to the changing pattern of inter-generational occupational mobility.

Table 5.9

Proportion in Four Social Strata by different occupational indices: Great Britain 1961, 1966 and 1971

Percentages

Strata [1]	All Economically Active Men and Women		Occupied Males		Household Chief Economic Supporters			All Husbands		
	1961[2]	1966[3]	1961[4]	1966[5]	1961[6]	1966[7]	1971[8]	1961[9]	1966[10]	1971[11]
Upper Middle Class	11.1	11.5	14.3	15.1	15.2	16.1	17.2	16.1	17.5	19.8
Lower Middle Class	29.7	31.5	20.9	21.4	23.9	23.7	24.4	20.9	21.6	22.3
Skilled Working Class	26.7	25.4	34.9	35.1	31.6	30.9	28.3	34.8	34.8	33.3
Semi-and Unskilled Working Class	32.4	31.6	29.9	28.3	29.3	29.3	30.1	28.1	26.1	24.6
Totals	99.9	100.0	100.0	99.9	100.0	100.0	100.0	99.9	100.0	100.0
N = 100 per cent (in thousands)	24,012	24,856	16,232	15,994	15,124	16,961	17,161	12,646	12,327	12,869

N.B. The notes to this table are printed opposite, on p. 169.

and at the same time recognizing the social realities of status group membership. It should be recognized, however, that the term household refers to a residential unit rather than a family and applies to typists living in bedsitters as well as married couples with their children. Some of the single person households especially, may derive their life-style from another and it may be argued that in the case of widows, divorced and separated wives as well as of some young people living alone, the individual's own occupation may still be misleading as an index of social status.

Taking all these considerations into account, Table 5.9 shows how the proportions in the upper and lower middle class and the skilled and semi- and unskilled working class vary according to the composition of the population on which the figures are based.

Briefly, it can be seen that sex is an important factor but that family or household status makes the greatest difference. In comparison with the distribution of all occupied males the inclusion of economically active women reduces the proportional size of the higher professional and managerial group, what I have called the 'upper middle class'. The size of the skilled working class also is substantially reduced while the proportion in the less skilled working class is greater and in the lower middle class very

[1] Strata are condensed from seventeen socio-economic groups as follows:
  Upper Middle Class: S.E.Gs. 1, 2, 3, 4, 13.
  Lower Middle Class: S.E.Gs. 5, 6, 12, 14.
  Skilled Working Class: S.E.Gs. 8, 9.
  Semi-and Unskilled Working Class: S.E.Gs. 7, 10, 11, 15, 16, 17.

[2] Calculated from *1961 Census of England and Wales, Occupation Tables*, Table 19. *1961 Census of Scotland, Occupation, Industry and Workplace Tables*, Table 19.

[3] Calculated from *1966 Census, Economic Activity Tables, Part III*, Table 30.

[4] Calculated from *1961 Census of England and Wales, Occupation Tables*, Table 28.
  1961 Census of Scotland, Occupation, Industry and Workplace Tables, Table 28.

[5] Calculated from *1966 Census Economic Activity Tables, Part III*, Table 25.

[6] Calculated from *1961 Census, Great Britain Summary Tables*, Table 39, including retired.

[7] Calculated from *1966 Census, Household Composition Tables*, Table 30. These figures are not available for Scotland for 1966 but only England and Wales and include the retired. The number of households given at the foot of the column refers to Great Britain as a whole however.

[8] Calculated from *1971 Census, Great Britain Summary Tables (One Per Cent Sample)*, Table 27, including retired.

[9] Calculated from *1961 Census, Great Britain Summary Tables*, Table 47, including retired.

[10] Calculated from *1966 Census, Household Composition Tables*, Table 25, including retired.

[11] Calculated from *1971 Census, Great Britain Summary Tables (One Per Cent Sample)*, Table 33, including retired.

much greater. If to accommodate the problem of manual workers' wives and daughters, we consider households, because everyone is a member of a household, we find distributions closer to those for occupied males but with fewer in the semi-skilled and unskilled working class and a larger proportion in the upper middle class. Even using this most comprehensive classification we omit three per cent of the population, including students and those with either independent or no visible means of support.[1] Again, the inclusion of women among these heads of households in the 'Household Chief Economic Supporters' may have the statistical effect of apparently enlarging the lower middle class and the semi-skilled and unskilled working class while depressing the proportions in the upper middle class and the skilled working class. If we consider only husbands the opposite occurs, but this excludes not only female heads of households but also the single population living alone.

The problem of choosing a basis for describing the shape of the class structure is a practical one. That is to say it has more than merely theoretical significance; more important, it has implications for the empirical conclusions we can reach about the past and current pattern of change in the structure of British society. On the ten-year comparison shown in Table 5.9, the general indication is that the middle class have been increasing in relation to the working classes. There are some exceptions however which I think justify labouring the point about defining the populations to be compared very carefully. The different occupational distributions and trends amongst men and women play a part here too. Though information is so far available only up to 1966 the pattern holds consistently for all economically active men and women, but when we consider only occupied males, it is apparent that there has been an increase in the proportion in the skilled working class as well as in the two middle class strata. Amongst Household Chief Economic Supporters, there was at first a slight decline in the proportion in lower middle class occupations as well as in the working class as a whole though this was confined to the skilled while the proportion in the less skilled stratum latterly increased. Amongst husbands the increase in the proportions in the middle class is evident but the decline in the working class proportion in contrast includes the semi-skilled and unskilled group.

It is clear that if, when we refer to classes and status groups, we intend to include their dependents along with the workers themselves, and at the same time recognize the realities and influences of family life, then we must encounter such problems in describing the relative size of these social strata. We can talk about the changing size of social classes or status groups but face the same issues. Certainly something is happening out there in society and this is connected with the changing distribution of occup-

---

[1] See *1971 Census Great Britain Summary Tables (One Per Cent Sample)*, General Explanatory Notes, VIII, p.xi.

ations. If we want to say in any detail at all what *is* happening, however, then both what we mean by the middle class or the working class and whom we count as involved in the stratification system must be very carefully defined indeed.

6 Wealth and Income

Introduction

In a society where more and more values appear to be expressed in pecuniary terms, where not only the power to acquire goods and services but also influence over others, and even time and aesthetic appreciation are often measured in such terms, money is clearly an important social fact and not merely a narrowly economic one. Its dispersion through society naturally reveals a great deal about the social structure, about the way of life of its members, about what is important to them, and not least about the distribution of power amongst them. If social stratification is broadly a matter of 'who gets what?' we must unavoidably include some examination of the distribution of wealth and income and make some attempt to discover what sorts of people get how much. I shall begin by looking at the evidence on the distribution of wealth and on the income it produces before going on to consider income from employment and other sources. There are many obstacles in our way, however, when we try to compare different sectors of society over time. The very reliability of the available information probably varies a good deal between social strata. Then there are problems of the presentation of data which have implications for the kinds of interpretation it leads us towards. As a measure of change in incomes, for instance, percentage increases or decreases are misleading when base amounts of widely different magnitude are involved while the general rise in living standards since the war together with the continuous decline in the domestic value of money since 1933 mean that it is seldom helpful to refer to actual sums. In the ten years up to 1970 the purchasing power of the pound declined to the equivalent of only 69 new pence at 1960 prices and the rate of inflation steepened after that.[1] In discussing the evidence on wealth and income at the opening of the 1970s therefore, it would seem more than ever necessary to look at proportionate distributions rather than the absolute quantities accruing to the different social strata.

[1] See David Butler and Jennie Freeman, *British Political Facts 1900-1967*, Macmillan, 1968, pp.224-5 and Central Statistical Office, *Facts in Focus*, Penguin, 1972, Table 153, p.192.

Wealth

J.E. Meade has pointed out that inequality in the ownership of wealth is significant apart from any income inequality which it implies.

'A man with much property has great bargaining strength and a great sense of security, independence and freedom; and he enjoys these things not only *vis-à-vis* his propertyless fellow citizens but also *vis-à-vis* the public authorities . . . An unequal distribution of property means an unequal distribution of power and status even if it is prevented from causing too unequal a distribution of income.'[1]

It is clear that in modern Britain wealth is still very unevenly distributed and this is not simply another quaint survival from a long and colourful history. The concentration of wealth has important sociological consequences in the present here and now. As an economic resource wealth may be readily converted into other forms of power, e.g. social status, political influence, etc. But besides the prestige of ownership and the security and independence it confers, property is still socially important as a source of further income through rents, interest on savings or dividends on investment. Wealth in private ownership is particularly important in the system of social stratification as it is transmittable at the will of the individual proprietor, and, inherited by his heirs, perpetuates economic and social differentiation from one generation to another. The inheritance of property is unevenly distributed, however, and statistically the distribution of income from property is probably more significant than the distribution of wealth itself as an indicator of the degree of concentration of private economic power and thus of how clearly the society is divided into classes.

All useful information on the distribution of personal wealth in Britain derives from the estimates now made annually by the Commissioners of Her Majesty's Inland Revenue on the basis of Estate Duty returns. The main difficulty encountered in dealing with such estimates of wealth, apart from the representativeness of the deaths in any one year, is that in addition to any evasion of estate duty — which is illegal — it is known that legal devices are operated to avoid death duties so that at least some private wealth escapes the Commissioners' assessment.[2]

The so-called death duties are paid on the estate or wealth which the deceased leaves behind him.

---

[1] J.E.Meade, *Efficiency, Equality and the Ownership of Property*, Allen and Unwin, 1964, p.39.

[2] See *Inland Revenue Statistics 1973*, p.170. Michael Meacher has argued that the Inland Revenue estimates are 'little more than ingenious fictions' and may indeed account for as little as a third of the wealth in private hands in Britain today, but his working assumptions may be as corrigible as those of H.M.Commissioners. In particular he appears to overlook the growing importance of the nationalized

'Estate duty is chargeable on the value of property, whether settled or not settled, which passes (i.e. changes hands) or is treated as passing on death. The charge to duty is thus not limited to property owned by the deceased but may extend to other property, e.g. to trust funds where the deceased received all or part of the income during his lifetime, and to gifts . . . made by the deceased within seven years of his death. The time limit is one year in the case of gifts for public or charitable purposes.'[1]

Estates with a net capital value of £15,000 or less are exempt from duty, but on estates of a higher value there is a progressive duty ranging up to 75 per cent. The consequence of such a progressive duty is that the incentive to avoidance or even evasion increases with the size of the fortune and it is likely on this account that, in the way Titmuss[2] showed for official income statistics, the estimates of the distribution of wealth made by the Commissioners of Inland Revenue on the basis of estate duty are likely to suffer severely from a tendency to underestimate the size and number of large fortunes. Estate duty is avoided in many ways. The gift of titles to the heirs well before the owner's death while he goes on enjoying the benefits of the property is very risky as heirs may die inconveniently early. Other more secure ways of avoiding duties almost all however depend on handing over the ownership of wealth to some legal fiction so that it is no longer subject to the risk of human mortality. A private company – which a man owns only in association with his heirs but which retains his services as a director – may survive him. Lord Denning (then Master of the Rolls) described the principle of varying a trust so that an interest is maintained beyond the death of its original beneficiaries and the payment of estate duty is avoided on the capital. Varying trusts mainly to avoid death duties had become, he said in the Court of Appeal in May, 1966,

'a game of chess played by lawyers and the revenue authorities with a subtlety and skill worthy of the schoolmen . . . You take an interest which is going to come to an end when an old lady dies. You treat it like the branch of a tree. You graft on to it an offshoot which will

industries and public investment when estimating the growth of total wealth between 1920 and 1969. His discussion nevertheless remains the best critical discussion of recent estimates of the distribution of wealth in Britain that I have seen. See Michael Meacher, 'Wealth: Labour's Achilles Heel' in Peter Townsend and Nicholas Bosanquet (eds), *Labour and Inequality*, Fabian Society, 1972, especially pp.193-6.

[1] The exemption level from Estate Duty was raised from £5,000 to £10,000 in the 1969 Finance Act, £12,500 in 1971 and £15,000 for surviving husbands or wives in 1972, together with an easing of the scale of rates. *Inland Revenue Statistics*, 1973, p.160.

[2] R.M. Titmuss, *Income Distribution and Social Change*, Allen & Unwin, 1962.

continue after her death, so that there is one continuous interest which will not cease on her death. By this means you avoid the Finance Act.'[1]

The two world wars seem to be associated with the greatest reductions in the concentration of wealth in private ownership at least until the late 1960s. In the postwar period little change occurred until the mid-1960s. though whether the figures since then indicate a genuine redistribution of wealth or the progressive improvement of the art of estate duty avoidance it is hard to judge. Strachey and others have argued that the degree of concentration still revealed by the Commissioners' estimates indicate a strongly persistent tendency towards inequality.[2]

Table 6.1 below shows the proportion of personal wealth held by the richest one, five and ten per cent of the population, according to the official estimates. On this basis one per cent of population, in 1971 about half a million people, owned more than £27,000,000,000. The actual amounts involved however, are so great as to be virtually inconceivable and it is the degree of concentration measured proportionately which is socially significant.

Table 6.1

Net Personal Wealth in Britain

Percentage of the population	Percentage of Total Net Personal Wealth					
	1911-13*	1936-38*	1946-47**	1961†	1966†	1971†
1	69	56	45	42	35	32
5	87	79	69	68	62	58
10	92	88	80	80	78	75

Sources: *J.E.Meade, *Efficiency, Equality and the Ownership of Property*, Allen and Unwin, 1964, Table 1, p.27.
**Calculated from K.M.Langley, 'The Distribution of Capital in Private Hands in 1936-38 and 1946-47 (Part 2)', *Bulletin of the Oxford University Institute of Statistics*, Feb. 1951, Table XVB, p.46.
†*Inland Revenue Statistics 1973*, HMSO, 1973, Table 92.

---

[1] See the *Guardian*, 13 May 1966. This particular expedient is likely to have ended as a consequence of changes introduced by the Chancellor of the Exchequer in the 1969 Finance Act. The purpose of the example is to illustrate the subtlety of the tactics involved. Whether the Exchequer's move has had any long-term strategic effects however, remains to be seen. One curious effect of the reduction of Estate Duty avoidance in this way would probably be to indicate an apparent increase in the inequality of the distribution of wealth due to the appearance in the Commissioner's returns of types of fortune such as those in the example, previously not taken into account. But there is no sign so far that this has occurred.

[2] See John Strachey, *Contemporary Capitalism*, Gollancz, 1956; T.B.Bottomore, *Elites and Society*, Watts 1964; and Michael Meacher, op.cit., 1972.

On the basis of Estate Duty returns the Board of Inland Revenue 'estimates the number of people with any wealth in 1971 as 18.6 million, about one third of the population; of the remainder, who either have no wealth at all or only . . . small amounts (usually less than £500) . . . about 60 per cent are below the age of 25'.[1]

The table indicates a substantial reduction in the degree to which personal wealth is concentrated in a very few hands since the 1914-18 war. The decline in the numbers and sizes of the great landed family estates and the overshadowing of the family firm by the joint stock corporations has, it seems, swelled the number and importance of the relatively smaller fortunes. This apparent levelling is no doubt to some extent misleading. The figures may in part reflect the increasing subtlety of avoidance though it seems improbable that this could entirely explain away such a marked trend. It is probable then, that the smaller fortunes have increased. But when we come to examine the dispersion of income from property it will be evident that the larger concentrations of property still have a disproportionately greater significance in the contribution they make to the system of social stratification and the influence they represent in the economic sphere.

In the most recent period covered by the table, ideologues of all shades will find material to grind their axes on. The decline in the concentration of personal wealth appears to have slowed down in the later 1960s, at least at the very top of the distribution. On the other hand, contrary to many theoretical expectations, the most important empirical point to note is that, as far as the evidence goes, the trend towards equalization did persist.

Income

The major and most reliable source of information on the distribution of income in Britain is also the Board of Inland Revenue. Their annual surveys of income tax assessments (quinquennial before 1966) suffer from a number of limitations however. Firstly, their figures only describe taxable incomes and so ignore all those below the exemption limit, in effect about £8 a week, and above this level those portions of some incomes not subject to income tax. Secondly, while regional, household composition, sex, marital status, source (i.e. income from employment or from investments) and other analyses are given, income is not related to occupation or socio-economic status. R.M. Titmuss[2] has discussed the limitations of figures based on taxable income at some length and though subsequent measures have out-dated some of his comments in respect of more recent estimates some are still significant, in particular at the upper

[1] *Inland Revenue Statistics*, 1973, p.170.

[2] op.cit., 1962.

end of the scale where the incentive to tax avoidance is increased by the incidence of surtax. Titmuss lists (a) covenants and marriage settlements which enable a man to spread a large income over all the members of his family; (b) so-called 'top hat' pension schemes which spread income smoothly over a man's lifetime. *The Times* described[1] the increasing popularity of such schemes in the 1960s and explained 'the main incentive to those on high tax scales is that the employee defers his remuneration till after his retirement, when he will be paying tax at a lower rate. If he dies before retirement the sum assured is payable free of estate duty (and should he survive) up to a quarter of the benefit can be commuted and taken as a capital sum tax free'; (c) fringe benefits (non-taxable income) enhance the effective spending power of the recipient but do not appear as taxable income. According to a survey of salaried jobs carried out in 1966 fringe benefits were higher in the higher income ranges. Company cars, share profits etc. accounted for 31 per cent of the incomes of those earning £7,000 p.a. or more but only 11 per cent of incomes at £1,000 p.a. Thus in industry those earning a basic salary of £1,000 per year could add a further £100, while those with a salary of £7,000 could on average expect additional fringe benefits worth about £2,000 per annum before tax.[2] A survey by the Prices and Incomes Board[3] also indicated that in the private sector members of boards of directors and senior executives receive benefits in addition to their salaries worth on average something in the region of £2,000 per year at current rates of tax.

For such reasons as these income distributions derived from tax assessments may be assumed to under-represent the differences in gross effective income. It is however necessary to make use of such information, lacking any better. First I shall discuss the figures for the overall distribution of personal incomes and then examine more closely income from property and thirdly, earned income.

Personal Incomes

Above the exemption limit the mean income before tax in 1971 was approximately £1,545 and the median income about £1,320; in other words, a skewed distribution where one almost might say only a minority are above average. Taxes on income are progressive in that, as the table shows, they fall somewhat more heavily on the larger incomes. However it also shows the relatively small extent to which direct taxes on income reduced the skew in the distribution of income in 1970-71.[4]

[1] *The Times*, 11 June 1966.

[2] Description of Hay-MSL Ltd Survey by Rudolph Klein and David Howarth in the *Observer*, 4 December 1966.

[3] *Top Salaries in the Private Sector and Nationalized Industries*, National Board for Prices and Incomes, HMSO, March 1969, Table 16, p.62.

[4] cf. Table 6.12.

Table 6.2

Personal Incomes in Britain 1970-71

Range of Annual Income before Tax	Proportion of All Incomes (above exemption limits)	Proportion of Total Amount of:		
		Income before Tax	Taxes paid on Incomes	Income after Tax
£	%	%	%	%
420-999	32.1	14.7	7.6	16.4
1000-1499	26.8	21.4	16,7	22.6
1500-1999	20.1	22.6	19.4	23.3
2000-4999	19.5	33.1	37.4	32.1
5000-9999	1.3	5.4	10.2	4.2
10000 and over	0.3	2.8	8.7	1.4

Total number of
incomes (thousands)   21,368
Total amount (£ million)   33,005   6,158   26,847

Source: Calculated from: Board of Inland Revenue *The Survey of Personal Incomes 1970-71*, Table 1.

Returning to incomes before tax, we can see from Table 6.3 how the shape of the income distribution has changed slightly in the later 1950s and 1960s.[1]

Table 6.3

The Distribution of Personal Incomes before Tax in the U.K. 1954-1970

Highest Incomes	Cumulative Proportion of Total Personal Income:			
	1954-5	1959-60	1964-5	1969-70
	%	%	%	%
1%	8.6	8.4	7.5	6.6
5%	19.4	18.5	18.1	16.6
10%	27.9	27.9	26.5	25.3
50%	76.3	72.0	71.5	71.7

Source: Calculated from *Annual Abstract of Statistics*, 105, 1968, Table 327; *Inland Revenue Statistics 1972*, Table 57.

[1] Some of the problems of evaluating these figures are referred to in A.R.Prest and T.Stark, who describe a similar trend, 'Some Aspects of Income Distribution in the U.K. since World War II', *Manchester School*, 35, 1967, pp.217-44;

There was a slight but nonetheless obvious and steepening decline in the proportion of personal income accounted for by the very highest incomes in the period 1954-70. This should perhaps more properly be understood, of course, as a relative improvement in the incomes in the lower ranges in this period. After 1965 however, it would seem that the change was limited to the top half of the income distribution though the levelling out at the bottom of the distribution of pre-tax incomes is partly to be explained by the raising of the exemption limit. In 1969 weekly incomes between £5.25 and £6.35 were no longer included in the survey and as we cannot be certain how many of these there were we shall have to wait a year or two to see if the slow trend toward a more equal distribution fully re-establishes itself.[1]

Investment Income

Many people have some capital or savings and earn interest from investment. In most cases, however, as we have noted, this is only a small proportion of their total income. The 1971 Family Expenditure Survey found that 52 per cent of all households had some income form investments if we take into account Post Office Savings Banks, money in a bank or building society as well as rents and dividends on stocks and shares. The average weekly income per household from all such sources together was £1.40.[2]

Above the mean level of incomes the proportion derived from property sharply increases. As the figures in Table 6.4 show, it is to the very richest that the lion's share of income from property accrues and it is amongst these largest incomes that the proportion of 'unearned income' is greatest. The accumulation of wealth it would seem is self-sustaining. It is not the result of savings from the salaries even of the highest paid. As A.J. Merrett concluded from his 1967 survey of directors' incomes '. . . the probability of the director ever achieving disposable wealth greater than about twice his before-tax salary are [sic] relatively small. In fact, less than one-third of salaried and professional directors ever achieve this small distinction.'[3] It is clear that the large fortunes of the present day are still usually founded on inherited wealth.[4]

[1] The exemption limit was again raised in 1970 and 1974.

[2] *Family Expenditure Survey for 1971*, Appendix 2, HMSO, 1972.

[3] A.J.Merrett, *Executive Remuneration in the United Kingdom*, Longman, 1968, p.41.

[4] See also C.D.Harbury, 'Inheritance and the Distribution of Personal Wealth in Britain', *Economic Journal*, 1962, 72, pp.845-68, reprinted as ch.19 in A.B.Atkinson (ed.), *Wealth, Income and Inequality*, Penguin, 1973, pp.323-47, and C.D.Harbury and P.C.McMahon, 'Intergenerational Wealth Transmission and the Characteristics of Top Wealth Leavers in Britain', ch.7 in Philip Stanworth and Anthony Giddens, *Elites and Power in British Society*, Cambridge, 1974.

Table 6.4 shows the distribution of personal income from property, i.e. rents, dividends and interest, as indicated by the Board of Inland Revenue's annual survey for 1971. I should emphasize that it is personal income which is being considered in this chapter so that the income of companies or public bodies from corporate property is not represented here. Some critics of the Board's estimates attribute such income to individual owners but this seems to me, as well as to many investors, a rather doubtful procedure which prejudges many of the most important arguments about the role of property ownership in contemporary society.[1] The first set of percentages in the table shows the proportion of all those with any property income whose total income, either from their investment or any other sources whatever, together falls within each range.

Table 6.4

Personal Income from Investment 1970-71

Range of annual net income before tax	Proportion of investment incomes in each range of total income	Proportion of all investment income	Proportion of all income in each range derived from investment
£	%	%	%
420-999	31.2	11.3	4.9
1000-1499	23.8	10.7	3.2
1500-1999	21.8	12.6	3.4
2000-4999	18.3	29.7	5.8
5000-9999	3.9	19.1	23.1
10000 and over	1.0	16.6	38.2

Number of investment incomes	4,895,300
Total income from investment (£ million)	2,117

Source: Calculated from *The Survey of Personal Incomes* 1970-71, Tables 1, 34 and 35.

The second set of figures refers to the proportion of all investment income which accrues to individuals whose total income, including that from other sources, lies within each range; while the third column shows the proportion of all personal income in each range deriving from property.

[1] See e.g. Meacher, 'Wealth: Labour's Achilles Heel', in Townsend and Bosanquet (eds), *Labour and Inequality*, Fabian Society, 1972; and cf. Alex Rubner, *The Ensnared Shareholder*, Macmillan, 1965.

For a number of technical reasons[1], but principally in omitting capital gains, the table may underestimate the skew in the distribution of income from property.

Income from property as a proportion of all personal income declined substantially after the Second World War. In 1938 rents, dividends and interest accounted for 22.4 per cent of the total United Kingdom personal income from all sources but only 13 per cent in 1946, falling to nine per cent in 1956. After 1961 the proportion rose, reaching 12 per cent in 1966, but fell again to 10.4 per cent in 1971. This proportionate decline is mainly to be accounted for by the much larger proportion of total personal income deriving from employment, in the region of 72 per cent since the early 1950s compared with only 61 per cent in 1938.[2] The ownership of property thus plays a less important part than it did while earnings from employment together with national insurance and other welfare benefits represent an increasing proportion of the social distribution of income.[3] This seems to be part of a long-term trend going back to the beginning of the industrial revolution. Soltow has shown however that for two centuries the pace of change was glacier slow and that it was mainly since the First World War that there has been any substantial decrease in inequality.[4] As these more recent figures indicate the upheavals of the Second World War gave some further impetus to the trend whose progress in peacetime has been slower and less certain.

We may infer from the increasing role of employment and welfare benefits in the social distribution of income as against property ownership that there has been some change in the nature of class relations over this period. We may provisionally assume, though it will be necessary at least to consider a much wider range of evidence, that as the importance of property ownership may have declined, Britain has therefore become a less rigidly stratified society. It may be on the other hand, simply that in a changing society the crucial dimensions of inequality have shifted elsewhere. At the same time we must not underestimate the continuing

---

[1] cf. John Hughes, 'The Increase in Inequality', *New Statesman*, 8 November 1968, p.620, who applies Meade's formula: ref. J.E.Meade, *Efficiency, Equality and the Ownership of Property*, Allen and Unwin, 1964, ch.2.

[2] *National Income and Expenditure 1963, 1972*, Table 2, and cf. A.J.Walsh, 'Tax Allowances and Fiscal Policy', pp.224-6 in Townsend and Bosanquet (eds), op.cit., 1972.

[3] National Insurance benefits and other payments from public authorities as a proportion of total personal income increased from 5.5 per cent in 1938 to 10.2 per cent in 1971, the remaining component of the distribution also involving to some degree an element of capital ownership, namely income from self-employment, declined from 12.8 per cent to 8.5 per cent as a proportion of total personal income in this period.

[4] L.Soltow, 'Long-Run Changes in British Income Inequality', *Economic History Review*, 1968, 21, pp.17-29, reprinted as ch. 5 in Atkinson, *Wealth, Income and Inequality*, Penguin, 1973, pp. 83-98.

significance of property ownership in a market economy. Property in private hands, as Meade suggests, confers power on the individual owners which has consequences which reach beyond the market place. It remains true that the ownership of wealth is highly concentrated and as a comparison of Table 6.4 with Table 6.2 makes clear, even on the evidence of income tax returns, the distribution of income from property is very much more skewed towards the top than the distribution of income as a whole. The parable of the talents – the one that concludes 'unto every one that hath shall be given'[1] – could easily be mistaken for a shrewd observation on property ownership in a modern economy.

Thus while on the one hand the changing structure of British society has led to a reduction in the importance of property ownership as a source of income as compared with the 1930s and before, private property in a form and in quantities sufficient to produce a substantial income remains highly concentrated. About 500,000 people, one per cent of the population, own just over a third of all private wealth in contemporary Britain and receive just over half of all the personal income derived from the possession of wealth. Within this stratum a smaller group of the very rich numbering about 12,600 owns property which produces for each of them £10,000 per annum or more before tax.[2] This group which, with dependent relatives should amount to fewer than 50,000 people or less than 0.1 per cent of the population, is numerically much too small to show up in most statistical accounts of the population. Some, especially the more flamboyant of them, may be familiar as individuals through the mass media's accounts of public occasions or private indulgences. Their importance however goes beyond the entertainment they provide, intentionally or otherwise, for the rest of the population. They are, in virtue of the rights by definition inherent in property as such, and the power which such resources necsssarily confer, a very significant element, as it were a keystone of the whole social structure. We shall return to further consideration of them in a later chapter.

Earned Income

From the propertied élite, the keystone, let us turn to the rest of the social structure. Maintaining the conventional distinction between income from the ownership of property, or investment income, on the one hand and earned income on the other, a term which may refer to income from employment, self-employment or pensions and other welfare benefits; as we have already seen the great bulk of society, its abutments and buttresses, is almost entirely supported on its earned income. For the majority investment income plays little or no part.

[1] Matthew, XXV, 29.

[2] *The Survey of Personal Incomes 1970-71*, Tables 34 and 35

Several sources of information are available on the distribution of earned income. Tax-based figures may be the most reliable but for making comparisons between different occupations or social strata the Department of Employment and its predecessors' surveys and various independent academic studies are more useful. Here again it is not changes in the absolute amounts of income which are most significant in showing social change or the lack of it but changes or lack of change in the income levels of the various social strata relatively to one another. A number of studies in fact testify to a great deal of inertia in relative income distributions over quite long periods. Thatcher, for example, showed that, though by the middle 1960s the earnings of male manual workers had increased to almost 16 times what they were in 1886, over that period the dispersion of earnings had remained remarkably stable.[1] It may be that though differentials in wage rates have perhaps narrowed there has been an increased opportunity for the more skilled to increase their earnings through overtime, piece rates and so forth. Routh's analysis based on wage rates over the period 1913-1960 does show that skilled manual working men lost some ground relative to other workers after the 1930s while semi- and unskilled manual working men maintained their position. Overall, however, Routh's

> 'most impressive finding was the rigidity of the inter-class and inter-occupational relationships . . . the average for semi-skilled men was 86 per cent of the all class average in 1913 and 85 per cent in 1960, for unskilled men, the percentage was the same in both years. The woman's average was 63 per cent of the all class average in 1913 and 64 per cent in 1960.'[2]

This is not to say that there have not been important changes in the relative distribution of income during the period since the First World War, but these have been surprisingly few and have not occurred smoothly or regularly over that whole period.

> 'During the half century', Routh concludes, 'the only really big changes have been the decline in the differential for professionals, clerks and foremen between 1935 and 1955 and for skilled manual workers between 1913 and 1924. The fall in the relative position of the professionals was substantial and affected both men and women; 1955 found them at between 60 and 70 per cent of their relative position in 1935. Between 1955 and 1960, however, they showed some gain.'[3]

[1] A.R.Thatcher, 'The Distribution of Earnings of Employees in Great Britain', *Journal of Royal Statistical Society*, Series A, vol. 131, 1968, pp.133-80.

[2] Guy Routh, *Occupation and Pay in Britain 1906-1960*, NIESR Economic and Social Studies XXIV, Cambridge, 1965, p.x.

[3] Routh, op.cit., 1965, p.106.

This recent gain was a little greater for the lower professions (e.g. teachers, social welfare workers etc.) than the higher (e.g. doctors, lawyers), but the decline of their relative income advantage since the 1930s was the greater. This is no doubt associated with the growth in these occupations in the intervening period. The higher professions remained the best paid group in 1960 with about three times the all-class average income, closely followed by managers and administrators whose relative position had changed little since 1935 and had improved since 1913. Male clerical workers, though holding their relative position in the later 1950s, according to Routh seemed to be less well paid than skilled manual workers in 1960 and had lost a great deal of ground since 1935 while women clerical workers had been relatively improving their earnings.[1]

Routh nevertheless argues that the evidence he has assembled does not support the view that there is an inherent tendency for income differences to decrease gradually within an industrial economy. The reductions in the degree of inequality of pay have occurred '. . . suddenly, within short periods and owing to an extraordinary conjuncture of circumstances. In intervening periods, egalitarian tendencies have disappeared or been reversed.'[2] He describes the circumstances in which major changes in pay structure occurred in the present century.

'There were three periods between 1913 and 1960 when this occurred in the form of a general narrowing of differentials: 1914-1920, 1934-1944 (in particular, 1938-1940) and 1951-1955. Between 1920 and 1924, there was a drastic widening of differentials so that, by the latter year, the pre-war position had generally been regained. After 1955, there was again a reversal of the narrowing process'.[3]

Figures published by the Department of Employment confirm Routh's estimation that after 1955 income differentials at first tended to widen. In the 1960s however, they indicate another reversal of this trend. Table 6.5 outlines these movements. Until 1961, though the incomes of both manual workers and salaried employees (white collar workers) were improving, salaries moved ahead faster than either weekly wage rates or even the average weekly earnings of manual workers. Manual workers' average weekly earnings have generally been somewhat higher than their weekly wage rates as it has been possible for many workers to improve on their basic wage through piece rates, bonus payments and overtime in a period of fairly high levels of employment. After 1961 the manual workers' weekly earnings rose faster than salary earnings, especially those of clerical workers. By 1967 the ground lost by manual workers after 1955 had been regained, and by 1968 the earnings of manual workers taken together were

[1] Ibid., Table 48, p.107.
[2] Ibid.
[3] Ibid.

increasing faster than those of salaried workers taken together. Thus the figures for 1970, when the series was discontinued, show manual workers' average weekly earnings ahead of salaries and suggest therefore some greater degree of income equality than in 1955. In some ways however, this may be statistically, if not also politically, misleading.

These indices for salaries and wage earnings of course refer to proportional increases. It is self-evident, as even the government's economic advisers have lately realized, that when salaries are on average higher than wages an equal proportional increase will represent a larger addition to salary earnings in absolute terms. Thus while money incomes have been increasing it follows that, except where income growth has been completely offset by inflation, proportionately equal improvements may imply a widening of the difference in actual income levels between the better and the worse paid.

Table 6.5

Prices, Salaries, Wages and Earnings

In October	Prices	Salaries	Average 1955 = 100 All manual workers	
			Average Weekly Earnings	Weekly Rates of Wages
1955	100.0	100.0	100.0	100.0
1960	113.9	133.4	130.1	123.7
1965	135.6	178.4	174.8	151.2
1970	169.3	251.6	259.2	207.4

Source: Department of Employment *Statistics on Incomes, Prices and Production*, Table B.1, and *Gazette*, Table 129. These series now discontinued.

There are in any case, unfortunately, a number of problems which arise in interpreting such figures. These indices are based on the earnings of men and women of all ages and may for that reason be somewhat misleading. Hamilton has pointed out that the large-scale employment of women and girls in the lower paid 'white-collar' jobs can depress salary earnings averages. In addition the inclusion of young employees usually paid at lower rates than adults creates difficulties in making comparisons between occupational groups. Hamilton considers that this misrepresents the dynamics of the earning situation by masking marked differences in the typical career patterns of manual and non-manual workers. Young white-collar workers, unlike young manual workers, will generally be at the beginning of an incremental salary scale and can expect their incomes to increase automatically year by year.[1] In a study of workers in manufacturing industry, Wedderburn and Craig found that between 80 and 90 per cent of non-manual workers could reasonably expect an annual rise compared with only about 20 per cent of manual workers.[2] The New Earnings Survey shows that manual workers' median earnings rise with age at first but reach their peak for men in their thirties, while the earnings of non-manual workers go on rising until they reach their forties. For both groups earnings decline in later life but the decline not only starts sooner but is steeper for manual workers. Median earnings are highest for women manual workers in their twenties but go on rising for women non-manual workers into their fifties.[3] The inclusion of young workers adds a further distorting element to the comparison since during the 1950s and 1960s the earnings of young workers increased at a faster rate than adults' earnings.[4]

Though more detailed tabulations are available distinguishing the earnings of men and women and salaried and wage earners, inconsistencies in the coverage of the various regular surveys on which they are based have made comparisons between different occupational groups hazardous. After 1968 the New Earnings Surveys of the Department of Employment provide much more detailed information on earnings in various occupations with subdivisions by age and sex. Sufficiently reliable comparisons between broad occupational strata which go back to 1962 can be made on the basis of the Family Expenditure Survey. This is carried out annually by the Government Social Survey for the Department of Employment and reports on a three-stage stratified random sample of over 10,000 households in Great Britain. Sampling households provides more sociologically meaningful information on the distribution of incomes and expenditure than any other source. Thatcher has shown that data on earnings in the survey tend to under-represent highest incomes slightly, as there is a relatively poor and erratic response rate amongst men earning in 1966 more than £50 per week.[5] Presumably some people are too busy getting and spending to complete the survey schedules. The survey-based estimates, despite this, compare very closely with national income

[1] See Richard Hamilton, 'The Income Difference: Skilled and White-collar Workers', *British Journal of Sociology*, XIV, 4, 1963, pp.363-73.

[2] Dorothy Wedderburn and Christine Craig, *Men in Manufacturing Industry*, Department of Applied Economics, Cambridge, 1969; Dorothy Wedderburn 'Workplace Inequality', *New Society*, 9 April 1970.

[3] *Social Trends*, 3, 1972, p.89. Prest and Stark pointed out that income differentials increase with age, being greatest among the over-65s. The ageing of the population therefore serves to maintain inequalities of income distribution op.cit., 1967, 238-9.

[4] *Annual Abstract of Statistics*, 105, 1968, Table 149; 109, 1972, Table 161; *Social Trends*, 3, 1972, Table 36.

[5] A.R.Thatcher, 'The Distribution of Earnings of Employees in Great Britain', *Journal of Royal Statistical Society*, Series A, vol. 131, 1968, pp.133-80.

statistics and can therefore be assumed to give a reasonably accurate account of the distribution of earnings. The quality of information from the Family Expenditure Survey was improved still further in 1967 when the size of the sample was doubled, so that since then, after sample losses and non-response, information has been available for over 7,000 households every year compared with about 3,200 for earlier years. The Family Expenditure Survey permits us to compare the earnings of individuals in different occupational groups for the period since 1963 and the incomes of households headed by workers in different groups since 1962. To pursue the question of the convergence of incomes in the 1960s we can compare the weekly earnings of men in full-time employment in the period after 1963.

Table 6.6

Median Weekly Earnings* of Men in Full-time Employment
U.K. 1963-71

	Amount in:			Increase		Percentage Increases	
	1963	1967	1971	63-67	67-71	63-67	67-71
	£	£	£	£	£	%	%
Manual Workers (inc. Shop Assistants)	15.03	19.72	27.77	4.69	8.05	31.02	40.08
Clerical Workers	16.35	20.35	28.64	4.00	8.29	24.05	40.07
Managerial, Administrative, Professional and Technical Workers (inc. Teachers)	23.82	28.75	40.15	4.93	11.40	20.07	39.07

*Median earnings in each group are lower than the mean earnings and median differences between groups are smaller than mean differences. The median is, however, a less misleading statistic when considering convergence.

Source: 1963 figures from Thatcher, *op.cit.*, Table 2; 1967 and 1971, from *Family Expenditure Surveys* for 1967, Table 32, and for 1971, Table 36.

Table 6.6 shows the progress of weekly earnings steepening with the increase in money incomes in the later 1960s. It is at once obvious that the earnings of manual workers have increased faster than those of the other two groups, though in the later 1960s the managerial and clerical earnings increased at almost the same rate as those of manual workers. On the other hand though the slowest proportionate increase was in the earnings of the Managerial and Professional group these nevertheless increased by the greatest amount in absolute terms and their advantage has lately been increasing. In the earlier period represented in the table, clerical workers' earnings increased least in absolute terms, but some of their lost ground *vis-à-vis* manual workers appears to have been regained after 1968. Their median income in 1967 was still somewhat higher than that of manual workers.[1] After 1963, then, there was a convergence between the incomes of manual and clerical workers at least until 1968, although thereafter they have regained some of their former advantage. On the other hand it is hard to maintain that there has been any convergence between the earnings of manual workers and those of managerial and professional groups who, despite a slower rate of increase before 1967, have throughout obtained greater absolute increases. Even in terms of proportional increase, as the overall Department of Employment figures (Table 6.5) show, if they show anything, the average weekly earnings of manual workers were increasing more slowly than salaries as a whole for over ten years until the later 1960s. They did not begin to improve on their relative position in 1955 until 1967. Of course structural factors render these gross comparisons hazardous. Changes in the numbers of young workers, an increasing proportion of women working generally on lower rates of pay and the tendency on the part of men towards earlier retirements as well as the changing proportions in different types of manual and non-manual employment (see Chapter 5) should all be taken into account. With the comparison of the earnings of full-time men summarized in Table 6.6 we are on surer ground. In fact, we find there that the picture revealed by the general movements of wage-earnings and salaries is broadly confirmed. The data for full-time men shows that the relative gains of manual workers were short-lived. Already by 1968, before the real take-off into inflation got under way, it would seem that income convergence had come to an end.

The three periods of narrowing differentials identified in Routh's analysis have the common characteristic of a higher rate of inflation. 'For

---

[1] It is true that in this comparison the inclusion of shop assistants with low median earnings for full-time men (see Tables 6.7 and 6.8) might be considered to exaggerate manual/non-manual differences. On the other hand the Survey's category of Manual Workers includes foremen, whose incomes in general seem to be higher than most manual workers, and who, Hamilton has argued (loc.cit.), should properly be considered as non-manual workers. In terms of their market situation, 'shop assistants would seem to be working class but their assignment is debatable.

the period 1914-1920, the average annual rise in the cost of living index was nearly 17 per cent; for 1935-1942, 6.2 per cent; for 1950-1955, 5.1 per cent. In the periods 1944-1950 and 1956-1960, when dispersion was stable or widening, the rise in prices was more moderate; 3.7 per cent and 2.7 per cent per year, respectively'.[1] The period of convergence in the 1960s — roughly between 1962 and 1967 — was in several respects different from these, therefore. There was throughout a continuing rise in the retail price index but when this began to steepen into the inflation of the late sixties and early seventies it seems that earnings differentials began to widen again.[2]

Not the least unusual feature of the situation at the beginning of the 1970s then, was that in a seriously inflationary period income differentials were widening.[3] The first three periods of inflation mentioned however, coincide of course with the First World War, the Second World War and the Korean War.[4] In wartime unemployment falls as industrial production rises and the armed forces absorb an increased proportion of society's available manpower resources. As a result it seems of this increased demand for labour the political and economic bargaining power of the industrial workers is improved as compared with other occupational groups. Even the social prestige of the working class is enhanced at such times though, it may be observed, the improvement is bought very dear. In the most recent period of inflation when neither industrial investment nor an increasing demand for labour have played a primary part, by contrast, income differentials both before and especially after tax have been widening.

If we examine the dispersion of incomes within each occupational group two things are apparent (see Table 6.7). Firstly the difference between the highest and lowest incomes of clerical and manual workers is similar, but the dispersion of earnings in the professional and managerial group is much wider and more skewed and, to that extent, the comparison of median earnings we have just made should be treated with some caution. Secondly the overlap between different occupational groups is

---

[1] Routh, op.cit., 1965, p.107.

[2] Between January 1962 and the end of 1967 the Retail Price Index increased by an average of 3.0 per cent per year. Between 1967 and 1971 it rose by 7.1 per cent per year, rising steadily from an increase of 4.7 per cent in 1967-68 to 9.4 per cent in 1970-71; see *Annual Abstract of Statistics*, 109, 1972, Table 403.

[3] See H.A.Turner, Dudley Jackson and F.H.Wilkinson, *Do Trade Unions Cause Inflation?*, Cambridge University Department of Applied Economics, C.U.P., 1972, pp.63 ff.

[4] The American war in Indo-China in the latest period may, through its effects on the United States' balance of payments and international trade, have had some effects on the British economy, but not such as would result from direct involvement. While it should be taken into account as a possibly exacerbating factor, the inflation of the late sixties and early seventies would seem to arise primarily from other causes.

considerable, especially if we compare clerical and manual workers. This is one of the facts which has been used in support of the 'embourgeoisement thesis', the argument that is, that the working class is becoming indistinguishable from at least the lower middle class. Although clerical workers are on average slightly better off the evidence clearly indicates a considerable amount of similarity in weekly incomes between them and manual workers. As we have seen however this seems to be the result of the relatively slow increase in earnings of the lower paid white collar workers in the late 1950s and the earlier 1960s when compared with other groups above and below. It may be that it is more plausible to construe these figures as an indication of the 'proletarianization' of the clerical workers rather than the embourgeoisement of the working class. This is a question we will return to in the next chapter. The more affluent members of the middle class, the professional and managerial group, have not lagged in the increase of earnings in this period, and though the interval between the upper and lower quartiles in their earnings distribution is almost double that of the manual workers, nevertheless, fewer than 10 per cent of all manual workers earn more than the median income of the professional and managerial group.

Table 6.7

Dispersion of Weekly Earnings of Full-Time Men Employees 1971

	Professional, Technical, Administrative, Managerial and Teaching Occupations	Clerks	Shop Assistants	Manual Workers
	£	£	£	£
Lower quartile	31.4	23.9	18.5	22.8
Median	40.1	28.6	24.0	27.8
Upper quartile	52.9	36.0	29.3	34.1
Number of men in each group	1,008	391	34	2,893

Source: *Family Expenditure Survey for 1971*, Table 36.

The Prices and Incomes Board concluded in 1971 that workers in lower paid industries were faring less well than other manual workers. These workers are less likely to be organised than other sections of the manual labour force and the unions seem not to have been very successful in improving the relative position of the lower paid workers. An analysis by the Board showed that in 106 industries and services, each with over 10,000 workers and ranked by the lowest national wage rates for adult male manual workers in force immediately before the latest increase up to the end of December 1970, settlements were at a lower level and at less frequent intervals for the lowest ranking industries.[1]

Table 6.8

Size of Latest Settlement up to December 31st 1970 and Time since Previous Settlement in Industries ranked by Level of Weekly Wage Rates

Weekly Wage Rates in Industry	Adult Male Manual Workers		
	Latest Gross Increase	Time since Last Increase	Implied Annual Average Rate of Increase
	%	Months	%
Lowest quarter	9.7	21.5	5.4
Third quarter	11.2	12.8	10.5
Second quarter	11.8	9.9	14.3
Highest quarter	9.5	8.6	13.2

Source: NBPI, op.cit., Table H, p.16.

Though the NBPI analysis refers to nationally negotiated wage rates their conclusions are confirmed by an examination of dispersion data for earnings which can be drawn from the Family Expenditure Survey figures such as those we looked at in Table 6.7. The evidence is, however, conflicting, as the New Earnings Survey for 1971 shows little or no change in the dispersion of earnings for either manual or non-manual men in full-time employment between 1968 and 1971[2], while as Table 6.9 shows, calculation from the Family Expenditure Surveys for those years produces quite a different picture. For each occupational group the inter-quartile range of earnings increased between 1968 and 1971. Despite the much larger sample size in the New Earnings Survey[3] the consistency of these figures in the table with the evidence on wages settlements from the NBPI gives some ground for accepting them even while the more direct discrepancy remains to puzzle us.

[1] National Board for Prices and Incomes, General Problems of Low Pay, H.M.S.O., 1971, pp.14-17 and 41-3.

[2] Department of Employment, New Earnings Survey 1971, H.M.S.O., 1972, Table 2, p.31.

[3] 96,000 full-time men in a total sample of over 170,000 – ibid., p.14.

Table 6.9

Dispersion of Weekly Earnings of Full-time Men
Employees 1968-71

		Lower Quartile	Median	Upper Quartile
Professional, Technical, Administrative, Manager-	1968	79.4	100.0	131.4
ial and Teaching	1971	78.3	100.0	131.9
Clerks	1968	84.0	100.0	122.8
	1971	83.6	100.0	125.9
Shop Assistants	1968	83.2	100.0	115.1
	1971	77.1	100.0	122.1
Manual Workers	1968	82.2	100.0	119.0
	1971	82.0	100.0	122.7

Source: Calculated from *Family Expenditure Survey for 1968*, Table 34, and *Family Expenditure Survey for 1971*, Table 36.

These figures further plausibly suggest that what was true of comparisons between occupational groups after 1968 was also true within them, namely, that income differentials were widening.

Households

The Family Expenditure Survey also produces information which enables us to make fairly detailed comparisons between broad occupational groups in terms of either individual or household earnings. Schumpeter has argued that it is the family that is the unit of social class rather than the individual. 'Class membership for the individual is ascribed.'[1] This has been echoed by R.M. Titmuss, Frank Parkin and by J.H. Goldthorpe who, discussing the re-distribution of wealth within families, observes '. . . it is, of course, the family, not the individual, that must be regarded as the basic unit of stratification'.[2] In empirical studies on stratification this important point is very rarely considered as the atomistic individualism of most survey research methodology subtly imposes itself upon the theoretical interpretation of what the sociologist observes. Though strictly speaking it

[1] 'Social Classes in an Ethnically Homogeneous Environment', in J.Schumpeter, *Imperialism and Social Classes*, Meridian Books, 1955, p.113.

[2] See R.M.Titmuss, op.cit., 1962, p.198; Frank Parkin *Class Inequality and Political Order*, MacGibbon and Kee, 1971 p.14; and J.H.Goldthorpe 'Social Structure in Industrial Society' in Paul Halmos (ed.), *Sociological Review Monograph No.8*, 1964, note 20, p.119, reprinted in R.Bendix and S.M.Lipset (eds), *Class, Status and Power* Routledge, 2nd Edition, 1967, pp.648-59, and in Celia Heller (ed.), *Structured Social Inequality*, Collier-Macmillan, 1969, pp.452-64.

describes households rather than families, the Family Expenditure Survey data, from this point of view, has an advantage over that from any other official source.

In comparing families in different social classes the usual convention is to assign them to the appropriate group according to the occupation of the head of household, that member who owns or is responsible for the rent of the family's accommodation. This is generally the senior working man. When we compare family earnings with those of men in full-time employment (Table 6.10) it seems that differences in the men's earnings are not evened out by the additional earnings of other members of the family or by income from other sources. On the contrary other family income in addition to the chief bread winner's earnings apparently contributes more to the family incomes of the better paid. And this is the case even when comparing clerical employees and manual workers.

Table 6.10

Median Weekly Earnings of Households* and Men 1971

	Median Household Earnings	Median Weekly Earnings of Full-time Men	Difference
	£	£	£
Professional, Technical, Administrative, Managerial and Teaching Occupations	52.9	40.1	12.8
Clerks	38.8	28.6	10.2
Shop Assistants	25.3	24.0	1.3
Manual Workers	37.3	27.8	9.5
Retired or Unoccupied	13.8	—	—

*Classified by occupational grouping of head of household.

Source: *Family Expenditure Survey for 1971*, Tables 48, 36.

If then we compare, as for the most part we have done, the earnings of individuals instead of whole families, we are likely to underestimate the differences between social classes rather than exaggerate them. In other words, figures on the earnings of individuals obscure some of the real difference in living standards which people experience in the course of real day-to-day life in Britain today.

Poverty

At the lower margin of the distribution of income we are faced with the question of poverty. If one cannot make one's money last through the week without going hungry or if there is not enough to pay for the heating to keep one from shivering in the winter months there is no question about poverty: it is all too real. The more affluent inquirer however finds it necessary to demarcate the limits of poverty somehow. There is however no amount of income which would be generally accepted as 'just enough'. Even for families of similar size and composition needs are given different priorities and even similar needs will be met in different ways. Since the pioneering surveys of the extent of poverty in the late nineteenth century, by Booth in London and Rowntree in York,[1] many attempts have been made to define an absolute minimum standard below which a family's income would clearly be inadequate to sustain physical health. In addition to the families in this state of 'primary poverty', Rowntree pointed out the existence of many more suffering perhaps equal hardships not entirely as a result of their low incomes or large numbers of children but either because of other demands on their resources or because they spent inexpertly, not getting value for money, or perhaps unwisely on strong drink or other luxuries. In his second York survey[2] Rowntree concluded that despite his earlier attempt in the 1899 survey it was not really feasible to measure this 'secondary poverty' in an objective way. Expenditure patterns indeed are socially determined and the interpretation of necessity in household expenditure is open to considerable variation. When times are hard people will not always sacrifice first those things that an outsider might consider luxuries, beer, fried fish and vinegar, cigarettes, television. They may be clung to the more fiercely because they make the hardships bearable.[3] Standards change through time and vary from subculture to subculture and it seems impossible to define finally and absolutely what is an essential minimum. As Professors Abel-Smith and Townsend remark, 'Saying who is in poverty is to make a relative statement — rather like saying who is short or heavy.'[4]

[1] Charles Booth, *Labour and Life of the People of London*, Macmillan, 1889-1902; B.S.Rowntree, *Poverty: a Study of Town Life*, Macmillan, 1901. Good brief accounts of these studies will be found in D.Caradog Jones, *Social Surveys*, Hutchinson, n.d., chs 4 and 5; and C.A.Moser, *Survey Methods in Social Investigation*, Heinemann, 1958, pp.19-23.

[2] B.S.Rowntree, *Poverty and Progress*, Longmans Green, 1941. There was a third postwar survey of York described in B.S.Rowntree and G.R.Lavers, *Poverty and the Welfare State*, Longmans Green, 1951.

[3] See e.g. George Orwell, *The Road to Wigan Pier*, Left Book Club, 1935, and John Yudkin, op.cit., *The Listener*, 30 January 1969.

[4] Brian Abel-Smith and Peter Townsend, *The Poor and the Poorest: a New Analysis of the Ministry of Labour's Family Expenditure Surveys of 1953-4 and 1960*, Occasional Papers on Social Administration, No.17, G.Bell, London, 1965, p.63.

As an operational definition of poverty, Abel-Smith and Townsend took the National Assistance Benefit scale (after 26 November 1966 national assistance grants were re-styled 'supplementary benefits'). This scale has changed from time to time in accord with how much the government of the day is prepared to set aside in relation to what may be generally considered to be a tolerable minimum level of family income. A statistical consequence of this relativism of course, is that, except where it is matched by increased welfare benefits, a more generous or humane definition of the minimal acceptable standard of provision can make it seem that there are initially more people in poverty than before. In consequence comparisons over time are hazardous. While this social relativism makes not only comparison over time but also between different societies more difficult, it at least avoids the unreality of arbitrary criteria which take no account of changing standards.

Between 1953 and 1960, while the cost of living in Britain increased by about 20 per cent, the National Assistance basic scale increased by almost 44 per cent, but personal income per head for the country as a whole increased by 51 per cent.[1] By this definition those families receiving national assistance benefits were better off in 1960 than before, but their position had worsened in relation to other less impoverished families. Between 1962 and 1971 however, while retail prices increased by 53 per cent and personal income per head for the country as a whole went up by 87 per cent, the basic level of supplementary benefits more than doubled.[2] Over the period of the 1960s, then, it would seem that not only were living standards raised for everyone, including the poorest, but that the gap between them and the rest of society was at least not allowed to widen.

Using a broad definition of a low level of living as income or expenditure at 140 per cent or less of the national assistance scale plus rent or housing costs, Abel-Smith and Townsend estimated that in the U.K. as a whole the total number of people in households at this level had increased between 1953 and 1960 from just under 4 million to nearly 7½ million, that is, from 7.8 per cent to 14.2 per cent of the population, At the same time the number of people who were living on less than the basic assistance scale for their kind of household increased from about 600,000 to almost 2 million.[3] A later discussion of the problem concluded that there were still not less than 2 million and possibly as many as 3 million people living on less than the appropriate Supplementary Benefit scale in

See also Social Science Research Council, *Research on Poverty*, Heinemann, 1968, pp.5-8; Department of Employment and Productivity, *A National Minimum Wage: an Inquiry*, H.M.S.O., 1969, paragraphs 11, 39; Martin Rein, 'Problems in the Definition and Measurement of Poverty', ch.2 in Peter Townsend (ed.), *The Concept of Poverty*, Heinemann, 1970, pp.61-62.

[1] See Abel-Smith and Townsend, op.cit., 1965, p.19.
[2] *Annual Abstract of Statistics*, No. 109, 1972, Tables 403, 57, 308 and 6.
[3] Abel-Smith and Townsend, 1965, p.588.

1967[1] and whatever improvement in the situation followed was painfully slow.[2]

Poverty is a circumstance to which all are not equally exposed. It is the already weakest and most defenceless of the flock who are most likely to fall its prey. Fatherless families, the chronically sick and disabled and the old are obviously vulnerable. In all five areas Hunt and her colleagues surveyed in 1970 about three in every four fatherless families could be considered to be in poverty, especially where the mothers were widowed or unmarried.[3] Turning to the old, in 1971 almost 2,000,000 out of the 8,700,000 people over pensionable age were receiving supplementary pensions and accounted for 70 per cent of all those receiving benefits in that year.[4] This must under-represent the proportions of the problem however. Not all old people who are eligible for supplementary pensions in fact receive them. On the basis of a survey carried out in 1963, the Allen Report[5] concluded that about 500,000 retired householders were apparently eligible for assistance but were not getting it. A further survey of 10,000 pensioners carried out for the MPNI[6] estimated that some 700,000 pensioner households in the country as a whole were eligible for assistance but not receiving it in the summer of 1965. About a quarter of a million pensioner households were in fact living appreciably below the National Assistance Board's standards in that year while the remainder were helped out by their relatives or other people. About a third of those not receiving the benefits they were entitled to did not know of the help they could get or misunderstood the situation in some way. The remainder were fairly evenly divided between those who said they were managing all right on what they had and those who were too proud to seek what they

[1] A.B. Atkinson, *Poverty in Britain and the Reform of Social Security*, Department of Applied Economics, Cambridge, 1969. Atkinson writes (p.38): 'It seems fair to conclude that the proportion of the population with incomes below the National Assistance/Supplementary Benefit Scale lies towards the upper end of the range 4%-9%. In other words, around 5 million people are living below the standard which the Government feels to be the national minimum. If we allow for the sharing of income among members of a household, then the number whose actual living standard is below the poverty line is probably rather smaller, although not less than 2 million.'

[2] See Editor's Note, Table 4 in A.B. Atkinson (ed.), *Wealth, Income and Inequality*, Penguin 1973, p.371.

[3] Audrey Hunt, Judith Fox and Margaret Morgan, *Families and their Needs*, H.M.S.O., 1973, vol.I, pp.33-6.

[4] *Annual Abstract of Statistics*, No. 109, 1972, Table 58.

[5] *Report of the Committee of Inquiry into the Impact of Rates on Households*, Cmnd. 2582, H.M.S.O., 1965.

[6] Ministry of Pensions and National Insurance, *The Financial and Other Circumstances of Retirement Pensioners*, H.M.S.O., 10 June 1966.

considered charity.[1] With the proportion of the population over retirement age growing at a faster rate than any other this is likely to prove a growing problem. But the global problem of poverty is much greater than even these estimates suggest. Poverty in contemporary Britain is not only a consequence of reduced income after retirement: while 70 per cent of all households receiving supplementary benefits and four out of five of all those households with incomes below the supplementary benefit level are pensioner households, pensioners only account for about half of all the individuals whose standard of living fell below this level in the later 1960s.

Among the economically active the needs of a young family may for a time reduce living standards. Incapacity for work through illness or accident as well as unemployment and other family crises, the chronic sickness of a dependent or the separation of a husband and wife may strain financial resources to or beyond the limit.[2] It is evident besides that the low level of earnings in some jobs and the consequent operation of the 'wage-stop' rule on sickness, unemployment and supplementary benefits was responsible for roughly half of the poverty of the 1960s, measured in terms of the number of individuals living on less than the minimum fixed by the level of supplementary benefits.

In June and July 1966 the then Ministry of Social Security carried out a survey of households in which there were two or more children. They found that in Great Britain as a whole an estimated 345,000 families with at least 1,000,000 children amongst them were living on initial incomes less than the supplementary benefit level.[3] Applying the higher assistance standard introduced later in 1966, Lafitte estimated that there must have been some 1,250,000 children with some 800,000 parents in *initial* poverty at that time.[4] Some 260,000 families, the Ministry estimated, had fathers who were disqualified from receiving supplementary benefits. These men either were in full-time work or receiving an allowance because they were unemployed or sick, but because of the wage-stop could not be paid enough to bridge the gap between their incomes and their needs, measured by supplementary benefit standards.[5] Four-fifths of the men

[1] See P. Townsend, *The Family Life of Old People*, Penguin, 1963, pp.183 and 235 for a moving description of just a few such cases. See also Dorothy Wedderburn, 'A Cross-National Study of Standards of Living of the Aged in Three Countries' in Townsend (ed.), *The Concept of Poverty*, Heinemann, 1970.

[2] See Social Science Research Council, *Research on Poverty*, Heinemann, 1968, pp.8-9.

[3] *Report on the Circumstances of Families*, H.M.S.O., July 1967.

[4] Francois Lafitte, 'Income Deprivation' in Robert Holman (ed.), *Socially Deprived Families in Britain*, National Council of Social Service, Bedford Square Press, 1970, p.29.

[5] ibid. The Supplementary Benefits Commission Report for 1967 noted '. . . the wage-stop is not . . . a cause of family poverty; it is a harsh reflection of the fact that there are many men in work living on incomes below the supplementary benefit standard'.

whose incomes from employment brought them less than the supplementary benefit scale assessment of their needs were manual workers, a
disproportionately large number of them agricultural workers; the
remainder were mainly self-employed. Working from the findings of the
1970 Family Expenditure Survey, the Department of Health and Social
Security, as it had become, estimated that in that year there were still over
100,000 families with children where the father was either in full-time
employment or was wage-stopped who were having to live on less than the
appropriate minimum laid down as necessary by the Supplementary
Benefit scale.[1] In her survey of the evidence on this point Judith
Marquand concluded, 'The problem of workers with resources insufficient
for their needs (defined as supplementary benefit rates) is not simply a
problem of large families, of fatherless families, or of ill-health. There are
some male workers in full-time employment in good health and with
relatively small families whose earnings fall below this minimal level'.[2] The
major factor in the generation of poverty in contemporary Britain
therefore remains, as it was at the time of Booth's and Rowntree's studies,
the low level of earnings of those in a weak position within a market
economy. These households not only lack the resources to cope with the
common crises of life, they are trapped in a cycle of impoverishment even
in the ordinary run of circumstances.

The very lowest levels of income are nevertheless mainly encountered
by those with no employment at all.[3] According to the 1971 Family
Expenditure Survey, four out of five of the 2,000,000 households where
the total income was under £15 a week contained no workers and nearly
two thirds were in fact people living alone.[4] For many more families the
experience of poverty is an episode brought on by illness, temporary
unemployment or other circumstances, rather than a permanent condition.
This, on the other hand, only shows the problem of poverty to be an even
greater one than it may at first appear. As Lafitte notes, '. . . the
experience of income deprivation, even in a single year and even if
short-lived, extends much beyond those affected by it at one moment in
time'.[5] About twice as many families have to be assisted in any one year as
will be found to be on Supplementary Benefit at a particular time. Then
there are those who, for one reason or another, are not assisted at all.

[1] Department of Health and Social Security, *Two-Parent Families*, H.M.S.O., 1971.

[2] Judith Marquand, 'Which are the Lower Paid Workers?', *British Journal of
Industrial Relations*, V, November 1967, pp.359-74.

[3] See e.g. Dennis Marsden, 'Fatherless Families on National Assistance' in Townsend
(ed.), op.cit., 1970.

[4] Family Expenditure Survey for 1971, Tables 38, 44 and 45. Of these households
with a weekly income of less than £15 eight per cent included dependent children.
cf. *A National Minimum Wage: An Enquiry*, H.M.S.O., 1969, para.66.

[5] Lafitte, op.cit., 1970, p.34.

The Redistribution of Income

The incidence of taxation and the distribution of welfare benefits of course serve to redress the inequalities of income to some extent. A minimal aim of income redistribution is the amelioration of market forces to bring the distribution of means somewhat more in line with the apparent distribution of needs. The quantification of the process in terms of how much is to be redistributed, in what forms, from whom and to whom is a matter of political decision. As the persistent problem of poverty demonstrates needs will not necessarily be fully met and the reputation the taxation authorities seem to have in some quarters as a kind of bureaucratic Robin Hood is not altogether deserved.

As we have already seen (Table 6.2) the effect of taxes on income is progressive and levels out some of the inequalities in the pre-tax distribution. The effect has been remarkably consistent since the mid-1950s, as Table 6.11 shows.

Table 6.11

*Distribution of Personal Incomes in the United Kingdom
after Tax: 1954-1970*

Cumulative Proportion of Total Personal Income

Highest Incomes	1954-55	1959-60	1964-65	1969-70
	%	%	%	%
1%	4.8	4.8	4.9	4.1
5%	14.6	14.4	14.4	13.5
10%	22.8	23.8	22.6	21.6
50%	69.5	.69.8	69.5	69.6

Source: Board of Inland Revenue: see *Annual Abstract of Statistics*, 105, 1968, Table 327; *Inland Revenue Statistics 1972*, Table 57.

It is interesting to observe how much more stable the proportions here have been than those representing the distribution of personal income before tax shown in Table 6.3 above. Over this period at least it would seem that while the before-tax distribution has changed, the shape of the post-tax distribution has somehow been maintained at least up to the middle 1960s.

The relatively small changes which have become apparent in the later 1960s, as with the distribution of pre-tax incomes, have mostly been the result of the growth of incomes in the middle of the range. Taxes on income alone thus would seem to have had very little, if any, overall redistributive effect. As R.J. Nicholson has commented, 'Indeed if, as is sometimes suggested, certain 'tax avoidance' incomes and other claims on wealth outside personal income have increased over the last decade and are concentrated more among higher income recipients, it is possible that the distribution of incomes on some wider definition may have moved towards greater inequality.'[1]

It is, of course, necessary to consider not just the incidence of direct taxes such as income tax and surtax but of indirect taxes such as purchase tax, tobacco duty and so forth as well as the redistributive effects of direct and indirect benefits. Direct benefits include unemployment and sickness benefits, retirement pensions, family allowances et cetera, while indirect benefits include those attributable to the provision of educational and medical services. Dorothy Wedderburn has reviewed a number of studies of the redistribution of income in Britain since 1945. The overall effect of all taxes and benefits seemed to be, she wrote,'that *horizontal redistribution* was more important than *vertical redistribution* i.e. there was more redistribution from smokers to non-smokers, or from people without children to people with children, rather than from rich to poor in the sense, simply, of income level'.[2]

Many benefits are not related to income level but are nevertheless, in general, much more progressive than taxes. They benefit people with larger families and those in the lower income ranges relatively more because they represent a larger proportion of their total resources. At the same time the taxes paid by the more affluent also provide for benefits received by the more affluent themselves.

From the findings of the Family Expenditure Surveys the Central Statistical Office has been able to make a series of estimates of how all these balance out. In the analysis of results from the 1971 survey[3] it is pointed out that while income tax and surtax are obviously progressive, national insurance and national health contributions and indirect taxes as a whole are regressive inasmuch as the latter absorb a larger proportion of lower incomes than of higher incomes and bear more heavily on large than on small families. In consequence the effect of all taxes taken together is only very slightly progressive.

The evidence on long-term trends is slightly conflicting. After examining the pattern of redistribution between 1961 and 1971 and comparing his findings with those of an earlier study, J.L. Nicholson concluded: 'Professor Barna's estimates for 1937 . . . showed a surprisingly similar

[1] R.J. Nicholson, 'The Distribution of Personal Income', *Lloyds Bank Review*, January 1967, p.18; also reprinted as Reading 6 in A.B. Atkinson, (ed.) *Wealth, Income and Inequality*, Penguin, 1973.

[2] Dorothy Wedderburn, 'Facts and Theories of the Welfare State', Part II, ch. 1 in Ralph Miliband and John Saville (eds), *The Socialist Register 1965*, Merlin Press, 1965.

[3] 'The Incidence of Taxes and Social Service Benefits in 1971', *Economic Trends*, No.229, H.M.S.O., November 1972, p.xi.

degree of inequality of income before and after redistribution, and a similar reduction in inequality from all taxes and benefits, to those shown in recent years'.[1] The high level of unemployment in 1937 compared with the 1960s however, must have contributed substantially to both the degree of original income inequality and, through unemployment benefits, to the amount of redistribution which was made in that year. In the face of the decline in the amount of unemployment since then it is evident that redistribution through other forms of welfare benefits have come to play an increasingly important part, while at the same time other sources of income inequality would appear to have increased. On the other hand, for those in employment however, the National Board for Prices and Incomes concluded that there had been a significant improvement in real net income for those with low earnings, most marked between 1938 and 1960. 'In 1970 the index number for the real net income of a married man with two children under 11 (1938 = 100) was 157 at the median but 176 at the bottom decile.'[2] Notwithstanding the experience of lower paid workers in the later 1960s this may be the result of the longer-term movements in relative earnings I referred to earlier and could possibly owe but little to the incidence of taxes and benefits. Part, at least, of the apparent conflict between these two findings can be resolved if we take into account the structural changes in the population which occurred during the period. The NBPI figures refer to men in similar circumstances but in the population dealt with in Nicholson's comparison a number of factors have probably tended to increase the amount of inequality between different kinds of household. Increasing numbers of women working, the declining age of marriage so that parents of young children are younger and relatively less prosperous and an increase in the proportion of semi-disabled and older people in the working population with low or declining earnings are likely to have had the effect of increasing the inequality which shows up in these comparisons.[3]

In the period between 1961 and 1971 improvements in direct benefits, especially national insurance benefits, have brought about some change. The analysis of 1971 data showed that since 1961 the result of the combined effects of changes in original income and the impact of all taxes and benefits, direct and indirect, was that single adult households of all types and households with three or four children showed considerable gains as compared with other types of household.[4] Vertical redistribution

[1] R.J. Nicholson, 'The Distribution of Personal Income', *Lloyds Bank Review*, Kingdom' in Dorothy Wedderburn (ed.), *Poverty, Inequality and Class Structure'*, Cambridge University Press, 1974, p.81, and cf. T. Barna, *Redistribution of Incomes through Public Finance in 1937*, Clarendon Press, 1945. See also J.L. Nicholson, *Redistribution of Income in the U.K. in 1959, 1957 and 1953*, Bowes and Bowes, 1965.

[2] NBPI, *General Problems of Low Pay*, H.M.S.O., 1971, p.17.

[3] See J.L. Nicholson, op.cit., 1974, pp.85-6.

[4] *Economic Trends*, 229, November 1972, p.xiv and Table 5, pp. xlii-xliv.

— that is between households at different income levels — increased too, but this was just about enough to offset the slight increase in original incomes after 1969. Thus, as Nicholson remarks, 'The degree of inequality of final income remained remarkably constant throughout the whole period 1961-71'.[1]

Whether this stability will continue trhough the 1970s is, of course, essentially a matter of political decision. If, as seems likely, Peter Kaim-Caudle is right that 'the passion for equality is a minority creed',[2] then at the time of writing the majority would seem to be very securely established and far from silent. The relatively small amount of redistribution in Britain up to the 1950s led T.B.Bottomore to the conclusion that, in evidently possessing the power to defend its economic interests, the upper class in Britain 'has maintained itself during the present century as a ruling class'.[3] Whether such an interpretation can be sustained on the evidence presented in this chapter is open to doubt. It is, however, relevant to note here that the distribution of wealth remains highly skewed and the distribution of income, especially after tax, changed very little in the 1950s and 1960s. On the other hand some slow but distinct movements in the distribution of wealth are apparent on the best evidence available to us. This *may* reflect a change taking place in the relations between classes or merely in the usefulness of our data. The balance of plausibilities here can only be judged in the context of a much wider range of evidence.

In the distribution of income the most striking feature of the evidence we have been able to consider is not any of the small changes which occur from time to time but the long-term stability of the overall pattern. In a society where more and more we measure things in terms of money values, however, we must be especially careful about inferring too much from figures of this kind. Some of the stability in income distributions is certainly illusory. It is the result of applying simple measures to complex phenomena and reflects the accidental product of a number of unrelated changes. Some of these are the achievement of actions on the part of interest groups or of particular measures taken by governments; others are the indirect consequences of change in the population and economy.

---

[1] J.L. Nicholson, op.cit., 1974, p.78.

[2] In Townsend and Bosanquet (eds.), op.cit., 1972, p.160.

[3] T.B.Bottomore, *Elites and Society*, 1964, p.35; cf. John Strachey, *Contemporary Capitalism*, 1956, pp.150-51.

7 Some Subjective Aspects of British Social Stratification

Introduction

The vernacular reference to 'the middle class' or 'the working class' may sometimes refer to economic strata or classes and sometimes to social status groups ranked in terms of the prestige they enjoy. These ordinary terms usually serve us well enough as descriptions of the pattern of social stratification until we encounter inconsistencies between class and status group membership or when we try to reconcile people's subjective perception of their own place in society with the sometimes different views of others.

In the everyday experience of most people it is this aspect of social stratification which is most directly encountered. Differential prestige is associated with different ways of life — the 'nice' and 'respectable' against the 'common' or 'rough' or, alternatively, the 'pretentious' or 'stuck-up' as aginst the 'just ordinary' or 'decent'. As a feature of the social structure what we can observe is a complex of interaction and avoidance patterns. When we try to analyse and take into account the cultural content of this behaviour we encounter distinctive sets of social norms and goals. The relationship between this and the class structure, though they do not exactly coincide, is generally close however. For the most part economic opportunities set limits to the style of life which is possible for a man and his family. In either respect a man's occupation is likely to be a major factor in determining to which social stratum he belongs.

The structure of society, in any case, is not just whatever anyone may like to believe it to be. The range and distribution of various subjective perceptions of a society among its members is itself a social fact. It is a fact of the very greatest importance to us in trying to give an account of the continuing relations between social strata. If we are to understand how the society works, the objectivity of market relations and the subjective perceptions which constitute the status hierarchy need to be disentangled and an attempt made to estimate the weight of their respective influence one upon the other.

The class structure based on the distribution of economic resources can, then, be distinguished from the hierarchy of social status groups differentiated from one another by their different life-styles and ranked on the basis of their relative prestige. Both features of the social structure have been selected by one writer or another as the basic pattern of social stratification in modern industrial societies. Both represent an aspect of a more complex reality which separately may be sufficient either to organize a writer's argument or to express the pressing concerns of a particular segment of society responding to the exigencies of a particular social situation. In their perception of their own society, individuals or communities are likely to emphasise the importance of inter-group relations in the context which is most salient for them. Manual workers' market insecurity may lead to an emphasis on class position for the working class, while the relative security and affluence but ambiguous prestige of the middle class may, in their experience, bring status group relations to the fore.

Deprivation or relative deprivation, that is the sense of deprivation whether justified in any absolute sense or not, within the status group hierarchy is as likely to be effective in political mobilization as deprivation in the economic order and more so when their social prestige has a higher degree of salience for the people concerned than their material circumstances.

The Persistence of Social Divisions

The individual's subjective appraisal of his social position has been a central concern in the debate about the embourgeoisement of the working class. The embourgeoisement thesis is, in simple terms, the argument that the rise in working class living standards after World War II had reduced the differences between them and at least the lower middle class to such an extent that they were likely to have come to regard themselves as no different. The large amount of working class support for the Conservative Party — the party of the middle classes — which permitted it to win three successive elections in the 1950s, was taken to be, at least in part, the result of this embourgeoisement of the newly affluent working class.[1]

The question of the embourgeoisement of at least the more affluent members of the working class has been the theme of a series of articles and books by John Goldthorpe and David Lockwood and their colleagues. The idea that the whole, or parts of, the working class have, or are becoming, assimilated into the middle class, involves more than an improvement in wages or a change in expenditure patterns. 'There are implied', Goldthorpe and Lockwood wrote, 'as well as economic changes, changes in values, attitudes and aspirations, in behavioural patterns and in the structure of relationships in associational and community life'.[1]

[1] See Mark Abrams and Richard Rose, *Must Labour Lose?* Penguin, 1961; David Butler and Richard Rose, *The British General Election of 1959*, Macmillan, 1960, pp.2, 15; C.A.R. Crosland, *Can Labour Win?*, Fabian Society, 1961; and Ferdynand Zweig, *The Worker in an Affluent Society*, Heinemann, 1961.
[2] John H. Goldthorpe and David Lockwood, 'Affluence and the British Class

There is little evidence, they point out, to suggest that even the most affluent workers have become bourgeois at the normative or relational level.

It was, I believe, Raymond Williams who in 1958 first pointed out that when working class people buy consumer goods previously only within reach of the middle class this has no necessary implications beyond the greater prosperity of those sections of the working class. Williams noted that

'It is argued . . . that the working class is becoming 'bourgeois' because it is dressing like the middle class, living in semi-detached houses, acquiring cars and washing machines and television sets. But it is not 'bourgeois' to possess objects of utility, nor to enjoy a high material standard of living. The great majority of English working people want only the middle-class material standard and for the rest want to go on being themselves.'[1]

Whatever the advertisements may say, social boundaries cannot be crossed simply by buying a lot of expensive consumer goods. Of course, differences in expenditure patterns are aspects of the general life style which distinguishes one status group from another. But it would seem that the possession of particular goods is not prestigious in itself, or only to a limited degree. Owning a particular make of car, drinking a particular brand of liquor, wearing a particular style in clothes, confer only a kind of 'as if' status because of the prestige attributed to those with whom the object is normally associated. Buying a dishwasher may make you the envy of your friends but it won't make them think of you as their social superior. Consumption patterns are a sign of status rather more than a source of status. Of more significance is mixing on terms of equality or mutual acceptance as social equals. In this connection affluence seems to have less effect than one might expect.

Structure', *Sociological Review*, 1963, 11, pp.133-63 and 'Not so Bourgeois after all' in *New Society*, 18 October 1962. Other important items in this series include David Lockwood, 'The New Working Class', *European Journal of Sociology*, 1960, 1, pp.248-59; D. Lockwood, 'Sources of Variation in Working Class Images of Society', *Sociological Review*, 1966, 14, pp.249-67; J.H. Goldthorpe, D. Lockwood, F. Bechhofer and J. Platt, 'The Affluent Worker and the Thesis of Embourgeoisement: Some Preliminary Research Findings', *Sociology*, 1967, 1, pp.11-31; J. H. Goldthorpe, D. Lockwood, F. Bechhofer and J. Platt, *The Affluent Worker: Industrial Attitudes and Behaviour; The Affluent Worker: Political Attitudes and Behaviour; The Affluent Worker in the Class Structure,* Cambridge Studies in Sociology 1-3, Cambridge, 1968-9; J.H. Goldthorpe 'Attitudes and Behaviour of Car Assembly Workers: A deviant case and theoretical critique', *British Journal of Sociology*, 1966, 17, pp.227-44.

[1] Raymond Williams, *Culture and Society 1780-1950*, Chatto, 1958. The quotation is from the Pelican edition 1961, p.311, cf.David Lockwood, op.cit., 1960 and W.G. Runciman, 'Embourgeoisement, Self-rated Class and Party Preference', *Sociological Review*, 1964, 12, p.138.

Of the Luton manual workers Goldthorpe and his colleagues studied —
'workers, who from the point of view of their economic aspirations, their
uprootedness from family and community of origin and their residential
location might be regarded as prime candidates for embourgeoisement'[1] —
only seven per cent seemed to associate mainly with members of the
middle class.[2] In the larger urban areas there tends in any case to be
considerable residential segregation with predominantly middle class or
predominantly working class neighbourhoods, but even in small towns or
within a socially mixed locality friendships are usually confined to social
equals, that is to say occur within the social boundaries of a single status
group.

In the North London suburb of Woodford the middle class were
unwilling to regard the greater prosperity of the working class residents of
the borough as having any effect on their relative social standing.[3] Social
status divisions are not overcome merely by a change in the level of
income or the pattern of expenditure on one side of the boundary. They
are much more resistant to change, though to be sure they do not always
take on the manifest solidity of the remarkable Cutteslow walls. These
seven-foot brick walls were erected in 1934 across two roads to prevent
the working class tenants of an Oxford council estate from going through
the adjoining mainly lower-middle-class private estate to reach the main
road and the nearest bus stop and shops. After long drawn out legal
disputes and disagreements the barriers were finally knocked down by the
City Council in 1959.[4]

Subjective Aspects of Stratification

Being less tangible than brick walls, for the most part the boundaries
between social status groups are harder to remove. Indeed for many
people, except those involved in attempts to cross the social boundaries,
they may scarcely be noticeable at all. Perhaps only in historically
exceptional circumstances are the majority of individuals in a common
class situation likely to become aware of their common interests. A similar
economic situation may accommodate a great diversity of effective social
environments. As Elizabeth Bott has pointed out, the individual's own
view of the system of social stratification is likely to reflect his personal
social experience. 'When an individual talks about class', she wrote, 'he is

[1] Goldthorpe et al., *The Affluent Worker: Political Attitudes and Behaviour*, 1968,
p.9.

[2] Goldthorpe et al., op.cit., 1967, p.22.

[3] See Peter Willmott and Michael Young, *Family and Class in a London Suburb*,
Routledge, 1960, ch.10.

[4] See Peter Collison, *The Cutteslow Walls*, Faber, 1963.

trying to say something . . . about his experiences of power and prestige in his actual membership groups and social relationships both past and present.'[1] It is clear, however, that in this context 'class' is not being used to refer to a group defined by its market situation but to subjectively perceived social divisions whose basis is the sense of social standing or denigration encountered in day-to-day social interaction. This interaction is patterned by implicit social rules that Margaret Stacey described in operation in her study of Banbury.[2] In brief these define that status differences are taken for granted but not spoken of. 'It is the existence of these rules which in part makes the class system workable,' she noted.[3] Stacey described how these unacknowledged but effective status group boundaries were maintained at the face-to-face level.

'The techniques of acceptance or rejection are subtle. You must possess appropriate characteristics: occupation, home, residence area, income (suitably spent), manners and attitudes. You must know or learn the language and the current private 'passwords' of the group. You must be introduced. If you fail in these particulars you will simply be 'not known'. Nothing is said or done. The barrier is one of silence.'[4]

Thus, the defining characteristics of the life-styles which distinguish status groups are diverse. The norms relating to the appropriate patterns of behaviour are implicit rather than explicit and the main negative sanction which enforces their observance is avoidance or ostracism.

The normative differences between social status groups in this way operate as social barriers. The pattern of overlapping associations with intermediate groups and avoidance of contact between the most extreme groups reduces the salience of social differences for most people. The sense of relative deprivation or privilege — and thus the likelihood of conflict — is reduced as comparisons tend to be made primarily between groups with some degree of contact and acquaintance.[5] This avoidance of large-scale comparison nevertheless does not prevent almost everyone being ready to assign themselves to a place in the social order, even if it does not always coincide with the way a sociologist might classify them.

Rosser and Harris found that 93 per cent of the large sample of Swansea people they interviewed readily assigned themselves to either the middle class or the working class.[6] In their sample of British electors,

[1] Elizabeth Bott, *Family and Social Network*, Tavistock, 1957; cf. David Lockwood. 'Sources of Variation in Working Class Images of Society', *Sociological Review*, 1966, 14, pp.249-67.

[2] See Chapter 3 above.

[3] Margaret Stacey, *Tradition and Change*, Oxford, 1960, p.145.

[4] ibid, p.148.

[5] See W.G.Runciman, *Relative Deprivation and Social Justice*, Routledge, 1966, and Margaret Stacey, op.cit., 1960.

[6] C. Rosser and C.C. Harris, *Family and Social Change*, Routledge, 1965, p.86, Table 3.1.

Butler and Stokes found as many as 11 out of 12 respondents described themselves as either middle class or working class. They concluded that 'British society is divided into two primary classes. This is more than a sociologist's simplification; it seems to be deeply rooted in the mind of the ordinary British citizen.'[1] Again, one might suspect some ambiguity in the term 'class' but the reality of the social division is the important emphasis. Though at least nine out of ten people seem ready to assign themselves to a place in the hierarchy of social strata, it should not be supposed they will all agree about how to assign one another. Young and Willmott found that some manual workers were not inclined to rank occupations in terms of the more usual criteria of social esteem. They thought that miners and other manual workers should rank high along with doctors and above lawyers or managers.[2] These workers were, however, a minority even amonst the working class, and it is not altogether clear whether they were describing the distribution of prestige in society as they saw it or rather as they thought it ought to be. Equally, as Parkin and later Goldthorpe and Hope have pointed out, when the majority of respondents to a survey describe the more conventional status hierarchy we cannot infer from their answers that they necessarily approve of that order without reservation. There may be a considerable degree of consensus regarding the character of the social order without the same degree of agreement about the desirability of such a state of affairs.[3]

There is an additional methodological difficulty encountered by the student of people's own views of their society and their place in it. The snag is an acute case of the general problem that apparently very similar questions can produce different distributions of answers even from the same sample of respondents. For instance, Willmott and Young asked two questions in their Woodford survey, about which class people thought they belonged to; first an open-ended question: 'Which class do you belong to?' and then again offering a list: 'Upper, Upper Middle, Middle, Lower Middle, Working, Can't say'. They found that the proportion of manual workers who said they were middle class was 34 per cent in answer to the first, open-ended question, but rose to 48 per cent in response to the forced-choice question.[4] Mark Abrams however, found a rather lower

---

[1] David Butler and Donald Stokes, *Political Change in Britain*, Macmillan, 1969, p.67.

[2] See M. Young and P. Willmott, 'Social Grading by Manual Workers', *British Journal of Sociology*, 1956, VII pp.337-45 and cf J. Hall and D. Jones, 'Social Grading of Occupations', *British Journal of Sociology*, 1950, I, pp.31-55; and also Mark Abrams, 'Some Measurements of Social Stratification in Britain', in John Jackson (ed.), *Social Stratification*, Cambridge, 1969, pp.133-44.

[3] See Frank Parkin, *Class, Inequality and Political Order*, McGibbon and Kee, 1971, pp.40-44; John H. Goldthorpe and K. Hope, 'Occupational Grading and Occupational Prestige', in K. Hope (ed.), *The Analysis of Social Mobility: Methods and Approaches*, Oxford, 1972, pp.34-5.

[4] Willmott and Young, op.cit., 1960, p.115, n.1.

proportion of working class respondents describing themselves as middle class in answer to a question presented with a list of two working class and three middle class alternatives in surveys carried out between 1962 and 1964.[1] Most studies however, have used open-ended questions and it is on these that I shall concentrate in the ensuing discussion.

A large number of studies now besides the Woodford survey have found that a substantial number of people who would be regarded as working class, judged either according to their own occupation or that of the head of their household, nevertheless regard themselves as middle class. For example, W.G. Runciman found that of 1,415 respondents in a random sample of the adult population of England and Wales in 1962, 919 were working class and 496 were middle class when classified by their occupation, or by their husbands' occupations in the case of married women. Ninety-nine per cent were able to classify themselves as middle class or as working class but the 'objective' and 'subjective' distributions did not match; thus of the objectively middle class 25 per cent thought of themselves as working class, while of the objectively working class 33 per cent thought of themselves as middle class.[2] The first study of the ideas commonly held in Britain about the structure of society still seems to me the best one. This study by F. M. Martin was carried out in 1950 as part of the L.S.E. survey of social mobility and used samples totalling just under 900 from the London Borough of Greenwich and from Hertford, a small county town north of London.[3] Less than four per cent of the respondents in this study were unwilling or unable to assign themselves to a social class. Two respondents said they were upper class; almost all the remainder thought of themselves as working class or some degree of middle class. The extreme groups on the occupational scale were most homogeneous in terms of the subjective class-attachment of their members. A diversity of self-assignment was progressively more common towards the middle of the scale so that the lowest grade of non-manual workers were almost evenly divided between those who thought of themselves as 'working class' and those who held themselves to be 'middle class'. Of those of professional and managerial status, 93 per cent thought of themselves as middle class compared with 65 per cent in the lower middle class. Thirty per cent of those objectively in the skilled working class thought themselves middle class, while 18 per cent of those in the less skilled working class did so. Only four per cent in the first category

[1] See Mark Abrams, 'Social Class and Politics', in Richard Mabey (ed.), *Class*, Anthony Blond, 1967, pp.19-32.

[2] See Runciman, 'Embourgeoisement, Self-rated Class and Party Preference', *Sociological Review*, 1964, 12, p.138, and *Relative Deprivation and Social Justice*, Routledge, 1966.

[3] See F.M. Martin 'Some Subjective Aspects of Social Stratification', pp. 51-75 in D.V. Glass (ed.), *Social Mobility in Britain*. Routledge, 1954.

described themselves as lower or working class but a third of the lower middle class did so. Two thirds of the skilled working class and three quarters of the less skilled working class described themselves as working class.

In their more recent study, Butler and Stokes found a larger proportion in all social strata assigning themselves to the working class. They classified the 1,757 respondents in a two-stage stratified random sample of electors in Britain interviewed in 1963-66 according to the occupations of the heads of their households. In the unskilled working class only nine per cent thought of themselves as middle class, while 17 per cent of the skilled working class 'up-graded' themselves in this way. In the upper middle class — the professional, managerial and administrative strata — 30 per cent thought of themselves as working class, while 51 per cent of the lower middle class did so.[1]

The apparent pattern of change which emerges from a comparison with Martin's 1950 findings could perhaps be explained as reflecting the change pattern of social mobility (see the next chapter), but the proportions identifying with the working class in Butler and Stokes' sample seem too high in comparison with the findings of Abrams or Runciman in surveys carried out at about the same time.[2] While we can therefore reasonably suspect some over-representation of 'working class' identification in Butler and Stokes' sample, this can naturally occur in any random sample of the population and while it calls for some caution in making use of their findings it should not necessarily lead us to distrust their data in general.

Like Martin, Butler and Stokes found that in the non-manual strata the lowest rank they distinguished were most likely to consider themselves working class; in fact they found a group including waiters, policemen, shop assistants, etc., were divided approximately 70 per cent self-rated 'working class' and 30 per cent self-rated 'middle class'.[3] As we have seen in Chapter 5, this range of occupations presents difficulties of classification for sociologists at least as much as for the people themselves. Butler and Stokes remark that the inclusion of this group with others predominantly regarding themselves as middle class in a general lower-middle class category as occurs in many occupation-based social classifications, 'involves lumping together people who diverge markedly in their subjective class identifications'.[4] On the other hand, the distinction may have only limited utility in other respects. For instance, in their political allegiance this group appears to resemble the rest of the lower middle class

[1] See David Butler and Donald Stokes, *Political Change in Britain,* Macmillan, 1969, Table 4.3, from which these percentages are calculated.

[2] See Abrams, op.cit., 1967, Runciman, op.cit., 1966.

[3] Butler and Stokes, 1969, Table 4.3, p.70.

[4] ibid., p.71.

much more than it does even the skilled working class.[1]

Martin found that in Hertford, with a larger proportion of middle class residents than Greenwich, a larger proportion in each stratum were likely to consider themselves middle class. This was most pronounced amongst those objectively assigned to the lower middle class. The effect of the class composition of the locality on people's image of themselves is confirmed in Willmott's finding that in Dagenham, where only 12 per cent of his General Sample were white-collar workers or the wives of white-collar workers, only 13 per cent of manual workers and their wives thought of themselves as middle class, and more of the white-collar workers described themselves as working class than claimed to be middle class. The area was so homogeneous however, that it seems class was of little salience and a third of the respondents were unable or unwilling to assign themselves to a class at all.[2] Runciman found that manual workers were least likely to think of themselves as middle class in the north – 26 per cent – while 35 per cent of manual workers in the south described themselves as middle class. In the Midlands, however, the proportion was even higher at 45 per cent.[3] Women are less likely to think of themselves as working class than are men,[4] but age appears to have no influence on class self-assignment.[5] Martin found that those in the middle class who regarded themselves as working class were more likely to have been upwardly mobile than middle class respondents in general – 45 per cent as against 31 per cent – while a slightly larger proportion – 19 per cent – of the working class respondents who claimed to be middle class had been downwardly mobile from middle class homes than among the working class as a whole, of whom 14 per cent had been downwardly mobile.[6]

There is apparently some degree of variation in the stability of such subjective identifications over time. People may change their mind about where they stand in the social order or they may say different things at different times because they haven't got any very clear or firm views on the matter anyway. This would suggest that, while in the relatively short-run, the proportion of, say, manual workers describing themselves as middle class may remain much the same, we should not assume even in the short term that these will remain the *same* manual workers and in the longer term the proportions may change a great deal. Using data from a 1963 panel study of over 500 men aged about 20 Abramson and Books

[1] See Michael Kahan, David Butler and Donald Stokes, 'On the Analytical Division of Social Class', *British Journal of Sociology*, 1966, 17, Table 6, p.129; but see also Table 7.3 below, where at least some of this group are included in the 'skilled working class'.

[2] Peter Willmott, *The Evolution of a Community*, Routledge, 1963, pp.102-3.

[3] See Runciman, op.cit., 1966, Table 6, p.166.

[4] See Martin, op.cit., 1954, p.58 and Table 5, and Runciman, op.cit., 1966.

[5] Martin, loc.cit.

[6] ibid., Table 5.

found that a third of those in the working class assigned themselves to a different class than they had when first interviewed three years earlier. Those who had been occupationally upwardly mobile out of the working class were only a little less likely to switch than were those downwardly mobile out of the middle class. The men of middle class origins who themselves remained in the middle class were only about half as likely to change their subjective class identification.[1] It was the stable middle class group, however, rather than the socially mobile who were most likely to think that class barriers were breaking down and this view was least common among the stable working class.[2]

In addition to all this, however, people differ in the concept of social structure they are inclined to employ. Consequently though they may all be prepared to tell an interviewer they tend to think of themselves as 'middle class' or as 'working class' they may not all have quite the same notions about what these terms mean. Butler and Stokes asked a randomly selected half of the sample they investigated in 1964 to describe the main social classes and found that most people thought of class in occupational terms. Sixty-one per cent described the middle class in occupational terms with a further 21 per cent thinking mainly in terms of income or level of living. No other descriptions accounted for more than five per cent of the answers and references to family background or political orientation each represented only one per cent. Descriptions of what sort of people belonged to the working class were even more homogeneous, with 74 per cent of the answers emphasizing occupational characteristics while income and level of living were referred to by only ten per cent.[3]

Martin's study retains its importance, however, from the fact that he not only describes the perceived characteristics of the social strata but also shows how these perceptions are related to both the individual's own position in the social hierarchy and to his perception of his own position. Thus three quarters of all respondents except for those manual workers or wives of manual workers describing themselves as 'middle class', describe the working class in occupational terms. However, manual workers and the wives of manual workers who thought of themselves as 'working class' scarcely mentioned any of the less skilled or least esteemed kinds of work in this connection, while amongst those describing themselves as 'middle class' descriptions of the working class referring to dustmen, navvies, etc. were frequent. Martin points out that mention of these occupations has the effect of maximizing social distance between the self-described 'middle class' respondent and his idea of the 'working class', and were particularly common in the answers from people whose occupational status was below

---

[1] Paul R. Abramson and John W. Books, 'Social Mobility and Political Attitudes', *Comparative Politics*, 1970-71, 3, p.420.

[2] ibid., p.427.

[3] See Butler and Stokes, op.cit., 1969, Table 4.2.

the professional level.[1] Those manual workers claiming to be middle class were more likely to make evaluative references to the 'working class', attributing to its members laziness, lack of ambition or irresponsibility. They were least inclined to describe the 'middle class' in occupational terms and most frequently (two thirds of the group) described the middle class in terms of income and standard of living.

Ideas about the middle class were otherwise relatively vague and ill-defined. About a third of all working class respondents could not give a description of the middle class at all. As in Butler and Stokes' study nearly 15 years later, occupation was less frequently mentioned in relation to the middle class then with reference to the working class. Income and the middle class standard of living however, were mentioned more by respondents not themselves claiming to be middle class. A series of surveys carried out between 1962 and 1964 by Mark Abrams indicated a considerable similarity between the ways in which manual and non-manual workers and their wives saw the classes to which, subjectively, they felt they belonged. In both manual and non-manual strata their occupation was the most frequently given reason for their self-assignment among those who thought of themselves as 'working class'. In contrast, but like Martin's 'middle class' manual workers, in all objective strata, references to their income and possessions were the reasons most often given by those describing themselves as 'middle class'.[2] In Martin's study evaluative accounts of the 'middle class' emphasized either their respectability and integrity or their snobbery and pretensions to superiority according to the social grade of the respondent.

Martin's most interesting finding was that manual workers who thought of themselves as 'middle class' often defined the middle class in just the terms used by 'working class' manual workers to define the working class, namely as including 'everyone who works for a living'. 'The frequency with which this is put forward as a description of the middle class', he wrote, 'strongly suggests that when a manual worker assesses himself as middle class he is not merely asserting his personal superiority; he carries with him a large proportion of his compeers, and in so doing he shifts the boundaries of the classes'. So that when a man tells us he is working class we must remember that he is placing himself within his own ideas about the social structure as a whole and it is only in that context that we can properly interpret his statement. However, the various images with which people operate are few and their frequency is socially distributed in a significant way. This emerges a little more clearly in the answers to Martin's questions about the 'upper class'. 'Within the sample', he found, '. . . two-thirds of all descriptions of the upper class are accounted for by two frames of reference.' The frequencies across the social hierarchy were

[1] F.M. Martin, 'Some Subjective Aspects of Social Stratification', pp.51-75 in D.V. Glass (ed.), *Social Mobility in Britain*, Routledge, 1954, Table 6.
[2] Mark Abrams, op.cit., 1967, Tables 4, 7 and 10.

however inversely related. At the top the members of the 'upper class' were mostly thought of 'in terms of their social prestige or familial status; they are the old landowning families, the hereditary aristocracy, or simply 'society' '. But this kind of description, with its emphasis on social status and deference, declines in frequency as one descends the social scale from the higher levels of the self-consciously middle class to the self-confessed working class. In the same descent an alternative image increases in frequency to become the majority view.

'The members of the upper class come to be thought of more and more as 'people with private incomes'. They are sometimes called simply the 'rich' or the 'very rich', though precise limits are scarcely ever stated. Most often, however, it is the source of their income to which reference is made; they are 'people who don't need to work for a living'.[1]

Thus, most people think of the social structure and their place in it in terms of occupation but at the upper, and possibly at the lower margins of their experience, the upper class on the one hand and possibly the poor on the other are distinguished in terms of their resources — mainly their abundance, or lack, of money. The names given to the strata differ. The middle class for many people includes everyone except the very rich and the very poor. For others the working class may overlap very considerably across the same occupations. But only a minority of non-manual workers, especially in the lower middle class and those who have been upwardly mobile from working class families or who have other personal connections with manual workers, regard the working class as including any white collar workers. At the same time a larger minority, especially among the skilled and better paid manual workers, often those living in middle class neighbourhoods or who have family connections with white collar workers, are likely to think of the middle class as including manual workers. Put in this way the overlapping identifications found in the various studies I have referred to seem less accidental or random. Clearly there is a predominantly middle class perspective which may be compared with the frame of reference of the majority of the working class. The former emphasizes style of life and the existence of a hierarchy of social status groups ranked in order of prestige but without any sharp opposition of interest between them. It may include the belief that the divisions between the social strata are breaking down. The latter point of view emphasizes the division of society between 'the haves' and 'the have-nots', between those who have to work for a living and those who apparently do not. It does not suggest that society is changing at all significantly in this respect.

Lockwood and Goldthorpe have given these frames of reference a

---

[1] Martin op.cit., 1954, p.62; again cf. Lockwood's discussion of the views of the supposedly 'privatised' workers of Luton in op.cit., 1966, pp.260-61.

central place in their discussion of the changing character of working class life in mid-twentieth century Britain. Lockwood has pointed out the connections between the view of society as a prestige hierarchy and the individualism of the middle class and between the dichotomous or conflict view and the collectivism characteristic of working class social movements. In discussing the idea that the class boundaries were shifting or disappearing altogether Goldthorpe and Lockwood have argued that while sections of the more affluent working class may have abandoned the 'proletarian' image of a society divided between two antagonistic classes, they have not yet adopted the typically individualistic middle class perspective.[1] Instead, they argue, many workers have become 'privatised'. Thus many workers and their families interpret their social situation neither in terms of a 'them and us' or 'power model', nor a 'prestige model' in terms of their relation to other more and less respectable strata, but rather in terms simply of an individual's or a family's possessions or more especially the money they have to spend. This 'pecuniary' model suggests a new basis for the evaluation of others, no longer 'Who is he?' nor even 'What does he do?' but rather 'How much has he got?'[2] As Lockwood put it, 'The daily social encounters of the privatised worker do not . . . lead him to think of a society divided up into either a hierarchy of status groups or an opposition of class. His model of society is one in which the individuals are associated with, and disassociated from one another less by any type of social exchange than by the magnitude of their incomes and possessions'[3] and further, 'the single, overwhelmingly important, and the most spontaneously conceived criterion of class division is money and the possessions, both material and immaterial, that money can buy'.[4] Of the Luton sample, 56 per cent responded in these terms.[5] This however, is not so different from the way the manual workers of Greenwich and Hertford thought of themselves and the upper class in 1950. The emphasis on possessions amongst these better off, geographically mobile workers also reminds us of the emphasis on 'keeping up with the Joneses' noted by Young and Willmott among the workers' families on the new Greenleigh estate.

Most of the highly skilled workers in a Tyneside shipyard described by Brown and his colleagues were similarly aware of some degree of complexity in the class structure, that it was not just 'us and them'. Brown and Brannen attributed this to the cooperation at work between men in sharply differentiated trades. In the sometimes confusing accounts of this

---

[1] See Lockwood, op.cit., 1960, and Goldthorpe and Lockwood, op.cit., 1963.

[2] See Lockwood, op.cit., 1966, p.250.

[3] Lockwood, 'The New Working Class', *European Journal of Sociology*, 1960, 1, p.259.

[4] ibid, p.260.

[5] See Goldthorpe et al., op.cit., 1969, Table 20, p.150 and pp.146ff.

research emphasis is placed on the number of strata named by the men rather than on their conceptions of the relations between them, but it is apparent that the diversity of responses occurred within what was for most a generally similar working-class orientation to society. These craftsmen had deep social roots in the locality and in the ship building industry. More than four out of every five were Labour voters and a similar proportion thought union membership should be compulsory. The majority did not think industrial relations in their yard were good while 70 per cent believed that strikes never achieved anything. Only a handful of the younger and most mobile differed significantly in their point of view.[1]

It is not after all necessary to invoke a further dimension or a qualitatively different subjective view of social structure. The social isolation of the affluent and geographically mobile worker is 'privatising' in that his social network density is reduced to a level where he no longer has a sense of residential or occupational community with which to identify. Neither from the locality he has come to live in nor from the factory he has come to work in 'will he derive more than a rudimentary awareness of belonging to a cohesive group and hence of the social distance between such groups'.[2] Jennifer Platt has pointed out that emphasis on money and possessions in the answers of the Luton workers is ambiguous and for many of them might be no more than a correlate of class position rather than a determinant of it.[3] She also notes that, as well as those referring to income levels or wealth, respondents were coded as having 'money' models of class if they emphasized differences in life-style characteristics such as possessions or material living standards.[4] In these cases it might be further argued that the 'pecuniary model' is after all only the limiting case of a status model where the hierarchy of social status groups has been lost sight of and this would adequately account for the lack of status aspirations among the Luton workers.[5] There was little hope of social betterment because the possibility of higher social status was not evident to most of these workers and their families. Their daily experience was in encounters with others like themselves, some with more money and

[1] Richard Brown and Peter Brannen, 'Social Relations and Social Perspectives Amongst Shipbuilding Workers', *Sociology*, 1970, 4, pp.71-84 and pp.197-211; Jim Cousins and Richard Brown, 'Patterns of Paradox: Shipbuilding Workers' Images of Society', *Working Papers in Sociology No.4*, University of Durham Department of Sociology and Social Administration, 1972.

[2] Lockwood, op.cit., 1966, p.258.

[3] Jennifer Platt, 'Variations in answers to different questions on Perception of Class', *Sociological Review*, 1971, 19, p.417.

[4] ibid., p.416.

[5] Goldthorpe et al., op cit., 1969 p.150. Runciman, for instance, noted that manual workers with the highest level of income were least likely of any group to feel that anyone was noticeably better off than themselves: see Runciman, *Relative Deprivation and Social Justice*, Routledge, 1966, p.197.

some with less. As a result of their lack of contact with other social strata and their consequent absence of experience of social exchanges across stratum boundaries these affluent and geographically mobile workers and their families have developed a view of society where everyone seems to have the same social status, where 'we're all working class these days' or 'everyone is middle class now'.

While the social isolation geographical mobility brings may make a special case of sections of the working class, and possibly a degree of 'privatisation' amongst sections of the middle class, there remain for the majority two most common frames of reference: the dichotomous power or class model and the hierarchy of open status groups or prestige model. These perspectives imply not only different interpretations of what society is like but also indicate different prescriptions for how we can conduct ourselves within that society. With these associated values and attitudes they still do not amount to 'political ideologies, but rather . . . the raw materials of social consciousness which political ideologies may articulate'.[1]

The extent to which these frames of reference fall short of political ideologies can be demonstrated by reference to the low salience which political issues have for most members of contemporary British society. Those who follow events closely, study the news and read widely or at all (or even write) in quest of a theoretical understanding of contemporary society, either from some academic curiosity or a political commitment that something ought to be done about things, may very readily over-estimate how far most of their fellow citizens subscribe to any coherent political doctrine. Disinterested observation or an examination of what evidence is available on the subject should convince us that, as for the majority, a clearly articulated and self-consistent set of beliefs is something of a rarity.

Political Perspectives

The Common Importance of Politics

Although one can argue that at a macro-social level politics is central to the integration of the social order, to many of the individual members of society politics, at least narrowly defined, if not positively distasteful, is not of any great interest. Fewer still are in any way politically active beyond perhaps voting in General Elections. Thus, in the 1964 electorate of about 36,000,000, it appears that 92 per cent took some interest in the

[1] Goldthorpe and Lockwood, 'Affluence and the British Class Structure', *Sociological Review* 1963, pp.146-7.

General Election campaign of that year, following it through the mass media or private conversation, and 81 per cent identified with a political party. Of those on the 1964 electoral rolls, 77 per cent voted in the General Election compared with only 43 per cent in local elections that year.[1] Though 25 per cent were nominally party members in 1964, many of them were so in virtue of their membership of a trade union affiliated to the Labour Party. Only about 0.3 per cent held some office in their local party but between 10 and 14 per cent paid subscriptions as individual party members and these accounted for most of those who could be described as politically well informed. As Richard Rose reports, in an election year with the press, radio and television all discussing the likelihood of a change of government, and despite the fact that 92 per cent had 'followed' the election campaign, 84 per cent of the electorate were unable to name six major politicians. This is not to be judged as a measure of intelligence or of the informativeness of the mass media. It is, however, a striking indication of the importance of politicians and political matters generally in the day-to-day concerns of most people. Rose concluded that, 'many Englishmen maintain a shallow, intermittent participation in politics; few are inclined to sustained participation'.[2] But not only do few actively participate in politics to any extent, large numbers – half of the electorate – are not interested in political matters anyway. Butler and Stokes asked how much interest the people in their large sample of electors had in politics and a third of the men and about 60 per cent of the women said 'not much'.[3] Abrams has indicated the peripheral importance of politics for a quota sample of 593 respondents interviewed in November 1971 in the seven largest conurbations. On the whole they were more satisfied than dissatisfied with the level of democracy in Britain. More than half thought Britain was very democratic and tolerant of minorities though similar proportions thought that local councillors were not very effective and that it was difficult for people like themselves to understand what was going on in politics. A striking contrast emerged between the evidence that 80 per cent thought that there was a great deal of freedom of speech while 74 per cent thought that voters had very little influence on the way the country is run. Much of the potential force of this depressing juxtaposition is dissipated by the fact that for all but seven per cent of this sample democratic institutions were rated as of very little importance in determining the respondents' overall level of satisfaction with life.[4]

This picture was generally confirmed in a 1972 study by Crewe and

---

[1] 79 per cent in February 1974, though in 1970, in the lowest turnout since 1935, only 72 per cent; the October 1974 poll was 73 per cent.

[2] Richard Rose, *Politics in England*, Faber, 1965, p.93.

[3] The sources of the preceding estimates are Rose, ibid., Table IV.2, p.94, and Butler and Stokes, *Political Change in Britain*, Macmillan, 1969, Table 2.1, p.25

[4] Mark Abrams, 'Subjective Social Indicators', *Social Trends No.4*, H.M.S.O., 1973, pp.35-50.

Spence who explored the attitudes to parliamentary affairs of a random sample of just under 2,000 electors from all over Great Britain. Moderation characterized the attitudes of the overwhelming majority. Eighty-one per cent were neither completely happy with the system nor very unhappy and 70 per cent were in favour of moderate or minor changes. Very few could recall any recent legislation likely to affect them, ten per cent mentioned the Housing Finance Act which raised council rents and, despite widespread coverage in the press and on television and the ardent opposition of most unions only 13 per cent of trade unionists and fewer still of the others could recall any parliamentary discussion of the Industrial Relations Act. 'These figures', Crewe and Spence commented, 'hardly expose a nation of alert and attentive citizens'. What matters to most people are more immediate, more concrete, more local issues. Significantly what most would like to see was more involvement on the part of their M.P.s with their constituencies.[1] For a majority, then, political issues have little connection with ordinary experience. This underlies one of Butler and Stokes' most striking findings which was their evidence of the considerable volatility of opinions even on fairly broad political policies, let alone on particular issues or matters of detail. They interviewed a large panel of electors from all over Britain three times, in 1963, 1964 and again in 1966. Over the three interviews only 50 per cent were consistent in either supporting or opposing further nationalization of industry and views on Britain's possession of nuclear weapons were equally unstable, with a correlation coefficient for responses over the three interviews of only 0.31.[2]

Butler and Stokes showed that political opinions are not only unstable over time but that opinions on any given matter cannot necessarily be taken as an indication of other attitudes. Political opinions do not reflect a self-consistent pattern of beliefs. Taking the questions 'Should Britain give up the Bomb?' and 'Should more industries be nationalized?' they found that only 30 per cent of their panel of electors gave consistent responses to both questions over all three interviews.[3] The attitudes of this 30 per cent on seven political issues were then inter-correlated to see if, even among this minority, attitudes were patterned in ways which would reflect the discernibly different positions of the major political parties. 'What emerges from the correlations obtained in this way is that there is no strong pattern linking the attitudes even of those who do have stable attitudes'. It is true that within this group, 'People who opposed the recent level of immigration were more likely to be for the death penalty and against the power of the trade unions. Those who discounted the importance of the Monarchy were likely to accept nationalization, oppose the Bomb, accept

[1] See Ivor Crewe and James Spence, 'Parliament and Public', *New Society*, 12 July 1973, pp.78-80.
[2] Butler and Stokes, *Political Change in Britain*, Macmillan, 1969, pp.178-81.
[3] ibid., p.197.

recent immigration, condemn hanging and the power of big business, and to be tolerant towards trade unions.'[1] The correlations between these opinions, however, were generally very low. Thus even for the 30 per cent of those whose views displayed some stability there hardly exists any coherent division of political perspective corresponding to the different-iation of principle and programmes presented by the political parties.

Reviewing the findings of two series of opinion polls from 1959 to 1961 and from 1965 to 1968 Blondel showed that Labour and Conservative supporters were very similar in their attitudes on a wide range of issues. On foreign affairs, the Common Market, disarmament, reform of the House of Lords, immigration or capital punishment, there was little or no difference. They were partisan on social and economic matters only and even there differences were not extreme.[2] This similarity in the attitudes of Conservative and Labour voters does not mean they do not distinguish between the parties in terms of their different policies or programmes. These differences between the parties are evident to most people but even among partisans there is little certain connection between the position they see taken by their party on some matter and their own attitudes or opinions on the subject. As Blondel noted, 'Electors hold views which are not those of their party and still vote for that party'.[3] Thus Moodie and Studdert-Kennedy observe, 'Whatever is translated across the representative process from mass following to party leadership, it is certainly not a clear structure of commonly shared opinions on those current issues that seem to call for decision'.[4] Blondel has argued that opinions on particular issues in any case play little part in the distribution of political allegiance. While the conduct of a party on the issues it faces may shape the image it has in the minds of its supporters or potential supporters, this image is built up over the long run of memory for many years and is unlikely to be drastically changed as a result of any specific policy at one particular point in time. More important than issues is a diffuse image of one party rather than the other one being for 'our sort'.

But there are signs of change here in recent years. The stable division between the two major parties which had characterized British politics for more than 30 years has weakened. While on the political fringes extremists may have become more vocal, the electorate as a whole has become less polarized between the two parties of left and right than at any time since the 1930s. The domination by the two major parties' was at its pinnacle in the General Election of 1951. Between them the Labour and Conservative Parties won 97 per cent of the vote on that occasion. In the election of

[1] ibid., pp.198 and 199.
[2] See Jean Blondel, *Voters, Parties and Leaders,* Penguin, 2nd Edition, 1974, pp.74-7.
[3] ibid., p.78, and cf. Butler and Stokes, op.cit., 1969, pp.194-5.
[4] Graeme Moodie and Gerald Studdert-Kennedy, *Opinions, Publics and Pressure Groups,* Allen and Unwin, 1970, p.50.

1970 they together accounted for only 89 per cent and in October 1974 they were down to 75 per cent. Most of the lost votes went to the Liberals who received more than 18 per cent of the votes cast, their largest vote since 1929, though they won only 13 seats. The 7 per cent of votes for other minor parties, being more locally concentrated, elected 26 M.P.s mainly from Northern Ireland, Scotland and Wales. Some of the increase in Liberal support, of course, reflects the greater availability of Liberal candidates to vote for in comparison with recent elections in other years, but most of the change appears to be a real gain at the expense of both the other parties.[1]

It would appear that for a quarter of the voters neither Labour nor Tory present an image of being the party for 'our sort'. Surveys carried out during the 1960s should, perhaps, have led us to expect as much, but the composition of the 1974 Parliaments makes the fact and its consequences vivid. It is a situation which raises many questions it is still much too soon to even begin to answer. For instance, were the results of February 1974, like the last minute swing to the Conservatives in 1970 which took all but one of the opinion polls by surprise, a sign only of the volatility of opinion caught off guard by a snap election in the February on top of the coal-strike, the three-day week, the oil-crisis, Ulster, rising prices and so on and so forth? The October results make this seem unlikely. Were they on the other hand a sign of more long-term change? Is there a new sort of political concern emerging which neither of the larger parties so far has had the flexibility to accommodate? Only another election will tell. Perhaps this is too negative an interpretation in any case. The growth for the Liberals may amount to rather more than a mere protest vote against the inadequacies of the other parties. The ebb and flow of social change may have created new political cross-currents. Is there in fact a new sort of citizen seeking political expression here? The two-party system has become adapted to a confrontation arising out of circumstances which in some degree may no longer hold. Only a great deal of research will permit us to answer these questions with any certainty. And by the time we can do that no doubt something else will have taken us by surprise.

Class and Party Support

At the general level where political opinion is manifest as identification with, or support for, one of the political parties it is closely associated with social class. In their account of the British General Election of February 1974 Butler and Kavanagh presented the figures shown here in Table 7.1 which are based on a series of pre-election polls of voting

---

[1] For February 1974 see Richard Rose, 'The Voting Surveyed', *The Times Guide to the House of Commons 1974*, Times Newspapers, 1974, pp.30, 31. In October 1974 Labour won 39.3%; Conservatives 35.7%. The Liberal percentage was down from 19.3% in February, their largest since 1929, to 18.3% and this cost them a seat. See the *Guardian*, 19 October 1974.

intention carried out by National Opinion Polls. The same degree of overall strength of party support would not of course be found in the polls of other years when their electoral success was greater or less.

Table 7.1

Social Class and Party Support in February 1974

	AB Upper Middle	01 Lower Middle	02 Skilled Working	DE Unskilled and 'Very Poor'
	%	%	%	%
Conservative	67.3	51.4	30.1	24.6
Labour	10.4	21.3	47.2	53.7
Liberal	19.6	24.7	19.6	16.6
Other	2.7	2.6	3.1	5.1

Source: David Butler and Dennis Kavanagh, *The British General Election of February 1974,* Macmillan, 1974, p.263.

In February 1974 38.1 per cent of the electorate voted Conservative, 37.2 per cent Labour, 19.3 per cent Liberal and 5.4 per cent for 'Others'. The smaller parties gained support at the expense of both Labour and, still more, the Conservatives. In the professional and managerial middle class Labour voters were outnumbered by Conservatives by seven or eight to one. In the much larger lower middle class the Conservatives are also in an overwhelming majority, outnumbering Labour supporters by more than two to one. In the skilled working class, the largest section of the electorate, Labour outnumbers Conservatives by a smaller margin, with Liberal Party supporters proportionately slightly fewer than in the lower middle class. Liberal and Conservative support was least common among the members of the unskilled working class group. Even in this group, however, a substantial proportion, about a quarter, supported the Conservative Party. These large Conservative minorities in the working class provide an important part of total Conservative support. In contrast, as a proportion of Labour votes, middle class support is much less significant, as not only are the minorities smaller but the middle classes are in any case a smaller proportion of the electorate. Though at present it has not been possible to make the calculation for 1974, the distribution of party support by social class in 1970 is shown in Table 7.2.

As we can see from Table 7.2, Conservative support was evenly divided between middle class and working class voters while more than four fifths of Labour's support came from the working class. Thus in a sense Labour can reasonably claim to be the working class party but at the same time a third of the working class votes Conservative.

Table 7.2

Party Support by Social Class in 1970

Class	Voting Intention		
	Conservative	Labour	Liberal
	%	%	%
Upper Middle (AB)	21.5	2.5	16.0
Lower Middle (C₁)	28.6	14.8	26.7
Working Class (C₂ DE)	49.9	82.7	57.3
	100.0	100.0	100.0

Source: Calculated from David Butler and Michael Pinto-Duchinsky, *The British General Election of 1970*, Macmillan 1971, p.342.

The large working class minority supporting the Conservatives is clearly of crucial importance in the outcome of the electoral competition between the political parties. If a larger proportion of the working class were to conform to the political views of the majority of their peers then the Conservatives could not hope to gain a parliamentary majority. The Labour Party, on the other hand, is overwhelmingly dependent on working class support and if a still larger minority of workers were to become Conservative supporters Labour could have no hope of maintaining a political balance by making reciprocal gains in the middle class. It is for this reason that working class voters, and especially working class Conservatives, have been the focus of a great deal of inquiry in recent years; it is why the debate about the possible embourgeoisement of some sections of the working class has been of more than academic significance. Though the Conservatives may have almost as many working class supporters as middle class supporters, the overwhelming strength of their support in the upper middle class exceeds Labour's strength in any sector of the working class and suggests a close identification of the interests of the upper middle class with those of the Conservative Party and makes that stratum appear to be the most 'class conscious' of all sections of society in their political allegiance.

The class distribution of Liberals corresponds more closely to the proportions in the population than that of either of the larger parties. Support for the Liberal party is clearly not so rooted in the class division of society as in the case of the others. Their main gains in February 1974 compared with 1970 were at the expense of the Conservative vote in the upper middle and the unskilled working classes and at the expense of the Labour vote in the lower middle and skilled working classes. It follows that a drift towards the Liberals and away from Labour and Conservatives indicates a weakening of the association between party preference and class.

Social Perception and Party Identification

While in general the middle classes vote Conservative and the Labour Party draws its votes from the working class, substantial minorities within each class either voting Liberal or with the majority in the other class casts some doubt upon a straightforward conscious identification of interests of class and party. If we make the usually reasonable assumption — though it is, we must acknowledge, sometimes fallacious — that a man is the best judge of his own interests, then we cannot retain the notion that voting represents class interests in any simple way. The increase in the Liberal vote between 1970 and 1974, though it may be related to changes in the significance of class divisions within the social structure, was too great and too sudden to reflect structural change in any direct way. The fact that there is not a complete identification of class position and party support indicates that somehow a large minority of the members of each class interpret their best interests in a different way from those apparently similarly socially located. In other words, political beliefs, such as they are, cannot be directly determined by 'objective' class position but must be a more complicated response to a perceived social situation. Rose identified an 'ideal typical' working class voter as someone who was a manual worker or married to one who thought of himself or herself as working class, lived in rented accommodation, was a trade unionist or a member of a trade unionist's family and had left school at the minimum age. Taking the results of three Gallup surveys carried out before the 1964 General Election he showed that of the 'ideal typical' working class voters, 75 per cent were Labour supporters but only 26 per cent of the working class had all these characteristics. Thirty-four per cent of the working class in fact, lacked two or more of these characteristics and of this group 44 per cent were Conservatives and only 40 per cent were Labour. Of the 40 per cent of the working class lacking only one or other of the 'ideal typical' characteristics about a quarter were Conservative and two thirds Labour. The exception were the small number having all the characteristics except that they had stayed beyond the minimum school leaving age who seemed to be almost lower middle class in their politics with more than half Conservative and only a third Labour.[1] This is a particularly important exception however, in that it underlines the association between political identification and family background in childhood and early adolescence. Preference for one political party or another, like religion, is for most people mainly the consequence of early socialization.

Though social class or social status is related to voting then, there is a clear link between the way people vote and the way they see their own place in society and this link is strong. From Mark Abrams' surveys of 1962 to 1964 and W. G. Runciman's 1962 survey we can clearly see that voting

---

[1] See R. Rose 'Class and Party Divisions: Britain as a Test Case', *Sociology*, 1968, 2, pp.129-62, Table 11.

intentions are more closely associated with class self-image than with objective class position. That is to say, whether a man thinks he is middle class or not is generally a better guide to the way he is likely to vote than whether in fact he is a manual worker or a white-collar worker. This, of course, does not imply that subjective factors have more causal significance than objective — in this case occupational — factors. The facts that a manual worker votes Conservative and thinks of himself as 'middle class' are more plausibly seen as facets of the same phenomenon, whether it is labelled embourgeoisement, false consciousness, status dissent or whatever, rather than as causally related in either direction.[1]

Table 7.3

Party Support and Subjective and Objective
'Class' in Great Britain 1962-4

Percentages

Voting Intention	Middle Class*		Skilled** Working-Class		Non-Skilled† Working-Class	
	Self-rated 'middle' class	Self-rated 'working' class	Self-rated 'middle' class	Self-rated 'working' class	Self-rated 'middle' class	Self-rated 'working' class
Labour	11	33	31	47	27	49
Conservative	58	27	38	21	37	19
Others***	29	40	31	32	36	32

*All non-manual workers and their dependents: about 30 per cent of the electorate.
**Includes skilled manual workers, foremen and senior shop assistants — 35 per cent of the electorate.
†Non-skilled manual workers and pensioners — 35 per cent of the electorate.
***Others include Liberals, Don't knows and Abstainers.
Source: Mark Abrams, 'Social Class and Politics', in Mabey (ed.), *Class*, Anthony Blond, 1967, Tables 2, 5 and 8.

As Table 7.3 shows, Abrams found that intending Labour and Conservative voters accounted for only about two thirds of his series of samples of the electorate and the proportions lying outside this division were perhaps at that time surprisingly large. Between the two major parties, the Conservatives had a 5 to 1 majority among those members of the middle class who also thought of themselves as 'middle class'. Among the minority in the middle class who described themselves as 'working class' there were more Labour voters than Tories. In the two objectively working class groups there were conversely more Conservative than Labour supporters among the 25 or 30 per cent who thought of themselves as 'middle class', while Labour supporters outnumber Conservatives by more than two to one among the rest. Runciman's figures present a similar pattern but with

[1] See Frank Parkin, 'Working Class Conservatives: A Theory of Political Deviance', *British Journal of Sociology*, 1967, 18, p.290, n.15.

even more Liberals and others and a balance between the major parties more favourable to Labour in all groups except the 'middle class' middle class.[1]

Abrams reminds us, however, that in both working class groups 'those who did *not* up-grade themselves still provide the Conservatives with more votes than they obtain from those who do up-grade themselves.' Fifty-six per cent of the Conservative vote in the skilled working class and 60 per cent in the non-skilled group came 'from electors who insist they are working class.'[2]

Among middle class Labour supporters, however, there is no complementary majority of those who regard themselves as being middle class.[3] The majority of middle class Labour voters, on the contrary, tend to think of themselves as 'working class' so that if we were to take subjective identification as the more significant factor, then Labour Party support is still more overwhelmingly working class than it appears in the objective terms of Table 7.2. In both middle class and working class, then, there is an association between cross-class self-assignment and cross-class party preference in which each set of beliefs probably supports the other. In the working class however, the majority of cross-class voters do not feel themselves to be anything other than working class but in the middle class cross-class voting seems to need the support of congruent views about social status. This pattern, together with the minorities in each subjective subdivision, the working class and middle class Labour voters who feel themselves to be 'middle class' and the subjectively 'working class' Conservatives in all strata, strongly suggests a complex chain of factors shaping political allegiances as well as subjective views of class psoition. Among these local tradition, work situation, age, sex, family background and affiliations, and religion have all been identified as influential by one writer or another.

Other Objective Factors

The association between self-assigned class and party preference varies with the objective structual and political characteristics of the social milieu. Thus NOP surveys from 1963 to 1966 showed that, among those who described themselves as middle class, Conservatives outnumbered Labour supporters by two to one in coal-mining constituencies but by 13 to one in resorts such as Eastbourne or Harrogate. At the same time, among those who thought of themselves as working class, Labour supporters outnumbered Conservatives by ten to one in the mining

---

[1] Abrams, op.cit., 1967, p.25, and Runciman, *Relative Deprivation and Social Justice,* Routledge, 1966, ch.9, especially p.178 and cf. Table 7.1 above.

[2] Abrams, op.cit., 1967, p.25 and cf. Runciman, op.cit., 1966, p.181.

[3] See also Runciman, 'Embourgeoisement, Self-rated Class and Party Preference', *Sociological Review,* 1964, 12, p.148, and 1966, p.171.

divisions but were more or less evenly divided in the resorts.[1] Earlier, in 1950, Benney, Gray and Pear had found in their Greenwich study that occupation was more closely correlated with voting than was self-rated class, but either things changed during the intervening period or perhaps in a predominantly working class constituency subjective perceptions are less influential.[2] In any case, local social structure appears to have a direct influence on voting so that, though the voters' subjective views of their class position may have a mediating and possibly augmentative effect, the relationship still holds even when class self-assignment is ignored. In a study of workers in five oil or chemical process plants in different regions of Great Britain Cotgrove and Vamplew found that despite the similar technology in all the plants self-assigned class and party preference varies with white collar affiliations and local or regional political tradition.[3]

In the south of England the dominance of the Conservative Party, both in terms of popular support and in their representation in the House of Commons, has been increasing[4] and this is, of course, partly due to the growing concentration of the middle classes there.[5] The effect is substantially amplified however, by a sort of bandwagon effect in which the proportion of votes from each class going to the Conservatives increases where the middle class is most common, while the Labour share is highest where the working class is most concentrated. In the north of England, Scotland and Wales the middle class is a little more inclined to vote Labour than in the south and the midlands, while the working class in the midlands and the south of England is much more likely to vote Conservative than elsewhere.[6] Thus a study in Newcastle-under-Lyme showed that more manual workers vote Labour in predominantly working class wards and more manual workers vote Tory in predominantly middle class wards.[7] Willmott and Young noted in their Woodford study that '... the more the middle class predominates in a district the more working-class people identify themselves with it and, incidentally, the more they vote Conservative.'[8]

[1] Cited in Butler and Stokes, *Political Change in Britain*, Macmillan, 1969, Table 6.17, p.145.
[2] See M. Benney, A.P. Gray and R.H. Pear, *How People Vote*, Routledge, 1956.
[3] S. Cotgrove and C. Vamplew, 'Technology, Class and Politics: the Case of the Process Workers', *Sociology*, 1972, 6, pp.169-85.
[4] See E. Hammond, *An Analysis of Regional Economic and Social Statistics*, Rowntree Research Unit, University of Durham, 1968.
[5] See Chapter 3 above.
[6] See Butler and Stokes, op.cit., 1969, p.142, reporting National Opinion Poll data from 1963-66.
[7] See F. Bealey, J. Blondel and W.P. McCann, *Constituency Politics*, 1965, Faber, p.183, and cf. Mark Benney and Phyllis Geiss, 'Social Class and Politics in Greenwich', *British Journal of Sociology*, 1950, 1, p.327.
[8] P. Willmott and M. Young, *Family and Class in a London Suburb*, Routledge, 1960, p.115.

A number of studies have sought to relate political partisanship to experience at work though the evidence is somewhat contradictory. Nordlinger found that the size of the works was correlated with the radicalism of the workers. Among the manual workers he studied, of those working in plants with not more than ten employees, 62 per cent were Conservative, while only 25 per cent of those working in plants with more than 1,000 employees were Conservatives.[1]

Margaret Stacey described how Labour strength was greater in the non-traditional firms, those firms that is to say, organized on a large scale and controlled by decisions made far away from Banbury.[2] It will be recalled that Lockwood explained the Conservativism of clerical workers by their close contact with management on a fairly personalized basis.[3] Geoffrey Ingham, however, unable to discover in his small sample of Bradford workers a relationship between voting and plant size, nevertheless concluded that size was associated with political attitude, with Conservatives in small firms generally expressing views to the right of Conservatives in large-firms while large-firm Labour men were generally to the left of Labour voters in small firms. He argues, in some ways like Lockwood, that the high visibility of behaviour in smaller firms contributes to an identification of the worker's interests with those of the firm.[4] Nordlinger, however, controlling for plant size, found that face-to-face relations between workers and their employers was not directly related to Conservative voting.[5]

Trade union membership is closely associated with Labour voting too but Goldthorpe and his colleagues argue that it is only relevant to consider union membership as a factor in Labour support in the case of those workers subject to conflicting 'cross pressures', and that when there are no middle class and hence Conservative influences seducing the workers from their Labour sympathies, belonging to a union adds nothing to their loyalty to the Labour Party.[6] Butler and Stokes, in fact, conclude from their survey that the correlation is close but support for Labour more often leads to union membership than vice versa.[7] Thus choosing to join a union or choosing to support the Labour Pary are both expressions of a set of attitudes relating the individual and his response to his place in society as he sees it. It is this response and the structural factors which shape it that we are concerned with. As we have seen the evidence on the work situation

---

[1] Eric Nordlinger, *Working Class Tories*, MacGibbon and Kee, 1967, Table 57, p.205.

[2] Stacey, *Tradition and Change,* Oxford, 1960, pp.21 and 46.

[3] Lockwood, *The Blackcoated Worker,* Allen and Unwin, 1957.

[4] Geoffrey K. Ingham, 'Plant Size: Political Attitudes and Behaviour', *Sociological Review,* 1968, 17, p.238.

[5] Nordlinger, op.cit., 1967, pp.190-94.

[6] Goldthorpe et al., *The Affluent Worker: Political Attitudes and Behaviour,* 1968, p.72.

[7] Butler and Stokes, *Political Change in Britain,* Macmillan, 1969, p.157.

itself is contradictory and we must look at a wider range of factors.

The demographic variables, age and sex, can refine the issues somewhat but do not in themselves offer an answer. We still have to account for, that is to say, any sex or age differences which we might discover. Indeed sex and age differences in voting behaviour can easily be misleading, as may be evident when we consider that evidence a little more closely.

Table 7.4

Voting in February 1974 by Age and Sex

	Age						Sex	
	18-24	25-34	35-44	45-54	55-64	65+	Men	Women
	%	%	%	%	%	%	%	%
Conservative	26.9	31.4	35.2	41.4	44.3	49.7	38.1	39.2
Labour	39.5	40.5	40.7	36.7	35.9	35.1	39.3	36.9
Liberal	37.7	24.6	20.6	19.0	16.6	12.6	17.9	21.4
Other	5.9	3.5	3.5	2.9	3.3	2.6	4.7	2.5

Source: Butler and Kavanagh, *op.cit.,* 1974, p.263.

Although we are advised that not too much weight should be given to any one figure in Table 7.4 it is quite evident that women were more likely to be Conservative than men. The election in 1966 was the only one so far in which more women voted Labour than Conservative. Part of this is explained by the fact that women outnumber men among the older age groups. It appears that in 1974 there was still a tendency for older people to vote for the Conservatives while support for Labour and Liberals is generally higher among the younger voters. The biggest change from earlier elections is the more than four-fold increase in the Liberal vote among new voters. This has mainly been to the cost as compared with 1970, of the Conservative vote in this age-group.[1] Butler and Stokes have argued that the association of age and party preference has generally been misconstrued. Youth is generally idealistic and age may bring caution, but Young Socialists generally mellow to become old Labour voters and Young Conservatives turn into old Tories. Allegiances change only rarely and the distribution of party strength across the age structure of the electorate is not the outcome of the progress of the life cycles of the individual voters but is the product of the changing historical fortunes of the parties. Thus every age cohort reflects the popularity of the parties as it was when they first became voters.

Butler and Stokes employ the concept of 'political generation' to account for the association between party preference and age. The

[1] See Butler and Pinto-Duchinsky, op.cit., 1971, pp.342-3.

experience of those who first voted between the wars is different and produced a different result as compared with that of the pre-1918 or post-1945 generations; and those who first became electors in the 1950s and 1960s did not share the same memories as those who first voted in the aftermath of the Second World War. In a period of electoral success for the Tory party new voters are much more likely to be swayed to the Conservative cause, and when Labour comes to look like the party of government new voters are more susceptible to the Labour image. Butler and Stokes divided their 1963 sample of voters into age cohorts according to when they first voted in a General Election. Among the working class almost half (48 per cent) of those who first voted before 1918 said they were Conservatives as compared with 34 per cent of those first voting between the two World Wars and 27 per cent of those who first voted in 1945 or since then. The Labour Party in this period has attracted increasing working class support but those Conservatives whose party allegiances were settled when the Parliamentary Labour Party was small have not changed. While attracting the support of a growing majority of the working class the Labour Party also at first gained the support of an increasing minority of middle class voters. In 1963 there were 15 per cent of the middle class who first voted before 1918 who were Labour supporters and 18 per cent among the inter-war cohort. The immediate postwar popularity of Labour attracted more middle class support and in 1963 25 per cent of those who first voted in 1945 were still Labour supporters, but of those who first voted in the Conservative elections of 1951, 1955 and 1959 only 21 per cent were Labour in 1963;[1] thus for the working class and perhaps latterly for the middle class, the link between class and party was becoming increasingly polarized. The existence of political generations in this way is, of course, very relevant to the embourgeoisement thesis we considered previously and suggests that long-run change in the structure of society is not the only area in which explanation for variations in working class social *Weltanschauungen* should be sought. The changing political climate as it is experienced by the new voter has to be taken into account together with his structural location as an influence upon his view of society and his political opinion.

It may be objected that if this thesis be true then on the one hand the division of political sympathies ought to be increasingly rather than decreasingly between the two major parties, while on the other Liberal voting ought to increase with age too as a number of older electors first voted when the Liberal Party was one of the major parliamentary parties. The fact that neither is the case indicates that the cohort thesis has not rendered other accounts wholly redundant but must be considered as representing one factor among the several operating to bring about change in social attitudes.

[1] op.cit., 1969, Table 5.11, p.109.

While the association of Labour voting with membership of the working class was increasing there may have been some reduction in the intensity of commitment to a party. Among working class Labour supporters, Butler and Stokes write,

'. . . the image of politics as the representation of opposing class interests is increasingly accepted as we move from the pre-1918 cohort (36 per cent) to the Interwar cohort (41 per cent) and reaches a peak in the cohort which entered the electorate over the Second World War and its aftermath (44 per cent). But such an image is accepted less frequently among Labour's working class supporters who entered the electorate more recently (31 per cent).'[1]

Although for working class voters a strong awareness of class produces a view of politics in terms of class interests and support for Labour, to middle class voters the awareness of class makes no difference to the division between the parties. Among the middle class both those for whom class has a high salience and those to whom it seems unimportant divided approximately 80 per cent Conservative to 20 per cent Labour.[2]

The Influence of the Family

In considering class and generation we may still be dealing with minor influences, or at least with factors which shape the views of only a susceptible minority, while family background remains a much more directly influential element in the situation. Certainly it is true that those of us who had Labour parents mostly vote Labour and those of us whose parents were Conservative generally vote Conservative.

The single most influential factor in structuring political opinion can, very briefly, thus be identified as fathers. This is particularly true in the case of first voters. A minority, mostly those exposed to conflicting loyalties of class and family may subsequently switch allegiance, but with age the consistency of voting and the strength of the individual's attachment to his party increases.[3] To begin with, however, in nine cases out of ten people say that when they voted for the first time they voted as their parents did. Butler and Stokes found that where both parents were remembered to be Conservative, 89 per cent of their respondents first preference was also Conservative. Where both parents had been Labour 92 per cent of their respondents had voted Labour the first time. Those respondents who had one parent who had been Conservative and the other Labour had been almost evenly divided in their own first party preference,

[1] ibid., p.117, figures inserted from Table 5.19.

[2] ibid., p.113.

[3] ibid., pp.55-6.

48 per cent having first voted Conservative and 52 per cent Labour.[1] In these 'mixed' families, fathers' views were generally the influential ones because men are most likely to be interested in politics, though the minority of mothers who were partisan had rather more influence than their husbands.[2] First-time voters are only likely to differ from their parents' views when their family is untypical of their own class. That is to say, the children of middle class rather than working class Labour supporters were likely to reject their parents' position and to favour the Conservatives when they themselves came to vote, and it was the children of working class rather than middle class Conservatives who were likely to become Labour themselves. In other words, in the few cases when new voters had abandoned the views prevailing in their own homes they had moved towards the norm for their own class. In the longer run this pattern of conformity to the views learned in the family and reinforced by the political climate of the parental family's social context is the major factor in determining political position. Where their parents had supported the party dominant in their class – i.e. were middle class Conservatives or working class Labour – 85 per cent of Butler and Stokes' respondents still agreed with their parents' party preference. Where their parents had been middle class Labour or working class Conservatives, 42 per cent supported the opposite party but a clear majority, 58 per cent, nevertheless still followed their parents' party preference.[3]

Labour's main inter-generational gains were voters from non-political backgrounds. Here the political effect of class position is unhindered. More than half of all new Labour support in the generation represented by Butler and Stokes' respondents came from manual workers or their wives with non-partisan parents, three quarters of whom became Labour voters.[4] There was also some gain from the downwardly mobile, but here a Conservative family background generally outweighed class position as did a Labour background for the upwardly mobile, though here the tendency to conform to the dominant politics of the respondent's own achieved class position was greater.[5] Butler and Stokes, however, point out that children of Conservative parents are more than twice as likely to be upwardly mobile as those of Labour parents so that some upward mobility 'simply makes middle class adults out of working class children who were already disposed to be Conservative'.[6]

---

[1] ibid., Table 3.1, p.47.

[2] ibid., Table 3.3 and p.50.

[3] Butler and Stokes, *Political Change in Britain*, 1969, Table 3.7, p.52.

[4] ibid., pp.110-12 and Table 5.15.

[5] ibid., Table 5.5

[6] ibid., p.100; see also B.G. Stacey 'Intergeneration Mobility and Voting', *Public Opinion Quarterly*. 1966, 30, p.138; and Abramson and Books, 'Social Mobility and Political Attitudes', *Comparative Politics*, 1970-71, p.411

Working Class Conservatism

As we have seen the low fortunes of the Labour Party in the 1950s led to a great deal of interest in working class Conservatism and even a substantial amount of research. One consequence was the revival after a hundred years of Engels' idea of the embourgeoisement of the English working class. The view that the workers were becoming middle class which we have discussed was advanced as a ready explanation for the third successive Conservative victory in the General Election of 1959. Despite the research it is a view still held to in some quarters with a doggedness largely attributable to its usefulness in explaining the failure of the working class to live up to theoretical expectations.

Working class Conservatism has been associated with the idea of working class affluence. In Runciman's sample, however, the group of manual workers most likely to be Conservative voters were those who thought of themselves as 'middle class' but were in the lowest income group.[1] Among the highly paid workers of Luton on the other hand, while Conservative support was generally no more than average for the working class in the country as a whole (though differences were small), it was positively associated with higher incomes and home ownership.[2]

Goldthorpe and his colleagues however, note that these differences are overshadowed by another. The strongest influence on voting behaviour among these workers was whether or not they had personal contacts in the middle class. Having what Goldthorpe and his colleagues described as 'white collar affiliations' was the greatest single factor making for Conservative support in this group. Whether a man or his wife came from a middle class home (that is if either of their fathers had been white-collar workers), or if the wife had or had had a non-manual job herself or if the husband had had such a job himself before seeking the high wages of the motor industry, exposed these manual workers to cross-pressures from which their colleagues were free.[3] Another idea which was much employed in accounting for the persistent Conservatism of a large proportion of the working class was the notion of deference. In Nordlinger's sample of 320 working class Tories 28 per cent believed they themselves would be better off with a Labour government but nevertheless voted Conservative on deferential grounds.[4] That is to say they accepted and supported the right of the party of the traditional élite, people born to govern. Professor Beer describes the Tory philosophy which rests on the notion that hierarchy is part of the order of nature and argues that for many Conservatives voting for their party is '. . . an act of renewed confidence in the governing class'.[5] Deferentials accept their subordinate

---

[1] Runciman, *Relative Deprivation and Social Justice,* 1966, Table 8, p.172.
[2] Goldthorpe, loc. cit., 1968, p.58.
[3] ibid., p.72.
[4] Nordlinger, *Working Class Tories,* MacGibbon and Kee, 1967.
[5] Samuel H. Beer, *Modern British Politics,* Methuen, 2nd rev. edition, 1969, p.101.

social position – they are in Mogey's terms status assenters[1] – but they do
not necessarily think of themselves as inferior on that account. McKenzie
and Silver in their study of English working class Conservative support
since the nineteenth century argue that

> 'English deferentials feel themselves the moral, if not the social equals
> of the élite because they appear to accept the classic doctrine that all
> who properly fulfil their stations in life contribute worthily to the
> common good . . . English working class deferentials are provided with
> a sense of esteem by the very ideas which justify and explain their
> social and political subordination.'[2]

On this Tory view the differentiation of society into social strata is seen
not as divisive or necessarily generating conflict but rather as a source of
cooperation. Again Beer refers to the '. . . classic Tory theory that class
serves to integrate society vertically rather than dividing it horizontally'.[3]
In the working class however McKenzie and Silver distinguished the
declining deferential Conservatism from the secular Conservatism of the
affluent, whose voting preference stems from a calculation that their
prosperity might be enhanced under a Tory government. Less than a third
of their 1958 sample of working class men and women from London,
Manchester, Halifax and Coventry were deferential voters and Ralph
Samuel found a similar proportion in his smaller investigation in
Stevenage[4] while in Nordlinger's study deference voters were a still
smaller minority.

The concept of deference is however more complex than it at first
appears. Graeme Moodie and Gerald Studdert-Kennedy suggest that
deference may be a consequence or rationalization of Conservative voting
rather than a cause of it, while the general acceptance of a subordinate
social and political position *vis-à-vis* the traditionally ruling groups may be
construed as no more than a certain kind of realism which, as McKenzie
and Silver imply, need not be confined to the working class. Butler and
Stokes too suggest that deference is not peculiar to those of a humble
station in life but may account for middle-class Conservative voting too[5]
and this has been confirmed in a study of three constituencies in
north-east London by R.D. Jessop, who found deferential attitudes
towards the Conservative leadership much more common among their
middle class supporters than among their followers in the working class.[6]

[1] See Chapter 3 above.
[2] R.T. McKenzie and A. Silver, *Angels in Marble*, Heinemann, 1968, p.249.
[3] Beer, loc.cit., 1969, p.412.
[4] R. Samuel, 'The Deference Voter', *New Left Review*, 1960, 1, pp.9-13; McKenzie,
and Silver, op.cit., and 'Conservatism, Industrialism and the Working Class Tory in
England' in Richard Rose (ed.), *Studies in British Politics*, Macmillan, 1966
pp.21ff.
[5] Butler and Stokes, op.cit., 1969, p.115.
[6] See R.D. Jessop, 'Civility and Traditionalism in English Political Culture', *British
Journal of Political Science*, 1971, 1, pp. 1-24.

He argues that a generally favourable attitude towards the prevailing social and political institutions and processes is much more characteristic of English political culture than a specifically deferential attitude towards the members of an élite group, and that what he calls socio-cultural deference or Traditionalism — as distinct from an ascriptive political deference towards an establshed élite — is closely associated with Conservatism, particularly in the middle class. Indeed, 60 per cent of the middle class Conservatives and only 11 per cent of the middle class Labour supporters in his sample were Traditionalist in this sense, compared with only 52 per cent of the working class Conservatives and 24 per cent of the working class Labour supporters.[1]

The use of the term Traditionalism in Jessop's study may itself be slightly misleading however, particularly in the context of those few studies of subcultural variation within the middle class we have referred to earlier.[2] Further research into normative subsystems among the middle class along the lines of what we already know about working class value systems is clearly desirable. It is, however, on the one hand uncertain how far the scale used by Jessop measures some value or attitude dimension which is independent of Conservative opinion, while on the other the hold of the class system and the major institutions of contemporary British culture, the monarchy, private property, Christianity etc., on the consciousness of those involved in it extends beyond those who deferentially accept the leadership of our traditional rulers. Indeed, as Jessop suggests, the concept of deference often serves to obscure this. But Beer goes further than Jessop in suggesting, like McKenzie and Silver, that the class system may have latent functions for many even amongst those most opposed to the material and social inequalities it produces. 'For many people . . . there is psychological security and comfort in class — in automatically having membership in a certain kind of human community by birth and breeding, in knowing exactly where one stands socially in relation to others, in not being continually driven by the social ethos to be 'upwardly mobile'.[3] Jessop's concept of traditionalism is clearly close to that of status assent or the position outlined in McKenzie and Silver's general discussion of English deferentials quoted above. It invokes a set of shared values and mutual obligations which are manifest in the existing and generally approved of social consensus.

It is this consensus and these values with which the Conservative Party has sought to identify itself and in the preservation of which it has sought to establish a monopoly in the minds of the electorate. Moodie and Studdert-Kennedy have argued that historically 'It has been the achievement of the Conservative Party . . . to succeed in identifying itself as an

[1] Calculated from ibid., Table 3, p.11 and cf. Table 6, p.14.

[2] e.g. Margaret Stacey, *Tradition and Change*, or Colin Bell, *Middle Class Families.*, see Chapters 3 and 4 above.

[3] Beer, loc.cit., p.431.

organisation with the commanding features of this national consensus . . .'
the general attitudes involved '. . . are associated with the group
identifications and polarizations that anchor the individual in his own
social reality, helping to structure his perceptions in ways that may at
times seem to be at odds with a simplistic notion of rationality as the
pursuit of economic self interest, but serving important purposes for the
quality of his day-to-day relationships within his family or at work and
satisfying other, non-economic priorities'.[1]

McKenzie and Silver, after analysing Conservative Party literature since
the turn of the century, concluded that 'The central argument which
emerges in the popular party literature is that the Conservatives are
uniquely qualified to govern Britain and that the institutions of the
country are safe in their hands alone.'[2] In this way, as Samuel Beer has
suggested, the strength of the Conservative Party lies in its identification in
the minds of its supporters with things as they are.[3] Unlike Labour, the
Tories have the advantage of, as it were, working with the grain of the
social structure. This may be regarded as an extension of Marx's remark
about the ruling ideas in society being the ideas of the ruling class.[4] The
values of Conservatism justify the social order and in the social order are
manifest the values of a Conservatism which adapts to the circumstances
of the time.

Parkin advanced the argument that because the values upon which the
major institutions of modern British society are built are just those with
which the Conservative Party has identified itself, even working class
support for the Labour Party and Socialism must be thought of as a form
of deviance. Labour support 'like other institutionalised forms of deviance'
is most likely to be found only where the social structural position
insulates the voter from the predominant Conservative values.

> '. . . It is not working class status in and of itself which is held to be the
> crucial determinant of socialist voting so much as the workers' access to
> a normative subsystem which provides the necessary buttresses against
> the dominant value system. Thus members of the working class who are
> not located in such a milieu will lack the normative protection, so to
> speak, necessary to sustain a Socialist commitment — notwithstanding
> their low status and class position. It is this latter category that could
> be expected to provide one major source of the Working Class
> Conservative vote.'[5]

[1] Moodie and Studdert-Kennedy, *Opinions, Publics and Pressure Groups*, Allen and
Unwin, 1970, p 40.
[2] McKenzie and Silver, *Angels in Marble*, 1968, p.72.
[3] Samuel Beer, *Modern British Politics*, 2nd Edition, 1969, pp.92-102.
[4] K. Marx, *The German Ideology*, quoted in T.B. Bottomore and Maximilien Rubel
(eds), *Karl Marx: Selected Writings in Sociology and Social Philosophy*, Watts,
1956, p.79.
[5] Parkin, 'Working-Class Conservatives: A Theory of Political Deviance; *British
Journal of Sociology*, 1967, 18, p.284.

I have already described how Labour support in the working class is more widespread in predominantly working class communities while in the large plant the structural isolation of the labour force from the dominant political value system appears to have similar effects. Beer too underlines the structural context of Labour support. In contrast with the radical individualism of the Liberal Party he emphasizes the collectivist view of politics held by Labour's working class supporters; as far as the working class Labour voter is concerned, he concluded 'the basis of his party allegiance is not so much that he *agrees,* as that he *belongs*'.[1] After the defection of its leaders in 1931, the Labour Party did not split. Ramsay MacDonald, Thomas and Snowden were expelled together with the handful of M.P.s who went with them to support the National Government. Despite this destructive experience the party renewed its strength and gathered support so as to become the main parliamentary opposition party, an important element in the wartime coalition and to form the government after 1945. Beer argues that in such circumstances similar solidarity would have been inconceivable for a party based on the individualism of Liberal or Radical ideals. Labour support was founded on class membership and 'Labour's class image of politics, as well as its Collectivist view of policy made it a distinctive type of political formation'.[2]

Mark Abrams notes that the minority in the middle class who were Labour supporters were 'concentrated in two socially extreme groups — those with considerable experience of higher education and those with low work status within the middle class group'.[3] The latter are generally those who having left school early nevertheless were upwardly mobile from a working class background and continue to think of themselves as working class. The highly educated group have frequently been upwardly mobile too and are concentrated particularly in what Parkin describes as the 'welfare' and 'creative' professions. Parkin argues that these academically highly qualified critics of society select careers which are more congenial or compatible with their beliefs than most middle class occupations in commerce, industry and administration would be.[4] As we have seen they are also likely to be the children of Labour parents.

---

[1] Beer, loc.cit., 1969, p.85.

[2] ibid., p.86.

[3] Mark Abrams in Mabey, *Class,* Anthony Blond, 1967, p.23, and see F. Parkin, *Middle Class Radicalism,* Manchester U.P., 1968.

[4] ibid.

Social Trends and Political Prospects

Support for a political party is associated with an individual's location within the social structure. But it is neither a simple function of any one aspect of his social position, neither his social class nor his age for instance, nor yet simply of his own perception of his social position. External and objective factors shape the way we understand our social environment without our being always sensitive to their influence. Among them material, structural and normative influences operate on the way we order our experience before we ever begin to make rational decisions about it. We have inherited values which have been slowly woven into the social fabric over the course of centuries of change and· these colour our responses to the issues of today. At the same time the present pattern of change, which we are at once making and trying to cope with, traces a new and different outline for succeeding generations with new emphases and new possibilities. The view that because of the congruence of the values they claim to advance with those institutionalized in the structure of British society, the Conservatives are the party most likely to govern 'unless there are quite exceptional circumstances'[1] should not be regarded as a secure assumption. In politics it is a good working assumption to regard all circumstances as exceptional and we can observe that the future of the parties has been subject to somewhat divergent prognoses. Following Parkin[2] we might expect that the gradual disappearance of the traditional working class communities would lead to the destruction of those sub-cultural normative subsystems within which support for Labour thrived, while on the other hand the growth in scale of organizations might be expected to reduce the workers' contact with the bearers of the dominant value system and consequently also reduce their sympathy for the values for which the Conservative Party might appear to stand.

Goldthorpe, Lockwood, Bechhofer and Platt (and W.G. Runciman) found no evidence of embourgeoisement among the working class but nevertheless suggest the likelihood of a long-run decline in Labour support as a result of the increase in the non-manual affiliations of manual workers through the growth of white-collar employment amongst their wives[3]. Grace Jones reinforces this point in reminding us that the overall pattern of change in the occupational structure with the growth of the non-manual sector and the declining size of the working class favours the Conservative Party.[4] Beer on the other hand shows how little reliability such inferences from extraneous social trends have, by pointing out that while non-manual employment increased and manual employment decreased as proportions

[1] See Bernard Crick, *The Reform of Parliament*, Weidenfeld, 1964, p.8.

[2] Parkin, loc.cit., 1967.

[3] Goldthorpe, Lockwood, Bechhofer, Platt, *The Affluent Worker: Political Attitudes and Behaviour, 1968, p.82*

[4] *The Political Structure*, Longmans, 1969, p.19.

of the labour force between 1931 and 1951 at the same time membership of the Labour Party doubled.[1] Of course this was mainly a matter of recruitment within the working class. The lesson we should draw is that the assumptions we are inclined to make on the basis of the current influence of particular social affiliations cannot be relied on to hold good through periods of considerable social change and may need to be revised.

The pattern of social mobility is complex[2] but seems likely to have something of a polarizing effect on the distribution of party support between the classes. Butler and Stokes, as we have seen, found the upwardly mobile into the middle class were particularly likely to be Conservative already, and Abramson and Books noted that downwardly mobile young men were more likely to be either the sons of middle class Labour parents or were especially likely to change their political allegiance to conform with their new social position.[3] The working class is likely therefore to become increasingly Labour and, while the Labour minority in the middle class and the proportion of Labour support they represent is likely to increase, the growing middle class is likely in general to be increasingly Conservative.

The cleavage between the middle class and the working class in their allegiance to the Conservative and Labour Parties however, as Butler and Stokes have emphasized, is very much a matter of the last 40 years or so. It is associated with the decline of the Liberal Party and its replacement by Labour as the other major parliamentary party along with the Conservatives. They demonstrate how the process has taken a generation or more to work itself out. The growth of Labour support means an increasing number of families in which voting Labour is normal. The link between parents' and their children's party preferences is therefore increasingly likely to favour the Labour Party . . . 'Commentaries on Tory voting in the working class', they argue, 'have tended to look for factors which might *de novo* deflect a working class voter to the opposite party and not to see the unequal strength of the two parties in the opposite classes as at least partially due to an evolutionary process by which the bars to Labour strength in its own class have been successively removed."[4] *Ex post facto* generalization is the easiest kind, but it is worth recalling that, while Labour strength grew despite the increase in the size of the middle class, similarly the enlargement of that proportion of the electorate who have grown up in Labour families did not prevent Mr Heath and the Tories winning the 1970 election. And somehow the trend towards the political polarization of the classes has to be reconciled with the two-and-a-half times growth in the Liberal vote between 1970 and 1974. We may perhaps

[1] *Modern British Politics*, 1969, p.414.
[2] See Chapter 8.
[3] 'Social Mobility and Political Attitudes', *Comparative Politics*, 1970-71 pp.411 and 420.
[4] Butler and Stokes, op.cit., 1969, p.109.

conclude that whatever the relevant social trends may be they offer no more than a framework for a more informed sort of speculation and the political future remains uncertain, thank God.

The available evidence on the determinants of party support suggests that for most of us in modern Britain our politics is a product of our social position rather than the outcome of a process of ratiocination and disinterested choice. While reasoned argument may prevail from time to time on specific issues, it operates upon a set of premises which derive from the values, predispositions, interpretations, attitudes and prejudices we already possess. These are not reached after careful deliberation but express our social being for better or worse as it is. The general position has been expressed by a number of writers with more or less emphasis on the structural determinants as against the individual's choice.

'Voting is clearly partly an emotional affair. It is based on prejudices as well as on a rational assessment of the structure of society in general. It is based on the view which the electors have of the future society which the parties are trying to build.'[1]

'For most people most of the time, political issues are remote and responses to them are shaped in complex and indirect ways by reference groups and the mass media.'[2]

'Political choice is an index of individuals' commitments not merely to parties and programmes, but to a wide range of social values; for obviously political allegiances are to an important extent a reflection of the values men subscribe to in areas of life outside politics.'[3]

'Party allegiance is less a conscious and deliberate choice than a by-product of the more primitive forms of collectivism in which he is involved at the workplace, the local Union Branch, in the working men's club, and, at an even deeper level, in the communal sociability of everyday life'[4] and '. . . the understanding of contemporary working class politics is to be found, first and foremost, in the structure of the workers' group attachments and not, as many have suggested, in the extent of his income and possessions'.[5]

We have here a number of accounts suggesting degrees of circumstantial determination ranging from the contention that there is an element of emotionalism in the views people form to the more profoundly deterministic sociology of Goldthorpe et al. The common drift of the argument

[1] Blondel, *Voters, Parties and Leaders,* Penguin, 1963, p.83
[2] Graeme Moodie and G. Studdert Kennedy, *Opinions, Publics and Pressure Groups,* Allen and Unwin, 1970, p.98
[3] Frank Parkin, op.cit., 1967, p.279.
[4] Goldthorpe et al., op.cit., 1968, p.75.
[5] ibid., p.82.

would seem to be that views on particular issues may arise in response to
the mass media or to the behaviour of a reference group, but overall
political orientation is only part of a general outlook which is shaped by
the individual's membership groups and their location within the interlocking relationships of the total social structure. That would seem to be a
fair interpretation of the evidence reviewed in this chapter. All the same it
is important not to overstep the proper limits of such a generalization. The
fact that most people conform to the common pattern should not be
taken to indicate their stupidity or helplessness in the face of their social
conditioning. The fact that people respond to situations in predictable
ways is not a sign of their lack of freedom or of irrationality, even if most
do not stop to work things out from first principles every time. Perhaps
that would be irrational or, if strictly speaking not irrational, at least
unreasonable. The typical patterns of voting, party preference, social
beliefs and world view which the various surveys have discovered are not
prescriptive laws by which men and women are bound. They are no more
than descriptions of the ways people with certain kinds of social
experience have actually thought and behaved. Conformity of itself
constrains no-one; it is only when people feel that they ought to conform
to some pattern that social pressures may override rational considerations. Even then to bow to the social pressures, to behave as might be
expected of one as a member of a particular group, is not itself a sign of
irrationality or a lack of will on the part of the individual. On the
contrary, as Moodie and Studdert-Kennedy put it,

> '. . . it is not necessarily a sign of voter irrationality (instrumentally) to
> vote with one's spouse for the sake of domestic peace (if the latter
> seems sufficiently valuable), to devote little or no time to the
> acquisition of information, or to remain largely uninterested provided
> that others take care of politics in acceptable ways . . .'[1]

The low level of political interest, which is condemned by some as apathy,
irrationality or alienation, may be a perfectly realistic response to their
social situation on the part of individuals with relatively little opportunity
to influence political events and perhaps many other more rewarding
things to do. Political beliefs and attitudes are not distinct from other
beliefs and attitudes. They are part of the way people respond to their
social environment.

As Parkin argued we should not 'treat voting behaviour as a self
contained activity' and so 'ignore the overall value system within which it
occurs'.[2] That value system itself represents a response to the experience
of the communities to which the individual belongs, to their position
within a social structure which is not merely stratified but stratified in

[1] loc.cit., 1970, p.111.
[2] loc.cit., 1967, p.289.

different ways and subject to a range of economic, demographic and cultural changes taking effect differentially at varying rates. Can one wonder that the resulting picture is complex?

8 Education and Social Mobility

Introduction

It sometimes seems as though education is aimed at the attainment of as many goals as there are participants in the process. It is not my purpose here to try to make any sense of the diversity of ideas about what education is or should be, or to weigh the effectiveness with which any of these aims may, in practice, be pursued. The kind of educational system which exists in any society is, in large part, the product of the structure of that society itself. The system, that is to say, will have been based on assumptions about what is normal or desirable and these are in turn partly reflections of the existing social order and partly a series of reactions to it. Particular institutional arrangements will have been contrived to achieve social ends as well as individual enlightenment or the pursuit of knowledge, but of course that still leaves a great deal of scope for a diversity of opinion.[1]

The educational system serves a wide range of interests. Politicians, parents, pedagogues, planners and pupils may seek quite different ends through the institutional framework of education as it may exist at any given time. Each group, within the changing contingencies of their interrelations, may be able, or seek, to frustrate the intentions of some of the others. Once established, however, an educational system acts as a set of constraints upon the activities of those who participate in it. It thus has consequences for the future development of the larger society itself, though these may not always be appreciated or welcomed by those responsible for instituting or maintaining the system in that particular form.

Modern Britain has a money economy and a technologically sophisticated material culture, a highly complex apparatus of legal and welfare obligations and rights and as a concomitant of all this an elaborately

---

[1] See Dennis Smith, 'Power, Ideology and the Transmission of Knowledge', ch.11 in Earl Hopper (ed.) *Readings in the Theory of Educational Systems,* Hutchinson, 1971, pp.240-61; and cf. Ioan Davies, 'The Management of Knowledge: A Critique of the Use of Typologies in Educational Sociology', *Sociology,* 1970, 4, pp.1-22. and reprinted in the same collection.

differentiated division of labour. In this type of society an individual lacking either in literacy or the ability to do simple arithmetic is socially handicapped. Without the possession of these minimal skills by the great majority of adults this kind of social organization would be impossible. Indeed more than this is needed in order to maintain the machine technology and complex commercial and administrative organization on which our present way of life depends. Continuing social and economic change bring about the rationalization of industrial techniques and social and productive innovation which demand an emphasis on training in cognitive skills for an increasingly large proportion of the population.[1] This is what universal primary and secondary education seeks to provide in addition to a more general socialization into the norms of society for those who must make up the mass of its citizens. But it has further consequences. Two, apparently contradictory, themes may be discerned in accounts of the function of education in the modern world. These emphasize either the levelling or the differentiating effects of education in contemporary industrial societies.

On the levelling side the egalitarian social and economic effects of education have been widely emphasized, notably, for example, by Clark Kerr and his colleagues. 'Education is intended to reduce the scarcity of skilled persons and this after a time reduces the wage and salary differentials they receive; it also pulls people out of the least skilled and most disagreeable occupations and raises wage levels there. It conduces to a new equality which has nothing to do with ideology.'[2] As we have seen there is some evidence that this has occurred in respect of the newer professions, particularly those in public employment and in routine non-manual employment, though this is less clearly the case within the manual sector where the restricted entrance to apprenticeship on the one side and the availability of immigrant labour on the other seem to have maintained differentials. A more general question of the primacy of factors arises here as to whether increased supply of skill through educational expansion or the changing demand for types of labour as a result of economic change has been the more important and it may be thought that Kerr and his colleagues claim too much for education in the passage quoted. It represents however – perhaps in an extreme form – one view of the role of educational institutions in an industrial society.

In contrast, and with increasing emphasis in recent years, others have stressed the socially differentiating effects of education in relation to the social structure within which it is provided. Jean Floud, for instance, has stressed the allocative function of education in modern society and has

---

[1] See H. Schelsky, 'Technical Change and Educational Consequence', in A.H. Halsey, J. Floud and C.A. Anderson (eds), *Education, Economy and Society*, Free Press, 1961, pp.31-6.

[2] Clark Kerr, J.T. Dunlop, F.H. Harbison and C.A. Myers, *Industrialism and Industrial Man*, Harvard University Press, 1960, p.286.

suggested that in this society a major task of education has been to train an elite.[1]

The point of view represented here in the quotation from Clark Kerr stresses the role of education as a factor in social change, the second its function in the conservation of the prevailing social order albeit within the pressures of innovative technological change. The resolution of this apparent contradiction requires only that we accept the role of education primarily as one of agent rather than of principal within the social structure. Understandably, this is a view which may rarely be represented adequately in the writings of professional educationalists. If we accept that the relationship of the educational system to the social structure at large is mainly mediated through its allocative functions, then it is evident that people are allocated to socio-economic positions within a changing occupational structure largely on the basis of their success within the educational system. Their starting points in that competition are by no means equal and the handicapping in the race for certificated educational qualification is socially distributed. Thus access to positions of privilege may be mediated through the educational system but the number of such positions and the privileges they confer are determined elsewhere. At the same time, who is most likely to succeed to these positions is already partly determined before they enter school even though a large part of the sorting takes place there.

Selection and Opportunity

In Britain, parents are required by law to ensure that their children receive full-time education, at school or elsewhere, from the age of five until the compulsory minimum leaving age. This has been the situation in England and Wales since the 'Forster' Elementary Education Act of 1870 and in Scotland since the corresponding measure of 1871. The formal foundation of the contemporary system of education as most people experience it today can be said, however, to be the Education Act of 1944. The provisions of this Act have been briefly described by D.E. Butler and J. Freeman as follows,

'The Act changed the title of the President of the Board of Education to the Minister of Education. Primary and secondary education were

[1] 'The processes of social selection and differentiation are heavily concentrated in the educational system, as is the nature of things in a technological society. . .', review by Jean Floud in *Sociological Review*, 1963, II, 1; cf.'Social Class Factors in educational achievement', ch.2 in M. Craft (ed.), *Family, Class and Education: A Reader*, Longman, 1970, pp.31ff.; see also 'The Sociology of Education', ch.29 in A.T. Welford et al. (eds), *Society: Problems and Methods of Study*, Routledge, 1963; and J. Floud and A.H. Halsey in Floud, Halsey and Anderson (eds), op. cit., 1961, p.6.

divided at '11 plus'. Provision was made for compulsory part-time education between the school-leaving age and 18 in county colleges, but this has not been implemented. The minimum school-leaving age was raised to 15 (in 1947) and provision was made for raising it to 16 ... No fees were to be charged in schools which were publicly provided or aided by grants from the local authority.'[1]

The abolition of fees made secondary education much more widely accessible, but the raising of the school-leaving age to 16 was not achieved until the educational year 1972-3. No particular pattern of organization of secondary education was prescribed by the Act, but until the later 1960s most local authorities adopted the tripartite division into grammar, secondary modern and technical schools, though with the frequent omission of the technical school element. By 1971 only 36 per cent of English secondary school pupils were in comprehensive schools though in Wales the proportion reached almost 59 per cent.[2]

T.H. Marshall had argued in 1953 that selection on grounds of academic ability for the different sorts of school designed to suit the pupils' aptitudes was in effect social selection determining the future social opportunities of children channelled into each of the different educational processes at 11. He argued that parents' reactions to this arrangement would subvert the 'separate but equal' ideals of the educational planners.[3] Ten years later Taylor's study of the secondary modern school showed that this was precisely what had occurred.[4] The original intentions had been to escape from the traditional, academically orientated, curriculum of the grammar school pattern and to provide less specialist, more flexible and more practically orientated education. On the one side however, as employment in clerical and higher status positions came more and more to depend on the possession of G.C.E. 'O' level certificates or higher qualifications, there were the demands from parents — particularly in the middle class — for parity of opportunity for their secondary modern school children to acquire formally certificated levels of education. At the same time, from the other side, secondary modern teachers were very ready to agree, predisposed as they were by their own educational success to recognize the virtues of an academic, examination-orientated sytem, and with a material interest in the opportunities for specialist teaching allowances which it provided.

The tripartite scheme, or at least the usual division between grammar and secondary modern schools, came to be criticized not only on account

[1] D.E. Butler and J. Freeman, *British Political Facts 1900-1967*, Macmillan, 1968, p.197.

[2] *Social Trends* No.3, 1972, Table 88.

[3] T.H. Marshall, 'Social Selection in the Welfare State' included as ch.14 in Halsey, Floud and Anderson, op.cit., 1961, and as ch.2 in Hopper, op.cit., 1971.

[4] William Taylor, *The Secondary Modern School*, Faber and Faber, 1963.

of the differential opportunities the schools provided but also because of the apparently socially unequal chances of getting to one or the other. Jean Floud emphasized that

> 'It is important to realise . . . that social selection disguised as academic selection is a process at work in all schools. By the time children reach the threshhold of secondary education at the age of eleven, those drawn from certain social groups have as a whole already begun to outstrip scholastically those from families at the other end of the scale, and the same process is continued among those selected for grammar schools during their time there.'[1]

The process of selection is in practice felt to be competitive and contributes to the production of failure at all levels. Selection for the secondary modern school was construed by parents, teachers and children as failure. Even among the minority selected for the grammar school, as Lacey has described, the lowest stream produces an antipathetic, rebellious minority growing in antagonism into their fourth year and leaving early, while even the express stream has its failures.[2]

Hargreaves showed how the institutionalization of streaming worked in a northern secondary modern school. The lower stream generally had teachers with poorer qualifications and weaker discipline and were not entered for external examinations. The effect, he concluded, was to polarize the two groups of similarly working-class pupils between the upper, academically orientated stream and a lower stream 'progressively retarded and alienated from the school's values' as they reach their fourth and final year.[3] Yet as Brian Jackson showed in a survey of 666 primary schools in England and Wales, 96 per cent were streamed and 91 per cent of teachers were in favour. Half of the children at school in England and Wales were already streamed in the infants school and three quarters were streamed by the age of seven.[4] A study of the attitudes of secondary modern and grammar school teachers throughout England in 1966 found that 64 per cent were in favour of retaining some selection for secondary schools.[5] But the pressure for higher qualifications and the changing occupational opportunities of the 1960s, together with the criticisms of inequalities within the tripartite system, led to the movement towards various kinds of comprehensive system under which selection of pupils for different kinds of school is in principle avoided.

[1] Jean Floud, 'Social Class Factors in Educational Achievement' in A.H. Halsey (ed.), *Ability and Educational Opportunity*, OECD, Paris, 1961 and Craft (ed.), op.cit., 1970. p.45.

[2] Colin Lacey, 'Some Sociological Concomitants of Academic Streaming in a Grammar School', *British Journal of Sociology*, 1969, 17, pp.245-62

[3] David Hargreaves, *Social Relations in a Secondary School*, Routledge, 1967.

[4] Brian Jackson, *Streaming: An Education System in Miniature*, Routledge, 1964.

[5] P.Biggin, C.R. Coast and J.M. Stansfield, *A Verdict on Comprehensives*, Wheelwright G.S., Dewsbury, 1966.

Table 8.1

Educational Expansion in Britain 1956-71

(a) *% Increase in Attendance at Grant Aided Schools in U.K. by Age*

	Increase in Pupils			Increase in Age Group	
	1956-61	1961-66	1966-71	1961-66	1966-71
Ages:	%	%	%	%	%
2 yrs to 4 yrs	+12.5	+10.0	+ 32.3	+15.9	−3.8
5 yrs to 14 yrs	+2.9	−0.6	+ 11.3	−1.3	+11.9
15 yrs and over	+50.6	+62.5	+ 15.7	+16.2	−9.4

(b) *Pupils in School as a percentage of Age Groups in U.K.*

% of Children Aged:	1961	1966	1971
2 yrs to 4 yrs	9.9	9.3	12.4
16 yrs	21.5	27.7	35.6
17 yrs	11.7	14.8	20.3
18 yrs and over (as % of 18-yr-olds)	4.1	5.1	7.0

(c) *Distribution of pupils in England Wales by Type of School*

% of All Pupils	1956	1961	1966	1971
in Maintained Schools	91.8	92.3	92.8	93.9
in Direct Grant Schools	1.3	1.4	1.5	1.4
in Independent Schools recognized as efficient	3.7	3.8	3.9	3.5
in Other Independent Schools	3.2	2.5	1.8	1.2
N = 100%	7.3m.	7.7m.	7.8m.	8.8m.

(d) *Distribution of pupils aged 15 years and over in England and Wales by Type of School*

% of Pupils aged 15 yrs to 19 yrs	1956	1961	1966	1971
in Maintained Schools	71.2	76.4	83.3	86.2
in Direct Grant Schools	7.7	7.2	5.3	4.9
in Independent Schools recognized as efficient	16.6	13.2	9.8	8.2
in Other Independent Schools	4.5	3.2	1.6	0.7
N = 100%	353,437	504,271	782,027	889,607

Source: Calculated from *Social Trends* 3, 1972, Table 82 and *Annual Abstract of Statistics* 104, Table 38 and 109, Table 124.

The spread of formal and compulsory education to the whole population is a story set in the nineteenth century. The twentieth century has seen the extension of the duration of education beyond the statutory minimum for an increasing proportion of the population. The more recent stages of this development, set out in Table 8.1, have to be set against the background of demographic, economic and social changes which have been in process over the same period.

As the table shows, during the late 1950s and early 1960s the number of pupils in schools increased in the younger and older age groups and declined slightly in the normal school age population. This decline was, of course, due to the decline in the size of the age group as the post-war 'bulge' passed on into employment or the later stages of education. The rising numbers of nursery school children at this time in fact represented a declining proportion of the increasing numbers in the age group and it was not until the later 1960s that with increasing provision of places there was a real improvement in the proportions under five years of age in schools. The effect of the increasing fertility rates of the later 1950s and early 1960s is apparent in the sharp rise in the school population in the later 1960s. These demographic trends have had some influence on the numbers in school over the statutory minimum age.[1] However an increasing proportion of pupils has been staying on at school so that by 1971 more than a third were remaining till 16 and C.S.E. or 'O' levels, while a fifth of all 17-year-olds were at school — almost double the proportion of ten years earlier.

An increasing proportion of this expanding school population, especially among the over 15s, has been provided for in the local authority schools. The decline in minor schools in the private sector is partly accounted for by some achieving official recognition and inspection which had not previously done so. In part, however, it is evident there has been a genuine decline in the numbers of small private schools for older pupils (mostly on account of their increasing costs) leaving in the 'other independent' category mostly the smaller private schools catering for the younger child. Schools recognized as efficient and direct grant schools have, however, increased in number and in the number of pupils they provide places for, though they have not kept pace with more recent expansion of demand and, in the later 1960s, accommodated a declining proportion of pupils. This is particularly clear when we consider the rapid growth of schooling for those over 15. Most of the increased demand here has had to be provided for within the state system (i.e. local authority schools) and though the private sector has expanded it has not had the resources to cope with a trend of these dimensions. A comparison of the percentages in sections (c) and (d) of the Table will indicate the Direct Grant and Independent (Efficient) school children stay on after 15 years of age to a much greater extent than do local authority schoolchildren.

---

[1] 15 in the period under discussion.

Nevertheless, despite their increasing numbers, they accommodate a decreasing proportion of all pupils over 15.

There are some signs that these trends may have been levelling off in the early 1970s and certainly the rate of increase slowed then.[1] Nevertheless, the proportion of young people undergoing education continued to grow as increasing proportions not only stayed beyond the statutory minimum school-leaving age but increasing proportions went on into higher or further full- and part-time education after school.

Table 8.2

Percentage of Young People of Both Sexes receiving full-time education 1870-1971

				Great Britain		
	1870*	1902*	1938*	1961**	1966†	1971***
10 year olds	40	100	100	100	100	100
14 year olds	2	9	38	100	100	100
17 year olds	1	2	4	18	22	30
19 year olds	1	1	2	10	10	16

*Approximate figures. Source: *Higher Education: Report* (Robbins Report), ch. III, Table 1, p.11.
**Source: *1961 Census Great Britain Summary Tables*, Table 32.
†Source: *1966 Census Economic Activity Tables, Part I*, Table 1.
***Source: *1971 Census Great Britain Summary Tables (One Per Cent Sample)*, Table 13.

Table 8.2 indicates the expansion of education into later age ranges of the population during the course of the past century. This is a trend which has been accelerated in the expansion of higher education in the late 1960s. As Table 8.3 demonstrates, more than one in every six 18-year-olds are now students in some form of full-time higher education, more than double the proportion ten years earlier. At the beginning of the 1970s, however, more than half of the school population was still leaving full-time education by the age of 16.[2] After 17, the proportion of girls in full-time education falls rather more steeply than that of boys, though among postwar generations the gap seems to be less great than before the war and is still narrowing.[3] As Table 8.4 shows, the proportion of school-leavers (particularly of girls) going directly into employment fell substantially during the 60s. In absolute terms the decline was very much greater among pupils attending the private sector schools where in 1971 only four in every ten boys left to

[1] See *New Society*, 10 August 1972, p.290.

[2] *1971 Census Great Britain Summary Tables (One Per Cent Sample)*, Table 13.

[3] ibid.; cf. *1966 Census Economic Activity Tables, Part I*, Table 1.

Table 8.3

The Growth of Higher Education in Britain 1900-1970*

The Percentage of the Age-Group Entering:**

Year	University	Teacher Training	Full-time Further Education	All Full Higher Education
1900	0.8	0.4	–	1.2
1938	1.7	0.7	0.3	2.7
1954	3.2	2.0	0.6	5.8
1960	4.1	2.7	1.5	8.3
1970	8.7	5.2	3.6	17.5

*Figures for 1900-1960 refer to Great Britain while those for 1970 refer to the United Kingdom.

**New students as a percentage of 18-year-olds figures for Full-Time Further Education are approximate.

Source: 1900-1960 *Higher Education*, ch. 3, Table 4.

1970 *Annual Abstract of Statistics 109*, 1972, Tables 127, 129, 136, 141 and 108, 1971, Table 10.

go into employment, compared with over eight out of every ten in the state sector, and only one third of the girls did not go on into further full-time education after school compared with almost eight in every ten in the state sector. The greatest proportionate changes have been local authority school boys and most spectacularly girls from both local authority and independent or assisted schools going on to university and also, to a lesser extent, girls from the public sector and boys from both sectors going into other full-time further education in colleges of technology and so forth. These trends also represent a distinct narrowing of differentials in the proportions from public and private sector schools going on into higher education and to universities in particular. There is, nevertheless, still a long way to go on the road to equality of opportunity when pupils in non-state schools still had better than a five times greater chance of getting to university in 1971. From all origins, the proportion of men going to university has increased from 3.7 per cent of all 18-years-olds in the period 1928 to 1947 to 5.6 per cent in 1962 and 12.3 per cent in 1972. The proportion of women going to university increased from 2.5 per cent in 1962 to 5.9 per cent in 1972. [1]

[1] *Higher Education*, 1963, Appendix I, Part II, Table 15, and Report Table 5, p.16; Universities Central Council on Admission, *Statistical Supplement to Tenth Report*, 1973, p.10 and *1971 Census*.

Table 8.4

Destination of School Leavers by Type of School

England and Wales

TYPE OF SCHOOL	Number of Leavers (Thousands) (= 100%)	Employment* %	Other Full-time Further Education %	Colleges of Education %	Universities** %
1961					
BOYS:					
A Public Sector Schools	290.8	90.4	5.2	0.9	3.5
B Assisted and Independent Schools†	21.4	51.7	16.8	1.7	29.8
All Schools	312.2	87.7	6.1	0.9	5.3
A : B			1 : 3.2	1 : 1.9	1 : 8.5
GIRLS:					
A Public Sector Schools	280.4	87.2	8.3	2.8	1.7
B Assisted and Independent Schools†	20.2	40.6	36.8	10.4	12.2
All Schools	300.6	84.0	10.2	3.4	2.4
A : B			1 : 4.4	1 : 3.7	1 : 7.2
1971					
BOYS:					
A Public Sector Schools	292.8	83.5	9.5	1.3	5.7
B Assisted and Independent Schools†	22.5	40.4	26.3	1.8	31.5
All Schools	315.3	80.6	10.6	1.3	7.5
A : B			1 : 2.8	1 : 1.4	1 : 5.5
GIRLS:					
A Public Sector Schools	279.2	78.6	13.0	4.9	3.5
B Assisted and Independent Schools†	18.9	35.9	33.1	10.5	20.5
All Schools	298.1	75.9	14.3	5.2	4.6
A : B			1 : 2.5	1 : 2.1	1 : 5.9

* In 1971 leavers going into temporary employment have been included in the Employment column as have those whose destinations were unknown.
** Including Colleges of Advanced Technology (which became universities on 1 April 1965).
† Excluding independent schools not recognised as efficient, and special schools.

Source: *Social Trends*, 3, 1972, Table 90.

Inequalities of Opportunity

The problem of equality of opportunity at all levels of the system has been the central concern of the sociology of education and indeed of educational reform in the postwar world. I shall return to the institutional division between the public and private sector later. Within the local authority maintained schools a wide variety of factors have been found to be influential in success. First Jahoda and then Douglas, Ross and Simpson found short-sighted children are academically more successful than those with normal vision,[1] while Dennis Child has shown that more introverted children are more likely to be successful in internal school examinations than others.[2] Indeed, earlier studies suggest that even neuroticism too can be an educationally felicitous trait.[3] These temperamental and physiological characteristics are associated with higher social status however, and such findings reflect and help to account for the consistent evidence from a large body of research indicating the tendency to greater educational achievements of children from middle class families. The association of attainment with birth weight and family size is similarly related to social status as longitudinal studies by The National Survey of Health and Development of Children and The National Child Development Study have shown.[4]

Though the abolition of fees in local authority secondary schools by the 1944 Education Act removed one of the more obvious sources of social inequality in education it soon became evident that middle class children enjoyed considerable advantages with regard to their attainments within the new system. As the study of 14,500 children born throughout Great Britain in the first week of March 1958 by the National Children's Bureau showed this is already evident in the infant schools. By the age of seven, when these children transferred to primary schools, class differences in attainment were already clearly apparent. In this study children were categorized according to their fathers' occupations, which were classified within the Registrar-General's five social classes with Class III divided between non-manual and manual occupations. From the attainment tests they used, the authors note two important points which emerge.

[1] See G. Jahoda, 'Refractive Errors, Intelligence and Social Mobility', *British Journal of Social and Clinical Psychology*, 1962, 1, p.96; J.W. B. Douglas, J.M. Ross and H.R. Simpson, 'The Ability and Attainment of Short Sighted Pupils', *Journal of the Royal Statistical Society; Ser. A,* 1967, 130, pp.479-503, and *All Our Future,* Peter Davies, 1968, ch.21

[2] Dennis Child, 'Personality and Social Status', *British Journal of Social and Clinical Psychology,* 1969, 5, pp.196-9.

[3] See summary in F. Musgrove, *The Migratory Elite,* Heinemann, 1963, pp.127-8.

[4] See J.W.B. Douglas, *The Home and the School,* McGibbon and Kee, 1964; and Ronald Davie, Neville Butler, Harvey Goldstein, *From Birth to Seven,* Longman, 1972.

'First there is clearly a strong association between social class and reading and arithmetic attainment at seven years of age. The chances of an unskilled manual worker's child (Social Class V) being a poor reader are six times greater than those of a professional worker's child (Social Class I). If the criterion of poor reading is made more stringent, the disparity is much larger. Thus, the chances of a Social Class V child being a *non*-reader are fifteen times greater than those of a Social Class I child.

'A second point which emerges is that the gradient from Social Class I through to Social Class V is not regular. There are little or no differences between the results for Social Class II and Social Class III (non-manual) children but very considerable differences between the results of these groups and those for Social Class III (manual) children . . . There appears to be a substantial division between the children from non-manual, or middle-class, homes on the one hand, and those from manual, or working-class, homes on the other. This suggests that whatever the factors are which social class indirectly measures, they are fairly sharply differentiated as between middle-class and working-class homes, at least as far as their effect on attainment or ability is concerned.'[1]

Within the working class there was a consistent gradient on these measures from children whose fathers were classified as skilled through the semi-skilled to the unskilled who were particularly likely to be of poor ability or attainment in school. Within the middle class the gradient of attainment was not a consistent one however and there was a distinct gap between the high average attainment of children from the professional group and that of the managerial, technical and routine clerical workers' children (Social Classes II and III non-manual).

The continuation of the process of differentiation through the primary school has been clearly described in an earlier longitudinal study of a sample of over 5,000 children born in the first week of March 1946. Douglas and his colleagues found that when they reached primary school middle class children had a higher average measured ability than working class children and therefore, unsurprisingly, a larger proportion of middle class children were allocated to the upper streams than of working class children. But when children of the same ability are concerned, middle class children tended to be allocated to the upper streams and working class children to the lower, As compared with their measured ability at eight years of age, Douglas showed there were 11 per cent more middle class children in the upper streams than should have been expected and twenty six per cent fewer in the lower streams. He concluded that academic streaming in the primary school was tending to produce self-fulfilling

[1] Davie, Butler and Goldstein, op.cit., 1972, pp.102-4.

prophecies because children in the upper streams were found to improve their scores on reading tests between the ages of eight and eleven while those in the lower streams deteriorate. Middle class children are not only favoured by the pattern of selection for the upper streams in school but were less adversely affected when not so selected. Working class children on the other hand, were found to be liable to particularly severe deterioration in their relative attainment when assigned to the B-stream.[1]

On transfer from primary to secondary schools at the age of eleven, there was, under the so-called tripartite system, a further sorting out which though in principle based on aptitude and ability in effect produced a further segregation of middle class and working class children. Reviewing the evidence of expansion in secondary education over the first half of the twentieth century, Little and Westergaard took a very pessimistic view of the attempts to improve equality of opportunity through such measures as the 1944 Act. 'Clearly . . . this long-term trend towards a reduction of social differentials in educational opportunity at the secondary stage is moderate and limited', they wrote.

'The differentials remain sharp. Indeed, if the proportion *not* going to grammar-type schools is taken as the measure of changing educational opportunity the persistence of inequalities stands out still more clearly. Less than two in every five children from homes in the (professional and managerial) group failed to obtain education of a grammar school type in the 1950's, compared with almost two in every three in the first decades of the century — a reduction of nearly half. By contrast, no less than nine in every ten of the lowest social group (semi- and unskilled workers' children) were still deprived of a grammar school education in the 1950's; the proportion so deprived was barely a tenth smaller than 30 or 40 years before'.[2]

In the academic year 1959-60, pupils in the grammar schools in England and Wales were roughly 55 per cent middle class and 45 per cent working class[3] and 54 per cent of upper middle class children went to grammar school or an equivalent compared with only 11 per cent of lower working class children.[4]

[1] J.W.B. Douglas, op. cit., 1964, ch. 14.

[2] Alan Little and John Westergaard, 'The Trend of Class Differentials in Educational Opportunity in England and Wales', *British Journal of Sociology*, 1964, XV, pp.309-10; see also John Westergaard and Alan Little, 'Educational Opportunity and Social Selection in England and Wales: Trends and Policy Implications', *Social Objectives in Educational Planning*, O.E.C.D., 1967, pp.215-32, reprinted in Maurice Craft (ed.), *Family, Class and Education: A Reader*, Longman, 1970, pp.49-71.

[3] Estimated from J.W.B. Douglas, op.cit., 1964, Appendix III, Table VI(f).

[4] ibid., p.77 and Appendix III, Table VI(g).

The process of selection does not end with entry to secondary education but continues and again reaches a crucial point at the time of transfer to post-secondary school education. The evidence to the Committee on Higher Education under the chairmanship of Lord Robbins extensively documented class differentials in educational attainment at that level.[1]

Table 8.5

Proportion of Children in Great Britain Born in 1940-41 reaching Full-Time Higher Education: by Fathers' Occupations

Percentages

Father's Occupation	Full-time Higher Education		No full-time Higher Education	All Children	Population Estimates based on Survey (= 100%)
	Degree Level	Other			
Boys & Girls:					
Non-Manual					
Higher					
Professional	33	12	55	100	15,000
Managerial & Other					
Professional	11	8	81	100	87,000
Clerical	6	4	90	100	38,000
Manual					
Skilled	2	2	96	100	248,000
Semi and unskilled	1	1	98	100	137,000
Boys:					
Non-Manual	15	4	81	100	70,000
Manual	3	2	95	100	189,000
Girls:					
Non-Manual	9	10	81	100	70,000
Manual	1	2	97	100	196,000

Source: *Higher Education* (The Robbins Report), 1963, Ch.VI, Table 21.

As Table 8.5 from the Report shows, there was a very steep gradient across the class hierarchy in the early 1960s, particularly for girls. Children whose fathers were in the higher professions were 33 times more likely to reach university level courses than the children of semi-skilled and unskilled manual workers.

---

[1] See *Higher Education,* Report of the Committee appointed by the Prime Minister under the Chairmanship of Lord Robbins 1961-63, H.M.S.O., 1963: see especially Appendix One, *The Demand for Places in Higher Education,* Part II: 'Factors Influencing Entry to Higher Education'.

Universities as a consequence remain predominantly middle class institutions. Thus, though about 58 per cent of all households in Great Britain were working class at the beginning of the 1970s[1], only 28 per cent of university students were from working class homes, as Table 8.6 shows.

Table 8.6

Percentage of Undergraduates with Fathers in Manual Occupations

	Men	Women	Men and Women
1928-47	27	13	23
1955	27	19	23
1961	26	23	25
1970	30	25	28

Sources: 1928-1947 Jean Floud in D.V.Glass (ed.), *Social Mobility in Britain*, 1954, p.137 (men in England and Wales who had attended universities).
1955 R.K.Kelsall, *Applications for Admission to Universities*, 1957 (G.B. entrants).
1961 Robbins' Undergraduate Survey (all G.B. undergraduates) see *Higher Education*, Appendix Two B, Part I, Table 6.
1970 Universities Central Council on Admissions, *Report 1969-70*, Statistical Supplement, Table E 1 (G.B. accepted home candidates).

It is true that with the expansion of higher education since the Second World War there has been a gradual improvement in the proportion of students from the working class, a trend which has reduced the additional class disadvantage of working class women to a level closer to that of working class men. The proportion varies quite widely between universities ranging among those graduating in 1960 from 13 per cent of the men and only 6 per cent of the women in Oxford and Cambridge through London and the Scottish universities with 24 per cent of men from working class homes and 30 and 35 per cent of men in the smaller and larger universities in the rest of England and 43 per cent in Wales respectively.[2] Overall there are high proportions of students from working class homes in universities in Britain compared at least with other Western European countries. In France, the Netherlands and West Germany the proportions of working

---

[1] *1971 Census Great Britain Summary Tables (One Per Cent Sample)*, Table 27; see Table 5.9 above.

[2] See R.K. Kelsall, Anne Poole and Annette Kuhn, *Graduates: The Sociology of an Elite*, Methuen, 1972, p.191, and cf. Kelsall, *Applications for Admission to Universities*, Association of Universities of the British Commonwealth, 1957.

class university students were only a third to a fifth of that in Britain and even among the Scandinavian countries only Norway reaches a similar degree of equality.[1]

Thus with relatively greater and improving, if only slowly, educational opportunities for working class children than in many comparable countries, the evidence so far considered indicates a tendency for children to be like their parents and could well be quite consistent with a process of fair selection in what is in the long run a competitive educational system. In order to see how far this is in fact all there is to the matter or whether there really are differential opportunities for middle class and working class children, it is not enough simply to show that middle class children tend to be more successful than working class children. It is necessary to control for the factor of ability. When this is done we discover a rather more alarming picture.

Factors in Differential Achievement

On the basis of surveys carried out in 1956-59 for the Central Advisory Council for Education it was estimated that there was a substantial pool of untapped ability. In their report '15 to 18' published in 1960, the Council identified, between the brightest 25 per cent and the majority of ordinary children, a second quartile of intelligent children whose education was described as 'inadequate both in its quality and duration'.[2] As D.V. Glass pointed out in his introduction to Douglas's The Home and the School, if all the children of equal intelligence as measured in tests at the age of eight had had an equal chance of going to a state grammar school as children from the upper middle class there would have to have been 56 per cent more grammar school places than were in fact available. 'This analysis applies only to "success" in the public system. If we take into account the chances, for given levels of measured intelligence at the age of eight years, of children of the upper middle classes entering all forms of selective secondary education (including the independent schools) then we should need to increase the allotment of grammar school places by 75 per cent'.[3]

The relative advantage of the middle class is more marked the further one follows the career of the children and most marked amongst the less able as Table 8.7 shows.

The growth of secondary education beyond the statutory minimum has meant that the proportion of pupils reaching any given level of attainment has been increasing. The Robbins Committee estimated, however, that

[1] See Frank Parkin, Class, Inequality and Political Order, McGibbon and Kee, 1971, Table 4.2, p.110.

[2] 15 to 18: A Report of the Central Advisory Council for Education: England (The 'Crowther' Report), H.M.S.O., 1960, Paragraph 694.

[3] In J.W.B. Douglas, op.cit., 1964, pp. 19-20 and Appendix III, Table VI(g).

despite this the differentials between the social classes remained as great in 1960 as they had been ten years earlier.[1] Table 8.6 of course indicates that there was a considerable wastage of ability amongst the children of non-manual workers too, though the subsequent expansion in the 1960s will have reduced the numbers of able children not proceeding to 'A' levels and beyond in all social classes.

Table 8;7

Academic Achievement of Children Born in 1940-41 and at Maintained Grammar Schools in England and Wales by I.Q. at 11 years and Fathers' Occupation

I.Q.	Father's Occupation	Degree Level Course	Percentages At least 2 'A' Levels	At least 5 'O' Levels
130+	A Non-manual	37	43	73
	B Manual	18	30	75
	A divided by B	2.06	1.43	0.97
115-129	A Non-manual	17	23	56
	B Manual	8	14	45
	A divided by B	2.12	1.64	1.24
100-114	A Non-manual	6	9	37
	B Manual	2	6	22
	A divided by B	3.00	1.50	1.68

Source: *Higher Education*, 1963, Appendix I, Part II, Table 5.

In response to criticism arising from the inequalities of educational provision in different regions or between different local authorities, the strains on children and parents of the selection procedures and criticism from educationists of the efficacy of the secondary modern schools, various alternative schemes were canvassed and tried out. Various attempts to combine institutional reform with minimal administrative inconvenience and the redeployment of existing resources led to various combinations of junior, high and middle schools, bilateral and multilateral secondary schemes etc. The general tendency, however, encouraged by the Labour Secretary of State for Education at the Department of Education and Science in the renowned *Circular 10/65,* has been to replace the so-called tripartite scheme by a system of comprehensive education within which transfer between streams would be facilitated while the invidious comparisons which came to be made between the different types of secondary school formerly in existence might be evaded. As yet little is known about the effects of this reform. The evidence is scattered, covers only a short period and does not so far permit comparison between the

[1] *Higher Education*, 1963, Appendix One, Part II, paragraph 27, and Table 14.

different ways in which 'comprehensivization' has been implemented. What there is suggests that the grouping together of secondary education under one roof is not likely on its own to end the social differentiation evident in the data on the first 25 years after the 1944 Education Act. In 1958-63 Eggleston found that in a group of eight Midland local education authority areas, there was no evidence that the introduction of comprehensive schools led to higher proportions of pupils staying beyond the statutory minimum leaving age when the socio-economic level of the schools' catchment areas was allowed for. Staying-on rates in unselective schools were higher in those areas which also had or had had a high grammar school intake.[1]

Analysing data from several school catchment areas in the Leicestershire plan Eggleston found that the social composition of the area was an important influence on the behaviour of both middle and working class. The pattern is analogous to what we observed in relation to party preference in the preceding chapter.

> 'In the plan', Eggleston writes, 'pupils have the opportunity to transfer at fourteen to the Upper School for an extended education or remain in the High School and leave at minimum leaving age. The only condition of transfer is that the pupil will remain until he is sixteen, a year after minimum school leaving age. Though in all areas, the transfer rate of the non-manual workers' children was higher than that of the manual workers' children, the manual workers' rate was highest in the most middle-class community and lowest in the most working-class community. Fifty-nine per cent of manual workers' children transferred in the middle-class suburb, only 30 per cent in the working-class area. Conversely, only 77 per cent of non-manual workers' children transferred in the working-class area as against 89 per cent in the middle-class suburb.'[2]

In a more localized study contrasting a secondary modern school and a grammar school with what she took to be a fairly typical comprehensive school comparable with them in terms of range of ability represented among its pupils Julienne Ford found that there was a higher rate of early leaving in the comprehensive school among both working class and middle class pupils of grammar school ability. Middle class children were more likely to be in the A-streams of the comprehensive school than working class children of similar ability and there was, if anything, less mixing between children from different social backgrounds in the comprehensive

---

[1] S. John Eggleston, 'Some Environmental Correlates of Extended Secondary Education in England', *Comparative Education*, 1967, III, pp.85-99.

[2] S. John Eggleston, *The Social Context of the School*, Routledge, 1967, p.36, see also Eggleston, 'How Comprehensive is the Leicestershire Plan?', *New Society*, 1965, no.130, p.17.

school than in the grammar school.[1] Douglas, Ross and Simpson, on the other hand, found that among the children in their sample who had gone to comprehensive schools there was some levelling out of the social differentiation evident in the tripartite system. In terms of staying on beyond the minimum leaving age, they observed, 'It is particularly those of around average ability from the manual working-classes who seem to benefit, whereas the middle-class pupils show the same pattern of leaving in each type of school. In contrast, the pupils of high ability leave comprehensive schools at an earlier age than those of similar ability at other maintained schools.' Children of high ability were likely to gain fewer 'O' level passes while those of average ability did rather better if they had gone to a comprehensive school, though in this case the differences were small and not statistically significant.[2]

While without noticeable exception, all agree that the determinants of educational achievement are many and that the relationship between achievement and social class is the product of a variety of intercorrelated factors, two main schools of thought concerning their relative importance are apparent. The first, and in recent years it would appear the dominant view stresses the socio-cultural features of class differentiation with especial emphasis on socio-linguistic and value differences in the backgrounds of middle class and working class pupils. The second and perhaps somewhat old-fashioned view stresses the socio-economic aspect of class differentiation and emphasizes differences in material resources and the institutional or more political characteristics of class relations. These two perspectives are not mutually exclusive in the sense that the evidence adduced by the one is denied by the other. They differ rather in terms of the importance they assign to the various factors and perhaps still more in the practical implications they tend to be used to support.

Socio-Cultural Factors

On the socio-cultural side discontinuities of culture between home and school, differences of value between working class and middle class sub-cultures or at a more individualistic level differences in parental attitude have been identified as factors in differential educational attainment. These factors form a complex and perhaps should not be distinguished too sharply from one another. To some extent they represent different ways of talking about the cultural background by which the child is shaped and which he brings with him into the educational situation. As Jean Floud puts it, 'Here we are not concerned with snobbery in education — with invidious social differences in school or overt social bias in selection procedures — but with the existence of

---

[1] Julienne Ford, *Social Class and the Comprehensive School*, Routledge, 1969.

[2] J.W.B. Douglas, J.M. Ross and H.R. Simpson, *All Our Future*, 1968, pp.74-5 and cf. Eggleston, op.cit., *Comparative Education*, 1967.

fundamental differences as between the classes in ways of life, values, attitudes and aspirations, as well as in material circumstances[1]. D.F. Swift[2] and Barry Sugarman[3] have stressed the importance of value orientation in academic success, especially in secondary education. Dennis Marsden has given an especially pungent exposition of the conflict between the values implicit in the sub-cultures of the traditional working class and the more typically middle class values embodied in the educational system. He writes,

> 'A primary working-class emotion is solidarity. Its uglier edges are conservatism or a narrow mistrust of simple difference; yet at its best this feeling of a common purpose gave rise to the unions and co-operative movements. Given any inside knowledge about the education system, a parent will be reluctant to take a course that will give the child 'unfair' advantage or preferment.'[4]

In the same vein J. B. Mays quotes a Liverpool primary school head who said of the working class in the neighbourhood his school served, 'They go through life with arms linked, holding one another up'. Mays describes how in predominantly working class communities, 'the teachers in the school find themselves at the nexus of two distinct cultures with a correspondingly difficult role to play. Being themselves mainly conditioned by the grammar school tradition and the middle-class system of values, they have to make a drastic mental adjustment to be able to deal sympathetically with the people whose attitudes and standards are so different'.[5] Eggleston comments that '. . . the critical responses of many teachers to aspects of the cultures of low socio-economic status areas may be one of the most significant causal factors in the social problems of the schools'.[6]

In an important early study Floud, Halsey and Martin explored the determinants of educational achievement in a comparison of Middlesbrough and south-west Hertfordshire. In Hertfordshire, where the standard of housing was good and incomes generally higher than in Middlesborough,

---

[1] In Craft (ed.), *Family, Class and Education,* 1970, p.33.

[2] Social Class, Mobility Ideology and 11+ Success', *British Journal of Sociology,* 1967, XVIII, pp.165-86.

[3] 'Involvement in Youth Culture, Academic Achievement and Conformity in School: an Empirical Study of London Schoolboys', *British Journal of Sociology,* 1967, XVIII, pp.151-64.

[4] D. Marsden, 'Social Class and the Parent's Dilemma' in R. Mabey (ed.), *Class,* Anthony Blond, 1967, p.45. For a more extended discussion of traditional working class value systems see e.g. Josephine Klein, *Samples from English Cultures,* Routledge, 1965, Vol.1, ch.2, 3 and 4 and Vol.II, pp.487-526, 585-611..

[5] John Barron Mays, *Education and the Urban Child,* Liverpool U.P., 1962, pp.93 and 180.

[6] Eggleston, *The Social Context of the School,* 1967, p.20.

they found parental attitudes and ambitions for their children were more important factors in discriminating between the children who were selected for the grammar school and those who were not. In Middlesborough, with poorer housing and lower incomes at each social level, they found material prosperity to be a precondition of success.[1] In the survey of 1954-5 school leavers carried out for the Crowther committee in 1957 it was found that amongst pupils at grammar and technical schools 30 per cent of those whose fathers' earnings were in the bottom sixth of the income distribution had stayed at school beyond the age of 16. On this evidence Mrs Banks observes that 'it is clear that poverty is not necessarily a handicap if other circumstances are favourable'.[2] From the research he carried out for the Plowden Committee on *Children and Their Primary Schools*, Professor Wiseman concluded that parents' attitudes accounted for more of the variation in children's school achievement than did the material circumstances of the home or the environment within the schools. Wiseman wrote 'Educational deprivation is *not* mainly the effect of poverty; parental attitudes and maternal care are more important than the level of material needs.'[3] He found that the effect of parental attitude bore most heavily on the brightest children and increased in importance as the children grew older. Douglas, on the other hand, found that parental interest made most difference at the margin of grammar school ability where, among the children in his longitudinal study, those whose parents were interested in their school work got 19 per cent more places while those with uninterested parents got 14 per cent fewer than expected on the grounds of their measured ability at age eight.[4]

Though Wiseman's methodology has been criticized there is a good deal of evidence which supports his emphasis on the importance of parental interest. Jean Floud identifies parental interest with the cultural values and expectations we have already referred to. 'Parental attitudes are the principal ingredient in the subculture which a social class represents from the point of view of a school. They are at once a symbol and a source of social differences in the educational performance of children at the same general level of ability.'[5]

[1] J. Floud, A.H. Halsey and F.M. Martin, *Social Class and Educational Opportunity*, Routledge, 1956.

[2] *15-18* (Crowther Report), Vol. II (SURVEYS), Table 6, p.19 and Olive Banks, *The Sociology of Education*, Batsford, 2nd Edition 1971, p.67.

[3] Stephen Wiseman in Department of Education and Science, Central Advisory Council for Education (England), *Children and Their Primary Schools*, H.M.S.O., 1967, Vol.2, Appendix 9, p.369.

[4] J.W.B. Douglas, *The Home and the School*, 1964, pp.87-8.

[5] Jean Floud in Craft (ed.), op.cit., 1970.

In their study of the 1946-born children during their secondary education, Douglas, Ross and Simpson found that the attitudes of parents towards their children's education is not a matter of the parents' age but is strongly associated with their own educational attainments. Parents with any formal education beyond the statutory minimum are much more likely to be ambitious for their children and encouraging in their attitudes towards their efforts at school.[1] Parents' ambitions for their children may not always be fulfilled however. Of parents who had pursued their own education beyond the statutory minimum, 45 per cent had sons of average ability and half of these parents expected their sons to seek professional employment. Douglas, Ross and Simpson note 'Here conflicts are to be expected between parental hopes and what the boys are actually capable of achieving'.[2] The problems of social mobility have been extensively discussed and some of them will be considered later in this chapter, but in cases like this we can foresee some of the problems which are likely to arise out of a failure to be socially mobile against the hopes and expectations of ambitious parents and those internalized by the individual himself.

Among the socio-cultural variables we have so far referred to parental attitudes and the conflict of values – particularly between the values of the sub-culture of the more traditional working class and those of the school. An additional area of cultural or sub-cultural variation which has been given a great deal of attention as a factor in working class under-achievement is the mode of language used. Socio-linguistic influences have been seen both as a source of educational handicap in themselves and as a vehicle for sub-cultural values inimical to high academic achievement.

The tendency for children of less skilled workers and generally from the lower income ranges of the working class to do less well within the educational system than children from other strata should in any case be seen in the context of the relative non-integration of such families as theirs in other areas of institutional provision of social services. Though it is broadly in these sectors of the community that need of the statutory services is greatest and most widespread, they are also those which tend to make resort least readily to the services which are available. In their child development study Davie, Butler and Goldstein bring out this feature most clearly and are worth quoting at some length. They write:

'. . . children from unskilled working-class families are, for example, least often brought to 'toddler' clinic, to child guidance clinics or to dental clinics. At seven, they are relatively poorly adjusted at school, their dental health is poor and they show signs of delayed development in, for example, bladder control, speech and physical co-ordination.

[1] *All Our Future*, 1968, ch.12.

[2] ibid., p. 101.

Furthermore their educational standard is low and their parents tend not to seek a discussion with the teacher. To a lesser extent this situation is also to be seen amongst semi-skilled working-class families. Yet there is no evidence to suggest that parents in these social groups have any less concern for their children's welfare.'[1]

Davie and his colleagues argue that their failure to use the statutory services indicates either that these parents do not think of them as relevant to the needs of their children or there are physical or psychological barriers to their attending. A factor which, it has been argued, contributes both to the handicaps of these families and hinders their seeking help through the health, welfare and educational services is their linguistic background. Not only working class values but also working class speech patterns tend to differ from those of the middle class, which for all practical purposes are those current in the statutory services and in schools in particular. This goes beyond mere superficial differences in pronunciation, accent and intonation, the use of regional dialect expressions and so forth. Systematic comparison indicates differences in the structure of the language ordinarily used in everyday speech in different social strata. As Lawton has pointed out verbal ability has an effect not only on performance in selection tests — and thus on access to selective schools — but also on performance and retention in school once there.[2] We may add that the criteria employed in the evaluation of verbal ability are broadly speaking the characteristics of the linguistic codes which already prevail within the educational institutions.[3]

In a series of papers since 1958 Basil Bernstein has developed an influential but apparently easily misunderstood theory of socio-linguistic codes which relates forms of speech, whether restricted in grammar and vocabulary, or more elaborated forms, to their social setting in different types of family, sub-culture and especially in different social strata. In his later exposition restricted or elaborated speech codes are understood as generally articulating different types of meaning system.[4] Thus more

[1] Davie, Butler and Goldstein, *From Birth to Seven,* 1972, pp.191-2. See also Chapter 2, pp.38-9 above.

[2] Denis Lawton, *Social Class, Language and Education,* Routledge 1968, p.6., but cf. Westergaard and Little in Craft, op.cit., 1970, p.58, who emphasize the importance of class in selection but argue that it has less influence on academic performance in selective schools and higher education.

[3] See E.J. Goodacre 'Teachers and Their Pupils' Home Background' reprinted in B.R. Cosin et al. (eds), *School and Society,* Routledge, 1971, pp.9-15.

[4] Bernstein's collected papers are published in book form as Basil Bernstein, *Class, Codes and Control; Theoretical studies towards a sociology of language,* Routledge, 1971; see in particular ch.9, 'Social Class, Language and Socialisation', pp.193-213, which also appears in Pier Paolo Giglioli (ed.), *Language and Social Context,* Penguin, 1972, pp.157-78. A good discussion of some of his earlier work will be found in Lawton, op.cit., 1968.

elaborated codes tend to realize universalistic meanings in which inferential operations and principles are made fairly explicit while more
restricted speech codes employ imagery more directly and inferential
relations are less explicit. Thus it is much easier to convey complex and
unfamiliar ideas with some degree of precision within an elaborated code.
Using a restricted speech code, meaning tends to be local in the sense that
only those familiar with the context will fully understand the significance
of what has been said while the speaker will equally find it hard to convey
subtle or complex meaning to others unfamiliar with the contextual stock
of assumptions and imagery which he ordinarily is able to employ. For
Bernstein, the forms of language and speech a person uses are at once the
outcome of his social situation and determinants of the way in which he is
likely to respond to that situation. 'Different speech forms or codes
symbolize the form of the social relationship, regulate the nature of the
speech encounters, and create for the speakers different orders of
relevance and relation. The experience of the speakers is then transformed
by what is made significant or relevant by the speech form.'[1] We may infer
that a restricted speech code symbolizes a somewhat restricted form of
social relationship and restricts the nature of the speech encounters within
such relationships while creating only a limited order of relevance for the
speaker and consequently adding relatively little to his direct experience.[2]

Bernstein and his colleagues and others such as Lawton have produced
evidence in support of his argument that in general restricted socio-
linguistic codes are more characteristic of working class speech, especially
perhaps the speech of the more traditional working class, while middle
class people more readily employ an elaborated code.[3] These differences
in the speech codes habitually employed, through the meaning systems
they articulate and the class values with which they become associated,
help to structure, it is argued, children's responses to their educational
experience. Though it may be something of an oversimplification to label
the schools as middle class institutions, education is carried on within an
elaborated speech code and to that extent may seem alien to children —
and these will mostly be working class children — for whom their mother
tongue is familiar only in a restricted code. As Bernstein comments:

'. . . a restricted code gives access to a vast potential of meanings, of
delicacy, subtlety and diversity of cultural forms, to a unique aesthetic
whose basis in condensed symbols may influence the form of the
imagining. Yet, in complex industrialized societies its differently
focused experience may be disvalued and humiliated within schools or

[1] Bernstein, op.cit., 1971 p.197, and see ibid., p.166.
[2] ibid., p.170.
[3] See ibid., pp.209ff; Robinson and Rackstraw, 'Variations in mothers' answers to
children's questions, as a function of social class, verbal intelligence test scores and
sex', *Sociology*, 1967, 1, pp.259-76; Lawton, op.cit., 1968, ch.VI; etc.

seen, at best, to be irrelevant to the educational endeavour. For the schools are predicated upon elaborated code and its systems of social relationships. Although an elaborated code does not entail any specific value system, the value system of the middle class penetrates the texture of the very learning context itself.'[1]

For perhaps the majority of working class children this discontinuity between the values and the language of their school and those of their home environment progressively diverge with the school becoming more alien as they grow older. On the basis of comparisons between groups of middle class and working class boys aged 12 and 15 in written work, group discussions and individual interviews, Lawton found that in each situation there were greater differences in the speech codes of the two social classes at 15 than at age 12.[2] It is easy to understand how this has been regarded as indicating a form of educational handicap on the working class child. Referring to Bernstein's work, Jean Floud noted 'the linguistic handicap of working-class children becomes a more general intellectual handicap at the secondary stage of education. Successful learning may, therefore, be dependent on different educational measures for children of different backgrounds.'[3] Whatever one may think of this particular suggestion there has been in this country as well as in the United States in recent years an extensive discussion of the need to provide pre-school and continuing compensatory education for the 'culturally underprivileged and deprived child', with particular emphasis on language development.[4] In response to recent criticism such as that of Labov, Bernstein has latterly decried the justification of compensatory education schemes with reference to his own earlier work.[5] Nevertheless, this interpretation has been extensively made

[1] *Class, Codes and Control*, 1971, pp.211-12 and cf. ibid., p.175 and Lawton, op.cit., pp.80-81. Bernstein's comment should not be restricted to industrialized societies however. The association of speech codes, values and social status was discerned in Spain at the beginning of the seventeenth century. Respect for elaborated speech codes and the disvaluation of restricted forms even at the cost of sense is an important theme in Cervantes, *Don Quixote*.

[2] Lawton, op.cit., 1968, p.142.

[3] Jean Floud, op.cit., in Maurice Craft (ed.), *Family, Class and Education*, 1970, p.47, and cf. Bernstein, op.cit., 1971, p.175, '. . . the relative backwardness of many working-class children who live in areas of high population density or in rural areas may well be a culturally induced backwardness transmitted by the linguistic process. Such children's low performance on verbal I.Q. tests, their difficulty with "abstract" concepts, their failures within the language area, their general inability to profit from the school, all may result from the limitations of a restricted code.'

[4] See comments by M.C. Kellmer Pringle and Stephen Wiseman quoted in Davie, Butler and Goldstein, *From Birth to Seven*, 1972, p.190.

[5] See his 'A Critique of the Concept of Compensatory Education', ch.10 in *Class, Codes and Control*, pp.214-26 and Postcript to the Paladin edition 1973, pp.257 ff. and ref. W. Labov, 'The Logic of Non-Standard English' in Giglioli, *'Language and Social Context*, 1972, pp.179-215.

and is readily assimilated to the argument that cultural factors are the principal determinants of educational attainment. If educational attainment is chiefly a function of cultural background then the under-achievement of working class children is only to be effectively avoided by changing or improving their cultural background. Those features of working-class sub-cultures which provide an insufficient basis or only hinder success within the educational system would have to be modified or compensated for. If speech code is the major component in restricting working class children's speech encounters and consequently narrowing their response to their educational experience or their environment as a whole then any such compensatory programme should aim at the elimination of their linguistic handicap by introducing them to more elaborated speech codes. All this may seem a matter of very old educational mutton dressed as lamb, but it is a not uncommon view and indeed may be regarded as a liberal policy given an interpretation of the evidence which sees the socio-cultural as the crucial dimension of differential educational achievement.

Socio-Economic Factors

There is another view. This emphasises the role of material factors very much more. In their examination of families and their needs in 1970 Audrey Hunt and her colleagues found that the lack of a parent had reduced the likelihood of a child reaching grammar school and increased the probability of going to a secondary modern. Where both were present, parents had higher hopes of their children's educational attainment than did the remaining parent of motherless or fatherless children. But the proportion of children from one-parent families who were in grammar school and in secondary modern school was almost exactly the same as that from the lowest income group of two-parent families. Parental loss may be associated with lower aspirations but Hunt et al. suggest that this poorer educational attainment '. . . may be an example of deprivation which is mainly a result of low income rather than of the loss of a parent in itself'.[1] Although the home circumstances of children have been widely considered important in recent years increasing attention has recently been paid to the educational resources available to children of different backgrounds through the provision of facilities by local education authorities and others. The private sector of course is virtually available only to those children whose parents can afford the fees involved. In the public sector however there is a considerable diversity of provision both in terms of the expenditure on school buildings and equipment and in the proportional provision of places in different kinds of school.

Douglas and his colleagues found that while the profile of measurable

---

[1] Audrey Hunt, Judith Fox and Margaret Morgan, *Families and their Needs*, H.M.S.O., 1973, Vol.I, pp.60-61.

abilities seems to be fixed in major outline before the age of eight (though how much earlier they were unable to determine), the characteristics of a child's primary and secondary schools were an important influence on his actual levels of attainment.

Parental interest in his progress was clearly important, though the more interested parents were generally those whose children attended better equipped and better staffed schools. These factors operate independently and both are associated with staying on beyond the minimum leaving age among pupils of borderline and above average ability from the lower working class. As Douglas and his colleagues observe, 'high parental interest alone is insufficient to counter the deficiencies of the schools'.[1] Dr Agnes Crawford found that in a central Liverpool slum area the distribution of intelligence among the children was similar to that among children in the rest of the city even though a largely verbal test was used, but their reading ability was much poorer.[2] This implies that however important cultural background might be in the explanation of poor achievement by working class children it is not a sufficient cause. The Newsom Committee similarly found that the average reading age of fourth-year pupils in slum area secondary modern schools was 17 months behind the average for the country as a whole.[3] But the schools in slum areas are often no better than educational slums themselves and the poor conditions, dark and damp classrooms, inadequate cloakroom and toilet facilities and lack of playing space are not their only or perhaps their worst disadvantages.[4] These schools not only tend to be least well provided with equipment, books and other teaching materials, they are also the worst staffed. More serious than lack of qualifications or experience perhaps is the high rate of turnover of staff in these schools. The Newsom Committee reported that in schools in these areas half the men and two thirds of the women teachers had been on the staff for less than three years compared with a third of men teachers and half the women in secondary modern schools generally.[5] Clearly schools such as these in decaying inner-urban areas are more likely to be attended by working class than middle class children.

The provision of selective secondary school places varies a good deal between local authorities, with a high proportion of such places in the south and east and poor provision mainly in the north and midlands.[6] As

[1] Douglas, Ross and Simpson, *All Our Future,*, pp.187-95.

[2] Described in J.B. Mays, *Education and the Urban Child,* Liverpool U.P., 1962.

[3] Report of the Central Advisory Council for Education (England), *Half Our Future,* H.M.S.O., 1963 (The Newsom Report), pp.24-5.

[4] Ministry of Education, *The School Buildings Survey, 1962,* H.M.S.O., 1965.

[5] ibid., and for a description of the problem within a school see K.R. Gray, 'Schools: the real crisis', *New Society,* 27 August 1963.

[6] See G. Taylor and N. Ayres, *Born and Bred Unequal,* Longman, 1969, Part 3; and B.E. Coates and E.M. Rawstron, *Regional Variations in Britain,* Batsford, 1971, ch.10.

Douglas, Ross and Simpson note, there are more middle class pupils in the areas which provided many selective school places and this obviously represents an initial advantage to the prospects of grammar school selection for middle class children. Allowing for the differences in the social composition of the areas of high and low provision, Douglas and his colleagues found that in both the middle class and the working class, parents took a greater interest in their children's education and children tended to stay on at school longer in areas with a high provision of selective secondary places. This applied even to children who were not themselves selected but went instead to secondary modern school, and in such areas more of these children obtained G.C.E. passes. The proportion of pupils in selective schools made least difference amongst children in the highest range of measured ability but results were consistently improved in all groups at all ability levels below this and were most markedly better for working class pupils and especially for girls.[1] In general however levels of performance between children from the different social classes continued to widen during the secondary school years, with half of the lower working class pupils in the highest ability group leaving before they were 16½; this progressive divergence can also be associated with educational provision and at least during the primary phase the divergence of test scores between the social classes in England and Wales was not evident in Scotland. This may be associated with the greater pressures of selection south of the border with a generally less generous provision of selective secondary school places, as a result of which Scots working class children were about as likely as children from the English middle class to find a place in a selective secondary school.[2]

The continuing trend toward staying on beyond the minimum age encourages some optimism with regard to the wastage of ability but whether this and the spread of comprehensive secondary schooling will themselves counter the divergence in test scores between pupils from different social circumstances is more doubtful.[3] Not merely reorganization but a re-distribution of resources seems called for. Douglas, Ross and Simpson concluded that:

'. . . in the selective secondary system which existed between 1957 and 1962, social inequalities in educational opportunity could have been greatly reduced by raising the provision of grammar, direct grant and technical schools and by removing local inequalities in the provision of selective places — these inequalities are largely historic and bear little

---

[1] Douglas, Ross and Simpson, op.cit., 1968, pp.90-91.

[2] ibid., pp.86-8, and J.W.B. Douglas, J.M. Ross, S.M.M. Maxwell and D.A. Wallzer, 'Differences in Test Score and the Gaining of Selective Places for Scottish Children and those in England and Wales', *British Journal of Educational Psychology*, 1969, 36, pp.150-57.

[3] J.M. Ross, W.J. Burton, P.Evison and T.S. Robertson, *A Critical Appraisal of Comprehensive Education*, National Foundation for Educational Research, 1972.

relation to the ability of the pupils living in each area. A general improvement in the staffing and amenities of many of the schools and the elimination of local discrepancies are, and will be, no less necessary in the comprehensive system of secondary education which is now evolving: it requires and will require an equally great investment and direction of both capital and staff.'[1]

Further support for this point of view comes from the analysis of attainment and variations in the level of local authority expenditure on education carried out by Byrne and Williamson.[2] There is of course little difference between the level of expenditure per pupil in primary schools from one local authority area to another as the rate support grant they receive from the Department of Education largely eliminates differences at this level. At secondary and particularly sixth-form level however the grant system favours those areas with larger proportions of pupils staying on beyond the minimum leaving age and thus indirectly those areas with a relatively more middle class population.[3]

To begin with Byrne and Williamson criticized the methodology of some of those studies which have stressed the major importance of socio-cultural explanations of unequal educational attainment. Wiseman's conclusions, they point out, were based on the technique of factor analysis which is inappropriate for evaluating the relative influence of factors which are not independently variable. Their own investigations however examined a range of factors not elsewhere considered and also proceeded on a rather different plane. In an analysis of local education resources and expenditure throughout England outside the Inner London area they set out to 'delimit precisely the *explanatory range* of socio-cultural explanations of attainment'.[4] As an index of educational attainment they found it necessary to take the proportion of pupils staying on beyond the statutory minimum leaving age in each LEA area. They found that 66% of the variation in attainment on this measure could be attributed to the proportion of middle class households in the local population. When the resources of the local authority as measured by the product of a penny rate per pupil for whom the LEA was responsible and the actual per capita LEA expenditure on all pupils and separately on secondary school pupils was controlled, the positive influence of high social class was reduced by almost half and the negative influence of low social class was reduced by

[1] Douglas, Ross and Simpson, op.cit., 1968, p.195.
[2] D.S. Byrne and W. Williamson, *The Myth of the Restricted Code,* Working Papers in Sociology 1,, Department of Sociology and Social Administration, University of Durham, 1972; and see also D.S. Byrne and W. Williamson, 'Some Intra-Regional Variations in Educational Provision and their Bearing upon Educational Attainment – the Case of the North-East', *Sociology,* 1972, 6, pp.71-87.
[3] See Howard Glennerster, 'Education and Inequality' in Peter Townsend and Nicholas Bosanquet (eds), *Labour and Inequality,* Fabian Society, 1972, pp.97-9.
[4] *The Myth of the Restricted Code,* University of Durham, 1972, p.3.

nearly 60 per cent. Thus even on these admittedly less than comprehensive measures of provision, together with their index of local authority resources, a major part of the variation between social classes in their educational attainment was accounted for, leaving only the residual variation to be accounted for by other, possibly cultural, factors. When, in addition to variations in resources and provision, they controlled for high social class too, they found less than three per cent of the variation in attainment remained 'to be assigned to the negative effect of low social class' but that there was a residue of 27 per cent of the variation in attainment between the classes after controlling for the negative effects of low social class and variations in LEA resources and provision.[1] They were led to conclude that linguistic or other socio-cultural handicaps therefore could account at best for only a very small proportion of the differences in attainment and 'that cultural compensation has become a substitute for redistribution of resources'.[2]

Though clearly a challenging argument it will be necessary, before it can be said to be established, to examine Byrne and Williamson's thesis not only in relation to some more elaborate measure of attainment but more crucially at an individual level. Variations between the performance of individual working class and middle class children are likely to be much greater than variations in staying-on rates for predominantly working class or predominantly middle class local authority areas. The kind of data they examined does not permit us to estimate how far this might be the case and it will most likely prove necessary for a fresh large-scale study to deal with this problem. It is quite evident that local authorities with a larger proportion of middle class rate payers in their area spend more on secondary education than can those with a proportionately more working class population.[3] The question really is whether the resource and provision factors which they have clearly shown to be important would account for such a large proportion of the inter-class variation at an individual level of analysis and therefore whether socio-cultural factors might not be more influential than their methodology allowed them to observe.

The complexity of the issue is evident when we consider the role and influence of education in the private sector where, for at least some of the pupils, the resources available and the level of provision is high, while on the other hand the limited range of social background from which pupils are drawn is likely to highlight their socio-cultural differentiation from the great majority of the school population in the state sector.

---

[1] ibid., pp.16-20.

[2] ibid., p.23.

[3] Byrne and Williamson, 'Some Intra-Regional Variations in Educational Provision and their Bearing upon Educational Attainment', *Sociology*, 1972, 6.

The Private Sector

As we saw earlier the private sector has accounted for a declining proportion of all pupils in recent years and, though in absolute terms the numbers have been growing, these schools accommodate a still more steeply declining proportion of pupils over 15. There has been an absolute decline among the smaller private secondary schools but the remainder of the sector has prospered, though it is important to remember that 94 per cent of all pupils are in state schools and even excluding the direct grant grammar schools 86 per cent of all pupils over the minimum leaving age were in state schools in 1971. The private sector then caters for a minority of pupils and it is fair to say in many respects this may be regarded as a privileged minority. It is not however absolutely privileged and, as we shall see, the preference of some parents for private sector schooling is not always to the advantage of their children. There is in fact a wide variation in the standard required of pupils at entry, in staffing ratios and in the quality of teaching offered. The private sector consists of all those schools independent of the local education authority system of maintenance and of these the best known and most influential element are those known as public schools. These, each controlled by its own board of governors, are often, though not always, boarding schools mostly providing an education for boys from the ages of 13 to 18. There is a tendency to emphasise the importance of character building, but such schools also have a high proportion of pupils doing advanced work and large sixth forms. Some schools take day pupils and there are some girls public schools which have been largely modelled on the older pattern of the boys schools. The private sector includes also preparatory schools for boys and girls usually from eight to 13 and designed, for boys in particular, for those intending to go on to public school. In addition there is a wide range of other day and boarding schools, some of them run by non-profit-making trusts, some as a source of income for their proprietors. It is among these smaller schools, some of them providing only an indifferent education for the less academically gifted children of parents mainly concerned with preserving their social standing, that there has been some contraction in recent years.

Taken together, the pupils of the independent schools display a wider range of ability than those in state grammar schools. As Philip Masters, Chairman of the Incorporated Association of Preparatory Schools, put it, 'It is one of the proudest boasts of both I.A.P.S. and H.M.C. schools[1] that they do not restrict themselves in any way to an intellectual elite, but make the best of boys of only very moderate ability.'[2] While this is true to an extent it should not lead us to believe that in terms of ability the private sector is already comprehensive as has sometimes been suggested.

[1] H.M.C. = Headmasters' Conference i.e. 'public' schools.

[2] Phillip L. Masters, *Preparatory Schools Today*, A. & C. Black, 1966, p.93.

Table 8.8

The Public Schools

(a) Father's Social Class of School Entrants 1962

Registrar General's Social Class	Independent Schools			Direct Grant Schools	Economically Active and retired Males in England and Wales 1961
	Total	Day Boys	Boarders		
I Professional etc.	34.4	33.2	34.8	26.1	4
II Intermediate	55.2	49.2	57.8	47.2	15
III Skilled					
i. non-manual	6.1	10.3	4.4	13.1 ⎫	51
ii. manual	3.1	5.7	2.0	11.0 ⎬	
IV Partly skilled	1.1	1.3	1.0	2.6	21
V Unskilled	0.1	0.3	–	–	9
N = 100%	9467	2714	6753	5263	

Source: Calculated from Kalton, *op. cit.*, Table 3:11.

(b) Schools Attended by Fathers of School Entrants

Father's School	Independent Schools			Direct Grant Schools
	Total	Day Boys	Boarders	
Same School	17.0	6.0	21.2	6.0
Another H.M.C. School	27.2	15.8	31.4	10.2
A non-H.M.C. School	33.3	40.1	30.7	40.8
Schooling not known	22.5	38.1	16.7	43.0
N = 100%	10,518	2,853	7,665	5,658

Source: *ibid.*, Table 3:10.

Douglas, Ross and Simpson found that while in the population as a whole and therefore in a truly comprehensive school one would expect to find roughly one child in four of 'grammar school' ability, in the public schools there were on average three boys out of every four of this level of ability.

The private sector and particularly the public schools not only separate their pupils from the majority academically but socially. In a survey commissioned by the Headmasters' Conference itself in 1964,[1] Graham Kalton found that 84 per cent of the boys in independent schools had never attended a maintained school. They were overwhelmingly middle class in background and, as Table 8.8 (b) shows, to a remarkable extent self-recruiting.

It is clear from these figures that not just a general sub-cultural pattern but strong family traditions operate here and this is particularly true in the case of the more prestigious and more exclusive independent boarding schools. But this is not just a matter of family preference, there are also strongly influential economic factors involved. The cost in school fees alone is substantial. The average for a boy at boarding school in 1971 was £626 per year.[2] At a time when only about five per cent of personal incomes exceeded £3,000 per year the prospect of an outlay of this amount over a period of five years from 13 to 18 for one child in fees alone is likely by and large to restrict free parental choice over boarding education in the private sector only to the rich. To this must generally be added the cost of preparatory school fees for the years from nine to 13.[3] It is true that there are a large number of endowed scholarships at public schools which wholly or in part cover the cost of fees and that some boys are enabled to attend whose parents could not otherwise afford to send them there. Glennerster and Pryke note that in 1964 100 schools awarded scholarships to about 870 boys. They sampled 28 of these schools and found that of the 210 boys who won scholarships 185 were at the school already or had attended one of the I.A.P.S. schools of which all the first-class preparatory schools are members. 'Only two boys were known to come from other schools,' they noted.[4] In the main then, the public schools help those who can already help themselves.

It appears that it is the advantages of their social class position that account for the higher level of attainment of pupils in independent schools, at least at the age of seven.[5] At later ages the evidence is less clear. Taking all independent schools together it is only to be expected that their inclusion of pupils of a lower measured ability than would have assigned

[1] Graham Kalton, *The Public Schools: A Factual Survey*, Longmans, 1966.

[2] Fees for H.M.C. fee-paying boarding schools in Great Britain. Calculated from *Whitaker's Almanack 1972*, J. Whitaker and Sons, 1971, pp.538-41. For fees in 1965-6 cf. Kalton, op.cit., 1966, pp.131-22.

[3] See Masters, op.cit., 1966, p.89.

[4] H. Glennester and R. Pryke, *The Public Schools*, Fabian Society, 1964, p.11.

[5] See Davie, Butler and Goldstein, *From Birth to Seven*, 1972, pp.130-31.

them to a place in a state grammar school should lead to worse overall
G.C.E. 'O' level results than for grammar schools. Boys stay on longer but
except for the most able get fewer 'O' levels in the private sector and girls
of all abilities in general do less well than in the grammar schools.[1] The
public schools by themselves however show a better performance than this
and Masters and Hockey found that in a sample of public schoolboys who
had in fact 'failed' the 11-plus grading examination and but for the private
sector would have been destined for a secondary modern school, 70 per
cent gained five or more 'O' level passes and 25 per cent gained two or
more 'A' levels.[2] Kalton found that while almost half of the pupils did
not sit the 11-plus examination, about 16½ per cent had, in fact, failed it. In
a comparison of their subsequent performance the astonishing result
emerged, as Table 8.9 shows, that the academic achievements, including
university places, of 11-plus failures educated at public schools were about
as good as those of those who were in fact selected for the grammar
schools in the state sector.

Table 8.9

Achievement of Leavers known to have passed
or failed the 11+ examination

Examination Achievements	Survey Schools		Maintained Schools* (boys only)	
	Passed 11+	Failed 11+	Grammar	Secondary Modern
'O' Level Passes	%	%	%	%
None (inc. none attempted)	2	8	11	92
4 or more	92	72	67	3
8 or more	47	20	20	–
'A' Level Passes				
1 or more	74	35	38	–
2 or more	67	27	33	–
Awarded a University place	50	15	17	–
N = 100%	4,923	913	58,290	218,890

*from *Statistics of Education 1963*, Part III.

Source: Kalton, *op.cit.*, 1966, Table 6:22.

[1] Douglas, Ross and Simpson, *All Our Future*, 1968, pp.64-5.

[2] P.L. Masters and S.W. Hockey, 'National Reserves of Ability – Some Evidence from Independent Schools', *Times Educational Supplement*, 17 May 1963.

However, as Douglas, Ross and Simpson point out, the schools themselves cannot take the whole of the credit for this. In comparing the performance of schools in the different sectors one must control for the class background of the pupils, and Kalton omitted to do this. Douglas and his colleagues showed that when the upper middle class public school boys in their sample were matched with those from a similar social background the differences between the public schools and the grammar schools disappeared. In their sample of children born in March 1946, 'there were 90 boys at grammar schools from the upper middle class; 90 per cent of these boys started the session 1962-3, compared with 92 per cent of the H.M.C. school boys. Thus up to the threshold of the sixth form our evidence does not support Kalton's interpretation.'[1]

In this connection then, the difference between the public and private sector would seem to be entirely due to the class background of the pupils and the differences in attainment between social classes as great within the state schools without any addition from the greater expenditure and resources of the private sector. We have thus further grounds for reservation before accepting Byrne and Williamson's interpretation of their findings, though clearly the issues for further research have been a good deal sharpened by these apparently contradictory sets of evidence.

Education and Social Mobility

All this, of course, is to deal with education only in a strictly limited way. I have dealt only with the allocative or placement functions of the educational system. As I pointed out at the beginning of the chapter education may be regarded as a value in its own right as well as merely a means of providing the training and skill necessary to the achievement of ends determined elsewhere. Educational institutions may serve a society's collective goals, the needs of other social institutions or interests, the aspirations or thirst for knowledge of their clients or the autonomously academic goals of scholarship, research and the pursuit of learning. Here however I have not so much been concerned with education, educational institutions or professional educators as with the way for each new generation participation in the educational process facilitates or hinders the achievement of status across the whole social hierarchy according to their different social origins. In other words education has been dealt with only as a medium of social mobility or whatever its opposite should be called.

The balance of evidence we have considered here seems to indicate that educational attainment is still strongly influenced by extrinsic factors. Whether these factors are chiefly socio-cultural or socio-economic perhaps

---

[1] *All Our Future*, 1968, p.69 and see p.197.

is open to further debate, but in general they may be considered characteristics of the social structure which the educational system serves. The educational system then, in its allocative functions at least, like the family, is an agent rather than a principal in the shaping of social structure. There are signs of a slow but nevertheless real move towards a greater degree of equality in educational opportunity. The trend towards staying on after the statutory minimum school leaving age has not only brought more children from all classes into sixth forms and higher education but has increased the proportion of state school as against private sector pupils and of working class as against middle class boys and girls going right through into higher education. The pursuit of more than minimum education is even more marked when we take into account the growth of the polytechnics and other colleges providing C.N.A.A. degrees and other non-vocational courses as well as diploma and certificate courses in technical subjects.

During the 1960s further education grew even more rapidly than secondary and higher education. The polytechnics, regional and other technical colleges not only provided increasing opportunities in evening classes but accommodated especially rapidly growing numbers of day-release and sandwich course students already in employment, together with early leavers from secondary schools taking full-time courses leading either to technical qualifications or to certificates like those they might have taken had they remained at school. As Table 8.10 shows, while evening and day-release courses have been growing rapidly, there were respectively more than twice and more than three times the number of students on full-time courses and sandwich courses in 1970 as ten years before.

The expansion of part-time education has coincided with a shrinking proportion of the population *not* going on with some form of full-time education after school. A large proportion of the increase in full-time further education has paralleled the expansion of the later phases of secondary schooling. The proportion of 15-17-year-olds in full-time further education grew from one per cent in 1951[1] to more than five-and-a-half per cent in 1970-71. In the age range covered by higher education the expansion outside the school, university or college of education system has been even greater. The proportion of full-time sandwich-course students aged 18-21 more than doubled in the 1960s, while the proportion of the age group becoming part-time day students continued to grow.[2]

[1] See *Annual Abstract of Statistics 90*, 1953, Table 86.

[2] For some of the earlier details of this area of educational growth see Irene Hordley and D.J. Lee, 'The "Alternative Route" — Social Change and Opportunity in Technical Education', *Sociology*, 1970, 4, pp.23-50.

Table 8.10

Further Education in England and Wales 1960-70

	1960-61*	1970-71**	Percentage Increase
(a) *Students* (thousands):			
Full-time	106.2	237.8	123.9
Sandwich Courses	11.3	36.5	223.0
Part-time day	487.8	748.7	55.2
Evening:			
Major Establishments	713.1	736.4	3.3
Evening Institutes	887.0	1421.8	60.3
(b) *Students aged 15-17 as a percentage of 15-17 age group*:			
Full-time or sandwich	3.14	5.54	
Part-time day	10.86	13.14	
(c) *Students aged 18-20 as a percentage of 18-20 age group*:			
Full-time or sandwich	1.70	4.53	
Part-time day	9.24	11.87	

Sources: **Annual Abstract of Statistics 100*, 1963, Table 95.
    **Annual Abstract of Statistics 109, 1972, Table 108.

Intragenerational Mobility

A good deal of doubt has been cast on the socially equalizing effects of the post-war expansion of secondary and higher education. Goldthorpe and Lockwood for instance, in their preliminary discussion of the embourge-oisement thesis in 1963, *en passant* argued that:

'for those who leave non-selective secondary schools at the age of fifteen for a manual occupation, this kind of work is becoming more than ever before a life sentence. The same factors that are making for greater intergenerational mobility — technological progress, increasing specialization and the growing importance of education in occupational placement — are also operating to reduce the possibility of 'working up from the bottom' in industry . . .'[1]

Little and Westergaard sustained and generalized this point through two important papers on class differentials in educational opportunity pub-

---

[1] John H. Goldthorpe and David Lockwood, 'Affluence and the British Class Structure', *Sociological Review*, 1963, 11, p.137.

lished in 1964 and 1967. They argued that improvements in the equality of educational opportunity were unlikely to have resulted in greater social mobility since the growth of secondary and higher education, with more and more pupils and students gaining qualifications at all sorts of levels, was matched by the narrowing opportunities for promotion of those outside the educational system lacking the increasingly essential certificates and diplomas.

'As professionalization, bureaucratization and automation of work proceed, so access to occupations of the middle and higher levels increasingly demands formal educational qualifications. Career prospect and social position come to depend less on experience and training acquired on the job than on the education obtained in childhood and adolescence. The range of occupational statuses over which promotion — or demotion — may be expected in the course of a normal working life becomes narrower than in the past. If this is so, increased 'educational mobility' may be counterbalanced by decreased 'career mobility'.[1]

Their later paper makes the point with still greater firmness: 'Evidently, the small but continuous widening of the educational 'channel' was roughly counterbalanced by a corresponding contraction of other avenues of social mobility. This is precisely what might be expected.'[2]

The main grounds for this expectation would appear to be a number of studies of industrial career structures. Scott, Banks, Halsey and Lupton, for example, found that in the steel firm they studied in the 1950s already professionally qualified managers were increasingly recruited from outside the firm rather than promoted within it.[3] From his survey of industrial managers in the Manchester area in 1965 D.G. Clark also concluded that 'the 'average manager' is increasingly coming from a middle class home and has received a grammar school and university education'.[4] Clark based his conclusions on the fact that the younger managers in his sample were more commonly grammar school educated and of middle class origins. If, however, those who had worked their way up in the firm from below generally reached a manager's job somewhat later in life than those who started out as management trainees, then the question arises of whether

---

[1] A. Little and J. Westergaard, 'The Trend of Class Differentials in Educational Opportunity in England and Wales', *British Journal of Sociology*, 1964, XV, p.302.

[2] Educational Opportunity and Social Selection in England and Wales: Trends and Policy Implications' in *Social Objectives in Educational Planning*, O.E.C.D., 1967, pp.65-6.

[3] W.H. Scott, J.A. Banks, A.H. Halsey and T. Lupton, *Technical Change and Industrial Relations*, Liverpool University Press, 1956.

[4] D.G. Clark, *The Industrial Manager — His Background and Career Pattern*, London Business Publications, 1966, p.66.

this apparent change over time would not disappear.[1]

The counterbalance argument is that the growth of formal education and training has displaced experience on the job as the essential prerequisite for appointment to higher positions in management and administration. Studies of technical education by Hordley and Lee have been used both to support and to question this position. On the basis of their surveys of sandwich course and day-release students in Salford and Birmingham, Lee and Hordley concluded that the tendency for firms to formalize the criteria by which they selected their young workers for technical college courses favoured those who had already been more successful in their secondary schooling and thus to a certain extent undermined the possibility of technical education performing its 'salvage function' for those whose attainments in secondary school were poorer.[2] Using data on the age of completion of full-time education from the 1961 census, Lee found the promotion prospects of working class early leavers to be fairly stable in the short run as they always had been poor in comparison with those from the middle class and those with more education. He anticipated a worsening situation for them in the long run but pointed out the difficulties in extricating changes in intragenerational mobility from the processes of intergenerational mobility so as to make any evaluation of counterbalance.[3] On the other hand in a later paper Hordley and Lee argued that '. . . if any "counterbalancing" is occurring between educational and non-educational channels of mobility it is the result of the expansion of industrial education at the expense of 'on the job' training'.[4]

The importance of technical education is often overlooked by those more familiar with the academic educational career – passing through the school to university or college of education. But though technical education generally more closely reflects the demands of the economy for trained and qualified manpower the correspondence is by no means exact. Thus technological change has created opportunities for the movement of technicians into technologists' jobs before and in some places despite the increasing accreditation of technological qualifications in recent years. The issue of whether this spread limits career mobility depends on assumptions about the relation between technological change and technical education

[1] Gerstl's similar comparison of age strata within his sample of graduate engineers, though not directly concerned with their career mobility, suggested that inter-generational mobility in this expanding occupational group was increasing – a finding which it would be difficult to account for plausibly in the same sort of way; see Joel Gerstl, 'Social Origins of Engineers', *New Society*, 6 June 1963 pp.19-20.

[2] D.J.Lee and I. Hordley, 'Technical Education: an Alternative Route', *Technical Education*, 1966, 8, pp.394-5.

[3] D.J. Lee, 'Class Differentials in Educational Opportunity and Promotions from the Ranks', *Sociology*, 1968, 2, pp.293-312.

[4] Irene Hordley and D.J. Lee, op.cit., 1970, p.42.

which have not be independently verified. Thus the rapid growth of technical education supplying formal qualifications may, for all we know to the contrary, still not be keeping pace with industrial change.

Roberts and his colleagues described how, especially in the provinces away from London and the south east of England, the labour market for technicians blurs at one end into that for technologists and at the other into that for skilled manual workers.[1] Of the technicians in the 14 firms they surveyed in 1968-9 more than half had been upwardly mobile in comparison with their manual worker fathers and, among those for whom evidence was available, more than half had been upwardly mobile in the course of their own careers.[2]

The occupational structure has been changing, though much of this is accommodated within the pattern of retirements and new recruitment rather than through job mobility during the careers of men at work. As we have seen in Chapter 5 the proportion of men in skilled manual occupations has been increasing and in less skilled jobs decreasing. Yet, as Harris and Clausen's survey showed[3], during their working lives more men move from skilled to less skilled jobs than from less skilled to skilled. Restrictions on retraining no doubt inhibit moves in the one direction while the redundancy of dying trades and the problems or ageing contribute to the flow the other way. Quite large proportions had been upwardly mobile too, especially surprising perhaps among the higher professionals and administrators group where one in seven had been manual workers ten years earlier.[4]

What little direct evidence we have on career mobility suggests it has been increasing rather than decreasing. J.W.B. Douglas reported that among the fathers of the children included in his large-scale longitudinal study between 1946 and 1957 five per cent changed from manual to non-manual jobs and three per cent moved from non-manual to manual jobs.[5] In Harris and Clausen's study just over two-and-a-half per cent of the men had changed from non-manual to manual jobs, but seven per cent had begun in manual jobs in 1953 and ended in non-manual jobs in 1963. Thus, comparing the two sets of data, the main direction of career mobility was still upward at the later date, and increasingly so.

Criticisms of the counterbalance theory can be summarized under three main headings: its lack of attention to middle class career mobility; the neglect of the growth of technical education; and the disregard of

---

[1] B.C. Roberts, Ray Loveridge, John Gennard et al., *Reluctant Militants*, Heinemann, 1972, p.205.

[2] ibid., see Tables 4.3, 7.7 and 7.8

[3] Amelia I. Harris and Rosemary Clausen, *Labour Mobility in Britain 1953-1963*, H.M.S.O., 1966, Table 52, p.51.

[4] ibid.

[5] J.W.B. Douglas, *The Home and the School*, ch.VI, p.70.

large-scale structural change.[1] Firstly, we know very little about intragenerational mobility in earlier times but a good deal of it must have been accounted for by middle class early leavers whose career mobility did not lead to social mobility but merely restored them to the social status of their parents. The growth of higher education and the use made of these expanding opportunities by middle class students still in far greater proportions than by those of working class origins may short-circuit some career mobility but does not reduce intergenerational mobility. Indeed it may remove some of the competition working class early leavers have to face in their pursuit of an 'alternative route' to higher education qualifications and promotion at work. Secondly, the counterbalance theory places too much emphasis on what happens in schools as compared with what happens in technical colleges. Technological and organizational change may have brought about a situation in which promotion increasingly depends on formal qualifications it is true, but to concentrate only on those provided in secondary school and university is to take too narrow a view. The rapid expansion of technical education in the 1960s has widened opportunities for school leavers who instead of staying on for sixth form courses have gone into industry or commerce to continue their education and training right through what has become the *other* half of a binary system of higher education. No-one would pretend that there is a primrose path for the day-release apprentice on an O.N.C. course to continue on through H.N.C. and into the realms of middle management, but his prospects probably never were very great, and as far as institutional provision can go they would seem to have been increasing rather than decreasing. Thirdly, and most importantly, the notion that increased upward mobility through education is almost entirely offset by decreased career promotion assumes a static situation and implies a neglect of the large-scale shifts in the distribution of occupations which are changing the structure of the society. It also implies an adaptivity on the part of the educational system to the needs of the economy and the society which is hardly apparent outside academic circles.

The pattern of social mobility, however, is not to be discovered by speculative extrapolation from what happens in the schools. The idea that it could be is often no more than a manifestation of that parochialism of educationalists which has always inclined them to see education as the locomotive of social change instead of, say, something rather nearer the guard's van.

---

[1] These points together with the foregoing evidence are discussed at somewhat greater length in Trevor Noble, 'Intragenerational Mobility in Britain: A Criticism of the Counterbalance Theory', *Sociology*, 1974, 8, pp.475-83. I would like to thank the editor of *Sociology* for permission to incorporate some passages from that paper in this discussion.

Intergenerational Mobility Trends

The Evidence

If we want to find out whether social mobility has been increasing or decreasing, the only sure way is to go and look for direct evidence. Inferences made from changes in educational provision may be misleading since we know that other factors such as changes in the occupational structure or fertility differentials between the classes are likely to be influential. Equally, starting from either of these, we could not be certain *a priori* that changes within the educational system might not have influenced mobility rates.

The major study of social mobility in Britain published so far was made in 1949 and consequently predates most of the major educational, economic and demographic changes which have taken place since the Second World War.[1] Until the results from the Nuffield College survey,[2] designed to bring that information up to date, are available we must make do with the fragmentary evidence which can be found in studies which have included social mobility as a variable. There are a number of sample surveys carried out since the 1949 L.S.E. study which present us with usable data on mobility which seem to be representative of the population. These have been carried out with a variety of different intentions and a variety of occupational classifications have been used, and they severally may be open to methodological criticisms of one kind or another. Yet the consistency of their results when considered together encourages confidence in the pattern of change in mobility rates which they indicate. I have been able to find four studies from the 1950s and 1960s which justify some comparison with the earlier data and these are summarized in the transition matrices presented in Table 8.11. For the sake of simplicity and the avoidance of ambiguity, since different occupational scales were used in the original studies, I have limited the present discussion to mobility between the middle class and the working class as indicated respectively by non-manual or manual occupations. I can, in addition, think of three studies which describe mobility rates within single and not necessarily very typical communities and a 1958 survey of rather pessimistic national servicemen who were asked about the jobs they

---

[1] See D.V.Glass (ed.), *Social Mobility in Britain*, Routledge, 1954. Some earlier attempts to estimate the amount of social mobility are briefly described in B.G.Stacey, 'Inter-Generation Occupational Mobility in Britain', *Occupational Psychology*, 1968, 42, pp.33-48.

[2] See Keith Hope (ed.) , *The Analysis of Social Mobility: Methods and Approaches*, Oxford Studies in Social Mobility: Working Papers I, O.U.P. 1972.

expected to have on their return to civilian life.[1] These, however, in one way or another seemed insufficiently representative of the population as a whole to warrant inclusion here.

Some of the surveys have included women respondents usually classified by their husbands' occupations. A sample like this might look slightly more middle class than a sample of occupied males.[2] Only in the case of the Five Boroughs Survey was it possible to estimate the effects of the inclusion or exclusion of women from the sample and in that case no significant difference was apparent when women were excluded. It does suggest however that where some men in the sample are compared with their fathers-in-law in this way more downward mobility is recorded. The figures in Table 8.13 for England and Wales 1962, Great Britain 1963 and Five Boroughs I 1967 on this score therefore possibly over-estimate downward mobility as compared with the England and Wales figures for 1949 and 1951.

The main problem with data of this kind, however, is the representativeness of the samples from which it is derived. If there are too many middle class men in the sample this will also distort the derived distribution of fathers' occupations and together these will possibly influence the numbers of both the upwardly mobile and the downwardly mobile. If we want to reach realistic conclusions about rates of social mobility as a check on this kind of bias we shall have to compare the various samples with the occupational structure of the population at about the same time. When we look at the figures in Table 8.12 it is at once clear that in both the earlier samples described in Table 8.11, non-manual workers are substantially over-represented as compared with the 1951 census figures. If the three later samples are thought of as mixtures of heads of household and other occupied males then non-manual workers are probably under-represented in all three except for the Five Boroughs II analysis. Occupations were taken from census returns for the 1951 sample, and it is clear that middle class sons are over-represented. The analysis, carried out wholly within the Registrar General's Department, compared them with their fathers' occupations as recorded on their birth registration forms.

---

[1] These are respectively a comparison of husbands' and fathers' occupations for women giving birth to a first child in Aberdeen between 1950 and 1954 – see R.Illsley, 'Social Class Selection and Class Difference in Relation to Stillbirths and Infant Deaths', *British Medical Journal*, 1955, pp.1520-24; Woodford in 1959 described in P.Willmott and M.Young *Family and Class in a London Suburb*, Routledge, 1960, Appendix 3, Table XXXIX; Swansea in 1960, described in C.Rosser and C.C.Harris, *The Family and Social Change*, Routledge, 1965, Table 3.2; and the survey of national servicemen carried out for the Crowther Commission, see *15 to 18: Report of the Central Advisory Council for Education – England*, H.M.S.O., 1960, Vol.II (Surveys) p.160.

[2] See Chapter 5, Table 5.9.

Table 8.11

Some Estimates of Social Mobility in Britain

England and Wales 1949

	Sons		
Fathers	Non-Manual	Manual	All
Non-Manual	21.5	15.6	37.1
Manual	15.5	47.4	62.9
All	37.0	63.0	100.0
			N = 3498

England and Wales 1951

	Sons		
Fathers	Non-Manual	Manual	All
Non-Manual	14.6	9.5	24.1
Manual	17.4	58.5	75.9
All	32.0	68.0	100.0
			N = 2600

England and Wales 1962

	Sons and Sons-in-Law		
Fathers	Non-Manual	Manual	All
Non-Manual	16.8	7.8	24.6
Manual	18.8	56.6	75.4
All	35.6	64.4	100.0
			N = 1346

Great Britain 1963

	Sons and Sons-in-Law		
Fathers	Non-Manual	Manual	All
Non-Manual	18.7	10.8	29.5
Manual	18.8	51.7	70.5
All	37.5	62.5	100.0
			N = 1603

Five Boroughs 1967-I

	Sons and Sons-in-Law		
Fathers	Non-Manual	Manual	All
Non-Manual	15.9	11.2	27.1
Manual	19.0	53.9	72.9
All	34.9	65.1	100.0
			N = 2390

Five Boroughs 1967-II

	Sons		
Fathers	Non-Manual	Manual	All
Non-Manual	15.9	8.9	24.8
Manual	20.1	55.1	75.2
All	36.0	64.0	100.0
			N = 1094

Sources:

England and Wales 1949: D.V. Glass *Social Mobility in Britain*, Routledge, 1954, and S.M. Miller, 'Comparative Social Mobility', *Current Sociology*, 1960, IX, 1, Appendix p.71.

England and Wales 1951: B. Benjamin, 'Intergeneration Differences in Occupation', *Population Studies*, 1957-8, II, pp.262-8. The non-manual stratum in the table opposite comprises the Registrar General's 1951 socio-economic groups 1, 3-7 and 9. The manual stratum consists of s.e.gs 2, 8 and 10-13.

England and Wales 1962: W.G. Runciman, *Relative Deprivation and Social Justice*, Routledge, 1966, Table 6, p.167 and Table 12, p.175.

Great Britain 1963: D. Butler and D. Stokes, *Political Change in Britain*, Macmillan, 1969, p.96, n.1.

Five Boroughs 1967: Faith Noble, 'Social Mobility and Prejudice', Sheffield University, an unpublished manuscript based on a secondary analysis of data gathered in the survey described in E.J.B. Rose, *Colour and Citizenship*, Institute of Race Relations, 1969, ch.28.

Note: Where the transition matrix is based on a sample of males categorized by their own and their fathers' occupations they are described as sons. Where the sample included men and women classified by their husbands' occupations, the categories are described as referring to sons and sons-in-law.

Table 8.12

Occupied Males in Britain by Social Class

	1951 %	1961 %	1966 %
Non-manual	26.4	32.5	34.2
Manual	73.6	67.5	65.8

Source: Censuses 1951, 1961, 1966 and see Tables 5.7 and 5.9 above.

In relation to the other studies, where fathers' main occupations are dealt with, this procedure probably excludes a good deal of the fathers' career mobility and so overestimates the amount of intergenerational upward mobility and underestimates the amount of downward mobility which occurred. It is however, the 1949 sample from the L.S.E. survey, the one on which most discussions of social mobility in Britain have been based, which most diverges from the nearest census figures. Non-manual workers are overrepresented by almost a third or 10½% in the sample as a whole.[1]

Before making any allowance for the distortions which these features of the sample introduce, a comparison between the 1949 figures and those

---

[1] These and other biases in the figures are discussed at slightly greater length in Trevor Noble, 'Social Mobility and Class Relations in Britain', *British Journal of Sociology*, 1972, XXIII, pp.422-36.

from the three later studies shows there has been an increase in upward mobility and a decrease in downward mobility, though the differences are smaller if we take the 1951 figures as a base. As I have been arguing however, the effect of the bias in the 1951 sample is to minimize the changes which have taken place since then while the peculiarities of the samples in the later studies are likely to produce the same effect. The changes we can observe directly are unlikely therefore to be spurious and more likely underemphasize the degree of change than magnify it. This will be clearer when we try to compensate for the middle class over-representation in the 1949 survey. We can do this by weighting the sample to bring it more in line with the occupational distribution for occupied males at the time. If this is done we must of course also preserve the symmetry of the class distribution in each generation which is the main characteristic of the survey results and determines the proportions in each cell of the transition matrix. Thus if, for the sake of making the arithmetic easier, we assume in each generation 25 per cent should have been non-manual workers and 75 per cent manual workers and weight the proportions accordingly, we find 11.0 per cent of the sample would have been non-manual worker sons of non-manual fathers, and 60 per cent manual sons of manual worker fathers while approximately 14 per cent would have been downwardly mobile and 14 per cent upwardly mobile. This is less downward mobility and less upward mobility than in the original table and in fact suggests a smaller, though still real, decline in downward mobility than the comparison made with the unweighted data but an even greater increase in upward mobility.

The use of only two categories here means of course that a great deal of mobility within either of the major divisions must go undetected so that again we can be sure we are dealing with minimal estimates of mobility rates. And despite the ambiguities and blurring of the class division around the manual/non-manual division the pattern of change since 1949 is one which is quite inconsistent with an explanation merely in terms of some shift in the class boundary such as the embourgeoisement thesis or the possible progressive proletarianization of the routine white-collar occupations might suggest. A shift in the class boundary away from the non-manual/manual line should have produced both more upward and more downward mobility across that line as a consequence but this has not been the case.

Implications

Such direct evidence as we so far have on intergenerational mobility indicates that upward mobility has been increasing while downward mobility has been decreasing. Looked at from a different point of view this also reflects on the homogeneity of the major social classes. At least in comparison with the 1949 survey, even when the figures are weighted, the proportion of manual workers whose fathers were middle class has gone down from about one fifth (weighted) to around one seventh. All the more recent surveys show a majority ot non-manual workers having been born in the working class and this was true in the weighted figures for 1949 too, a conclusion confirmed by the 1951 estimate and in line with its probable bias. The pattern of change, therefore, while increasing the amount of upward mobility has made little difference to the composition of the middle class, though it draws our attention to the fact unsuspected by most sociologists, though perhaps only by them, that at least since the Second World War, the majority of men in non-manual jobs have been the sons of manual workers.[1] On the other hand, together with the decline in downward mobility this has produced a more homogeneous working class with fewer of its members having a middle class family background and possibly fewer with whatever the characteristics might be that conduce to upward mobility.

At the societal or structural level this is a rather paradoxical situation. The increased movement of men brought up in the working class into middle class occupations *prima facie* suggests some reduction in the salience of the class boundary. The greater homogeneity of background amongst the members of the working class in particular suggests an increasing polarization. The recruitment of membership to social positions (inflows) is clearly intimately connected with the pattern of social mobility (outflows), but is only a direct reflection of it in a society with a more or less stable occupational structure. This is not the case in contemporary Britain and the odd consequences of the situation we find ourselves in I shall return to in the final chapter.

Things are a bit less puzzling at the level of individual experience but this is in part because we know so little about the effects of social mobility. One thing we do know now is that in this society about 30 per cent of occupied males have been intergenerationally socially mobile between the working class and the middle class. Just after the Second World War probably as many were downwardly mobile as had been upwardly mobile, but now twice as many have been upwardly mobile from the working class as have been downwardly mobile out of the middle class.

We can be less sure about women. For those women who are in employment we might expect that mobility patterns would be similar to those of men. But a woman's position in the class structure is usually reckoned to be more closely connected with that of her husband or her father if she is still living in the bosom of her family of origin. As I pointed out above, the Five Boroughs survey, rather surprisingly perhaps, suggests that the balance of their mobility at marriage for women seemed to be downward. Either this is a fortuitous product of that particular sampling

---

[1] Among men aged 40 and over in the London region in 1970, Young and Wilmott found that 48 per cent of the professional and managerial group alone had fathers who were manual workers. See Young and Willmott, *The Symmetrical Family*, Routledge, 1973, p.242.

operation or we must consider the possibility of change since Berent's study based on data from the 1949 survey.[1] The first alternative would seem more consistent with the changes in the shape of the class structure I have been emphasizing in other connections but has no other recent direct evidence to support it. Preference for the second alternative perhaps depends on our faith in the reliability of the 1949 sample too.

Social Mobility and the Individual

It is hard to discover how mobile people differ from those who remain at the same level of society their parents had. For the most part those who become or have been socially mobile are not remarkably different from other people. They can be distinguished from their original peers or their ultimate social equals in terms of the distribution of material privilege, access to educational and occupational opportunities, values and attitudes in much the same terms which differentiate those who remain in one class or status group for life from the members of other, different, social strata. To account for the causes or the consequences of individual social mobility we are brought directly back to the structure of privilege and social differentiation which characterize the social order in general. Thus, as one might expect, those who already enjoy some of the advantages of the system are more likely to achieve individual upward mobility, while those already handicapped by lack of funds, abilities or health as compared with their original social peers are more likely to find their situation worsened by a downward career.

Most of the sparse evidence on individual social mobility relates to the background factors rather than to the consequences of the experience. As the educational system represents a major channel of mobility in contemporary Britain the findings on class differences in educational attainment reviewed above are generally relevant in this connection. Just as with selection for grammar schools or universities or the achievement of success in the public examinations the evidence from intergenerational occupational comparisons shows that those who have been upwardly mobile from the working class into the middle class are much more likely to have a skilled father than a semi-skilled or an unskilled one. What is more those favourably placed to begin with are more likely to achieve the more privileged and prestigious positions. Kelsall, Poole and Kuhn found that even amongst graduates those from families in the more prosperous sections of the middle class were more likely to have higher occupational ambitions and to gain entry to the professions in general, the legal

[1] See Jerzy Berent, 'Social Mobility and Marriage: A Study of Trends in England and Wales', in D.V.Glass (ed.), *Social Mobility in Britain*, 1954. Unfortunately the Oxford Mobility Survey only describes the mobility of men.

profession in particular, and the higher civil service or general management. Even amongst graduates, those with unskilled working class fathers seemed to be relatively handicapped in their occupational achievements. Kelsall, Poole and Kuhn point out that this casts some serious doubt on Turner's belief that upward mobility in Britain has been mysteriously 'sponsored' so that once selected for the grammar school the pupil was systematically socialized for elite membership. If this were the case the final achievements of all those selected should have been indistinguishable with reference to their social origins. It is now clear that for those reaching and graduating from university this is not true and that life chances are still conditioned by family background.[1] The same distribution of inequalities structure the probabilities of downward mobility. Those born into the middle class who have moved into the working class are disproportionately likely to have had fathers in routine clerical or lower non-manual jobs rather than in a professional or managerial occupation.[2]

Among those upwardly mobile from the working class a large proportion, though it is uncertain how large, have at least one parent who had been downwardly mobile in the first place. In a city in the north of England, out of 86 working class families with a child who had gone through grammar school and on into the middle or upper middle class, Jackson and Marsden identified 34 which were 'sunken middle class' in this sense.[3] Though it is impossible to estimate the proportion with any precision it is clearly stated that this was also a common sort of family background among the working class children who went to grammar school in the 1946 cohort studied by J.W.B. Douglas.[4] In their sample of the British graduates of 1960 Kelsall, Poole and Kuhn too found this a statistically highly significant pattern amongst those born in working class families, especially in the case of women, even though they did not consider the graduates' mothers' mobility experience in this connection.[5]

[1] *Graduates: The Sociology of an Elite*, Methuen, 1972, p.59, and Tables 3, 25 and 42-7, and see A.H.Halsey, 'Theoretical Advance and Empirical Challenge', ch.12 in Earl Hopper (ed.), *Readings in the Theory of Educational Systems*, Hutchinson, 1971, pp.270-72; cf. R.H.Turner 'Modes of Social Ascent through Education: Sponsored and Contest Mobility', in A.H.Halsey, J.Floud and C.A.Anderson (eds), *Education, Economy and Society,* Free Press, 1961, and Hopper (ed.), op.cit., 1971.

[2] See D.V.Glass, *Social Mobility in Britain,* Routledge, 1954; B.Benjamin, op.cit., 1957-8; Brian Jackson and Dennis Marsden, *Education and the Working Class,* Pelican, rev.edn., 1966, p.66; D.Butler and D.Stokes, op.cit., p.96; B.G.Stacey, 'Some Psychological Aspects of Inter-Generation Occupational Mobility', *British Journal of Social and Clinical Psychology*, 1965, 4, pp.275-86, and op.cit., 1968.

[3] loc.cit., p.68

[4] Douglas, op.cit., 1964, pp.70-74.

[5] Kelsall et al., loc.cit., p.34 and Table 7, p.182.

Douglas's study suggests that mothers' downward mobility is equally influential with fathers' in the subsequent upward mobility of their children, while others have argued that mothers are even more influential.[1] Thus for perhaps something in the region of 40 per cent of those moving up out of the working class this represents a return over three generations to a social status already familiar, at least indirectly, through the recollections of parents and close relatives. For many such people the sense of return to a lost position must mitigate the feelings of uprootedness and uncertainty often supposed to be a consequence of upward social mobility.

This is no doubt also associated with differences in values between the parents of upwardly mobile children and those of people who remain in the working class. The upwardly mobile tend to come from smaller than average families where parents take a particular interest in their activities and achievements. Typically these families live in neighbourhoods where there is a mixture of middle class and working class rather than ones which are homogeneously working class.[2]

The consequences of mobility for the individual have been fairly widely discussed although the evidence is contradictory and uncertain. Social mobility across class lines may have less general effect on people than the geographical mobility it usually entails. Among the 120 middle middle and upper middle class families Colin Bell studied in a western suburb of Swansea only 20 had not been geographically mobile. Of the 31 where the husband had been upwardly socially mobile however, 'there were none that had been socially mobile without some, usually considerable, geographical mobility'.[3]

As far as neighbourly contacts and a sense of their common interests was concerned, their experience of or lack of geographical mobility made much more difference among these educationally and occupationally successful families than whether or not they had originated in the working class.[4]

Otis Dudley Duncan has argued that we need to distinguish between the social influences operating on the original positions of the mobile individual on the one hand and and the effects of the experience of

---

[1] E.g. B.G.Stacey, op.cit. 1965; Jackson and Marsden, op.cit., 1966; M.Young and P.Willmott, *Family and Kinship in East London*, 1957, ch.11.

[2] See J.W.B. Douglas, op.cit., 1964 and B.G. Stacey, op.cit., 1965.

[3] Colin Bell, *Middle Class Families*, Routledge, 1968, p.44; see also ch. 3 above and Young and Willmott, op.cit., 1957, ch. 11; Frank Musgrove, *The Migratory Elite*, 1963, ch. 2, 3; A.H. Birch *Small Town Politics*, Oxford, 1959, p.35, and W. Watson, 'Social Mobility and Social Class in Industrial Communities' in Max Gluckman and Ely Devons (eds), *Closed Systems and Open Minds*, Oliver and Boyd, 1964.

[4] Bell, op.cit., 1969, p.160.

mobility itself on the other.[1] Thus in many respects we find that the behaviour of socially mobile people falls somewhere between that of their original peers and that of their new social equals, though in some cases closer to the one or the other. Thus in many areas of experience mobility exposes people to two sets of influences but does not in itself produce any distinctive effects. Duncan demonstrated this additive effect in a re-analysis of data on the fertility of socially mobile families from the 1949 sample in England and Wales. In the original study Berent showed that upwardly mobile people had fewer children than those who remained in the working class while the downwardly mobile had more than those who remained in the middle class.[2] Duncan showed that this could be entirely accounted for as a result of the additive effect of the two sets of social influences on the mobile individual, namely those making for conformity to the level of fertility prevailing in their original social position and those operating in the stratum which they had moved into. No effect over and above this which could be attributed to the experience of mobility itself was apparent.

Using the same material Hope has succeeded in confirming Duncan's conclusion, though he showed that there was a directional effect so that in this respect the mobile conform more to the social stratum they have joined than to the one they have left.[3] This is not universally the case and in many other respects, though in no so far apparently systematic way, original status frequently has more influence over attitudes or behaviour than current position. In general it may be said, however, that most of the apparent effects of social mobility derive from the exposure of the mobile individual to different sets of influences with the net result, for the mobile as a group, of some sort of compromise between the extremes defined by their initial and ultimate social milieux.[4] Thus the experience of social mobility often has little evident impact on its own beyond those influences which are already at work upon those who remain in the same social stratum they were born into. There are exceptions to this rule, however, though they raise their own additional problems of

[1] O.D. Duncan, 'Methodological Issues in the Analysis of Social Mobility' in N.J. Smelser and S.M. Lipset (eds), *Social Structure and Mobility in Economic Development,* Routledge, 1966.

[2] J.Berent, 'Fertility and Social Mobility', *Population Studies* 1952,5, pp.244-60.

[3] K.Hope, 'Social Mobility and Fertility' in K.Hope (ed.), *The analysis of Social Mobility: Methods and Approaches,* Oxford, 1972.

[4] See e.g. Chapter 7 above with reference to social mobility and class identification and party preference – ref.D.Butler and D.Stokes, op.cit., 1969, pp.95-101; Paul R.Abramson and John W.Books , 'Social Mobility and Political Attitudes', *Comparative Politics,* 1970-71, 3, pp. 403-428; Kenneth H.Thompson, 'A Cross-National Analysis of Intergenerational Social Mobility and Political Orientation', *Comparative Political Studies,* 1971-2, 4, pp.3-20.

interpretation. While few studies as yet have set out with Duncan's additive model in mind some in the U.S.A. have entertained this as a potential explanation of their results. Aiken and Goldberg found no effects of either upward or downward mobility on the extent of participation in family relationships which could not be accounted for simply by the cumulative influence of their respondents' original and current social status.[1] Similarly, but in the context of employment, Barbara Laslett found that mobility was quite unrelated to satisfaction with earnings while again the additive model adequately accounted for variations in overall work satisfaction and satisfaction with the kind of work done.[2]

Kessin on the other hand presents data which, however sceptical one may be of particular analytic procedures he deploys, clearly demonstrates effects, particularly for the extremely downwardly mobile, which fall quite outside the range of additive effects of origin and destination conformity. Some of these results are most surprising. Using a four category scale of socio-economic status in a survey of men in Washington D.C. he found their involvement with friends and neighbours in the local community increased as one descends from professional and technical workers through managerial and clerical, skilled manual workers to semi-skilled and unskilled manual workers. But the small group of those extremely downwardly mobile, just over three per cent of his sample, scored more highly on this measure than any of the stationary groups. They were also more involved with their friends and reported fewer symptoms of anxiety and stress than any stationary group.[3] It will be interesting to see whether these conflicting results can be replicated in Britain. Here few findings clearly demonstrate mobility effects as such. Runciman and Bagley showed that upwardly mobile people were much less likely to be prejudiced against coloured immigrants than any other group while the downwardly mobile were almost as likely to be prejudiced as the stationary working class.[4]

The main difficulty with this material, American and British, is in deciding whether it tells us anything about the consequences of social mobility at all or whether it only reflects some of the characteristics of the sort of people who become socially mobile anyway and which distinguish

---

[1] Michael Aiken and David Goldberg, 'Social Mobility and Kinship. A re-examination of the Hypothesis', *American Anthropologist*, 1969, 71, pp.261-70.

[2] Barbara Laslett, 'Mobility and Work Satisfaction: A Discussion of the Use and Interpretation of Mobility Models', *American Journal of Sociology*, 1971, 77, pp.19-34.

[3] Kenneth Kessin, 'Social and Psychological Consequences of Intergenerational Occupational Mobility', *American Journal of Sociology*, 1971, 77, pp.1-18.

[4] W.G.Runciman and C.R.Bagley, 'Status Inconsistency, Relative Deprivation and Attitudes to Immigrants', *Sociology*, 1969, 3, pp.359-75.

them from everyone else. In other words these may perhaps more plausibly be considered as causal factors themselves, or at least to derive from other causal factors in social mobility, rather than being effects or consequences of mobility. Whether socially mobile people are different from others before the event or after, and even allowing for the convincing success of the additive model in accounting for many of the supposed effects of the process, there remains an important difference which has not been explored. Socially mobile people have direct personal experience of a wider array of alternative norms than most other people — even than other geographically mobile people. It is unlikely therefore that they should be able to take conformity to any particular culture pattern for granted in the same way as other people. Whether this would generally bring about a greater uncertainty on their part about themselves and their place in society or whether it provides them with an opportunity for a more conscious and deliberate commitment to a way of life must remain a question for further research. In the light of the trend towards an increasing amount of upward social mobility it is not a question to which we can afford simply to assume we know the answer.

We can ask why rates of mobility stand at the particular level they do in this society now and why they are changing in the way observed. The anwers to these questions appear to involve the demands for recruitment to a changing occupational structure, the extent to which social strata are open or closed, the relative fertility of the members of the various social classes, the willingness or interest that people have in moving, their ability and readiness to adapt to changes in their personal circumstances. The consequences of mobility for the individual equally depend on the nature of the social system within which he or she moves, while the consequences for society of changing rates of mobility depend on the quality of individual experience in the course of mobility and the changing psychological demands which increased mobility within a changing society will necessarily make.[1]

In summary I think it is worth restating the obvious. So far, we know very little about the consequences of social mobility and only a very little more about its causes. While there is a premium on educational attainment, the unequal distribution of advantages in the class system determines the likelihood of social mobility for individuals in the various social strata. But this structuring occurs within a changing technological and economic environment which since the 1950s has required a social redistribution of labour and brought about an increasing amount of upward social mobility and a decline in downward mobility. This redistribution has mainly been mediated through the allocative functions of the educational system, though there is no good evidence that this has been at the expense of post-educational movement within the system of

---

[1] See B.G.Stacey, 'Some Psychological Consequences of Intergeneration Mobility', *Human Relations*, 1967, 20, pp.3-5.

employment itself. The technological changes of the 1960s have been heralded as the second industrial revolution and although that may be something of an historical exaggeration there would seem to be no obvious limits in the short run to the changes now in progress in Britain. In the long run, of course, a situation where continuing mobility transformed the present class structure out of all recognition would require fresh consideration, but that still lies a long way off.

9 Conclusions: Power and Structure

Introduction

The people of Britain do not simply follow diverse patterns of customary behaviour but are subject to inequalities of material provision and social regard. As a result they are not equally in command of their own circumstances. Some enjoy a measure of security from at least most of the social ills and though money may not be able to buy everything it can make unhappiness a great deal more comfortable. Others are much more vulnerable to the socially determined catastrophes: redundancy and unemployment, poor housing or even homelessness, deprivation and poverty. Property, profession or membership of an organised interest group provide the individual members of society with different and unequal degrees of influence over one another's lives. It is this complex, and to a certain extent changing, pattern of inequality which has been referred to as the system of social stratification. All the different but persistent structured social inequalities are gathered together and re-focused when we examine the distribution of power. This is not a separate area of study but rather a matter of looking at the same questions from a rather different perspective. Under this rubric our attention is drawn towards the more political dimensions of stratification and the way in which the various social inequalities operate as origin and outcome of a process of social relations.

Looked at in this way, any attempt at an account of social structure must raise the issue of identifying the sources and then outlining the distribution of power in society. It always seems much easier to do this when thinking about societies structurally dissimilar from that of our own contemporary experience. It may be that modern urbanized and industrialized societies are increasingly more complex than anything that preceded them and it is, of course, always difficult to be objective about a topic on which it is impossible to be disinterested. With few exceptions, most accounts of modern British social structure either make little effort in the direction of objectivity or else they avoid discussing the problem of power altogether. In the present chapter I have tried to look at the question of whether it is possible to draw any firm conclusions about the social location of the major concentrations of power and secondly how far the domain within which influence is exercised might currently be subject to change.

It must be apparent from the account of British social structure I have given so far that it is a society whose processes can be understood only in terms of the differentiation, though not necessarily the distinct separation, of social strata. The reader may recall that in the Introduction I followed Weber's distinction between the kinds of differentiating processes at work in industrialized societies which divided them into classes, status groups and parties. Which of these concepts is most helpful in ordering our sparse information about the distribution of power in Britain? In a sense there must always, by definition, be a ruling party. The question is what are the resources upon which its power is based? Within our parliamentary system the parties which compete to form our government, as was shown in Chapter 7, are rooted in social forces which outreach those purely political resources which suffice the ruling party in undemocratic states. But is some element of subjective experience, the sense of solidarity with one's social peers the important factor or are the more impersonal forces of the market the crucial thing? In the first place we should have to explore the character of the dominant status groups, in the second we should be looking for a ruling class.

This is a useful distinction and provides the basis for the discussion in the present chapter. Of course we must not expect that the facts should fall neatly into the categories of our theoretical expectations. This is not the kind of work in which all can be made blindingly clear in the last chapter. In the quest for understanding there is always further to go.

Anthony Sampson has argued that there is, in fact, no pinnacle or centre to the social hierarchy. In the arts, the churches, education and finance, industry the mass media, politics and the professions, science, trade and the unions, in each institutional order there is a separate élite. These various élite groups may tend to have some things in common but they are primarily concerned each with their own activities in their own field of action and encounter one another only peripherally.[1] The political leadership is perhaps exceptional to the extent that contact with other groups of interests is a primary object of their activity. In Britain the political leadership of the major parties which is to legitimate the outcome brought to bear upon the process of bargaining among all these separate sectional interests. This is mediated through the parliamentary role of the political leadership of the major parties which is to ligitimate the outcome of the bargaining process which they try to conduct and control. Reviewing the positions adopted by a wide range of interest groups over 24 issues of economic, foreign, social and welfare policy between 1944 and 1964, Christopher Hewitt concluded that not only was 'each interest limited in the range of its involvement', but that 'neither the business

[1] See Anthony Sampson, *Anatomy of Britain*, Hodder and Stoughton, 1962, p.624.

group nor any other appears to be especially favoured by the government'.[1] Appearances may in any case be misleading. On the one hand the distribution of power is not always a clear guide to the manner of its use. Writing of the liberalism of the nineteenth-century landed aristocracy F.M.L. Thompson pointed out that '. . . different answers must be returned to the questions, who holds power and in whose interest is power exercised'.[2] On the other it has become a sociological truism that formal authority is not the same as effective influence. Michels' 'iron law of oligarchy' was that in all complex organizations the full-time administrator gradually gains control; and Max Weber, writing of the administrative bureaucracies of the modern state, argued that 'Generally speaking, the trained permanent official is more likely to get his way in the long run than his nominal superior, the Cabinet Minister, who is not a specialist.'[3] Power is not always what nor where it appears to be on the surface. The concepts and methods we employ in its analysis and the emphasis we should give to the evidence we turn up are all uncertain. I shall tread carefully and try to avoid jumping to conclusions.

Economic Power: A Ruling Class?

Finding the Right Questions

In a society such as this one, dependent as it is for the very survival of its people on the workings of an industrial economy, control over its industrial and commercial resources will clearly be a major source of social power just as control over the land was in feudal times with an agrarian economy. But other factors may have to be taken into account too. Administrative and organizational resources, expertise, and commonly accepted right or legitimacy for instance, are all important in the highly differentiated, large-scale and technologically sophisticated social apparatus on which life as we now know it depends. The question still arises, however, as to the nature of the control over the economic resources of society and where it lies. Can it be said to lie with identifiable individuals or categories of individuals at all, or is the operation of large organizations, as well as the small firm dependent upon the state of its markets, so

[1] Christopher J.Hewitt, 'Elites and the Distribution of Power in British Society', ch.3 in Philip Stanworth and Anthony Giddens (eds), *Elites and Power in British Society*, Cambridge, 1974, pp.60-61.

[2] F.M.L. Thomson, *English Landed Society in the Nineteenth Century*, Routledge, 1963, p.279.

[3] Max Weber, *The Theory of Social and Economic Organisation*, Free Press and Falcon's Wing Press, 1947, p.338; Robert Michels, *Political Parties*, Free Press, 1949.

controlled by the impersonal necessities of the economic system that the question becomes meaningless? The growing concentration of economic power through the increasing domination of society by fewer and larger organizations described in Chapter 5 is likely to have far reaching effects on the future of British society. In the present and even for the future the exact significance of this tendency is hard to gauge.

The issues which arise in this context have been principally focused on the question wealth and ownership. Are these massive concentrations of capital increasingly under the control of a tiny and closely-knit group of capitalists or do they signify the depersonalization of institutionalized capital which, though it certainly confers great power on some of its senior employees, has itself ceased to depend on their social indentity as an independently self-interested class? Has not the management of corporate bodies taken the place of the self aggrandizement of wealthy men? Reliable evidence here is elusive, sparse and inconclusive. This partly derives from the difficulties involved in gathering accurate information, partly perhaps from the uncertainty and complexity of the real situation and partly from the fact that the questions themselves are posed in too simple terms. They are too simple because the either/or alternatives offered overlook some of the possible dimensions of change which must be considered if the current situation is not to be merely decked out in the threadbare categories of some outworn analysis. In this area there are relatively few facts around to feed a large number of competitive theories. Most of the theoretical accounts seem plausible but are mutually discrediting. For the purposes of political theory it is perhaps possible to choose among these contradictory interpretations according to their affinity with the assumptions one starts with. From the different perspective of sociology, however, there is little direct help to be offered. Instead of being able to build the whole analysis of social structure on the empirical outcome of these most basic questions one is driven back to ideological presumption or guesswork. Only provisional interpretative judgements of the inadequate evidence in the light of what is more confidently known about other aspects of society can be made at this stage. This is of course a very unsatisfactory situation, but it seems to me less satisfactory still to be offered speculation in the guise of knowledge and, while I shall try to keep the distinction between them as clear as I can, the end result is likely to seem a good deal less decisively clear-cut than might be achieved by deciding on the answers first before looking at the evidence.

As usual with summary diagnoses of the condition of contemporary society the major positions appear to seize on different aspects of the truth. The political or moral issue may involve which alternative view one wishes to take as the basis for evaluation and action. The sociological issue is to decide how different points of view which seem to be sustained by the available evidence can nevertheless appear to be contradictory. The answer seems to lie partly in the level of generality at which enquiry is conducted. Here Dahrendorf has reminded us of the useful distinction between Industrial Society on the one hand and Capitalism on the other. To be concerned with the structure and dynamics of Industrial Society is to treat Capitalism as only a particular type or case.[1] A capitalist society is one in which there is private property in the productive resources of the economy and where productive processes are regulated by private contract or managment initiative and the creation of credit rather than through central planning on the part of agencies of the state under political control.[2] The coordination and control of industrial organization, though it entails the continuous accummulation of capital for investment in renewal and development, does not depend on private ownership. The extent to which they coincide may have consequences for other aspects of the wider social context, but this itself is a question to which there is no final answer.

The growth of large corporate industrial, commercial and administrative organizations is now one of the facts of economic and social life in contemporary industrial societies. With this development the power which individuals or groups were able to wield in a less complex social structure has been constrained within the institutional necessities of long-term planning and control imposed by the problems consequent on large-scale organization. Large-scale organizations present especially difficult problems of coordination and management. Decisions have to be taken which involve the activities of many differentiated departments. Planning has to be in the long term if the organization is not to be thrown out of joint and valuable resources of skill, manpower and material employed wastefully. Management becomes a technically complex task involving large numbers of specialists. Among the problems this raises for the historical development of our social structure are: firstly, whether and how far this brings about a more diffused or pluralist distribution of effective power in society as a whole; and/or secondly, whether it means that power is shifted away from the old capitalist class who owned the productive resources of society, and into the hands of the salaried managerial employees of the great corporations whose expertise provides them alone with the capacity for making the decisions which are required in the running of an increasingly complex economy.

This argument is closely related to Burnham's idea of the 'Managerial Revolution'.[3] This coinage was intended to describe a situation in which capitalism of the type that existed in Marx's day has apparently disappeared to be replaced by a society in which industrial organizations

[1] Ralf Dahrendorf, *Class and Class Conflict in Industrial Society*, Routledge, 1964, p.40.

[2] J.Schumpeter, *Capitalism, Socialism and Democracy*, Allen and Unwin, 1943, p.167.

[3] See James Burnham, *The Managerial Revolution*, Pelican, 1945.

of vast size and either nominally owned by shareholders or nationalized organs of a collectivist state, remain the sources of effective power in society but are controlled by a new class of professional salaried managers.

Needless to say these arguments have attacted considerable criticism and not only on account of their political implications. Rothschild argues that ' . . . while real conflicts of interest may exist in minor affairs — for example on dividend policy, scale of operations etc. — there is little reason to expect any serious differences between owners and managers on the fundamental question of strengthening and exercising big business power'.[1] Nichols has argued more sweepingly that the behaviour of owner-capitalists, propertied directors and non-propertied managers is unlikely to differ. None are likely to go exclusively for short-term profit maximization; all are equally likely to benefit from and therefore to be interested in promoting the growth of their firm and the long-term security of its market position.[2] Managers in private industry generally enjoy higher salaries and a freer hand than those in nationalized undertakings and as a consequence are likely to share with private owners a concern for the preservation of private property.[3] Whatever the identity of interests between the propertied élite and the managerial élite, increasingly, however, they have to operate within a common political climate and their activities are increasingly circumscribed by governmental action. In the modern state political power is able to, and on occasion does, overrule economic interest.[4] The transfer of influence from economic to political resources is the outcome of just that process of the growth in scale of organizations and the closer interlocking of the several sectors of the economy which is generated as a reaction towards and an attempt to control irrational market forces and which Galbraith has identified with the growth of the technostructure.[5]

Ownership is a crucial issue where private property rights are a basis of legitimate decision-making in economic affairs. The questions which arise concern the location and concentration of such power, whether private property rights are regarded as the only basis of such authority and how far they are hedged about by other powers. The political powers of the state, which has assumed through its elected leaders and permanent

---

[1] K.W.Rothschild (ed.), *Power in Economics*, Penguin, 1971, p.167.

[2] Theo Nichols, *Ownership, Control and Ideology*, Allen and Unwin, 1969, ch.9, especially p.99.

[3] See National Board for Prices and Incomes, *Top Salaries in the Private Sector and Nationalized Industries*, Report No.107, H.M.S.O., 1969. Roy Lewis and Rosemary Steward *The Boss: The Life and Times of the British Business Man*, Dent, 1963, and G.Lenski, *Power and Privilege*, McGraw-Hill, 1966, p.359.

[4] See Andrew Shonfield, *Modern Capitalism: The Changing Balance of Public and Private Power*, Oxford, 1965; cf. Lenski, op.cit., p.341.

[5] J.K. Galbraith, *The New Industrial State*, Houghton Mifflin, 1967.

apparatus the right to control the country's economic affairs, obviously represent one sort of limitation on the power of property. Managerial and technocratic expertise and professionalism within the economic institutions themselves are another important resource in any complex industrial society without which mere ownership would be hamstrung. Nevertheless in a capitalist society property rights are the basis for access to positions of strategic significance in the economic institutions of society and hence are, within limits, transmutable into other forms of social influence.

The Concentration of Economic Power

In whose hands are the reins of economic power? The organized workers, about half the total working population, through the unions on the one hand wield the blunt instrument of industrial action which may sometimes hinder the operation of a firm, an industry or occasionally the whole economy and on the other, through wage-bargaining, they may sometimes improve their position as consumers and hence increase the overall level of demand. They are the cylinders of the economic engine, it is their activity which makes it go but they do not command either the supply of steam or what load it will have to pull. Influential as they may be on particular issues the unions for the most part operate within the framework of a labour market over whose structural determinants they have very little control.

In theory there are no restrictions on the internal power of the state. It has far-reaching and growing influence through its control of the money supply, through public investment and as an employer in the publicly-owned sector of the economy. In addition, assistance to ailing industries in the private sector, such as shipbuilding during the 1960s, and the placing of contracts for the supply of equipment to the armed services, the nationalized industries and departments of state, together provide considerable leverage on the economy. There is little sign that goverments systematically exploit this and with only about a quarter of the labour force in the public sector, the state's direct involvement is less than may sometimes appear. Government of the remainder of the economy is a political process in which the party in power has to negotiate the cooperation of the various interest groups in the pursuit of its own political aims. These may already coincide, but where there is some degree of conflict the avoidance of direct confrontation and compulsion is likely to prove a matter of practical necessity if the disruption of the economic life of the country and the frustration of the party's programme are to be avoided.

Economic power lies in control of the major economic institutions, and despite the strategic importance of the nationalized industries and public services, where the decisions of the elected government of the day are of major significance, the far larger portion of industrial and commercial activity is in the private sector. Even there however it may not be easy to find a readily identifiable section of the population who as far as their part of the economy is concerned, might be labelled 'the ruling class'. To begin with no economy is an island and the British economy is far from unalloyed with foreign interests. According to a United Nations estimate in 1973 one fifth of the gross fixed capital in manufacturing industry in Britain was American owned.[1] Foreign investment in British industry is particularly concentrated in the more technologically advanced and more rapidly growing fields — electronics, motor vehicles and the pharmaceutical industry (which is 80 per cent foreign owned).[2] Thus in Britain, whoever the holders of economic power are, they have to operate within the substantial constraints and competing interests of organized labour, the government and extensive foreign influence on their own doorstep.

Though the powers of British business are not then unfettered they are still important in the balance we are trying to strike. The right to participate in the crucial decisions, not merely on the design of toasters or the number of workers on the night shift, but about the merging or submerging of whole industrial enterprises, rests with the boards of directors and, in the private sector, membership of the board is legitimated on the basis of a property qualification. Of course, many directors have no more than a nominal holding in their company while, with rare exceptions, the large industrial or commercial corporation of today is run by directors whose own share in the firm is no more than a tiny fraction of its share capital.

As we have already observed, however, power and position are not synonymous. Pahl and Winkler emphasized this in their account of the directors and their influence in a wide range of firms in different sectors of British industry and commerce. Not all directors are equally influential and some are scarely influential at all. They concluded,

' . . . the board actions we observed are better interpreted, we feel, merely as ratifications of decisions made earlier and elsewhere, sometimes by much more junior men, about which the board had no practical alternative. The distinction between 'making' and 'taking' decisions is relevant. Boards of directors are, we feel, best conceived as decision-taking institutions, that is, as legitimating institutions rather than as decision-making ones'.[3]

[1] United Nations, *Multinational Corporations in World Development*, U.N., 1973; see also Michael Hughes, 'American Investment in Britain', in John Urry and John Wakeford (eds), *Power in Britain*, Heinemann, 1973, pp.157-79.

[2] See M.D.Steuer et al., *The Impact of Foreign Direct Investment in the United Kingdom*, H.M.S.O., 1973.

[3] R.E.Pahl and J.T.Winkler, 'The Economic Elite: Theory and Practice', ch.6 in Stanworth and Giddens, op.cit., 1974, p.110.

Nevertheless even though in many cases operational control of the firm's affairs may be in the hands of management and some proportion of those holding directorships may be ineffective 'window dressing' for the company's prospectus, the disposal of the firm's capital assets still remains the prerogative of the board and those who can determine the exercise of that prerogative will predominantly be directors.[1]

Nichols carried out a re-analysis of data on the shareholdings of directors of large British companies and concluded that the proportion of their firms' ordinary shares owned by board members and the size of their individual holdings were generally so small that it, 'disqualifies them from being termed "capitalists" in any meaningful sense'[2]. But as he emphasized, this was not to imply that these directors were 'non-propertied'.

The distribution of personal wealth has already been briefly described in Chapter 6. When it comes to the influence the ownership of wealth entails, over and above the financial security it confers, the picture is regrettably still more obscure. To begin with, as Moyle has shown, personal holdings are declining as a proportion of company share ownership in favour of institutional holdings by banks, insurance companies, pension funds and trusts. Between 1957 and 1970 the proportion of all British ordinary (voting) shares quoted on the stock exchange which was owned personally by individuals declined from 66 per cent to less than 48 per cent. Furthermore about a quarter of the total value of personal holdings is held by executors or trustees on behalf of the beneficial owner.[3]

In 1970 the role of the individual shareholder was declining but some shareholders were still very influential individuals. About 18,000,000 people, just over a third of the population, were regarded by the Board of Inland Revenue as owners of wealth in 1971. Of these 23 per cent had less than £1,000 and 12 per cent had more than £10,000 but owned 55 per cent of the total. Within this extremely lop-sided distribution, the ownership of stocks and shares is still more unevenly dispersed and only about one in seven of these 'wealthy' individuals were ordinary shareholders.[4] As we have already seen investment income provides the largest share in the income of the already wealthiest. The rich are also much more likely to derive their investment income from company stocks and shares than are people with more modest fortunes. In 1966 *The*

[1] ibid., p.115.

[2] *Ownership, Control and Ideology*, 1969, p.78. Nichols re-examined data from P.Sargant Florence, *The Ownership, Control and Success of Large Companies*, Sweet and Maxwell, 1961, with especial reference to companies with assets over £50 million in 1951; see Nichols, op.cit., Table 6.3, p.76.

[3] See John Moyle, *The Pattern of Ordinary Share Ownership 1957-1970*, Cambridge, 1971, pp.16 and 18, and Jack Revell and John Moyle, *The Owners of Quoted Ordinary Shares*, Chapman and Hall, 1966, p.9.

[4] See *Annual Abstract of Statistics No.110*, 1973, Table 326.

Economist estimated that 56 per cent of the wealth of those with fortunes of a quarter of a million pounds or more was in equities compared with only 5 per cent of the wealth of those with less than £10,000. These less wealthy individuals are more likely to have their funds in fixed interest bonds or in only slowly appreciating cash. It was calculated that between 1950 and 1964 the capital of those with between £3,000 and £10,000 must, on average, have appreciated by about 48 per cent, but in the same period the average appreciation of the capital of the wealthiest group must have averaged 114 per cent.[1] The survey carried out for the London Stock Exchange in 1966 showed that about five per cent of the adult British population, about 2,000,000 people, held industrial or commercial stocks and shares. Two thirds of them owned less than a thousand pounds' worth.[2]

By these standards company directors, at least those on the boards of the larger firms, must generally be counted as wealthy men, and increasingly so. Nichols showed that even 15 years before this only a fifth of the directors of the largest companies – companies with nominal assets over £50 million in 1951 – possessed less than a thousand pounds' worth of shares in their own company and 42 per cent had a shareholding of £5,000 or more. Allowing for the fall in the value of money this would be a little over £12,000 worth or more at 1972 prices.[3] A 1972 survey of the directors of 200 of Britain's largest companies found that 45 per cent owned shares in their company worth £20,000 or more, though this advance may reflect the state of the stockmarket rather than a rise in shareholdings.[4] Nichols' comment therefore has added force, 'In comparison with the population as a whole,' he wrote, ' . . . and even when compared to shareholders generally, there is some justification for regarding directors as "men of property" '.[5] But though the majority of company directors still fall some way short of being 'capitalists' except in the loosest sense, that species is not yet wholly extinct within these shores. In 1967, *The Times* listed 40 directors each with £1,000,000 or more in a single company, totalling amongst all of them almost £400,000,000 capital.[6]

[1] *The Economist*, 15 January 1966, p.218; British Market Research Bureau, *How Does Britain Save?*, London Stock Exchange, 1966. It is probable that large shareholders are not the last to dispose of their holdings when stockmarket prices fall.

[2] ibid., pp.13 and 27.

[3] This estimate is based on figures for the purchasing power of the pound given in David Butler and Jennie Freeman, *British Political Facts 1900-1967*, Macmillan, 1968, pp.223-4 and *Annual Abstract of Statistics 110*, H.M.S.O., 1973, Table 403.

[4] Robert H Heller, 'The State of British Boardrooms', *Management Today*, May 1973, pp.81-3.

[5] loc.cit., pp.78-9.

[6] *The Times*, 15 December 1967.

Here we have fallen among the super-rich, men whose financial resources alone could be the basis of considerable influence upon the destinies of the undertakings they invest in. When we extend our horizon to include the range of directors the surveys refer to we are still considering the wealthy. Somewhere between we come within hail of that band of British taxpayers whose wealth beings them an income of £10,000 or more a year before tax.[1] Some of them, no doubt, are content to sit back and enjoy their fortune while others prefer to make use of the security wealth brings to pursue an active life far removed from the world of business. There is, it seems, an increasing tendency for this to happen. Rubinstein concluded from his analysis of wills declared at half a million pounds or more that a much higher proportion of the directors and chairmen of the largest companies were wealthholders of this order at the beginning of the century than today.[2] At the same time, though it cannot be said of half-millionaires, the proportion of millionaires who were the sons of very rich fathers decreased among those dying in the 1960s. As these very large fortunes are only likely to be made in business, it would appear that the inheritors of great wealth are increasingly abandoning that scene to the salaried professionals on the one hand and the self-made entrepreneurs on the other.[3] From the point of view of the distribution of economic power, however, the most consequential members of this stratum are those who cultivate their wealth, taking not only an interest in its continuing investment but engaging directly in the running of the companies they invest in. Those with a seat on the board of a large firm link property with decision making. Those with several directorships are in a position to exercise an augmented influence, deriving from their involvement in a wider range of decision-making situations.

The degree of overlap that exists between the boards of the larger corporations represents the possibility at least of a more coherent understanding of common concerns even if it does not always amount to the active coordination of policies. The 1972 *Management Today* survey found that 45 per cent of directors had other directorships outside the firm sampled.[4] Among the 40 largest industrial firms in 1971 Whitley found 21 were linked with another by having at least one director in common. When he included 27 major financial firms in the analysis however, 56 out of the 67 were connected in this way. Only predominantly family or 'tycoon' controlled firms remained largely isolated from this network of

[1] See Chapter 6 above.

[2] W.D.Rubinstein, 'Men of Property: Some Aspects of Occupation, Inheritance and Power among Top British Wealthholders', ch.8 in Stanworth and Giddens, op.cit., 1974, p.169.

[3] ibid., p.163.

[4] loc.cit., 1973, p.82.

overlapping directorships.[1] The particular closeness of the connections which persist amongst the directors of the more important financial institutions, the Bank of England, the major clearing banks, the largest merchant banks and discount houses and the principal insurance companies emerges clearly from this study. Of the 402 directors of the 27 financial concerns he studied, there were in 1971 only 89 who were not also directors of other companies.[2] Michael Barratt-Brown found that in 1966 the 146 directors of merchant banks he studied sat on the boards of 400 other companies including 60 banks and trusts, 12 of the 20 biggest insurance companies, 45 or the 150 biggest British industrial companies and 32 big companies operating overseas including Shell, B.P., Burmah Oil, P. & O., Hudson's Bay and Rio Tinto Zinc.[3] This clearly adds up to a good deal of interconnectedness between industry and finance, and especially among the financial undertakings themselves, even when we are only concerned with the links which include the merchant banks, It would appear to fall short, however, of the decisive control by finance capital discerned, for instance, by Aaronovitch.[4] Pahl and Winkler came to the view that it was the executive directors who exercised most influence on the boards they observed. Those with seats on more than one board were there, of necessity, in a non-executive capacity and therefore were much less *au fait* with the activities of the company than its full-time directors. Interlocking directorships, they suggested, were 'not, in our experience, a significant instrument of shareholder-owner control; non-executive directors were easily manipulated'.[5] Nor should the linkages be deemed to operate only in one direction. As Parry pointed out in criticizing an earlier account by Barratt-Brown, the interconnections are often through directors from industry who 'for the sake of financial advice and business contacts . . . take up seats on the boards of the major financial institutions'.[6] And as Barratt-Brown's later study confirms, 'many of the largest firms in Britain have no directors in common with financial institutions whilst the very largest companies can be financially independent independent of the banks'.[7]

If the direction of the affairs of the financial institutions of the country

[1] Richard Whitley, 'The City and Industry: The Directors of Large Companies, their Characteristics and Connections', ch.4 in Stanworth and Giddens (eds.), *Elites and Power in British Society,* Cambridge pp.72-3.

[2] Richard Whitley, 'Commonalities and Connections Among Directors of Large Financial Institutions', *Sociological Review,* 1973, 21, p.622.

[3] See Michael Barratt-Brown, 'The Controllers of British Industry', Table 13 in Ken Coates (ed.), *Can The Workers Run Industry?,* Sphere, 1969.

[4] S.Aaronovitch, *The Ruling Class,* Lawrence and Wishart, 1961.

[5] loc.cit., 1974, p.119.

[6] Geraint Parry, *Political Elites,* Allen and Unwin, 1969, p.79.

[7] ibid.

is clearly still an immensely important source of influence on the available evidence it does not of itself amount to the exercise of finally decisive power.

Thus all that we can say of the social characteristics of the economically influential is that they are often wealthy men. Though that is hardly surprising it does indicate that wealth and power are still associated but it does not tell us very much one way or the other about what kind of association that is. The increasing concentration of capital in the private sector of the British economy documented in the 1970 Monopolies Commission Survey[1] means that the ultimate decisions on the deployment of these vast resources are increasingly located within fewer and fewer organizations, though not necessarily in the hands of fewer and fewer people. As organizations grow decisions become more long-term and more complex and more people may be involved rather than fewer. And as Barratt-Brown has pointed out, whether the directors of large companies are 'themselves private owners of great wealth or controllers of other people's wealth is in fact not important'.[2] Among the directors interviewed by Pahl and Winkler those who were salaried did distinguish themselves from the owners, especially the owners of family firms. However this was chiefly because they saw themselves as more professional in their attitude to business, that is to say they regarded themselves as more thoroughly profit-orientated.[3] Yet if the assumptions of businessmen remain largely unchanged that is not to say they are still applied within an unchanging set of circumstances.

As a factor in the total distribution of income the ownership of wealth is of declining importance. We might infer that therefore the class structure has become less rigid. On the other hand differentials within earned income have been widening and the same may be true of all incomes if tax avoidance on unearned personal income could be taken into account. This apparent paradox, together with Moyle's evidence of the decling proportion of personal ownership of ordinary shares, seems to indicate that the role of personal wealth in the structure of social inequality is being overshadowed by the growth of organizational size and the massive influence of corporate wealth. The individual, even the very very wealthy individual, is less influential in a society increasingly dominated by the corporate power of large-scale organizations, public and private. The distribution of power within society may still be construed as a zero-sum game but some of the rules have been changing. It may be that we have come to a time when it is necessary to consider whether the crucial dimensions of stratification have not shifted.

[1] The Monopolies Commission, *A Survey of Mergers 1958-1968*, H.M.S.O., 1970, and see Moyle, op.cit., 1971, Table 3.1, p.11.

[2] loc.cit., p.78.

[3] loc.cit., p.119.

A Dominant Status Group?

Before we can decide that the basis of stratification has shifted there are other dimensions to be considered. There is, moreover, little more evidence of change when we turn from the economic to the social characteristics of the élite. There is little enough known about life-styles among the 'upper crust', though various interesting but more or less impressionistic accounts of what 'top people' are like have appeared in recent years. In terms of their manners, behaviour and style of life generally, Nancy Mitford tells us, the aristocracy shade imperceptibly into the upper middle class, though there are clear differences between the latter and the rest of the middle class, which is continually betrayed by an immeasureable host of attitudes and assumptions, tastes, habits of speech, gesture and manner.[1] It is clear that there must be more to relations among the influential than a common market situation. Economic interest alone would not go very far to unite the diversity of élite groups in industry, finance, politics, administration, the services, education and the professions. In England however, most of the senior men in each sphere outside the Labour movement share a similar education, common social assumptions and fairly similar social backgrounds. Though at the same time this distinguishes them from the vast majority of the population it does not entail agreement on particular issues. Its significance is that they are able to accept one another at least as social equals and can take a great deal for granted in their relationships with one another even when their spheres of activity diverge and their interests conflict. Recruitment to these positions still reflects the importance of social inequality not only in economic terms but also in terms of status differentiation. This can readily be indicated by the role of private education outside the state system in the perpetuation of privilege from generation to generation.

The public schools, indeed the whole of the private sector of education but the public schools in particular, have never been concerned only with academic attainment, however successful their achievements in that direction may have been. They have always been profoundly concerned with the training of character with especial emphasis on the qualities of leadership. In a stratified society the positions of leadership toward which the pupils of the public schools are expected to proceed are roughly those in which their parents are already so heavily concentrated. Thus, in some contrast with the expanding state sector in education, the private sector fundamentally is aimed at the preservation of the social status of the

---

[1] See 'The English Aristocracy' in Nancy Mitford (ed.), *Noblesse Oblige*, Penguin, 1959, p.37 and see also e.g. Roy Perrott, *The Aristocrats*, Weidenfeld and Nicolson, 1968; Anthony Sampson, op.cit., 1962; *Anatomy of Britain Today*, Hodder and Stoughton, 1965, and *The New Anatomy of Britain*, Hodder and Stoughton, 1971.

children of the already advantaged few.[1]

To have been educated at a public school is a sign of privilege. It usually indicates a background of a family of well above average prosperity and suggests the possibility in later life of access easier than is available to the majority through former school fellows and others of similar social standing to people in positions of influence. As the then headmaster of Eton said in 1965, 'This is an extraordinarily happy school. People remember it and their friends with great affection and they do tend to stick together in later life.'[2] Too much should not be read into the irony of this remark however. Having been to school together does not automatically make men co-conspirators against the rest of society, still less when they have merely been to similar schools and at different times. Over and above their purely academic functions and the encouragement of aspirations to leadership the public schools inculcate a particular idea of decorous behaviour, of responsibility and of good manners, a way of life that is the medium, if not always the substance, of interaction amongst those born into the upper middle class. They do not determine the membership of that class as a socio-economic entity, rather they define the life-style of a status group.

Membership of a status group is mainly apparent in the way an individual conducts himself in his relations with his social equals and with others. It carries with it only limited implications for the relationships he will in fact maintain or the goals he is likely to pursue.[3] Just the same, this

[1] See in general Ian Weinberg, *The English Public Schools: The Sociology of An Elite*, Atherton Press, 1967; R. Wilkinson and T.J.H. Bishop, *Winchester and the Public School Elite*, Faber and Faber, 1967, and John Wakeford, *The Cloistered Elite: A Sociological Analysis of the English Public Boarding School*, Macmillan, 1969.

[2] A.Chenevix-Trench, quoted in the *Observer*, 14 February 1965.

[3] Fairlie and Budge have argued that social background (especially father's occupation) may play a more influential part in the determination of political attitudes in Britain than for elites elsewhere, though the important common characteristics seem to vary from issue to issue and are never wholly predictable in their effects. See Denis Fairlie and Ian Budge, 'Elite Background and Issue Preferences: A Comparison of British and Foreign Data using a New Technique' in Ivor Crewe (ed.), *British Political Sociology Yearbook Volume 1: Elites in Western Democracy*, Croom Helm, 1974, pp.199-240. Graeme Moodie and Gerald Studdert Kennedy have also pointed out that 'common membership does not necessarily carry with it political agreement, mutual friendship, conspiracy or even unqualified acceptance, although it sometimes does. But it does facilitate understanding (and, hence, on occasion, mutual antagonism) and does enlarge the possibilities of communication'. They remind us that even in the betrayal of official secrets the public schools and our ancient universities have provided the elite. Burgess, McLean and Philby demonstrate that one cannot safely assume anything about a man's political loyalties simply on the basis of his class or educational background; see *Opinions, Publics and Pressure Groups*, Allen and Unwin, 1970, pp.70-71. Similar points have been made by Parry, op.cit., 1969, p.101, and Anthony Giddens, 'Elites in the British Class Structure', *Sociological Review*, 1972, 20, p.362.

is not to deny the structural importance of the pattern of recruitment to élites nor, in rejecting a crudely deterministic account of their members' responses to their social position, is it intended to imply that they typically have no common interests. We can reasonably assume that it is only exceptionally that the beneficiaries of any situation will seek radically to change it, and then usually in a way which will benefit themselves still more.

The expansion of higher education and the slowly increasing access of lower middle class and working class children to university places has not ended the pattern of inequality of access to positions of influence. Kelsall and his colleagues found that, even among university graduates, class of origin remained an important factor in recruitment to higher status occupations, notably in the legal profession, the higher civil service and management. In part this was the result of the higher aspirations of graduates from higher status homes. They were more likely to have had clear ideas about future careers at the beginning of their university courses and aimed higher than students from working class homes.[1] The aspirations students have are passed on from their parents. Douglas, Ross and Simpson found that middle class parents are a good deal more ambitious for their children than are working class parents. More than twice the proportion of upper middle class boys of high ability were expected by their parents to enter the professions compared with lower working class boys of similar ability; the differences were even more pronounced for the less able.[2] Douglas et al. however point out that these differing aspirations may derive from their differing experience of social inequality. 'The low expectations of the manual working class parents may reflect the real diffifulties that many talented pupils have in attempting to enter the professions when they lack skilled advice and encouragement from their parents and schools.'[3] Success is not simply a matter of aiming high. This was demonstrated by the findings of Kelsall et al. that even among graduates with similar aspirations regarding their careers, higher class of origin was favourable to success.[4]

The advantage of a good start in life are too numerous and should be too obvious to need further summary here. The advantages of the kind of start signalized by a public school education do not end there but may endure throughout a subsequent career. This is clearly the case at least for those who come under our gaze when we examine the social origins of men in leading positions in modern England.

[1] See R.K.Kelsall, Anne Poole and Annette Kuhn, *Graduates: The Sociology of an Elite*, Methuen, 1972, pp.71, 91-9 and Tables 42-47.

[1] J.W.B. Douglas J.M. Ross and H.R. Simpson, *All Our Future,* Panther, 1971, p.100; cf. D.F.Swift, 'Social Class, Mobility Ideology and 11-plus Success', *British Journal of Sociology*, 1967, XVIII, pp.165-86.

[3] loc.cit., 1971, p.101.

[4] loc.cit., 1972, p.86.

From *Who's Who 1971* Wakeford et al. abstracted background information on 934 people holding high rank or influential appointments. These included: the Cabinet; senior civil servants; the 40 wealthiest businessmen; members of the boards of the major nationalized industries; admirals, generals and air-marshals; directors of the Bank of England; directors of the four major clearing banks and the four biggest insurance companies; members of the Monopolies Commission; Anglican bishops; university vice-chancellors and principals; the governors of the B.B.C. and the I.T.A.; the proprietors of seven major national daily papers; High Court judges; royal dukes; dukes and life peers. Seventy per cent had been educated outside the state school system, 47 per cent at public boarding schools. In fact 13 per cent were Old Etonians and another 14 per cent had attended one of five other schools.[1] The Newson Commission on the public schools, reporting in 1968, along with much other evidence presented statistical data on the predominance of former public schoolboys amongst the leadership in many particular spheres of British public life[2], while apart from the studies of the financial and business élite by Whitley[3] more recent evidence has also been gathered in a study of the educational background of several other leading cadres by Boyd.[4]

As Table 9.1, which summarizes some of these findings, shows, about two and a half per cent of the population are educated in the public schools but this fraction is hugely magnified in every one of the groups on which information is provided. Of course this comparison reflects a situation that existed a considerable time before the dates given in the table. Away from the world of entertainment, and even there it is only performers themselves who are sometimes exceptions, eminence in public life mostly comes after middle age. In each of the groups Boyd described the average age was in the fifties or sixties and Wakeford et al. found that 97 per cent of their élite group were men aged between 50 and 70. Thus the current membership of most élite groups will broadly reflect the outcome of educational attitudes of 40 years ago or more. Few postwar social changes therefore, in educational provision for instance, are likely to have begun to affect the situation indicated in Table 9.1.

[1] Charterhouse, Harrow, Marlborough, Rugby and Winchester; see John and Frances Wakeford and Douglas Benson, 'Some Social and Educational Characteristics of Selected Elite Groups in Contemporary Britain', in Ivor Crewe (ed.), op.cit., 1973, pp.172-98.

[2] See The Public Schools Commission, *First Report*, H.M.S.O., 1968, Vol.II, Appendix 8; earlier information in this area is to be found in *The Public Schools and the General Educational System*, (The Fleming Report), H.M.S.O., 1944, in Glennerster and Pryke, *The Public Schools*, Fabian Society, 1964, and most extensively in W.L.Guttsman, *The British Political Elite*, MacGibbon and Kee, 1963.

[3] loc.cit., 1974.

[4] David Boyd, *Elites and their Education*, National Foundation for Educational Research, 1973.

Table 9.1

Public School Background and Elite Groups in Britain

	Total	Percentage from all Public Schools*
14 year olds at school in England and Wales (1967)	642,977	2.6
Conservative M.P.s (1966)	253	76.6
Conservative M.P.s (1970)	330	64.4
Labour M.P.s (1966)	363	19.5
Labour M.P.s (1970)	287	8.0
Conservative Cabinet (1963)	23	90.9
Conservative Cabinet (1970)	18	77.7
Labour Cabinet (1967)	21	42.0
Labour Cabinet (1970)	21	28.6
Royal Navy: Rear Admirals and above (1970)	76	88.9**
Army: Major-Generals and above (1970)	117	86.1
Royal Air Force: Air Vice-Marshals and above (1971)	85	62.5
Civil Service: Under Secretaries and above (1970)	301	61.7
Ambassadors (1971)	80	82.5
Judiciary: High Court and Appeal Court Judges (1971)	91	80.2
Church of England: Diocesan, Sufragan and Assistant Bishops (1971)	133	67.4
Vice Chancellors, Heads of Colleges, Professors of all English and Welsh Universities (1967)	1,646	32.5
Heads of Colleges, Professors of Oxford and Cambridge (1967)	256	49.3
Fellows of the Royal Society elected between 1962 and 1966†	138	24.6
Physicians and Surgeons at London teaching hospitals and on General Medical Council (1967)	244	68.0
Directors of 40 major industrial firms (1971)	261	67.8
Directors of Clearing Banks (1971)	99	79.9
Directors of Merchant Banks (1971)	106	77.4
Directors of major Insurance Companies (1971)	118	83.1
Governor and Directors of the Bank of England (1967)	18	77.7
Governor and Directors of the Bank of England (1971)	18	55.5

*The percentages are taken of the total whose school is known.
**Including Royal Naval College, Dartmouth.
† Excluding three non-scientific members of the Royal Society elected in this period.

Sources: i. Pupils in school; M.P.s 1966; Cabinets 1963, 1967; Vice Chancellors and Professors; Fellows of Royal Society; Physicians and Surgeons; Bank of England 1967. The Public Schools Commission, *First Report*, H.M.S.O. 1968, Vol. II Appendix 8 p. 236.

ii. M.P.s 1970: *The Times House of Commons,* 1970, p.257.

iii. Cabinets in June 1970: R.M. Punnett, *British Government and Politics,* Heinemann, 1971, Table XX, p.97.

iv. Royal Navy; Army; Royal Air Force; Civil Service; Ambassadors; Judiciary; Church of England: David Boyd, op.cit., 1973, Tables 4-11, pp. 80-84.

v. Directors of Bank of England, Clearing Banks, Merchant Banks, Insurance Companies and 40 major industrial firms 1971: Whitley, op.cit., 1974.

The Conservative members of parliament were very much more drawn from the public schools than were Labour M.P.s, though in both cases the party leadership, as represented by their cabinet ministers, was socially less broadly based than the parliamentary party. In both parties, however, there was some sign of widening recruitment both of M.P.s and to cabinet office, even though the proportion of Labour M.P.s with personal experience of manual work has declined, especially in comparison with the inter-war period.[1] Among the other groups it was amongst the scientific élite, those elected Fellows of the Royal Society on their outstanding merit, that a public school education was of least account. The academic élite follows a little further behind in this respect and then it is clear from these figures that scholarship in Oxford and Cambridge is, at least socially, more rarified than in the other universities of England and Wales. It is noteworthy that the proportion of former public schoolboys among the directors of the Bank of England fell very considerably after 1967, but the social background of bank directors was generally more exclusive – as it remained among those in leading positions in the services, the Law, the Church, industry and medicine. This is not a matter of public school education alone. These schools educate the children of the already privileged minority and a high proportion of their pupils go on to those universities which provide them with the best access to top jobs in the civil service, the higher professions, industry and finance.[2] Reviewing their evidence the Public Schools Commission concluded:

---

[1] See W.L.Guttsman, 'The British Political Elite and the Class Structure' in Stanworth and Giddens, *Elites and Power in British Society*, 1974, pp.33-4, and R.W.Johnson 'The British Political Elite 1955-1972', *European Journal of Sociology* 1973, 14, pp.35-77.

[2] See Boyd, *Elites and their Education*, 1973, p.112.

' . . . the hold of public school men on senior posts in many fields is the outcome of a process which begins in the home and leads through preparatory school to the universities and beyond. The public schools play a central part in this process. Their success in securing entry to Oxford and Cambridge is one of the biggest advantages they offer to those who pay their fees, and one of the main reasons for the subsequent success of their pupils. While they recruit from so limited a section of the population, these advantages will remain a divisive influence.'[1]

As we saw in Table 8.3 just under a third of the boys and a fifth of the girls from private sector schools go on to university, almost six times the proportion from state schools. From the socially more exclusive independent boarding schools the proportion is higher, and of these half go to Oxford or Cambridge as compared with less than ten per cent of university entrants from maintained schools.[2] It appears that the main reason for this discrepancy is the unwillingness of pupils from state schools to apply rather than any bias in Oxbridge selection procedures[3] and the proportion of entrants to these two universities from independent schools has been declining. Where in 1955 schools in the private sector provided 57 per cent of Oxbridge entrants in 1965-6 the proportion was down to 40 per cent.[4] But this is still more than double the proportion of independent school leavers amongst those going on to university in general. As the decline suggests this is not entirely a matter of the greater academic excellence or superior ability of the public schoolboy to cope with Oxbridge education. Glennerster and Pryke quote a study by Newfield which showed that in 1958 a much high proportion of men from L.E.A. grammar schools achieved first or upper second class honours degrees at Oxford and Cambridge and fewer had thirds, pass degrees and failures than among former pupils in H.M.C. and Direct Grant boarding schools.[5]

As a passport to many subsequent careers this kind of educational background is clearly still an immense advantage, although to a decreasing

---

[1] The Public Schools Commission, *First Report*, Vol.I, H.M.S.O., 1968, para 96, pp. 60-61.

[2] ibid.

[3] See J.M.Ross and P.Case, 'Who Goes to Oxbridge?', *New Society*, 19 May 1966.

[4] R.K. Kelsall, *Applications for Admission to Universities*, Association of Universities of the British Commonwealth, 1957; Committee on Higher Education, *Higher Education* (The Robbins Report), H.M.S.O., 1963, Table 32, p.80; Public Schools Commission, *First Report*, H.M.S.O., 1968, Vol.II, Appendix 8, p.236.

[5] See J.G.H.Newfield quoted' in H.Glennerster and R.Pryke, op.cit., 1964, p.22.On the other hand, as J.Eggleston has shown, public schoolboys are conspicuously more successful in selection for university team games. 'Secondary Schools and Oxbridge Blues', *British Journal of Sociology*, 1965, XVI, pp. 232-42.

extent. In 1949-52 only 26 per cent of entrants to the Administrative Class of the Civil Service, excluding promotions, had last attended an L.E.A. school, but this rose to 38 per cent in 1968-70. In the same period the proportion who had degrees from Oxford or Cambridge fell from 74 per cent to 59 per cent.[1] This hardly amounts to revolutionary change and on these figures it is clear that men and women with a public school and Oxbridge education will continue to predominate in the upper échelons of the civil service for a considerable time to come. On the other hand it would be purblind to ignore the fact that some change has already occurred and may, possibly, continue.

Among an older generation Oxbridge men declined among the members of the boards of the largest companies between 1966 and 1972 but the public school contingent maintained its position with 71 per cent throughout the six years.[2] Some groups, particularly in the world of finance are still more socially exclusive. Wilson and Lupton's celebrated study of top decision makers in the 1950s detailed their shared background of public school and Oxbridge education as well as extensive kinship links between the leadership of the Conservative Party, the directors of the five major clearing banks, the fourteen largest merchant banks and discount houses and the eight largest insurance companies.[3] Whitley has shown how in 1971 the financial élite, i.e. directors of large financial institutions, was still overwhelmingly drawn from the same limited educational background and through common directorships, the membership of exclusive London clubs and through family connections remained a very closely knit group of men.[4] Yet in 1957, the six leading public schools — Charterhouse, Eton, Harrow, Marlborough, Rugby and Winchester — provided 67 per cent of the directors of the Bank of England but only 39 per cent in 1971.[5] Other comparisons must be less exact

[1] R.K.Kelsall, 'Recruitment to the Higher Civil Service: How Has the Pattern Changed?', ch.9 in Stanworth and Giddens, op.cit., 1974, Table 1, p.173; and see also Royal Commission on the Civil Service (The Fulton Commission), *Report*, H.M.S.O., 1969, Vol. 4, Appendix 2, Table B1, which shows that Oxbridge graduates increased to 87 per cent of new appointments in 1957-60 so that the liberalization of recruitment should perhaps be dated since then. An unfortunate result of the reforms introduced following the Royal Commission's recommendations is that it has become difficult to see whether this trend toward a slightly wider recruitment to top positions in the public service has been continued since 1970.

[2] Heller, 'The State of British Boardrooms', *Management Today*, May 1973.

[3] C.S. Wilson and T. Lupton, 'The Social Background and Connections of Top Decision Makers', *Manchester School of Economic and Social Studies*, 1959, 27, pp.30-51, reprinted in Rothschild (ed.), op.cit., pp.220-41 and Urry and Wakeford (eds), op.cit., pp.185-204.

[4] loc.cit., 1973, 1974, and see Anthony Sampson, *Anatomy of Britain Today*, 1965, pp.411-34.

[5] This was actually 2 more than in 1967 though the proportion from all public schools was down from 77.7 per cent to 55.5 per cent; see table 9.1.

because of differences in the composition of the samples as a result of change in the intervening period but are worth making for the sake of historical comparison. In 14 years these six schools' representation fell from 48 per cent of the directors of the major clearing banks in 1957 to 47 per cent in 1971; from 43 per cent of the directors of merchant banks and discount houses in 1957 to 37 per cent in 1971 and from 47 per cent of the directors of insurance companies in 1957 to 40 per cent in 1971. Only in the Conservative cabinet was there a rise in the proportion from these six schools, from 50 per cent in 1957 to 52 per cent in 1970.[1]

Boyd's study is, potentially at least, especially valuable in this context because he has attempted to deal directly with the question of change. He presented data on the educational background of the membership of eight influential cadres at four points in time, namely 1939, 1950, 1960 and either 1970 or 1971. These were senior civil servants of the rank of under-secretary and above; heads of embassies and legations; high court and appeal court judges; Admirals, Vice-Admirals and Rear-Admirals; Major-Generals and above in the Army; Air Vice-Marshals and above in the R.A.F.; assistant bishops and above in the Church of England, and, lastly, the directors of the Bank of England, the Bank of Scotland and the clearing banks. Allowing for the probable age-range of men in these positions[2], they would generally have completed their education in the region of 30 to 50 years earlier and probably only in the 1970/71 group would a clear majority have left school since the First World War. Only, therefore, if the relationship between élite recruitment and social background should have been radically disturbed by the upheavals of war and political change intervening in the normal career structures of these various groups, would we expect any dramatic change over this period. Educational change alone would be unlikely to have made a very great difference. The possible effects of World War II and other crises however call in question Boyd's use of trend analysis over only four points in time in this study and there are other grounds for paying closer attention to his data than to the conclusions he drew from them. Briefly, in the first place, his use of Chi-squared tests to evaluate the proportion of élite group members with public school or Oxbridge education and so forth over the years is inappropriate because the membership of the several élites is not independent for each of the years considered. A judge, bishop, ambassador or whatever in 1960 might very well have already held such an appointment in 1950 or still have remained a member of the élite group of ten years later. One cannot therefore estimate the number of judges etc. with the relevant characteristics which, given the proportion over all the

---

[1] See Wilson and Lupton op.cit., 1959, Table 1; Whitley 'Commonalities and Connections Among Directors of Large Financial Institutions', *Sociological Review*, 1973, 21, Table II and R.M.Punnett, *British Government and Politics*, Heinemann, 1971, Table XX, p.97.

[2] See Boyd, op.cit., 1973, Appendix I, p.147.

four years examined, would be expected by chance alone in any one year and the Chi-squared statistic measures the extent to which the observed frequencies diverge from this. In any case the data presented refers to all the members of the various élite categories and not merely to samples drawn from them, so that this sort of calculation was unnecessary. Because of the completeness of Boyd's data all the differences or changes which emerge are real and cannot be attributed to sampling errors, whatever their apparent statistical 'significance' or lack of it.

His findings permit us to observe the extent to which the members of these eight cadres have increasingly or decreasingly been the products of different kinds of school and the universities. They do not, of course, tell us about the rising or declining importance over time of the groups selected for study either relatively to one another or in relation to other groups not included. Nor, without considerable caution can we infer much about the changing exclusiveness of the groups over time since the social significance of education in the different educational institutions has itself been subject to change. Thus if the upper middle classes increasingly came to send their sons to public school the fact that the proportion of former public schoolboys among these élite groups has increased does not imply. that their membership is socially more narrowly recruited. Taking those for whom information was available in all eight élite groups together, the proportion who had attended public or independent fee-paying but non-H.M.C. schools increased from 65.4 per cent in 1939 to 70.7 per cent in 1970-71. At the same time the proportion of former grammar school boys increased from 3.3 per cent in 1939 to 9.7 per cent in 1950, 10.9 per cent in 1960 and 15.9 per cent in 1970/71. The explanation for this apparently simultaneous increase and decrease in exclusiveness lies in the decline of the residual 'other' category from 5.2 per cent to 1.4 per cent and in particular the contraction in the proportion whose education was described simply as presumably non-public' from 24 per cent in 1939 to only 6 per cent in 1970/71. These declines render interpretations of other changes uncertain but since, for instance, almost three quarters of the 1939 admirals were included in these categories, it is probable that they chiefly accommodate private sector schooling of one sort or another around the turn of the century which has subsequently been displaced as the public school ethos has extended its grip on the minds of the upper middle class. Some approximate indication of the social exclusiveness of recruitment to the various élite groups can be gained by comparing the proportion from independent and public schools with that from grammar schools. Table 9.2 shows the generally increasing proportion of those educated in the grammar schools in comparison with men educated in fee-paying schools. The exclusion of the 'presumably non-public' category of schools from this calculation means that the tendency towards greater openness in recruitment is almost certainly under-represented in this table.

Table 9.2

Grammar School Education in Eight Elite Groups.

Percentage of élite members who attended grammar school among those educated either in grammar school or public and fee-paying non-H.M.C. schools.

Elite Group	1939	1950	1960	1970/71
Civil Service: Under-Secretaries and above	6.6	25.5	25.8	31.4
Ambassadors	0.0	11.8	9.5	12.0
High Court and Appeal Court Judges	5.0	6.1	10.3	9.5
Royal Navy: Rear-Admirals and above	19.0	6.3	5.0	12.9
Army: Major-Generals and above	4.6	10.2	4.2	8.3
R.A.F.: Air Vice-Marshals and above	0.0	5.5	8.6	23.5
C. of E.: Assistant Bishops and above	4.5	11.5	15.1	17.9
Directors of Clearing Banks	3.9	5.8	10.1	9.0

Source: calculated from David Boyd, *Elites and their Education,* 1973, Tables 4-11, pp.80-84.

In seven cases out of eight there was an increase in the grammar school representation following the Second World War, though in the cases of the judiciary and the banks the increase was modest. The exceptional case of the Royal Navy reflects the sudden increase in the importance of the Royal Naval College Dartmouth among the post-war admiralty, 60 per cent of whom had attended compared with only two per cent of their predecessors in 1939. Since 1950 the proportion from other schools has increased again though the majority are still former Dartmouth boys. Between 1950 and 1960 the old order showed signs of re-establishing itself with an increasing representation of old public school boys at the top of the foreign service, the Army and the Navy. By 1970 however the widening process was generally restored though the bankers and top judiciary had retreated from the position of 1960. Boyd's comparison of 26 well-known schools with the remainder of less well known public schools broadly confirms this picture. Throughout the period among public school bishops there was a trend towards increasing representation of the less well-known schools. The same was true among the top judges, army, R.A.F. and banking groups before 1960 and the foreign and civil service élites since then. The exceptional case of the Royal Navy is attributable to a postwar trend towards élite recruitment of men from the well-known public schools rather than the Royal Naval College Dartmouth.[1]

These developments are less than drastic; in all these élite groups there remains a colossal predominance of men from very exclusive social origins. Nonetheless the colossus is not quite monolithic and it would be seriously misleading to ignore the signs of change. Britain is still a stratified society, one, that is, in which there is not merely social inequality but where inequalities are inherited. Yet the structure is not unchanging. The inequalities may, in some respects, even be increasing, but their perpetuation from one generation to the next shows signs of becoming less inflexible. If we can catch glimpses of this at the level of the élite, when we look at the social structure as a whole the movement becomes unmistakeable. The increasing amount of occupational mobility which was described in the preceding chapter can tell us something more about the sort of changes that are taking place.

Mobility and Change

The theme of change is strikingly manifested at the level of our individual experience by both social and geographical mobility. In Chapter 3 I suggested some of the possible consequences of increasing geographical mobility for the society as a whole and, through the communities in which people live, for the character of individual relationships. Vertical social mobility, considered in Chapter 8 similarly may be of profound importance for the individual who undergoes the experience but perhaps has more obvious consequences for the overall structure of society. Social mobility gives us a measure of the rigidity of that structure, of the relative extent to which it is possible for members of one or other social stratum to move into another and the degree of restriction and resistance to access from other parts of society which will be met with. As S.M. Miller pointed out, a large amount of vertical society mobility does not necessarily imply a large degree of equality.[2] Even where it is possible for the ambitious, the clever, the industrious or the lucky to rise in society without being handicapped by whatever their fathers did or were, there may still be great disparities in the rewards and privileges of people at different points in the social hierarchy. Good opportunities for people to move from one class to another do not imply that there are no classes nor do they necessarily entail any loss of class consciousness either on the part of those who are pleased to remain in the estate to which they were born or on the part of those proudly aware of their new style and the new loyalties which go with it.[3] On the other hand we should not go too far along with Miller in

[1] ibid., Tables 4-11 pp.80-84.
[2] S.M. Miller, 'Comparative Social Mobility', *Current Sociology*, 1963, 4, p.4.
[3] ibid., pp.3-4.

assuming that the overall amount of mobility is *not* related to the structure of class relations. A small amount of mobility may be consistent with a rigid social hierarchy but there are grounds for doubting whether a great deal of mobility could be compatible with a marked degree of inequality between status groups or even a very wide division between classes.

The amount or frequency of social mobility does indicate something of the rigidity of the class or status system and the extent to which life-chances are determined by the accident of birth or by the achievements of the individual. The fact that we can talk about mobility between social strata at all presupposes that there is some degree of stratification. In a completely classless society equality of opportunity would be complete and it would make little sense to talk about mobility at all precisely because there would be no restraints upon movement.

At the societal level it has been suggested that we should distinguish between demand mobility — the amount of mobility necessary to fill the vacancies in the occupational structure after the children of the generation incumbent at each level have been accommodated — and fluidity, which measures the openness of the class system over and above the requirements of demand mobility.[1] This, however, is a less useful distinction than it appears. Fluidity is a residual category and depends on how well we can define 'demand'. Demand varies as a function of the changing occupational structure and differential class fertility. But these are not necessarily independent. Fertility can be influenced by parents' perceptions of the opportunities there may be for their children while opportunities may be created or curtailed according to the availability of suitable recruits. What is apparently 'demand' mobility thus becomes, in part at least, the product of the relative openness of social strata — which is what 'fluidity' is supposed to measure. Fluidity of movement between classes only measures the openness of the stratification system if it can be assumed that, somehow, other social mobility has no effect on class relations. Changes in class membership, even as a result of economic or technological change, are likely to have extensive effects on class relations however, so that the sociological independence of fluidity and demand mobility seems very doubtful except as some kind of arbitrary statistical exercise.

The immense number of factors involved and the difficulty of specifying them with any precision prevents us in practice from saying what determines the prevailing rate of social mobility at any particular point in time. The current pattern of change seems mainly to be the result of the changing structure of the economy and it is from observations of the direction of concurrent trends in vertical mobility, rather than the absolute amount, that we will best be able to offer an interpretation of class relations. How could one decide whether any given mobility rate was high or low? What can be done, on the other hand, at least in principle, is

[1] Nathalie Rogoff, *Recent Trends in Occupational Mobility*, Free Press, 1953.

to observe whether vertical mobility is increasing or decreasing. Unquestionably if the possibility of both intragenerational and intergenerational social mobility for individuals was decreasing we might plausibly infer that society was becoming more sharply divided. If upward and downward mobility were both to increase, *prima facie* it would suggest that, though we must still recognize the existence of stratification, the boundaries between strata were weakening.[1] In the real world however, things rarely turn out to be so simple.

Blau and Duncan's study of occupational mobility in the U.S.A. between 1951 and 1962 showed a similar increase in upward mobility (blue collar to white collar) and a decrease in downward mobility, as are evident in Britain. On the basis of what were more reliable samples and a considerably more elaborate analysis, they also concluded that the blue-collar/white-collar division remained a significant 'frontier' of occupational groupings. That is to say the pattern of mobility change is not merely a spurious product of changing class boundaries; the boundary between effective strata had *not* shifted.[2] If this is also true of Britain, as it seems to be, then it has certain curious implications for arguments about the significance of occupational stratification in the structure of power.

The increasing proportion of all employment accounted for by non-manual occupations[3] has provided for a substantial increase in upward mobility mediated through the allocative functions of our educational system. That is to say the educational institutions have played a part in deciding who should be mobile rather than in determining how many should be. The continuing educational advantages of the middle class have meant that they have been about equally able to take advantage of this pattern of occupational change. As a consequence the downward mobility of middle class children into manual jobs has been considerably reduced. The changing occupational structure thus appears to have generated a situation in which the boundaries between the social strata have become more open in one direction and more closed in another.

By the later 1960s about ten per cent of occupied males in Britain had been downwardly mobile and about 20 per cent had been upwardly mobile across the manual/non-manual frontier. At the same time a little more than half of all men in non-manual jobs and more than eight out of ten in manual jobs have had fathers who were manual workers, proportions which have scarely changed since the Second World War. The stability of class recruitment indicated by inflow analyses is reconciled with the changing outflows when we recognize the dynamic of the

[1] See Trevor Noble, 'Social Mobility and Class Relations in Britain', *British Journal of Sociology*, 1972, XXIII, pp.422-36.

[2] P.M. Blau and O.D. Duncan, *The American Occupational Structure*, Wiley, 1967, p.421 and cf. Noble, op.cit., 1972, pp.422 ff.

[3] See Chapter 5.

changing occupational structure. The inflow analyses leave out of account the changing sizes of the strata whose recruitment they measure. They demonstrate the persistence of inequalities within a society undergoing structural change. The degree of inequality of opportunity is hard to measure, it all depends on what one takes as a starting point. From the point of view of the middle class the better access of their children to non-manual jobs has been maintained and the risk of downward mobility has declined. From the point of view of the working class access to non-manual jobs for their children has been improving. It is not so much that the inequality between the two classes has been directly confronted and reduced as that it has been bypassed by structural changes which have made the established class differences a little less critically central in the distribution of opportunities.

Power and the Consensus

Changes of the sort I have been describing make a brief summing-up of an already complex social system still more difficult than before. This is acutely so when we attempt to characterize their impact on people's values and the sense of mutual obligations which has united them both within and across the social divisions. The increasing difficulty of comprehending the changing social order is not merely something for sociologists to worry about but is itself an important social fact colouring the experience of all of us. If the social structure is harder to understand it provides more scope for disagreement amongst its members, not only about what should be done, but also about what has been and is being done. The outcomes of increasing misunderstanding amongst people are hard to predict with the exception that one certain consequence will be more misunderstanding still.

The material inequalities which remain, as we have seen, are still substantial and they are reinforced by the kind of apolitical traditionalism I referred to in Chapters 3, 4 and 7. The feeling of belonging among our own sort of people is something we generally value because it contributes to the security of our sense of identity and well being. It also helps to keep us in our place. It serves to reduce possible descrepancies between the social distribution of ambition and the socially unequal structure of opportunities. I referred to the large measure of agreement which exists, despite differences of emphasis, on basic social values. This may sometimes manifest itself as paternalism amongst the upper middle class and its complementary deference in the lower middle and working class or even in the distinctly conservative proletarianism which survives here and there,[1] but the traditional respect for the individual, for constitutionalism and fair play is general on all sides and all shades of political opinion. The political

[1] See Samuel H. Beer, *Modern British Politics*, Methuen, 1969, p.422.

process goes on within this general social consensus and is confined by it to well established channels. Attempts to widen the scope of debate or act in untraditional ways, demonstrations, sit ins and so forth, are not so much opposed at a political level as seen as failures of respect for commonly accepted rights recognized in established procedures. People in parliament and local government may not be admired overmuch and a majority of people might like to see some moderate changes, but there remains a deep and widespread respect for the institutions.[1] On the other hand it seems to be commonly agreed throughout Britain that, as far as possible, serious matters should not be made into political issues anyway. At each new crisis men and women of age and experience will be heard calling for the practical problems of, say, education or industrial relations to be 'taken out of politics'. The parliamentarian who is held to be making political capital out of matters of 'national' concern will be almost universally condemned.

This consensus is not, however, one of wholly equal partners. Martin and Crouch, for instance, are either too idealistic or disingenuous when they compare the power structure of contemporary England with the constitutional arrangements of our parliamentary monarchy. 'Like the Sovereign', they suggest, 'the British elite reigns, ensconced as the apex of a hierarchy of wealth and status, but it only rules by the grace of a liberal consensus and by virtue of the pragmatic test.'[2] I have presented evidence of the élite in the hierarchy of wealth and status here and in Chapter 6, but the absence of revolutionary resentment amongst all but a tiny minority of the non-élite is no indication of anything more than their acquiescence in this state of affairs. Whereas the monarchy has been challenged but has continued to exist since the seventeenth century as a symbolic focus for national sentiment,[3] this is not at all the case with the élite. It is partly the good fortune of the élite in Britain, partly the achievement of its political skills, that it has never had to face a direct challenge from social forces capable of matching it politically. Whether we regard it as a coherent and self-conscious ruling class or only as a loose federation of functional 'establishments' merging imperceptibly at the edges with the rest of society, the material and organizational resources of the élite are immense; it defines its own legitimacy and is in the position to choose the occasions when it has to meet its opponents. In times of general prosperity conflict can be avoided. In times of hardship or war, criticism can be made to seem opposed to the national interest.

[1] See Chapter 7 and G. Almond and S. Verba, *The Civic Culture*, Little, Brown, 1965.

[2] David Martin and Colin Crouch, 'England', ch.8 in Margaret Scotford Archer and Salvador Giner, *Contemporary Europe: Class, Status and Power*, Weidenfeld and Nicolson, 1971, p.274.

[3] See Edward Shils and Michael Young, 'The Meaning of the Coronation', *Sociological Review*, 1953, 1, pp.63-8.

Martin and Crouch are correct in emphasizing the importance of historical continuity in maintaining the consensus. The recent past in England has seen the dialectic of history proceed with scarcely a raised voice.

'Changes were forthcoming from the Establishment itself; the rivals of socialism put forward attractive alternatives or eventually acquiesced in many of its achievements; and in any case the debate was suffused with appeals for change based on morality, not class conflict, on universal brotherhood, not proletarian solidarity.'[1]

According to F.M.L. Thompson this prudent liberalism maintained the power of the English aristocracy without serious direct challenge throughout the nineteenth century, enabling them to merge peaceably with the bourgeois interests which in other European states displaced them.[2] The same flexibility has preserved the popularity of Conservative administrations with large sections of the working class into the present. For a century and a half this strategy was pursued, if sometimes inadvertently, and through a period of profound socio-economic change maintained an unequalled degree of political moderation in social affairs. As a result, until the inflationary period of the early 1970s the structure of class relations in Britain had become generally accepted as reasonably fair, the odd glaring exceptions only proving the rule of mutual give and take. Martin and Crouch sum up this political culture in an admirable epigram to the effect that 'English people are more prone to queues than barricades'.[3]

Even after all that, however, this tolerant reasonableness on the part of the less privileged has been sustained by structural factors. The pattern of occupational opportunities and the educational system have had an important part to play in this. The distribution of incomes, the conditions of employment and the limitations on occupational mobility which the less privileged experience may not be felt as deprivations by those socialized into wanting no more, or only a little more, than they are likely to achieve anyway.

The socialization of workers for their place within the division of labour begins with the handed-down experience of parents passed on in the home, but its generalization and reinforcement has been identified as one of the principal achievements of the educational system in twentieth-century England. The increasing possibility of some success for an academically gifted minority has, all too commonly, co-existed with the boredom and frustration of the less able children in the lower streams of non-selective schools. Some sociologically orientated critics of the

---

[1] Martin and Crouch, op.cit., 1971, p.243.

[2] F.M.L. Thompson, *English Landed Society in the Nineteenth Century,* Routledge 1963, p.272.

[3] loc.cit., 1971, p.272.

secondary modern schools in the 1950s and early 1960s pointed out, however, that the imposition of dull, routine tasks which lacked any apparent relevance to, or significance for, the lives of the children was in effect training them to accept the sorts of demands they would encounter in industrial employment after leaving school. As Carter commented, 'Perhaps it is as well that school does make such small impact on these children — otherwise they would be due for a shock when they started work, and found they were little more than extensions to machines, for example, and required to do routine work unquestioningly.'[1] For many children the transition from school to work still often involves only the change of routine. Expecting little from work because they have learned at school to expect little from the situations they find themselves obliged to be in, many of the non-skilled are satisfied with what they find even though the work is repetitive and makes few demands. Cotgrove and Parker in the early 1960s argued that

'The secondary modern boy leaving school at 15 has received early training in dissociating himself from the demands which 'they' make upon him. He simply doesn't care. It is not surprising that psychologists have discovered that many are content to carry out routine tasks. Dissatisfaction is a measure of the gap between aspiration and achievement. For many, no such gap exists — their expectations and aspirations are centred on the world outside the factory.'[2]

How far the reorganization of secondary education along comprehensive lines and the raising of the school-leaving age since then may have changed things remains to be seen. On the other hand expectations and aspirations are not centred in the sphere of political concern either. The feelings of powerlessness in political affairs especially among the young but also among the more highly educated are related to the relatively low importance in their lives most people attribute to their educational experience and to political matters alike.[3] This training in dissociation from the external circumstances which shape their lives which is received by the least privileged members of society, in so far as it is not an altogether out of date or inaccurate picture, casts some shadows on the notion of the liberal consensus referred to by Martin and Crouch. Of course the operation of the educational system and the conditions of employment experienced by the less skilled and less affluent majority do not necessarily imply the existence of a sinister programme of brainwashing carried out on behalf of a powerful and unscrupulous élite. The normal operation of 'good sense' and a practical adjustment to the

[1] M.P. Carter, *Into Work,* Penguin, 1966, p.115.

[2] S. Cotgrove and S.R. Parker, 'Work and Non-Work', *New Society,* 11 July 1963.

[3] See Mark Abrams, 'Subjective Social Indicators' in *Social Trends,* 4, H.M.S.O., 1973, pp.41 and 43.

sometimes unpleasant realities which everyone has to accept provides sufficient explanation of the situation. In a stratified society they have much the same effect.

The sort of social changes I was describing earlier will no doubt affect the social consensus too. Increasing mobility and more open recruitment to élites, together with technological change and educational reform, may improve class relations and either reduce or divert conflicts. They may, however, raise questions about the inequalities that remain, reducing deference and traditionalism while increasing discontent about the distribution of opportunities and reward. Both outcomes are likely and are not wholly mutually exclusive. The present situation is uncertain and the past hard to interpret; who can foretell the future?

Some Final Observations

This study began with a discussion of some of the demographic aspects of social structure. Demographic change is one of the best documented aspects of society yet there is still a great deal we do not understand about it. The general significance of this is, however, far too often overlooked in contemporary sociology. To begin with there have occurred a number of reversals of demographic trends in the recent past which have taken observers by surprise and whose origins and implications it has been impossible to determine with any degree of certainty. It is apparent that population change in many ways remains mysterious in the sense that we are still in no position to explain satisfactorily a great deal of what occurs. And yet changes in the size and composition of the population, in age structure, fertility and family size and the propensity of different groups to marry, is one of the best and most reliably documented areas of our knowledge about society and social change. This being the case, how much less certain should we be about the huge remainder of our notions about the dynamics of social interaction and social structure?

The great bulk of published accounts of the nature of society is largely speculative hypothesis advanced all too often, if not always, under the influence of wishful thinking and all the human passions, prejudgements and misunderstandings that thoughtful men and women, like all the rest, are subject to. There are added risks in the investigation of the very recent past. Things are more likely to turn out to be other than what they seem as compared with the study of more distant times where interpretations have had a chance to mature. As Sir Walter Raleigh wrote 'Whosoever . . . shall follow truth too near the heels, it may haply strike out his teeth.'[1] Fortunately, in England, the worldly dangers are much less than in his day but the problems of scholarship are still severe. The evidence we have cannot always be relied on and, at best, only demonstrates for certain that

[1] Sir Walter Raleigh, *History of the World*, 1614.

some generalizations can *not* be maintained, though it may indicate that some others may be, just possibly or even probably, true. But the uncertainty of our knowledge does not render it useless or imply that one man's opinions are as worthy of attention as any others. It is not necessary to rely on the impressions of any one individual except for an account of his own subjective experience. Instead we can employ the impersonal conventions which judicious men have developed in order to arrive at a degree of objectivity in their appraisal of their environment. In the peculiarly difficult task of employing these conventions in the study of their own society sociologists, beset by their moral, emotional and conceptual entanglements with the object of their enquiry, face a challenge which all must sometimes doubt their ability to meet. Yet it is not necessary to do so alone. We have the resources of a collective intelligence and imagination in the critical conventions which the founders of the discipline, Weber, Durkheim and all the others, have created for us. The employment of a scientific methodology provides us with a system by which some of the claims to represent the truth about social experience can be tested. The sort of evidence I have tried to assemble in this study has this virtue, that its reliability can be critically examined. After all one of the valuable characteristics of an empirical sociology, as distinct from other kinds of discussion about society, is that it shows us that raising questions is not all there is to discovering the truth.

The plausibility of the interpretation I have placed on this evidence is for the reader to judge. The main thing to recognize is that certainty is incompatible with a scientific approach to anything at all – including the study of society. Too many, even among those of us calling ourselves sociologists, have been convinced of the final truth of our theorizing. Some of the theories of course may *be* true, it is the conviction which renders them unsociological. Dogmatic theorists apart, however, the study of modern British society is still fraught with many disagreements. Often the arguments on both sides are persuasive and are backed with a certain amount of evidence, though not enough to be decisive. Most of what can be said is not a matter of finally established truths but of better or worse arguments, questions to be gone further into.

The analysis I have pursued in this book, though tentative, has nevertheless convinced me of some particular probabilities and has led to some more or less interpretive general conclusions. Discussion of the distribution of economic resources was found to be beset by inadequacies of data and uncertainties of interpretation. The examination of poverty and riches entailed not only the methodological problems of comparison between essentially relativistic measures but inherent conceptual difficulties in delineating these measures at all. Having reviewed some of the evidence on possibly the most 'objective' area of social differentiation, I next turned to some of the more clearly subjective aspects of stratification. Nevertheless even in the areas of political opinion, social self-perception and their shifting determinants, some broad outlines of the structure of British society emerged. These recognized the problematic nature of the individual's inclinations and outlook and engaged the historically changing structure of the economy and society as constraints upon his social circumstances and, if only less directly, upon his response to them.

What we have been able to learn about the structure of British society reveals how much we do not yet know, but it also suggests something of how much we might know which is not ordinarily apparent to us in our day-to-day lives. This is fairly readily apparent in some of the topics I have already discussed. Changes in family size, for instance, have been brought about by the deliberate decisions of parents, though the larger consequences in the changing size and composition of the population do not, for the most part, enter into their calculations. The loosening of social networks as a result of increasing geographical mobility may be of the most profound importance in changing the structure of meaning in ordinary social relations; it is the outcome of purposive moves on the part of the people who have no conception of the general structural consequences of their actions and who may remain blind to its significance, even when rationalizing about the changes which it induces in their own lives. The growth in scale and the bureaucratization of organizations in the economic order are the unconsidered but possibly the most socially dynamic outcomes of a range of particular decisions in the pursuit of other and more particular goals. Social stratification itself, whether seen in terms of class situation or of status situation, cannot be accounted for as other than the by-product, the more important by-product, of behaviour which is directed towards particular ends and not the maintenance of general institutionalized structures. As I argued in the Introduction, the social structure of Britain is a pattern made by people pursuing their own particular purposes in their own particular ways. The nature of social action has led some writers into denying the reality of general structural characteristics altogether as though the refusal to acknowledge their existence would make them go away. Unhappily, an unwillingness to recognize the constraints on our behaviour is only likely to bring us the enjoyment of the semblance of freedom, never an effective control of our collective destinies.

Further Reading

Since most selections of recommended reading seem calculated to daunt the most voracious of rapid readers, I offer only six titles for each chapter. Some choices will seem obvious but most have been made only with difficulty from amongst equally worthy alternatives. Even then a list of more than 50 starting-points for further reading is probably still far too long for most purposes. Some browsing and sampling will aid selection within the list, however, while the reader whose appetite remains unsatisfied on any topic should find the notes in the text helpful.

Chapter 1:
Eric Butterworth and David Weir (eds), *The Sociology of Modern Britain,* Collins, 1970
Central Statistical Office, *Facts in Focus,* Penguin, 2nd Edition 1974.
Central Office of Information, *Britain: An Official Handbook,* H.M.S.O. Annually
A.H. Halsey (ed.), *Trends in British Society since 1900,* Macmillan, 1972
Judith Ryder and Harold Silver, *Modern English Society: History and Structure 1850-1970,* Methuen, 1970
Barbara Wootton, *Contemporary Britain: Three Lectures,* Allen and Unwin, 1971

Chapter 2:
Central Statistical Office, *Social Trends,* H.M.S.O., Annually
House of Commons, *Report of the Population Panel,* Cmnd. 5258, H.M.S.O., 1973
Peter Laslett, *The World We Have Lost,* Methuen, 1965
R.M. Titmuss, *Essays on the Welfare State,* Allen and Unwin, 1958
Neil Tranter, *Population since the Industrial Revolution; the Case of England and Wales,* Croom Helm, 1973
Michael Young and Peter Willmott, *The Symmetrical Family*, Routledge, 1973

Chapter 3:
Michael Banton, *Racial Minorities*, Collins, 1972
Ernest Krausz, *Ethnic Minorities in Britain*, MacGibbon and Kee, 1971
Frank Musgrove, *The Migratory Elite*, Heinemann, 1963
John Rex and Robert Moore, *Race, Community and Conflict*, Oxford, 1967
Margaret Stacey, *Tradition and Change*, Oxford 1960
George Taylor and N. Ayres, *Born and Bred Unequal*, Longmans, 1969

Chapter 4:
Michael Anderson (ed.), *Sociology of the Family*, Penguin, 1971
Colin Bell, *Middle Class Families*, Routledge, 1969
Elizabeth Bott, *Family and Social Network*, Tavistock, 1957, 1971
C.C. Harris, *The Family*, Allen and Unwin, 1969
Josephine Klein, *Samples from English Cultures*, Routledge, 2 vols, 1965
John and Elizabeth Newson, *Four Years Old in an Urban Community*, Allen and Unwin, 1968, and Penguin, 1970.

Chapter 5:
George Bain, David Coates and Valerie Ellis, *Social Stratification and Trade Unionism*, Heinemann, 1973
M.P. Fogarty, R. Rapoport and R.N. Rapoport, *Sex, Career and Family*, Allen and Unwin, 1971
E.J. Hobsbawm, *Industry and Empire*, Weidenfeld and Nicolson, 1968
Theo Nichols, *Ownership Control and Ideology*, Allen and Unwin, 1969
S.R. Parker, R.K. Brown, J. Child and M:A. Smith, *The Sociology of Industry*, Allen and Unwin, 1967
David Weir (ed.), *Men and Work in Modern Britain*, Collins, 1973

Chapter 6:
A.B. Atkinson (ed.), *Wealth, Income and Inequality*, Penguin, 1973
Robert Holman (ed.), *Socially Deprived Families in Britain*, National Council of Social Service, Bedford Square Press, 1970
George Polanyi and John B. Wood, *How Much Inequality?*, Institute of Economic Affairs, 1974.
W.G. Runciman, *Relative Deprivation and Social Justice*, Routledge, 1966
Peter Townsend (ed.), *The Concept of Poverty*, Heinemann, 1970
Dorothy Wedderburn (ed.), *Poverty, Inequality and Class Structure*, Cambridge, 1974

Chapter 7:
Samuel H. Beer *Modern British Politics,* Methuen, 1965, 2nd Rev. Edition
1969
David Butler and Donald Stokes, *Political Change in Britain*, Macmillan,
1969, 2nd Rev. Edition 1974.
J.H. Goldthorpe, D. Lockwood, F. Bechhofer and J. Platt. *The Affluent
Worker in the Class Structure*, Cambridge, 1969
Michael Mann, *Consciousness and Action among the Western Working
Class,* Macmillan, 1973
Graeme Moodie and Gerald Studdert-Kennedy, *Opinions, Publics and
Pressure Groups,* Allen and Unwin, 1970
Richard Rose (ed.), *Studies in British Politics,* Macmillan, 1966

Chapter 8:
Olive Banks, *The Sociology of Education,* Batsford, 2nd. Rev. Edition
1971
Basil Bernstein, *Class, Codes and Control: Theoretical Studies towards a
Sociology of Language,* Routledge, 1971
B.R. Cosin et al. (eds.), *School and Society*, Routledge, 1971
M. Craft (ed.) *Family, Class and Education: A Reader,* Longman, 1970
J.W.B. Douglas, J.M. Ross and H.R. Simpson, *All Our Future*, Peter Davies,
1968
R.K. Kelsall, Anne Poole and Annette Kuhn, *Graduates: The Sociology of
an Elite,* Methuen, 1972

Chapter 9:
S. Aaronovitch, *The Ruling Class,* Lawrence and Wishart, 1961
T.B. Bottomore, *Elites and Society,* Watts, 1964
Ivor Crewe (ed.), *British Political Sociology Year Book Vol. 1: Elites in
Western Democracy,* Croom Helm, 1974
Geraint Parry, *Political Elites,* Allen and Unwin, 1969
Philip Stanworth and Anthony Giddens (eds.), *Elites and Power in British
Society,* Cambridge, 1974
John Urry and John Wakeford (eds.), *Power in Britain,* Heinemann, 1973

Author Index

(including publishing organizations in cases where material has been published anonymously – e.g. United Nations).

337

338

MACKAY, D.I. 46n, 82
MANN, Michael, 333
MANPOWER RESEARCH UNIT,
  136-7
MARQUAND, Judith, 198
MARSDEN, Dennis, 141n, 198n, 262
MARSDEN, Dennis. See also Jackson
  and *Marsden*
MARSH, A.I. and E.E. Cocker, 155n
MARSHALL, T.H, 246
MARTIN, David and Colin Crouch,
  325-7
MARTIN, F.M. 209-214
MARTIN, F.M. See also Floud,
  Halsey and *Martin*
MARX, Karl, 236, 301
MASON, W.S. See Gross, *Mason* and
  McEachern
MASTERS, Philip L, 273, 275n
MASTERS, P.L. and S.W. Hockey, 276
MATTHEW, St, 182n
MAXWELL, S.M.M. See Douglas,
  Ross, *Maxwell* and Wallzer
MAYS, John Barron, 107n, 262, 269
McCANN, W.T. See Bealey, Blondel
  and *McCann*
McEACHERN, A.W. See Gross,
  Mason and *McEachern*
McKENZIE, R.T. and A. Silver, 234-5,
  236
McMAHON, P.C. See Harbury and
  McMahon
MEACHER, Michael, 173n, 175n,
  180n
MEADE, J.E, 173, 175, 181n, 182
MERRETT, A.J, 179
MERTON, R.K, 88n
MICHELS, Robert, 299
MILLER, S.M, 286-7, 321
*THE MILNER HOLLAND REPORT
  (Housing in Greater London)*, 71-2,
  73
MINISTRY OF EDUCATION, 269n
*MINISTRY OF PENSIONS AND
  NATIONAL INSURANCE*, 196
MINISTRY OF SOCIAL SECURITY, 197
MITFORD, Nancy, 310
MOGEY, John, 88n, 89-90, 92n,
  110, 119n, 120-1, 125, 234
MONOPOLIES COMMISSION, 152,
  309
MOODIE, Graeme and Gerald
  Studdert-Kennedy, 220, 234,
  235-6, 240n, 241, 311n, 333
MOORE, Robert. See Rex and *Moore*
MOORE, W.E, 100n
MORGAN, Margaret. See Hunt, Fox
  and *Morgan*
MORNING TELEGRAPH, 73n
MOSER, C.A, 194n
MOYLE, John, 305, 309
MOYLE, John. See also Revell and
  Moyle

MURDOCK, G.P, 101n
MUSGROVE, F.M, 26, 83, 91, 92n, 95n
  130n, 253n, 292n, 332
MYERS, C.A. See Kerr, Dunlop,
  Harbison and *Myers*
MYRDAL, Alva and Viola Klein, 143n

NALSON, J.S, 108, 128n
*NATIONAL BOARD FOR PRICES
  AND INCOMES*, 177, 190-1, 201,
  302n
NATIONWIDE BUILDING SOCIETY,
  70
NEWBY, Howard, 149n
NEWBY, Howard. See also Bell and
  Newby
NEWFIELD, J.G.H, 316
NEW SOCIETY, 250
*THE NEWSOM REPORT – (Half
  our Future)*: 269
NEWSON, Elizabeth. See Newson
  and *Newson*
NEWSON, John and Elizabeth
  Newson, 119n, 121-22, 129-31,
  332
NICHOLS, Theo, 302, 305, 306, 332
NICHOLSON, J.H, 89n, 90
NICHOLSON, J.L, 200-01
NICHOLSON, R.J, 199-200
NOBLE, Faith, 286-7
NOBLE, Trevor, 81n, 126n, 167n,
  283n, 287n, 323n
NORDLINGER, Eric, 228, 233, 234

*OFFICE OF POPULATION CENSUSES
  AND SURVEYS: SOCIAL SURVEY
  DIVISION*, 22n, 38n, 55n, 72n,
  74-5, 82-4, 164n
ORWELL, George, 12n, 73n, 93n,
  194n

PAGE, Dilys. See Greve, *Page* and
  Greve
PAHL, J.M. and R.E. Pahl, 123, 131n,
  142n, 146, 147
PAHL, R.E, 83
PAHL, R.E. and J.T. Winkler, 304-5,
  308-9
PAHL, R.E. See also Pahl and *Pahl*
PARKER, S.R, 146
PARKER, S.R. et al, 145n, 147,
  148n, 332
PARKER, S.R. See also Cotgrove
  and *Parker*
PARKIN, Frank, 208, 225n, 236-7,
  238, 240n, 241, 258n
PARRY, Geraint, 308, 311n, 333
PATTERSON, Sheila, 61
PEAR, R.H. See Benney, Gray and
  Pear
PEEL, John, 22, 31
PERKIN, Harold, 149n
PERROTT, Roy, 310n

339

342

Subject Index